THE DESIGN BOOK

THE
DESIGN
BOOK

DK LONDON

SENIOR ART EDITOR
Duncan Turner

SENIOR EDITOR
Helen Fewster

EDITORS
Tom Booth, Katie John, Annie Moss

ILLUSTRATIONS
James Graham

JACKET DESIGNER
Stephanie Cheng Hui Tan

JACKET DESIGN
DEVELOPMENT MANAGER
Sophia MTT

PICTURE RESEARCHER
Sarah Smithies, Myriam Meguarbi

SENIOR PRODUCTION CONTROLLER
Meskerem Berhane

MANAGING ART EDITOR
Michael Duffy

MANAGING EDITOR
Angeles Gavira Guerrero

ART DIRECTOR
Maxine Pedliham

PUBLISHING DIRECTOR
Liz Wheeler

DESIGN DIRECTOR
Phil Ormerod

MANAGING DIRECTOR
Liz Gough

DK DELHI

SENIOR ART EDITOR
Pooja Pipil

ART EDITORS
Debjyoti Mukherjee, Mitravinda V K

SENIOR EDITOR
Suefa Lee

EDITOR
Aashline R. Avarachan

ILLUSTRATOR
Rupanki Kaushik

SENIOR MANAGING EDITOR
Rohan Sinha

MANAGING ART EDITOR
Sudakshina Basu

DTP DESIGNERS
Rakesh Kumar, Mrinmoy Mazumdar

HI-RES COORDINATOR
Neeraj Bhatia

PRODUCTION EDITOR
Anita Yadav

SENIOR JACKETS DESIGNER
Suhita Dharamjit

SENIOR JACKETS COORDINATOR
Priyanka Sharma Saddi

PRE-PRODUCTION MANAGER
Balwant Singh

PRODUCTION MANAGER
Pankaj Sharma

CREATIVE HEAD
Malavika Talukder

SANDS PUBLISHING
SOLUTIONS

EDITORIAL PARTNERS
David and Sylvia Tombesi-Walton

DESIGN PARTNER
Simon Murrell

original styling by
STUDIO 8

First published in Great Britain in 2024 by
Dorling Kindersley Limited
DK, One Embassy Gardens,
8 Viaduct Gardens, London, SW11 7BW

The authorised representative in the EEA is
Dorling Kindersley Verlag GmbH. Arnulfstr. 124,
80636 Munich, Germany

Copyright © 2024 Dorling Kindersley Limited
A Penguin Random House Company
10 9 8 7 6 5 4 3 2 1
001–294568–Sep/2024

A CIP catalogue record for this book
is available from the British Library.
ISBN 978-0-2412-5707-4

Printed and bound in China

www.dk.com

This book was made with Forest
Stewardship Council™ certified
paper – one small step in DK's
commitment to a sustainable future.
Learn more at **www.dk.com/uk/
information/sustainability**

CONTRIBUTORS

LYNDA RELPH-KNIGHT (CONSULTANT)

Lynda Relph-Knight has worked in design and architecture for most of her career. As a journalist she edited magazines including *The Architect* and *Design Week*, which she ran for 22 years. Lynda continues to work in design as a writer and consultant, advising design leaders and working on projects.

MILLY BURROUGHS

Milly Burroughs is a writer, editor, and strategist specializing in art, design and architecture. She has a degree in Product Design from Nottingham Trent School of Architecture, Design and the Built Environment, and has worked with numerous publications and publishers, including *AnOther*, *The Spaces*, and Gestalten.

PENNY CRASWELL

Penny Craswell is a writer and editor with a Masters of Design from the University of NSW, Sydney, Australia. She is the author of *Reclaimed: New homes from old materials* (2022) and *Design Lives Here: Australian interiors, furniture and lighting* (2020). A former magazine editor, Penny contributes regularly to a number of design magazines, including *Houses* and *Green* magazines.

FIONA GLEN

Fiona Glen is a freelance writer and editor who holds an MA in Writing from the Royal College of Art. She has contributed to a range of art and culture publications, including *ArtReview* and *Art & the Public Sphere*.

ELEANOR HERRING

Eleanor Herring studied the History of Design at the Royal College of Art, and has a PhD in Architectural Theory and Cultural Studies from the University of Edinburgh. She is the author of *Street Furniture Design* (2017), and currently works as a lecturer at Glasgow School of Art.

BRUCE PETER

Bruce Peter is Professor of Design History at The Glasgow School of Art. He is a graduate of the GSA, the Royal College of Art, and the University of Glasgow. His interests encompass modern architecture, design, and decorative art in the contexts of travel and leisure, and he has written extensively about ships, hotels, railways, and entertainment architecture.

ANGELA RIECHERS

Angela Riechers holds an MFA in Design Criticism from the School of Visual Arts and a BFA in Illustration from the Rhode Island School of Design. She is an award-winning writer, art director, and educator. Her most recent book is *The Elements of Visual Grammar* (2024).

ELEANOR ROBERTSON

Eleanor Robertson is a graphic designer and design writer. She works across branding, packaging and editorial design, and is editor of the website BP&O. She has mentored through D&AD's Shift programme and the Creative Mentor Network. Before training as a designer, she studied English language and literature at Oxford University.

ALEXIE SOMMER

Alexie Somer is a designer, sustainability strategist, and communication expert working the intersection between business creativity, environmental sustainability and authentic communication. Alexie is co-founder of URGE Collective and Design Declares.

SIMON SPIER

Simon Spier is a curator at the Victoria & Albert Museum, London. He has a PhD in History of Art from the University of Leeds, and in the past has worked with collections including Royal Collection Trust, The Bowes Museum, and York Museums Trust.

SOPHIE TOLHURST

Sophie Tolhurst is a writer and editor interested in all things design. Following a pivot from fashion design to writing, via an MA from the Royal College of Art, she has written on design for publications such as *Creative Review*, *Design Week*, *Disegno*, the *Financial Times*, and *Frieze*.

6

CONTENTS

THE AGE OF INDUSTRY
1900–1950

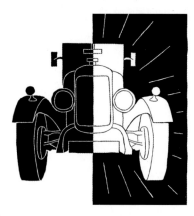

THE CONSUMER AGE
1950–2000

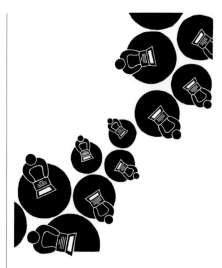

DIGITAL TO SUSTAINABLE
2000 ONWARDS

INTRODU

CTION

Design is in everything we do and make. It has shaped our world from time immemorial – and continues to do so. Design is complex: it crosses over with art, architecture, advertising, and craft, but it retains its own integrity. It is essentially what gives form and delight to functional objects and a tone of voice to how we express ourselves as individuals or businesses.

Initially, design was concerned with fulfilling basic needs – how we feed and clothe ourselves and create shelter as well as how we communicate with each other. These themes underpin the way the discipline has developed over the ages as it has embraced new media and materials, from the original clay, wood, iron, and papyrus, to plastics, plastic substitutes, and digital platforms.

Design through time
This book explores how design has evolved over the centuries, but across the ages, there are common themes. A remarkable legacy of cave art in Europe and Asia – including handprints and paintings that date to more than 40,000 years ago – testifies to the human desire to communicate and leave a mark on the world.

Similarly, parallels may be drawn between the use of ornaments worn by individuals in the prehistoric and ancient worlds to express their personal style or declare their status, and the development of corporate branding during the 20th century.

Refinement in the design of objects follows a similar trajectory. A simple beaker makes a perfectly adequate drinking vessel. It could perhaps be decorated as a mark of ownership, or for aesthetic reasons. Maybe, for practical purposes it might be useful to add a handle,

Design is a plan for arranging elements in such a way as to best accomplish a particular purpose.
Charles Eames
Design Q&A with Charles Eames, 1972

or have it set on a stem to make it look more pleasing and easier to hold. Then there is the question of the material from which it could be made: should it be pottery, metal, plastic, or a cut crystal glass? Any one of these variables could serve to elevate the beaker from a functional solution to a practical problem into a desirable, aesthetically pleasing item to own – perhaps even one that is purely just for decoration.

Another recurring theme is the manner in which designers adapt their creations according to the materials and technology available at the time. Early humans, for example, began to make weapons from bronze instead of stone. In areas such as transport the quest to increase speed, capacity, and comfort can result in a high level innovation, and a near constant drive for improvement. And for better or worse, in the 20th century, the development of plastics and synthetic fibres was transformative in a number of different fields – from furniture design to fashion. Each new innovation has inspired designers to create new styles and find new ways of doing things. It is a trend that looks set to continue as eco-friendly materials have become more widely available.

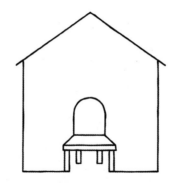

Invention and innovation

The story of design, then, is one of constant innovation. It tracks the creativity of our ancestors as they made tools, pots, and textiles through to the Industrial Revolution which transformed the industrial landscape.

During the 20th century, the new field of industrial design expanded the design remit to include savvy marketing strategies and the creation of advertising material, packaging, and interiors. The development of plastics and synthetic fabrics also created new opportunities for designers.

From the 1950s, in a world geared towards consumption, corporate brand identities became increasingly significant. Transport companies, for example, promoted waiting rooms and lounges as an essential part of a luxury lifestyle. Technical innovations such as miniaturization led to the creation of personal electronic devices.

In the 21st century, the Internet became more widely accessible, and consumerism moved online. Website design and e-commerce systems became more advanced as designers focused on the "user experience" to build traffic.

The issue of sustainability has now become a big factor in design, as the problem of plastic waste becomes ever more apparent. Meanwhile the development of "smart materials" that respond to their environment heralds an exciting new era in product design and construction.

Areas of design

Design is often subdivided into a number of different fields.

Visual communication covers everything from graphics, posters, typography, and print magazines to the design of digital media.

Branding encompasses the design of corporate marques and logos, packaging, and consumer promotions.

Environments involve the design of interiors for homes, offices, shops, bars, restaurants, and cultural venues.

Product design embraces the design of mass-produced artefacts and appliances, furniture, and technology products.

Transport design includes the design of cars and road vehicles, planes, boats, and trains, as well as traffic networks and routes.

Service design relates to the way in which companies and organizations conduct their business and serve their customers and stakeholders.

Design thinking

In recent years design has also become associated with a way of thinking and an approach to life – problem-solving is one way of putting it, blue-sky thinking another. Essentially, it is about exploring "What if?".

From its humble, need-driven origins design has become big business. It is no longer confined to objects and artefacts, but is also concerned with how organizations conduct themselves and how they are portrayed in the wider world. ■

Thinking about design is hard, but not thinking about it can be disastrous.
Ralph Caplan
PRINT Magazine
June 2020

INVENTI

THROUG

NECESS

BEFORE 1000 CE

ON
H
H
ITY

Homo erectus creates multifunctional Acheulean tools.

The **Jōmon people** use clay to create **ceramic pots** and **figurines** in Japan.

The **pottery wheel** is invented in Mesopotamia.

c. **1.9** MYA

c. **12,500** YA

c. **4000** BCE

c. **17,000** YA

c. **6000** BCE

c. **3500** BCE

Coloured pigments are used to create **rock art paintings** in the Lascaux Cave in France.

In southern China, the **Austronesian people** use **pulp from trees** to make **barkcloth**.

In Mesopotamia, the **Sumerians** develop the **cuneiform writing system**.

D esign can mean many things. In the widest sense, any object that has been altered by humans to use for a particular purpose may be considered to have been "designed". At its most basic, a stone,w shaped by an early human in prehistoric times to make a simple tool, could be considered an example of design.

In more than three millenia explored in this book, humans have accomplished extraordinary things. They began by exploiting the resources around them to provide the essentials of food, warmth, and shelter. They made tools for hunting – first from stone, then from metals – and textiles for clothing from plant fibres and animal skins. They created pottery for storage and used coloured pigments to record details of their lives on cave walls. They learned how to harness fire, cook food, make paper and glass, and sledges for transport. All these things demonstrate a capacity for sophisticated reasoning, planning and making – and some of the techniques developed – such as weaving – remained in use for thousands of years, right up to the Industrial Revolution.

Early ships
At the Viking Ship Museum in Oslo, Norway, there are vessels that are more than a thousand years old. However, their clinker-clad hulls display extraordinarily complex geometries: slender bows and sterns for cutting through waves while minimizing drag, and wider midbodies to aid buoyancy and stability. These robust vessels were able to traverse the Atlantic Ocean. They also reached the Mediterranean, where shipbuilding techniques were comparably refined. The museum also houses displays of intricate jewellery, utensils, and storage containers made by the Norse in the Middle Ages, all of which point to a culture rich in design imagination and skill in production.

Ancient craftsmanship
At the Egyptian Museum in Cairo, even more extraordinary treasures, dating from over 3,300 years ago, are on display. The finest of these were excavated in the mid-1920s from a tomb within a giant pyramid where the body of the Pharaoh Tutankhamun was interred. Today's visitors gaze in awe at the

Bronze is used to make **objects** and **weapons** such as swords and daggers.

c. 3000 BCE

Ancient Egyptians use **sails** to propel their **ships** and travel further **out to sea**.

c. 3000 BCE

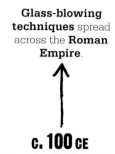

Glass-blowing techniques spread across the **Roman Empire**.

c. 100 CE

c. 3000 BCE

Chopsticks are used as **cooking aids** in ancient China.

c. 200 BCE

In China, **paper** is produced from **plant fibres** during the Han Dynasty.

c. 1000 CE

Vikings sail their **longships** across the **Atlantic Ocean**, from Europe to North America.

extraordinarily rich craftsmanship and striking, opulent-looking forms and materials of the items made to accompany him into the next world. Many will wonder how people back then were able to conceive of such things.

Design and evolution

Although humans themselves may have altered little since the earliest period addressed here, design has changed greatly. Indeed, the concept of "evolution" has become strongly attached to modern ideas of progress within design. The many contemporary practitioners and commentators who like to think of design as exhibiting Darwinian traits will often point to development within certain archetypes – such as ships – over long time-spans. Their aim is to show how each generation has improved upon the previous in what they would argue to be a logical and inevitable way. Popular and widespread though this mode of explanation may be, it surely provides only a partial explanation.

In reality, progress is often halting, and the emergence of new approaches is often affected by a variety of complex factors. Some of these are cultural, relating to the structures and priorities of different societies, and some are governed by what materials are available in particular geographical contexts, or the results of trade and conquest.

Creative differences

As a category of objects, ships are relatively easy to compare: all must interact with water, which means it is possible to assess how effective one hull form is relative to others. However, items such as jewellery are largely symbolic. The different styles and forms that are found relate much more to matters of culture and taste than to any objectively functional criterion.

Historians of the ancient and medieval worlds have written at length about the multitudinous factors informing the making of objects within the cultures and contexts of the distant past. In all instances, what was produced emerged through means that were considerably more convoluted than the basic struggles for survival observed within the animal kingdom by Charles Darwin. All of this makes early design a fascinating subject for study. ■

STONE TOOLS ARE FOSSILIZED HUMAN BEHAVIOUR
TOOLS AND WEAPONS

IN CONTEXT

FOCUS
Objects can do the work of human hands

FIELD
Product design, material design, industrial design

BEFORE
c. 3.3 MYA Rudimentary stone tools, thought to be used for cutting and processing meat, provide evidence of early humans in Africa.

AFTER
c. 8000 BCE Polished stone tools, sickles, grinding stones, and evidence of pottery being used to store food indicate more settled communities and a shift to agriculture.

c. 3000 BCE Bronze swords, axes, daggers, and spearheads show how the availability of new technology can transform design and craftsmanship.

Millions of years ago, human ancestors were driven to create tools and weapons that extended their capabilities beyond the limitations of their hands. These implements distinguished early humans from other species and this innate urge to solve problems through purposeful crafting illustrates that human instincts have always had the essence of what is now recognized as design.

The oldest recorded tools shaped from rocks – mainly flint, quartz, and obsidian – were used more than 3 million years ago. Primitive implements were crude, but developed in sophistication and complexity over time, alongside the evolution of various human species.

Long development
Homo habilis (the "handy man"), who lived around 2.3 million years ago, chipped stones to create sharp

Stone tool making is often depicted as a male activity, as in this etching from *Primitive Man* by Louis Figuier (1870). However, evidence shows that women also crafted stone tools.

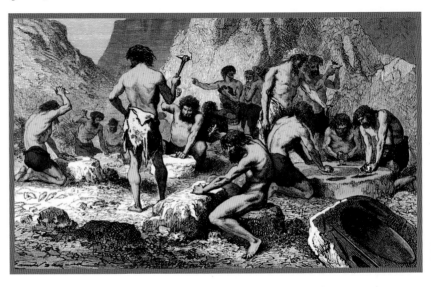

See also: Early ceramics 22–23 ▪ Tools for cooking and eating 30–31 ▪ Bronzeware 42–45 ▪ Early mass production 64–65 ▪ Industrial design 146–47

Toolmaking techniques

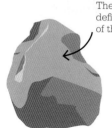

The tool shape is defined by the shape of the original stone

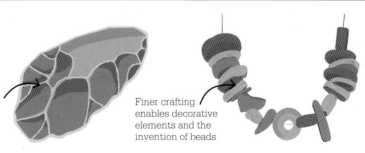

Flakes are removed from the sides to create a teardrop-shaped handaxe

Finer crafting enables decorative elements and the invention of beads

Stone knapping demanded motor and cognitive skills. The toolmaker had to choose a rock, strike it at the correct angle, and use an appropriate amount of force. These tools included choppers, scrapers, and pounders.

Bifacial flaking required a greater level of skill and patience. The toolmaker had to have a clear idea of what they wanted to make, such as a handaxe. The tool would be methodically shaped and then refined.

Pressure flaking was a technique that required the use of a sharp, hard flaking tool for finer, more precise shaping. Creative thinking brought the development of new tools to create basic clothing, etchings, and sculpture.

---

edges in a technique known as "stone knapping". Later, around 1.9 million years ago, *Homo erectus* ("upright man") displayed further advances in toolmaking by fashioning handaxes and cleavers. These tools, known as Acheulean tools, were symmetrical, double-sided, and multi-functional. The technique was used to make tools for more than a million years, and transformed the way human ancestors interacted with their environment – from hunting and butchering meat, to digging roots and hacking wood.

During the Middle Palaeolithic era, from around 300,000 years ago, *Homo sapiens* – the first modern humans – built on this legacy by inventing more diverse and specialized devices, such as flint-headed arrows and spears. These weapons were crafted with sharp, durable tips that vastly enhanced their efficacy in hunting, and in safeguarding against predators. "Hafting" – the practice of attaching stone or bone tools to

wooden handles to improve the utility and versatility of various implements – also emerged in this era.

Prestigious artefacts

It is likely that tools and weapons were not merely utilitarian objects, but also held cultural significance, representing hard-won survival, hunting prowess, and social status. Toolmaking involved innovation, refinement, and experimentation. As early humans improved their toolmaking techniques, they developed skills that extended beyond survival, improving their problem-solving and manual dexterity. This evolutionary transformation, over the gradual course of nearly 2 million years, was accompanied by a tripling of the size of the brain.

The Upper Palaeolithic period, from around 50,000 years ago, contains evidence of early settlements, and is considered to mark the start of "behavioural modernity", the point at which

humans developed behaviours and thoughts similar to modern humans. There were rapid strides in tool technology, such as fine blades, darts, and harpoons. In addition to stone, humans began to craft a variety of tools such as needles and fish hooks from bone, antler, and ivory. The desire to design, once started, could not be stopped. ▪

When you look at an array of these new tool types, you sense a different kind of mind at work, a qualitatively different interaction with the world.
Richard Leakey
Origins Reconsidered, 1993

THE EARTH LEAKED RED OCHRE

PIGMENTS AND COLOURS

The use of pigments –
coloured substances – is
deep-rooted in humanity.
From the earliest times, rocks were
scraped across surfaces to leave
coloured marks, and ground minerals
were smeared on to rock to create
patterns and images.

Materials from nature

Homo sapiens began by using
elements readily available in their
environment. Archaeological
findings suggest that people used
simple tools to obtain colours from
rocks, minerals, clay, plants, and
charcoal. Pigments and paint-
grinding tools dated at 350–
400,000 years old have been found
in a cave at Twin Rivers in Zambia,
southern Africa, and the earliest
known paintings, found in
Sulawesi, Indonesia, date to
around 45,500 years ago.

Early humans discovered that
certain materials produce colours
when ground into a powder. For
instance, ochre was made from clay
containing reddish or yellowish
iron oxide, and charcoal provided
black. Colours were fixed with
binders such as water, saliva,

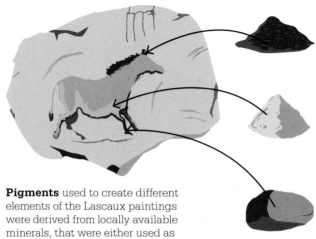

Pigments used to create different
elements of the Lascaux paintings
were derived from locally available
minerals, that were either used as
solid lumps, or ground into powder.

Manganese oxide
possibly applied
with a "brush" of
moss or hair, was
used to create the
mane and forelock.

Yellow ochre
(goethite) paint
was blown onto
rock to make the
main areas of body.

**A solid lump of
manganese oxide**
may have been used
to create the lines
of the horse's face,
neck, legs, and tail.

See also: Written communication 34–41 ▪ Theory of colours 94–101 ▪ Pantone colours 250–51 ▪ Memphis Milano and Maximalism 268–69

animal fats, or plant saps and applied with fingers, sticks, or other tools to surfaces such as cave walls, animal hides, or human skin.

The designs created with these techniques ranged from simple lines and hand prints to human figures and stylized drawings of animals. People may also have decorated their bodies. It is not known why this art was created, but the fact that the images on rock are so durable suggests a ritual or spiritual significance. Even today, many Indigenous peoples use natural pigments for ritual art, or as a marker of status or identity. Some see certain colours as having a particular meaning: for example, among some Aboriginal Australian people, red represents blood and black stands for earth.

Colour and meaning

With the rise of migration and trade, and the emergence of cities, human use of colour became more sophisticated. New pigments were discovered and transported long distances. In societies across the world, colour was used in clothing and furnishing, and to adorn houses, palaces, and temples.

Some colours acquired a special significance due to their richness and rarity. One example is Tyrian purple, from Tyre on the eastern Mediterranean coast, in use from the 16th century BCE. The pigment was extracted from snails; it took many thousands of snails to produce a tiny amount of colour, so purple was extremely expensive and reserved for the highest in society, such as emperors, kings, and priests. Another significant colour is lapis lazuli, a deep-blue mineral extracted from rocks in what is now Afghanistan. In ancient Egypt, the colour was associated with immortality, and included in jewellery and artefacts such as the funeral mask of Pharaoh Tutankhamun. In Asia and Europe, lapis lazuli was ground to make ultramarine, a deep blue. Because it was so expensive and hard to obtain, it was considered more precious than gold and reserved for the most significant parts of a

We love to contemplate blue, not because it advances to us, but because it draws us after it.
Johann Wolfgang von Goethe
Theory of Colours, 1810

painting – notably, for the Virgin Mary's robe in Christian art.

Continuing influence

Even now, we respond to the status signals of Roman gold and purple, and to the primal emotions first stirred tens of thousands of years ago by red ochre and black charcoal. These principles are still incorporated in clothing, objects, and brands across the world. ▪

The Lascaux caves

One of the most powerful examples of prehistoric art is found in the caves at Lascaux, in southwestern France. The caves were discovered in 1940 by 18-year-old Marcel Ravidat and three of his friends, who found a hole leading to a shaft 15 m (50 ft) deep. Marcel Ravidat's friend Jacques Marsal described what they found as "a cavalcade of animals larger than life" that "seemed to be moving". The complex was found to contain more than 6,000 paintings of animals such as horses, bison, deer, bears, and wolves. One figure is of a man with a bird's head, thought by some experts to be a shaman. The images, dated at around 17,000 years old, were made over many generations. Nobody knows why the paintings were made; they could have been a record of past hunting trips, or been part of a ritual to ensure successful hunting in the future.

Lascaux is now a UNESCO World Heritage Site, but it has been closed to the public since 1963 to protect the paintings from damage by visitors.

Larger-than-life animals tower above Jacques Marsal and Marcel Ravidat (seated) and Abbé Henri Breuil, an expert on prehistoric art.

THE RIDGED LINES RISE, FALL, AND SWIRL

EARLY CERAMICS

IN CONTEXT

FOCUS
Making and firing ceramic vessels and other objects

FIELD
Materials and material innovation

BEFORE
***c.* 29,000–25,000 BCE** In Central Europe, the Gravettian people manufacture clay figurines, such as the Venus of Dolní Věstonice.

***c.* 18,000 BCE** Pottery is produced in the Jiangxi province of south China.

AFTER
***c.* 300 BCE–250 CE** During Japan's Yayoi period, pottery-makers develop a smooth, minimal, undecorated style, using reddish clay.

***c.* 250–538 CE** Influenced by stoneware arriving from Korea, ceramicists during Japan's Kofun period use potters' wheels and Korean-style kilns to make Sueki stoneware.

Ceramics – both practical and decorative – have a lineage that can be traced back more than 30,000 years. While methods of manufacture have changed over time, pottery is still one of the oldest crafts. Many different peoples across the ancient world were able to develop pottery independently of each other because the required clay is abundant in soils around the globe.

At least 12,500 years ago, the society living in present-day Japan started to produce some of the first ceramic vessels. This was the beginning of the Jōmon pottery tradition, which lasted more than 10,000 years and evolved through many distinct stages.

The Jōmon people were semi-nomadic, shifting their settlements to cooler, warmer, or more resource-rich areas according to their needs. They discovered how to mix local earthenware clay with organic materials such as crushed shells to make it more workable. They then fired the ceramic objects they made in outdoor fires that could reach up to 900°C (1,650°F). As hot as this is, it is a low temperature for firing ceramics, which means that Jōmon pottery is not as hard or durable as the kiln-fired wares of later cultures.

Design evolution

Archaeologists believe that Jōmon potters were women. Working without potters' wheels, these artisans crafted their wares by hand, often using coils of clay to construct vessels from the bottom up, before smoothing them out and adding decoration. Many pots were

This fire-flame (*ka'en doki*) cooking vessel dates from *c.* 2500 BCE. When in use, its base would have been set in a hole in the ground. However, most fire-flame pottery was probably decorative.

See also: Tools for cooking and eating 30–31 ▪ Standardizing pottery 48–49 ▪ Mass-produced ceramics 92–93
▪ The Arts and Crafts movement 112–19 ▪ Art pottery 122–23

The vessels shake the
viewer to their depths
with their aura …
They have a pulsing strength
and sturdy balance.
Okamoto Taro
Japanese artist and writer, 1952

patterned by pressing rope into
the wet clay at intervals, giving the
era its name: in Japanese, *jōmon*
means "cord-marked".

In the early stages of Jōmon
pottery, designs were simple and
functional. Potters made deep
vessels for carrying, storing, and
cooking liquids and foods. In an
age before metal pots existed, the
production of earthenware vessels
that could withstand high heat
would have revolutionized cooking.

This terracotta statuette is typical
of the 11th–4th century BCE Jōmon
dogū style. It has large eyes, a wide
waist, and markings on the torso.
It may have represented a goddess.

Through the millennia, Jōmon
potters continued to make
functional ceramics, but their
designs became increasingly
decorative. By the Middle Jōmon
period (2500–1500 BCE), the upper
half of most pots was covered in
elaborate swirls and often had
distinctive flame-like edges.

Spiritual value
Jōmon ceramics served cultural
and spiritual purposes, as well as
fulfilling practical needs. People
sometimes buried human remains
in clay pots, and from 5000–300 BCE,
Jōmon potters created increasing
numbers of masks and figurines
known as dogū, which are believed
to have been used in rituals. The
exaggerated characteristics of
these stylized items reveal that the
potters were both highly skilled
and accustomed to working with
specific symbolism.

As well as transforming the daily
practicalities of cooking and eating,
the Jōmon people's innovation with
ceramics profoundly influenced
their cultural practices and perhaps
even the development of their
religion. Their extraordinary pottery
continues to inspire artists and
designers, and raises questions
about the lives and beliefs of the
people who produced it. ▪

Coil-building technique

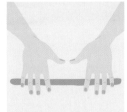

1: The consistency of
the clay is important – it
must be soft and pliable
without being sticky
or wet.

2: The clay coils are
moulded on a slightly
damp surface into long,
thin, cylindrical shapes
with an even diameter.

3: The circular clay base
is scored to ensure that
the first coil attaches to
it before the other coils
are added.

4: Further coils are added
carefully to build the
vessel. If they are pressed
too hard, the lower coils
become flattened.

5: Once the vessel
reaches the desired
height, the coils are
smoothed. Then the clay
is dried, ready for firing.

TWISTED, SEWN, AND PLAITED

EARLY TEXTILES

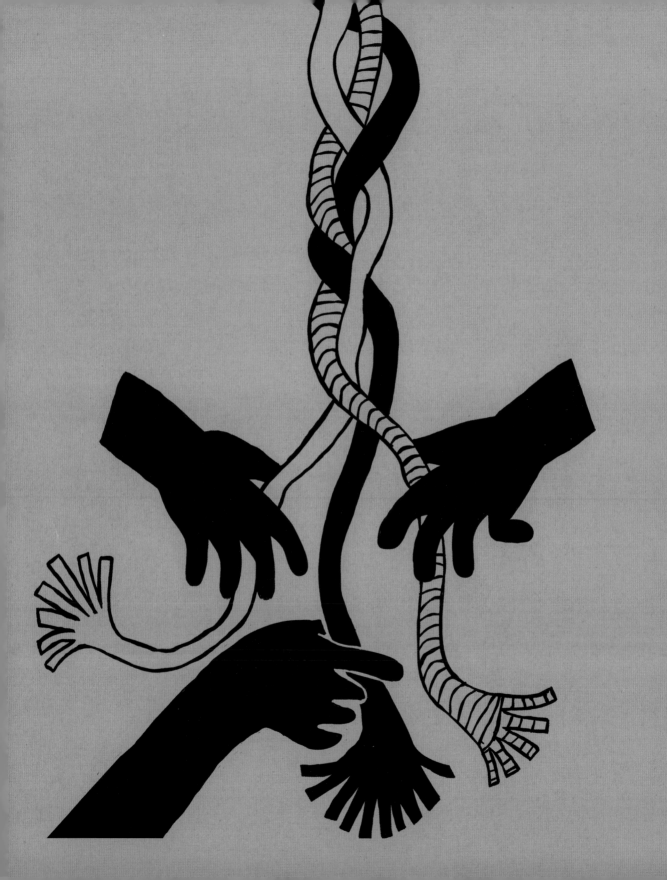

Textile-making was one of the earliest crafts to be developed by humans. Textiles provided warmth and protection in the form of clothing and shelter but were also used in communication, ritual, and worship. The spinning of thread and the figure of the weaver are frequently referenced in ancient mythology and language: in Latin, the words for "text" and "textile" come from the same root – *texere*, meaning "to weave" – and the early Buddhist sacred texts known as Sutras and Tantras take their names from words linked to "thread" and "loom" to represent strands and bodies of knowledge.

Unearthing textiles

Textiles are more likely to break down and decay than pottery and metal items, so estimates of when humans first started to produce them vary widely.

Where textiles have survived, it is usually due to specific environmental conditions. Plant fibres tend to fare less well over long periods of time, but some have been preserved in the alkaline-rich chalk beds of alpine lakes.

Now the first and chief of our needs is the provision of food for existence and life. The second is housing and the third is raiment.
Plato
Republic **(Book II),** *c.***370 BCE**

Similarly, acidic conditions such as those found in peat bogs can help to preserve fibres of animal origin. Unfortunately, these fibres deteriorate rapidly as soon as they are removed from the ground. When Grewelthorpe Man – the mummified body of an ancient Roman found wearing a green toga and yellow stockings – was unearthed from a bog in Yorkshire, in the UK, in 1850, his clothing disintegrated so quickly that only a fragment of stockings and the sole of a sandal survived.

Images of weavers on ancient pottery provide a wealth of detail about the tools and techniques used to create fabric.

Weavers of life

The importance of textiles through the ages is confirmed by the presence of goddesses of weaving in every ancient culture – from Athena for the Greeks, to Frigg in Norse mythology and Amaterasu in Japanese legends.

Another recurrent trope is the spider, a natural-born spinner of fine, strong threads, and weaver of well-constructed webs. In ancient Sumer, the goddess of weaving, Utta, was imagined as a spider spinning a web; and in pre-dynastic Egypt, the goddess Neith, described as the spinner and weaver of destiny, is also associated with the spider.

The story of Arachne derives from Greek mythology but was popularized by the Roman poet Ovid. An accomplished mortal weaver, Arachne boastfully compared her work to that of Athena, goddess of weaving (as well as of wisdom and warfare). The two engaged in a contest, which Arachne won. A raging Athena turned her challenger into a spider, allowing Arachne to practise her craft but lose her human form.

See also: Pigments and colours 20–21 ▪ Woodblock textile printing 78–79 ▪ Manufacturing textiles 84–91 ▪ Dawn of synthetic fabrics 194–95 ▪ Safety fabrics 244–47 ▪ Smart materials 314–17

Humans have used the resources around them to create textiles and fabrics since prehistoric times. One commonly used material was bast – a soft fibre from the bark and stems of plants such as flax and hemp. The earliest microscopic flax threads, believed to date from some 34,000 years ago, were found in a cave in the Caucasus Mountains of Georgia in 2009. It is thought that these fibres were braided into ropes, woven into baskets, and used to craft garments. Some of them had been dyed, which indicates that the inhabitants of the cave were already familiar with plant and animal pigments and colouring techniques.

Evidence of a strong cord dating from around 15,000 BCE was found fossilized in the Lascaux Cave of southwestern France in 1953. The clay imprint reveals a two-ply cord, where two separate strands of fibre are each twisted in one direction before being twisted together in the opposite direction for strength – a simple technique that is still in use today. The rope would have been used in conjunction with stone to create tools, or made into fishing and hunting nets.

While flax was the earliest and most widely used plant fibre, DNA sequencing suggests that cotton has been around for 10 to 20 million years. The first evidence of its cultivation, however, dates from around 3000 BCE in Mohenjo-daro, a settlement of the Indus Valley Civilization, now in Pakistan.

Fibres of animal origin

Wool and silk were among the first animal fibres to be widely used. Among the advantages they offered were greater warmth and an increased ability to take dye, which in turn brought greater decorative opportunities.

Sheep were domesticated from around 11,000–9000 BCE in Mesopotamia. These early »

Strands of rope found in the Lascaux Cave are seen in fossilized form on the positive plate on the left; the corresponding imprint is visible on the negative plate on the right.

Early humans use **animal hides** for **clothing and shelter** to provide warmth and comfort.

Fibres taken from **plant stems** are used to make **fabrics**.

Humans discover **animal fibres** and domesticate sheep and the **silk moth**.

Different **cloth-making techniques** – such as **felting, netting, and weaving** – are developed.

Continuous advances in dyes, techniques, and materials prompt new fashions in textile production.

animals were mouflons, which are less woolly than their modern counterparts, so they were initially bred only for meat, milk, and hides. The earliest carbonized traces of woven wool fabrics were found in Çatalhöyük, Anatolia, on the site of a Neolithic settlement that was occupied from *c.* 7400–6200 BCE.

There is evidence of silk production in China as early as the 4th millennium BCE, but the manufacturing process was a fiercely guarded secret that was kept from the rest of the world for a further 5,000 years.

Creating fabrics

For most fabrics – with the exception of barkcloth and felted wool – raw material must first be made into thread. When working with shorter fibres such as wool or cotton, a technique called spinning is used to twist the fibres into a regular, continuous filament. In their simplest form, the two main tools needed for this process were first developed during prehistoric times. The first is the spindle – a stick to spin the fibre, which is sometimes weighted with a disc called a whorl. The second tool is

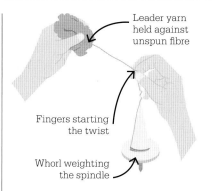

When preparing to make yarn, the spinner teases a few fibres out of the bundle and attaches them to the hook at the top of the spindle.

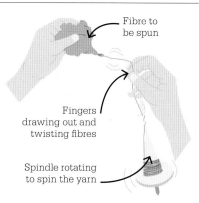

To spin the yarn, the spinner rotates the spindle while continuing to draw out and twist the fibres, which wind around the spindle.

called a distaff: this is a secondary stick that is used to hold the unspun fibre.

The resulting thread can then be worked into a fabric through netting, knitting, plaiting, or basketry, but the most widely used technique is weaving, which is defined by its separate warp and weft fibres. The device for weaving is the loom, which functions by allowing the warp – a series of parallel threads that run in one direction – to be held tight, and then enabling weft threads to be passed under and over one by one, at a 90-degree angle, until the fabric is created.

There were several different types of loom used in ancient civilizations: floor looms, where weavers crouched on the ground; vertical looms, which often featured weights on the end of the warp threads to hold them taut; and back-strap looms, where the weaver created tension by positioning the loom between a fixed point, such as a tree, and a strap around their back.

Dyeing and the significance of colour

Early natural dyes came from a variety of plants and animals: reds from the madder plant, the saffron lily, or an insect called kermes, which gives crimson; blues from the woad plant; and brown-purple hues from fermenting lichen. The dyeing process also required a mordant, such as alum or iron salts, to fix the colour to a fabric; the use of such fixatives increased the range of colours that could be derived from the dye.

Textiles were also bleached. One method involved draping linen or wool over burning sulphur, while in ancient Egypt a substance called natron – also used in the mummification process – was used to bleach and brighten fabric.

Colour was a way of indicating status, and restrictions on dress, known as sumptuary laws, helped to maintain social hierarchies. For example, in ancient Rome only senators and magistrates were entitled to wear robes in Tyrian purple, a rich colour extracted in small amounts and at great expense from a sea snail.

These colourful fibres – created using dyes from natural pigments – will be woven into baskets at a market in Peru.

The time-consuming nature of making textiles – whether for household, community, or trading purposes – meant that a large proportion of the population was involved in their production. The responsibility for gathering suitable material – either growing crops or tending sheep – was often the province of men, but spinning and weaving were generally considered to be women's work; along with food preparation, it was perhaps more compatible with child-rearing.

Symbols and patterns

Although textiles may primarily have been developed for essentials, such as clothing, they were also used for ornamental purposes – and in both cases decoration was an important element. The so-called Venus figurines – statues of female forms dating from the Palaeolithic era – sometimes feature string skirts or other items of clothing too skimpy to provide warmth or protect modesty. It is more likely that such garments had a symbolic value or were intended to draw attention to the body. More widely, depictions of clothing show developing techniques and changing fashions.

> Go, then, within the house and busy yourself with your daily duties, your loom, your distaff, and the ordering of your servants.
> **Homer**
> ***The Odyssey* (Book XXI), 8th century** BCE

The oldest surviving woven garment is the Tarkhan Dress, which dates from around 3000 BCE. Found at a burial site in Egypt, this linen tunic reveals sophisticated detailing – from decorative edging, to fine pleats around the shoulders.

Neolithic and Bronze Age textiles were often patterned. In Neolithic Europe, textile scraps have been found to be decorated with stripes, checks, and triangles, while Bronze Age Minoan women were depicted wearing patterns of stripes, dots, and wavy lines. Other archaeological finds reveal decorative elements such as fringing and embellishments with gold thread, shells, and beads – all of which required time, skill, and clear design intention.

Barkcloth was made in a variety of different textures. Depending on the materials used, the fabric could be coarse and oily, or fine and delicate, almost like muslin. The finished cloth was often painted with patterns and symbols related to the community making it.

Sometimes, textiles were patterned for narrative purposes. Stories from ancient Greece tell of woven friezes depicting historical or mythological scenes. While embroidery was most often used to add pattern to textiles, it could also be used for pictorial work – a famous, if much later, example is the Bayeux Tapestry, more accurately defined as an embroidery of wool thread on linen cloth.

Unchanged methods

Working with information from archaeological discoveries, modern weavers are sometimes able to replicate ancient garments, using their knowledge of the craft to fill gaps in the historical record. Cave paintings and drawings on ancient pottery are a valuable source of

The young woman depicted in this Minoan fresco of *c.* 1600 BCE is wearing a short-sleeved gown decorated with colourful stripes that provides evidence of contemporary fashion.

information: not only do they provide details of contemporary clothing, but they also show looms and spindles in use. These sources, in addition to later written records, reveal how widespread and important the making and trading of textiles were to early civilizations – and how, right up until the Industrial Revolution of the mid-18th century, fabric-making methods remained largely unchanged. ∎

THE EXTENSION OF A MAN'S HAND
TOOLS FOR COOKING AND EATING

IN CONTEXT

FOCUS
**The development
of cooking utensils**

FIELD
Product design

BEFORE
c.1.6 MYA Early humans
create handaxes from stone,
and use them to cut meat
and vegetables.

c.10,000 BCE The invention
of pottery provides new ways
to cook, store, and serve food.

c.3500 BCE Chopsticks
are used in China.

AFTER
1600 The city of Sheffield,
UK, becomes famous for
the production of cutlery.

1950s Disposable cutlery
is developed and becomes
widely used as fast food
grows in popularity.

1954 The non-stick pan is
developed, allowing food
to brown without sticking.

The earliest known tools used for cooking and eating were crafted by our ancestors around 1.6 million years ago. A prime example is the handaxe, a stone tool skilfully flaked on both sides to create a sharp, knife-like edge, that could be used for cutting and chopping raw food. These early utensils allowed our ancestors to process raw food more effectively; they could cut it into manageable pieces or use tools to break down tough plant fibres. Tools not only expanded people's dietary options – they also changed how people behaved around food, transforming cooking and eating into key aspects of human culture.

Ancient humans **begin to cook** food using fire.

A shortage of fuel leads to the discovery that smaller pieces of food cook **faster, using less fuel**.

Small pieces of food are **hard to pick up** during and after cooking, when they are **very hot** and likely to **burn the skin**.

**Carved wooden sticks can take the place of
fingers and be manipulated to pick up small
pieces of hot food safely.**

See also: Tools and weapons 18–19 ▪ Early ceramics 22–23 ▪ Standardizing pottery 48–49
▪ Interchangeable parts 106–07 ▪ Multifunctional tools 136–37 ▪ Ergonomics 278–85

Over time, ancient tools and culinary practices slowly evolved, setting the stage for the diverse culinary traditions that can be found around the world today. Initially, stone, wood, bone, and clay were the main materials used for utensils, with metal becoming more common later on.

Mastering materials

Stone mortars and pestles were used for grinding grains, seeds, and herbs. Clay pots and vessels could be used for either cooking or storage. Wooden tools, such as

A man uses a peel – a shovel-like tool used to slide baked goods into and out of an oven – in this mosaic from a Roman villa near Saint-Romain-en-Gal, France.

spatulas and stirring sticks, were crafted for preparing food in pots over open flames. All these tools reflected a practical understanding of the materials available and the needs of basic food preparation.

Unique tools and approaches developed in each part of the world. Ancient Mesopotamians, for instance, used clay ovens for baking bread. In ancient China, meanwhile, the development of woks and clay steamers provided quite different methods of cooking.

Elegant eating

The earliest eating utensils were very simple – people used their hands or basic tools made from carved wood, bone, and later metal to consume food. Chopsticks were used in ancient China as long as 3,500 years ago. They were initially used for

cooking, stirring, and serving food, rather than for eating. As Chinese cuisine changed, the popularity of finely chopped ingredients and bite-sized portions made chopsticks a practical choice for bringing food to the mouth. Chopsticks were made from bamboo, wood, or even bronze depending on the materials available, local cultural preferences, and the social status of the diner.

Forks, meanwhile, were first used for dining in the noble courts of Persia, the Middle East, and the Byzantine Empire, becoming common among wealthy families by the 10th century. From there, their use in dining spread to Europe in the late middle ages.

Cooking utensils have been further refined in more recent times. The 20th century saw the discovery of stainless steel and the invention of non-stick cookware. New technology, coupled with the globalization of tastes, will continue to shape our culinary practices, and transform how we prepare and consume food. ▪

How forks became fashionable in Europe

The dining fork was introduced to Italian courts in the 11th century via the Byzantine Empire. It gained wider acceptance in Europe during the Renaissance, partly due to the influence of Catherine de' Medici, an Italian noblewoman, whose marriage to Henry II of France in 1533 marked the introduction of the fork to the French court.

Initially met with scepticism and gentle ridicule, the fork gradually found its place in the dining customs of Europe,

evolving from a novelty to a symbol of refinement. By the 17th century, the fork was increasingly prevalent in European upper-class dining rooms, and over time, it became a standard part of table settings. This marked a cultural shift towards more formal European dining etiquette, reflecting changing social attitudes towards hygiene.

Early forks had two or three prongs; the four-pronged version familiar today only became popular in the 19th century.

A nobleman spears his food with an early type of fork in this illustration from an Italian religious manuscript dating from the 11th century.

THE WORLD BECAME SMALLER
TRANSPORT AND PORTABILITY

Human ingenuity in transportation has allowed people to traverse land, seas, skies, and even space – and these developments have influenced societies and the spread of ideas. Three important innovations were made before 2000 BCE: the boat, the wheel, and harnessing the power of animals.

This ancient Egyptian fresco found in the tomb of Pharaoh Seti I shows the ram-headed god Khnum on a boat with a sail. Khnum was closely associated with water, and was thought to play a part in the inundation of the Nile.

A way over water

Humans travelled and fished on water from around 10,000 BCE, first venturing out on logs and simple rafts, buoyed by inflated animal skins. The first boats and canoes, made from hollowed-out tree trunks and woven reeds were created around 7000 BCE. They were easier to steer, and could carry more weight. Animal skins and pitch – a black resin made from tar – kept the boats waterproof.

The ancient Egyptians added sails to their vessels by 3000 BCE, building larger boats and voyaging further out to sea. Two main types

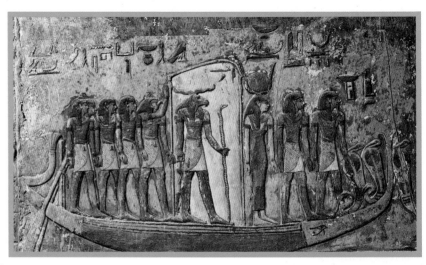

See also: Importing materials 46–47 ▪ Early mass production 64–65 ▪ Ford Model T 154–55 ▪ Promoting travel 182–83

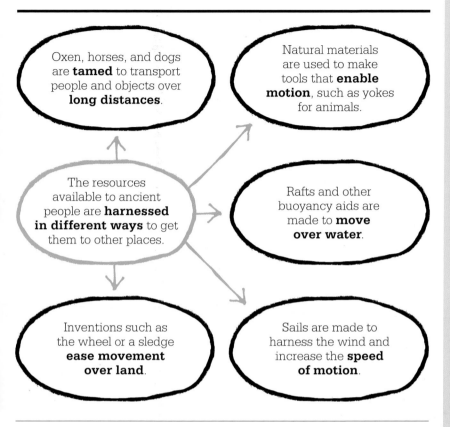

Oxen, horses, and dogs are **tamed** to transport people and objects over **long distances**.

Natural materials are used to make tools that **enable motion**, such as yokes for animals.

The resources available to ancient people are **harnessed in different ways** to get them to other places.

Rafts and other buoyancy aids are made to **move over water**.

Inventions such as the wheel or a sledge **ease movement over land**.

Sails are made to harness the wind and increase the **speed of motion**.

of ship developed: long, sleek ships powered by rowers, and broad, deep vessels powered by sail.

Using animal strength
Humans began to domesticate animals for carrying goods around 5000 BCE. The earliest pack animals were donkeys, camels, llamas, and elephants. Farmers also began to use livestock to transport crops, and oxen were yoked to simple ploughs and used to prepare land for cultivation. Harnesses helped to distribute weight, which allowed the animals to pull larger loads.

Another significant development occurred when people tamed and rode horses. Initially, riding was done bareback, but by around 1300 BCE, riding tack including

halters, bridles, and basic saddles, provided greater control. Horses were used for high-speed transport, hunting, and in battle.

The invention of the wheel
Around 3200 BCE, solid wooden wheels were fitted to simple wagons. Spoked wheels appeared from around 2000 BCE, which made vehicles much lighter and faster. Around 100 BCE, bearings were introduced to reduce friction, which allowed the wheel to turn more easily.

These innovations in transport were instrumental to trade and cultural exchange across vast distances, and shaped the movement of goods and people for thousands of years. ▪

The chariot

A light-weight, two-wheeled cart used for ancient warfare – the chariot was made possible by the combination of horse, harness, and the spoked wheel. Thought to have originated in Sumer (in modern Iraq) around 2000 BCE, chariots quickly spread to ancient Egypt and China, and reached Europe by 1000 BCE. The chariot revolutionized battle tactics and became an object of ceremonial status, especially for Egyptian pharaohs – four specimens were discovered in the tomb of Tutankhamun.

The chariot fell out of use in combat by 1000 CE as riding on horseback became more common. However, it continued to hold a prestigious role in processions and public races such as the Olympic games in Greece. Mosaics from the Roman empire depict Bacchus, the god of wine, driving chariots pulled by tigers and leopards, surrounded by other wild animals. This gives an indication of the chariot's continued significance as a symbol of power, intertwined with mythology.

Emperor Mu Wang (c.985–c.907 BCE) of China's Zhou dynasty is depicted in his chariot in this illustration from the 17th century.

LANGUAGE DOES NOT LEAVE FOSSILS UNTIL IT HAS BECOME WRITTEN

WRITTEN COMMUNICATION

Language – a mutually agreed system of sounds and signs that convey meaning – is the feature that distinguishes human beings from other animals. Some scholars think that humans may have been using language for at least 150,000 years. It evolved from basic signals common to most animals – such as alarm calls or babies' cries – to systems of meaning used for passing on ideas.

Hunter-gatherers may have used basic sounds and gestures to share information about activities such as hunting, foraging, toolmaking, or survival techniques. This may have taken the form of storytelling, songs, gestures, facial expressions, and imitation, along with practical demonstrations.

They also expressed themselves through body and tool decoration, cave paintings, and rock art. These decorations may have served as a way to preserve stories and cultural or spiritual practices, and to pass on these ideas from one generation to the next. This practice saw the beginning of humans intentionally creating symbolic designs.

The emergence of written communication

Writing was a conceptual leap that allowed humans to store information and transmit it to people in other places. It required communities to learn the same system of symbols, so texts could

The epic of Gilgamesh is the most important work of Mesopotamian literature. This tablet, describing Gilgamesh's meeting with the goddess Ishtar, is dated to the 7th century BCE.

be read as well as written. It also needed durable surfaces to write on, and methods for creating symbols that would last.

The precursors of writing, in which certain symbols stood for specific words or signs, arose independently in Mesopotamia (present-day Iraq), Egypt, China, and central America. The oldest by far is the "token system" used in Mesopotamia from 8000 BCE, in which discs and cylinders were used as counters for trade, with different shapes representing specific goods, such as oil, wheat, and livestock. The number of tokens represented the number or amount of each item. As physical symbols, they could be understood by people in different regions, speaking different languages.

The tokens were transmitted inside "envelopes" made from balls of clay. This system evolved into one in which the shapes of the

See also: Movable type and early graphic design 70–77 ▪ Design catalogues 82–83 ▪ Sans serif fonts 102–03 ▪ Vizualizing data 108–09 ▪ Information design 144–45 ▪ Political messaging 164–69 ▪ Branding 200–07 ▪ Pictograms 256–57

counters were impressed into clay tablets. Later, pictograms – images created as symbols for objects or names – would be inscribed on clay using a stylus (a sharpened rod similar to a pen). Over the centuries the symbols became simplified. They could also be combined to create ideograms – symbols that express ideas.

Finally, around 3500–3300 BCE, the Sumerians of Mesopotamia developed the system of marks that we know as cuneiform. This system, rediscovered in the late 17th century by German traveller Engelbert Kämpfer and named by him after the Latin *cuneus* (wedge), derived its shapes from the writing implement used to make the marks: a reed stylus with a triangular end.

The next innovation appeared around 3000 BCE – the use of symbols to represent the sounds of speech ("phonetic" symbols). These were combined as a rebus – a kind of visual pun in which the sounds associated with each symbol would make up a name or a concept.

In hieroglyphics, the names of pharaohs and other important people would be written inside an oval shape called a *shenu*, or a cartouche. This cartouche contains the birth name of the pharaoh Tutankhamun, together with his title "Ruler of On of Upper Egypt".

The symbols at the top represent the god Amun – written first even if they are not pronounced first.

This symbol represents the consonant "t".

The bird represents the sound "w"; combined with the two semicircles, this makes "twt".

The ankh – symbol of life.

These symbols represent Tutankhamun's title as ruler.

Cartouche of Tutankhamun

Cuneiform became a complex system in which ideograms were mixed with phonetic symbols, with additional "determinative" marks so readers could distinguish the two. As a result, it came to be used for purposes including religion, law, and literature. This phonetic system also spread to neighbouring peoples such as the Akkadians and Assyrians, and to others who used very different languages – reaching as far as the Canaanite language in Palestine and the Urartian language of Armenia.

Sacred writing

Hieroglyphics, the writing system of ancient Egypt, appeared around 3300 BCE and remained in use until »

Jean-François Champollion

Born in Figeac, France, in 1790, Champollion, at just 16 years old, presented a paper to the Grenoble Academy in which he argued that Coptic, the language of Christians in Egypt, was the same language spoken by the ancient Egyptians.

In 1799, a French lieutenant at Rashid (Rosetta) in the Nile Delta discovered a stone slab with inscriptions in hieroglyphics, ancient Greek, and an unknown language. The last sentence indicated that the three sets of text gave the same information. Champollion solved the puzzle in 1822, when he cross-checked the names Kleopatra and Ptolemy on other inscriptions with the same names on the Rosetta stone, and worked out that the hieroglyphs consisted of a combination of pictograms and phonetic signs.

Key works

1821 *De l'Écriture Hiératique des anciens Égyptiens*
1822 *Lettre à M. Dacier Relative à l'Alphabet des Hiéroglyphes Phonétiques*
1824 *Précis du système hiéroglyphique des anciens Égyptiens*

The Pharaoh Narmer is named on this carving with a rebus: a catfish (top), for the sound nar, and a chisel (bottom centre) for mer.

The rebus principle

The rebus principle is a technique in which a word is "written" using pictograms of objects whose names make up the sounds of that word. In this way pictograms are used to represent a sound or syllable, or combined to make an entire word or phrase that may not have its own pictogram.

The term "rebus" comes from the Latin phrase *non verbis sed rebus*, which translates to mean "not by words but by things". As an example, the English sentence "I can see you" could be "written" by using drawings of an eye, a tin can, the sea, and a ewe.

The rebus principle enabled writing to represent more than just objects that could be shown as pictures or amounts. Writing systems from hieroglyphs to Chinese and Mayan script used it to represent abstract words, which otherwise would be hard to draw. The rebus principle is still used today in various contexts, from games and puzzles to brand logos (such as the "Eye-bee-M" logo for IBM).

the Romans closed the Egyptian temples in 391 CE. Hieroglyphics are the first full writing system, in which symbols corresponded to spoken language, and which could be used to express abstract as well as concrete concepts. The system consists of three kinds of symbol: pictograms, visually representing a whole word; phonograms, which stand for the sounds of syllables; and symbols for single letters (consonants). As in Sumerian writing, determinative marks were used to show whether a symbol should be interpreted as an image or a sound. From the ancient Greek words *hieros* (sacred) and *glyphein* (to carve), hieroglyphics were initially used for religious inscriptions on temples, tombs, and statues. This led to their use in decorating daily and ritual objects, and to create administrative documents and literature. With continued use, and the application of writing – on easily available

papyrus – in everyday life, two further systems developed from hieroglyphs, to make writing easier and faster. Hieratic script was a cursive (joined-up) script originally used by priests, while Demotic script – from the ancient Greek *demotikos*, meaning "popular" – was an even quicker way of writing that spread to ordinary people.

Chinese characters and calligraphy

The Chinese script is formed from logograms – characters that each represent a word or part of a word.

The oldest known form of Chinese characters can be traced back to the Shang Dynasty (c.1600 to 1046 BCE), but some of the characters are still in use today. The earliest known writing was used on "oracle bones". This is a form of divination in which questions to the gods were engraved as pictograms on ox shoulder blades or tortoise plastrons (shells); a hot poker would then be applied to the bone or shell to crack it, and the pattern of cracks was interpreted. The interpretation was also recorded on the bone or shell. Like Egyptian hieroglyphics,

Chinese calligraphy fused art with meaning, as in the *Lanting Xu* (Orchard Pavilion Preface), written by Wang Xizhi in 353 CE, in which the flow of the script echoes the rhythm of the poem.

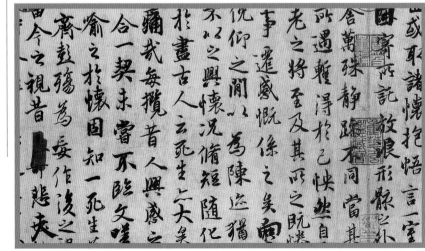

Evolution of alphabets

Hieroglyph	Proto-Sinaitic	Phoenician	Greek	Latin	
 Ox's head	 Aleph	Aleph	 Alpha	A	**The development** of the first two letters of the Latin alphabet can be traced from simplified Egyptian hieroglyphs adapted by the Proto-Sinaitic, Phoenician, and Greek alphabets to inform the Latin alphabet we know today. The images here show the pictographic evolution of letters A and B.
House	Bet	Beth	Beta	B	

Chinese script consisted of pictograms and phonograms and made use of the rebus principle. Chinese characters could also have more than one meaning, so extra determinative signs were used to help interpret the meaning. This system is still in use today.

Information was conveyed not just by the words themselves but also by the style in which they were written. Even today, in Chinese calligraphy each character must fit into a perfect square, and the strokes must be made in a particular sequence. The shape and strength of each stroke, and even the colour of the ink, all contribute to the meaning.

Central American scripts

On the other side of the world from Asia, the peoples of central America independently developed their own writing systems during the second millennium BCE. Like their Asian counterparts, cultures including the Olmec, the Mayans, and the Zapotec based their systems on pictograms and conveyed meaning using the rebus principle to spell out words such as names. Writing systems such as Mayan also used determinatives to give guidance on meaning.

The first alphabetic systems

The development of alphabets was another conceptual leap. In these systems, a small number of symbols represented individual letters, and could be combined to spell words in a wide range of languages. Unlike the pictographic systems that arose across the world, the alphabet was only invented once.

Perfection of handwriting needs proper education, regular exercises, and purity of the soul.
Yaqut al-Musta'simi
(d.1298)

The earliest known precursor to the alphabet is the Proto-Sinaitic script. It was developed in the Sinai Peninsula of ancient Egypt around c. 1900 BCE to represent the language of Semitic-speaking workers and enslaved people from Canaan (Palestine). These people created a very simplified form of the Egyptian hieroglyphic system, comprising a small number of the most commonly used pictograms of the time, such as the sign for "ox" (*aleph* in the Canaanite language) and "house" (*bet*). The system was initially used to give the sounds of people's or deities' names. This is the first example of an acrophonic alphabet – a development of the rebus principle in which a symbol is used to represent just the first sound of the associated word (thus a, b, and so on).

This script, taken back to Canaan, was developed further by the Phoenicians, from around 1300 BCE. The Phoenician script is an abjad – a writing system in which only consonants are represented, leaving the vowel sounds to be interpreted by the reader. It was also the first "linear" script, written and read horizontally from right »

to left, in contrast to previous multi-directional systems. The alphabet was well suited for trade and communication, and Phoenician merchants spread it throughout the Mediterranean region on sea routes to places as far away as Italy and the shores of north Africa.

The Phoenician script would, in turn, give rise to the Hebrew, Aramaic, Arabic, Italic, and Anatolian alphabets. By around 800 BCE it had reached the Greeks, who adapted it into a full alphabet, with vowels being given the same status as consonants, and writing that ran from left to right instead of right to left.

The people who became the Romans modified the alphabet to create the foundations of the writing system used across the world today. Literary culture flourished in the Roman Empire, with bookshops and public libraries, and with plentiful supplies of papyrus from Egypt making texts cheap and easily accessible to ordinary people. In addition, the Romans set up the first postal system in the Western world, enabling written communications to be sent across the empire.

The origins of Western script

With the fall of the Roman Empire in the 5th century CE, reading and writing were once again restricted to the elite. As information was lost to the Western world, however, it was preserved in the Islamic empire, notably in the Arabic language. The most significant text in Arabic was the Qur'an: the centrepiece of Islam, it was and still is believed to be the word of Allah. The ornate calligraphy that the Muslims developed to express the word of God embellished not just books but artwork and even buildings, from the Alhambra in Spain to the madrasahs (schools) of Samarkand in Uzbekistan.

Despite the eclipse of European civilization, during the dark ages and into medieval times the Latin alphabet had a crucial role to play in relaying information, through the emergence of the medieval manuscript culture, which placed great emphasis on preserving the written word. At the time, Catholic monasteries and cathedrals were centres for learning the skills of reading and writing. Scribes or monks would meticulously record

and copy information not just on religious subjects but also on topics including philosophy, medicine, literature, and history; this work included translating ancient Greek writings, preserved in the Islamic world, from Arabic into Latin.

Many of the most valuable works produced by the monks, notably bibles and Books of Hours – books containing prayers to be said at particular times of the day – were illuminated manuscripts, often embellished with intricate calligraphic designs, illustrations, and other decorative elements. A series of manuscripts would be bound together into handwritten books. This practice spread from religious institutions to the market in cities and to the emerging universities.

During this time, the features of modern Western script emerged. Modern capital letters are derived

Out of the simple consonants of the alphabet and our eleven vowels and diphthongs all possible syllables of a certain sort were constructed, a vowel sound being placed between two consonants.
Hermann Ebbinghaus
Memory: A Contribution to Psychology, 1913

from the "majuscule" (all-capital) scripts used by the Romans. Chief among them was the lettering carved on Roman monuments: a style known as *capitalis quadrata*, for the squared shapes of the letters. Features such as the variation between thick and thin strokes, and the serifs (short lines finishing off particular strokes), are still seen in many typefaces today.

Lower-case (minuscule) letters developed from the scripts used for literature and legal documents and in everyday life. One distinctive style of writing was insular script, which arose in 7th-century Ireland and spread to continental Europe. It comprises both a majuscule style, seen most famously in the *Book of Kells* and the *Lindisfarne Gospels*, and various minuscule styles for documents and record-keeping. These insular minuscule styles led to the development of Carolingian minuscule in 8th-century Europe during the reign of the Emperor Charlemagne (768–814). With its clear, legible letterforms and distinct spaces between words, it became the standard style in Europe, facilitating the spread of knowledge. Although it was superseded by Gothic blackletter, during the 14th and 15th centuries "humanist" scholars adopted it once more for its classic shapes and ease of reading. Thus, Carolingian minuscule forms the foundation for modern Western alphabets.

In addition to letter styles, Latin scripts developed features such as ligatures (lines joining one letter to another) and abbreviations, as well as punctuation marks such as the *interpunct*, which separated words, and the *punctus elevatus*, which resembled the modern semi-colon.

From handwriting to print

Printed letters with movable type were invented during the 11th century in China by Chinese artisan, engineer, and inventor Bi-Sheng, who created individual characters from fired clay and set them into metal frames. Letters were later carved from wood, and eventually metal type was invented in 12th-century Korea to provide more durable forms. However, early movable type technology did not spread beyond east and central Asia. In Europe, calligraphy remained essential for manuscript production and communication until the invention of the printing press and the resulting rise of mass publishing in Germany.

The design of letterforms later became known as typography (from the Greek *typos*, "form" or "impression", and *graphein*, "to write"). Its features are a delicate hand-crafted balance of aesthetics, functionality, and communication to help convey meaning and guide the reader's eye across the text. Beyond aesthetics, the design of letterforms influenced readability, hierarchy, and visual rhythm.■

The Tilya-Kori madrasah, a mosque and Islamic college in Samarkand's famous Registan Square, Uzbekistan, is adorned with Quranic calligraphy – a visual representation of the divine.

THEIR ARMOUR WAS BRONZE, AND OF BRONZE WERE THEIR IMPLEMENTS

BRONZEWARE

IN CONTEXT

FOCUS
Combining materials for greater durability

FIELD
Material design, product design

BEFORE
c. **10,000–***c.* **4500** BCE Tools and weapons are made of stone, but malleable metals such as gold and copper are used for ornamentation.

c. **5000–***c.* **3000** BCE Some societies begin smelting copper to use for tools and weapons.

AFTER
c. **1400–***c.* **1600** CE Italian Renaissance artists such as Benvenuto Cellini and Donatello revive interest in bronze sculptures.

1760 Hand tools are replaced by power-driven machines during the Industrial Age.

Bronze is an alloy – a mixture of copper and another metal. These days, the copper is mixed with around 12 per cent tin, but historically other elements such as zinc, silver, or arsenic were used in addition to or instead of tin. The exact composition of bronze varied according to the availability of easily accessible local materials.

During the Bronze Age (*c.* 3300–1000 BCE), bronze was the hardest metal in common use. Its strength and versatility, the ease with which it can be forged and worked, and its resistance to corrosion meant that it could be used for a wide variety of purposes, including tools, weapons, and decorative items.

See also: Tools and weapons 18–19 ▪ Early textiles 24–29 ▪ Tools for cooking and eating 30–31 ▪ Importing materials 46–47

> In his hands he held a club all of bronze, ever unbroken.
> **Homer**
> *The Odyssey*, Book XI

The first societies to enter the Bronze Age were those in West Asia and India. This momentous development took place much later elsewhere.

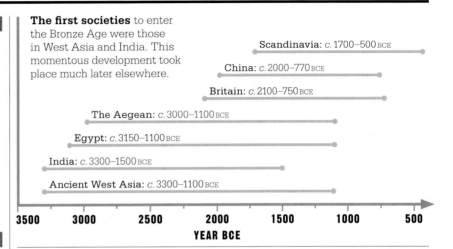

Scandinavia: *c.* 1700–500 BCE

China: *c.* 2000–770 BCE

Britain: *c.* 2100–750 BCE

The Aegean: *c.* 3000–1100 BCE

Egypt: *c.* 3150–1100 BCE

India: *c.* 3300–1500 BCE

Ancient West Asia: *c.* 3300–1100 BCE

| 3500 | 3000 | 2500 | 2000 | 1500 | 1000 | 500 |

YEAR BCE

Earlier, in the 5th millennium BCE, bronze was produced by combining copper and arsenic, because mixed ores of both metals occur naturally in some places. However, arsenical bronze produces toxic fumes during the smelting process, and it is not as strong or as easy to cast as bronze made with tin.

Tin became the main non-copper ingredient of bronze in the late 3rd millennium BCE. It is a relatively rare metal, and copper and tin ores are found together only in a few parts of the world, including Devon and Cornwall in the UK. Consequently, while Neolithic communities were entirely self-sufficient, the production of bronze always involved some level of trade and travel to obtain the necessary ores. In Europe, Cornish tin was traded as far as Phoenicia, in the eastern Mediterranean, indicating how highly valued bronze was. The development of trade in tin helped to spread bronze-making technology across a vast geographical range.

Improved weaponry

The introduction of bronze led to the development of more lethal weapons, including daggers and spearheads. These ranged in size from a few centimetres to more than 30 cm (12 in) long. Spearheads were attached to a wooden shaft, so they could be thrown like javelins.

Bronze swords were a much later invention. Considerably lighter than medieval long swords, they were too soft to sustain repeated blade-to-blade contact, and they were mainly used to stab or slash an enemy. Some surviving weapons also appear to have been ceremonial pieces. Most Bronze Age shields would have been made from wood or leather, although sheets of beaten bronze were used to make shields and armour for elite warriors.

Communities that had access to bronze weapons were more powerful than those still using stone weapons, and archaeological evidence suggests that the first large-scale battles in human history took place in the Bronze Age. A site in the Tollense Valley of northeastern Germany has yielded thousands of bones, together with bronze and stone weapons. It is estimated that perhaps 4,000 warriors clashed here in the 13th century BCE. »

These bronze sword blades dating from the 14th century BCE were found at a burial site in modern Greece. Their markings indicate evidence of combat.

The axe was the most important tool of the Bronze Age: it could be used to chop down trees and shape timber for a wide range of purposes, including dwellings, animal enclosures, and boats. Chopped wood was also essential for fuel, to achieve the kiln temperatures to smelt metal.

Axes were made in different sizes and styles, and the head was sometimes decorated with simple designs. The large numbers of unused bronze axes found in ancient graves suggests that they were also prestige items and indicators of wealth and power.

Decorative items

Bronze was used in the crafting of ornamental items, too. Many cultures made bronze mirrors, which were highly polished on one side and decorated on the other. Mirrors may have had religious significance in some ancient societies, with the Greeks using them for divining, and the Chinese placing them in graves.

One of the earliest-known bronze statues is *Dancing Girl*, which dates from around 2500 BCE and was found at Mohenjo-daro,

in modern Pakistan. The statue depicts a naked young woman standing in a naturalistic pose, wearing bracelets and a necklace, and it was produced using the lost-wax casting method.

From about 500 BCE, lost-wax casting became the main technique for producing bronze statues in Greece, too. Until then, the Greeks had favoured the sphyrelaton method, in which thin sheets of metal were hammered over a core of carved wood. Since

Dancing Girl is a diminutive statue (10.5 cm/4 in) that shows how bronze-workers had refined the lost-wax casting method by the 3rd century BCE.

bronze is not suitable for large solid casting, the Greeks developed the process of hollow lost-wax casting to make large, free-standing statues, which were typically cast in several pieces.

Many statues were melted down for their bronze in later periods. One that has survived is *Victorious Youth*, a life-sized bronze of an athletic young man, made in Greece in around 300–100 BCE. The statue would originally have been gleaming and colourful: its lips and nipples are copper, its eyes would have been made of ivory and glass, and there is evidence of silver on the athlete's wreath.

Ritual objects

In China, bronze was used to craft weapons, agricultural tools, and other utilitarian objects. However, during the Shang and Western Zhou dynasties (c. 1600–1046 BCE and 1046–771 BCE respectively), large numbers of ritual bronze items were also

A museum curator holds up an axe head unearthed in 2018 as part of the Havering Hoard, the largest Bronze Age hoard found in London.

Bronze Age hoarding

During the Bronze Age in Europe, it was common practice to bury large collections of bronze objects. More than 350 such hoards have been discovered in the UK alone.

The Migdale Hoard contains bronze jewellery and a bronze axe, and it is one of the earliest British hoards, dating from 2250–1950 BCE, when bronze was first being made in the British Isles. The largest is the Isleham Hoard (c. 1000 BCE), which contains more than 6,500 objects, including weapons and armour, in a huge ceramic jar.

Hoards were not always buried in one go. At Flag Fen, which appears to have been an important ritual site, weapons, tools, and jewellery were buried over the course of 1,200 years, from 1350–150 BCE.

The Boughton Malherbe Hoard (c. 850 BCE) contains more than 350 fragments of tools and weapons, many intentionally broken, suggesting a metal-recycling industry. Meanwhile, the Near Lewes Hoard (c. 1400–1250 BCE) has objects from France and Germany that are evidence of international trade.

This wine vessel is one of hundreds of bronze items found in the tomb of Fu Hao, a warrior queen from the Shang Dynasty who lived around 1200 BCE.

made. These included dings (three-legged cauldrons for ritual offerings) and vessels for food and drink that were placed inside royal tombs.

During the Shang dynasty, bronze objects were made by piece-mould casting, an elaborate technique that involves building a model of the item and taking a clay mould of the model. The mould is then cut into sections to release the model, and the sections are reassembled to form the mould for casting. This technique enables the bronze-worker to achieve a high degree of definition in even the most intricate designs. Many ritual bronze vessels feature geometric and zoomorphic designs, and the dominating motif is the *taotie*, a full-faced animal head with prominent eyes.

Iron smelts at higher temperatures than copper and tin, and this was not within the capabilities of ancient kilns until the end of the 2nd century BCE. As metalworking techniques improved, though, forged iron implements – which are much harder and more durable than bronze, and therefore better suited for use in weapons and tools – replaced cast bronze tools. However, bronze continued to be used during the Iron Age (*c*. 1000–600 BCE). ∎

The lost-wax casting technique has been in use since at least 3700 BCE. The process involves making a detailed model in solid wax of the object to be cast. This model is surrounded with clay, which is then heated to harden the clay and melt, or remove, the wax. Molten metal is then poured into the empty mould. When the metal has cooled, the clay is broken open to reveal a solid bronze object.

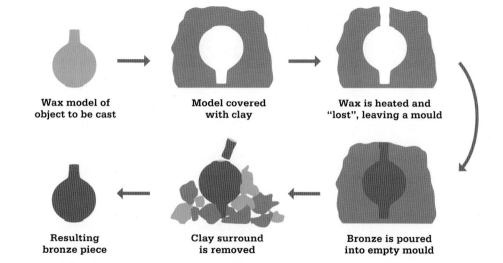

Wax model of object to be cast

Model covered with clay

Wax is heated and "lost", leaving a mould

Bronze is poured into empty mould

Clay surround is removed

Resulting bronze piece

MAY THE WIDE SEA YIELD YOU ITS WEALTH

IMPORTING MATERIALS

Trade has played a fundamental role in human society since prehistoric times, with people initially exchanging or gifting materials, foods, and objects, before later using currency. With the rise of the first cities, sophisticated trade routes were established, often under powerful dynasties. These routes allowed for the import of valuable materials from distant lands, sparking a revolution in local design and helping to reshape the material cultures of different regions.

One of the first regions where cities appeared was Sumer, located in Mesopotamia (present-day Iraq). Blessed with rich soils and favourable farming conditions, the people of Sumer were able to cultivate grains so successfully that they produced a surplus. This abundance paved the way for complex societies and cities to flourish, allowing people to take on increasingly diverse roles, such as artisans or priests.

Class distinction

As Sumerian societies became more stratified, the elite, including city leaders and priests, sought to set themselves apart. One of the ways they did this was through the exchange of gifts – either among themselves or to their gods. However, Sumer lacked the precious metals and gemstones needed for these elaborate gifts.

As a result, during the Uruk Period (c.4100–2900 BCE), Sumerian city-states began trading with other

A goat, intricately crafted from gold, copper, and lapis lazuli, grazes on leaves. Often known as the Ram in the Thicket, this artifact from c.2500 BCE, was discovered in the Royal Cemetery at Ur.

See also: Early ceramics 22–23 ▪ Transport and portability 32–33 ▪ Bronzeware 42–45
▪ Glass-blowing 50–55 ▪ Natural luxury 174

regions, such as ancient Egypt, the Indus Valley, and Dilmun, in eastern Arabia. The Sumerians exported products, including ceramics, textiles, and vegetable oils, and imported gold, silver, copper, lapis lazuli, ivory, pearls, and gemstones.

Sacred splendour

By 2600 BCE, Sumer was trading prolifically. Although it was not native to Mesopotamia, gold developed a deep local significance. It was almost exclusively used for religious rituals, and to adorn esteemed individuals.

Many examples of Sumerian gold artifacts come from one location – the Royal Cemetery in the city of Ur, excavated between 1922 and 1934. The burials here not only indicate the power and wealth of the elite – they reveal a culture in which foreign materials such as gold and lapis lazuli had taken on a symbolic or near-sacred power. These materials were used by Sumerian artisans to make extraordinarily intricate items with their own specific visual language and meaning.

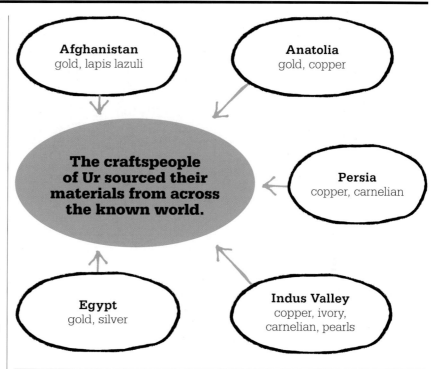

Afghanistan
gold, lapis lazuli

Anatolia
gold, copper

The craftspeople of Ur sourced their materials from across the known world.

Persia
copper, carnelian

Egypt
gold, silver

Indus Valley
copper, ivory, carnelian, pearls

Importing precious materials did more than just enrich the Sumerian culture. It also sparked the development of extensive trade networks, which became conduits for the exchange of ideas in art, design, technology, religion, and politics. This dynamic interplay of trade and cultural exchange would continue to transform the ancient world. ▪

The Ziggurat of Ur, built around 2100 BCE, is a prominent example of Sumerian religious architecture. Ziggurats supported a shrine on a platform, which was accessed by a system of ramps. They were sacred places – only priests were allowed to enter them.

Material religion

Material religion is a field within religious studies that focuses on the physical aspects of religion, including objects, words, and actions. It views religion as a lived experience, rooted in our sensory interactions with the world, rather than a purely conceptual or philosophical phenomenon.

Societies have always produced religious objects, ranging from statues and paintings to clothing and architecture. They also produce the rituals and words that activate them. Material religion attempts to look at how these two aspects interact, while also looking at how religion intersects with economics – from the flow of money that allows religions to function to the buying and selling of religious objects and materials.

Material religion can be used to examine both the religions of the past and how religions function in today's world. In our current era of mass production, scholars are particularly interested in understanding how religious commodities shape religious practices and influence believers' perceptions.

OFFSPRING OF WHEEL, EARTH, AND OVEN

STANDARDIZING POTTERY

IN CONTEXT

FOCUS
Producing ceramics with regular forms and styles

FIELD
Ceramics, crafts

BEFORE
c. **4000 BCE** The pottery wheel is invented in Mesopotamia, and its use soon spreads into the Levant.

3000–1900 BCE Longshan culture potters in ancient China create standardized items and increasingly delicate pieces on pottery wheels.

AFTER
1000–400 BCE In ancient Greece, potters develop defined shapes for wares that often feature important artwork.

625 BCE–476 CE Vast amounts of pottery are produced for everyday use in the Roman Empire, which standardizes the volume of vessels and assimilates conquered societies into its culture.

Today, we take the uniform shapes and sizes of mass-produced crockery for granted. Across the world, the form and volume of a ceramic object with a specific function – such as an espresso cup or a ramen bowl – remains largely the same. These items, produced with precision according to expectations, are a long way from the earliest ceramics in history, which were modelled by hand and varied greatly.

Over the millennia, societies in diverse regions found ways to standardize their own ceramics,

reproducing items with the same shape, size, and finish. Potters working across the Hittite Empire – which ruled a large part of Anatolia (in present-day Türkiye) from 1700 to 1180 BCE – produced ceramics in an increasingly uniform way on pottery wheels. Whether they lived in an administrative city or in a town near the edge of the territory, Hittites could buy roughly the same beaked pitcher or libation jug.

Fixed standards
During the Hittite period, ceramics became less decorative and more functional. The vessels were made in workshops by professional potters who followed specific standards. Pottery was being mass-produced across an empire, and archaeologists believe that the Hittite court controlled the industry for its economic benefit.

Pottery became standardized in different contexts for a number of reasons. In some cases, it helped to make the measurement and trade of goods easier and fairer,

The spouted pitcher is a form commonly seen in ceramics of the Hittite period. This example dates from 1650–1450 BCE.

See also: Early ceramics 22–23 ▪ Tools for cooking and eating 30–31 ▪ Early mass production 64–65 ▪ Mass-produced ceramics 92–93 ▪ Art pottery 122–23

In addition to standardized objects, such as the jug on the right, Longshan potters also made unusual works. The three-legged cooking pot, or *li*, on the left was made around 2000–1700 BCE.

while at other historic moments, cultural preferences or social status seem to have driven the development of specific types. For example, elites within the Longshan societies of ancient China sought out highly standardized forms of serving dishes to use for feasts, even though the jugs they bought remained more varied.

The wheel
Longshan potters developed a distinctive style of black vessels with "eggshell-thin" walls. Using a fast-turning pottery wheel, they trimmed clay down with sharp tools. Although some civilizations that never used the pottery wheel – such as the Incas – also created standardized ceramics, this invention helped to regularize pottery in many contexts. Its

mechanism has remained roughly the same since it originated in Mesopotamia, although many contemporary wheels are electric. The turning wheel creates centrifugal force, which potters use to shape their clay into vessels and components with curved sides.

Throwing on a wheel requires skill, but experienced potters build sensitivity and muscle memory, which they use to repeatedly wheel-throw items with the

same dimensions. This process is usually far quicker than hand-building items, and it helped pottery to become a specialism in many societies, since a smaller workforce could produce more.

Ceramics preserve well in the archaeological record, which helps us to piece together what everyday life was like in past eras and cultures. It has also led to various styles becoming emblematic of diverse ancient civilizations. ■

The works of humanity from prehistoric times have reached us … through slabs of pottery.
Bernard Leach
A Potter's Book, **1940**

Ceramic moulding

Moulds have been used to create ceramics in consistent shapes for millennia. In many ancient civilizations, potters used press moulds to reproduce the same shape repeatedly.

Press moulding involves pushing layers of clay into a negative shape before removing the mould and sometimes assembling segments into larger items. This technique can be used to make simple plates and vessels with several curved parts.

Today, moulding techniques are still used by artisans and artists who hand-make works in small quantities, but manufacturers also use moulding on an industrial scale for objects ranging from toilets and sinks to delicate porcelain figurines.

Sanitary-ware and intricate objects are often made using slip casting. In this technique, a porous mould made of plaster is filled with a liquid clay, called slip, to form a precise shape. Once the clay body has hardened enough, it is removed, dried fully, and fired in a kiln.

A STRANGE TRANSLUCENT LIQUID FLOWED FORTH IN STREAMS

GLASS-BLOWING

IN CONTEXT

FOCUS
How inflating glass revolutionized its use in manufacture

FIELD
Product design

BEFORE
2500 BCE The first glass objects – beads – are made in Mesopotamia.

1550 BCE Core-formed glass vessels are crafted in Egypt and Mesopotamia.

AFTER
c. 1271 Venetian glass-makers agree to protect the secret of their manufacturing trade, heralding the global dominance of Venetian glass.

1962 American glass-makers Harvey Littleton and Dominick Labino hold a workshop in Toledo, Ohio, which signals the arrival of the studio glass movement – creating glass for sculptural expression.

… a glass-blower blows and finishes a vessel using processes that have never altered … since glass-blowing originated.
D.B. Harden
Glass of the Caesars, 1987

Bridge of Glass by American glass-blower Dale Chihuly showcases his modern take on the art form. The 30-m- (100-ft-) long installation is one of Chihuly's largest suspended works.

Blowing molten glass has long been the foremost method of making glass vessels by hand. Before this technique was discovered, glass-makers would gather molten glass – created by heating sand or crushed quartz in a furnace – around a predetermined shape called a core. Once the glass had cooled and hardened, the core could be removed manually to reveal the vessel.

Around 50–40 BCE, glass-makers in the Syro-Palestinian region (Israel, Lebanon, Palestine, and Syria) discovered that molten glass in a plastic state could be inflated by air pressure – their own breath blown through a clay pipe – and began to develop a new manufacturing technique. During excavations in Jerusalem, archaeologists found evidence of blown-glass vessels dating from the second half of the 1st century BCE. These consist of small bottles with long necks, indicating that the earliest glass-blowers simply inflated tubes of glass that had been stretched using a small, localized heat source.

Later, with the introduction of larger furnaces and tools such as metal blowpipes, they could produce a considerably wider variety of forms.

Developing the process

The tools, techniques, and processes for making blown-glass objects developed over a century or more after the first long-necked bottles were made, and glass-blowing became commonplace in the Roman Empire during the 1st century CE. A new type of furnace was invented that allowed for a horizontal rather than a vertical heat source; this made working with molten glass much easier. Other key innovations included the development of the marver, for rolling blown glass.

Another significant advance in the forms that blown glass could take occurred around 25 CE, with

See also: Early ceramics 22–23 ▪ Tools for cooking and eating 30–31 ▪ Bronzeware 42–45 ▪ Art pottery 122–23 ▪ Lighting design 222–23

Before 2000 BCE in **Mesopotamia** (now Iraq and northern Syria), craftspeople **manipulate glass** by applying heat to create small objects.

In the 1st century BCE, glass in its heated, **malleable** form is first shaped by **blowing** into and inflating it.

Glass-blowing increases the **speed and efficiency** of glass production.

Glass becomes a viable medium for a wide range of vessels and products.

the introduction of mould-blown glass. In contrast to the technique used to make "free-blown" glass – in which only gravity and hand tools defined the shape of a vessel – in mould-blown glass, a partly inflated bubble of glass was inserted into a multipart mould made of terracotta, plaster, wood, or metal. The bubble was blown to fill the void inside and take on its shape. Once the glass was cool enough to retain its shape, the mould was removed. Moulds were often quite complicated to make, because they needed to be made from parts that were easy to separate once the blown vessel had been produced. However, the new technique enabled the creation of ever more complex decorative designs. The introduction and subsequent widespread use of moulds show that glass-work became a more specialized craft during the course of the 1st century CE.

Given the complicated contortions that are required to blow and manipulate glass at the same time, or at least in very quick succession, glass-blowing was done in teams of two or more people, using specialized furniture to support the glass-workers and their **»**

Glass-blowing step-by-step

Heat the glass in a furnace to at least 1,090°C (2,000°F) so that it melts. Once molten, the glass is malleable and easier to "gather".

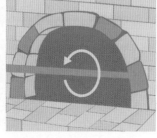

Gather the molten glass by rotating the blowpipe in the furnace two or three times, or until you have as much as you need.

Roll the glass on the marver to form a cylinder. The marver is a kind of smooth tabletop often made of polished steel or graphite.

Blow into the pipe while turning the shaft to expand the glass. Continue blowing until it is the required size and shape, then cool it down.

This illustration from the 15th-century *Tractatus de Herbis*, depicts two workers blowing glass in front of a roaring furnace.

equipment. Although there is no supporting archaeological evidence from the early years of glass production, centuries-old illustrations show that this workshop practice was certainly employed during the Middle Ages.

The use of glass

Following the discovery of the blowing technique, glass could be produced much more quickly. This improved process, and the endless array of forms and uses, meant that glass soon began to replace other materials, including ceramics and metal.

It was through the relentless spread of the Roman Empire, when the Syro-Palestinian region and its glass-blowing manufactories were annexed, that the glass-blowing industry expanded. This took place towards the end of the 1st century CE. Adopted by the Roman world, glass became central to the daily life of the population, and its production was arguably perfected in Italy. Perfume bottles, vessels in the shape of animals, beads for trading, and window glass were all made by glass-blowing.

It was on the dining table that glass became ubiquitous. A novel by Roman courtier Petronius describes how, in the middle of the 1st century CE, glass vessels for eating and drinking were preferred over those made from precious metals, because glass was odourless and cheaper to buy. Only its fragility prevented glass from superseding metal.

Blown glass also replaced terracotta or clay as a container for candles, thereby improving light sources. Glass lamps burned for longer and much more brightly than their clay counterparts and became widely used from the 4th century onwards.

Cut glass and cameos

The process of engraving or cutting into blown glass added further prestige to the material's status. By layering different colours of glass over each other and carving them away, glass began to imitate the naturally layered semi-precious stones that were worked into vessels and decorative objects.

One of the earliest and most famous examples of such decorative glass work is the so-called Portland Vase. Dating from the early 1st century CE and probably crafted near Rome, this deep-blue amphora is partially covered in opaque white glass that has been carved into a cameo scene showing several human figures and Eros carrying a bow. The cameo's true meaning has not been interpreted, but such a high-status object may have been a gift to commemorate a marriage.

Decorative processes

In addition to the revolutionary impact of inflating glass, and the limitless possibilities of moulding it into new forms, many other decorative processes emerged in the Roman Empire from the 1st century CE.

Flourishes were added to blown vessels, including trails of molten glass in contrasting colours, and moulded forms such as medallions were then applied to the vessel surface. Decorating the surface of glass with other materials also became a viable practice. The 2nd century witnessed the re-emergence of enamelling – mixing powdered, coloured glass with a binder, then heating it to fuse to the surface.

In the 4th century, glass artisans invented a technique called gold glass. Gold leaf engraved with a portrait was layered between two discs of glass, and inset into blown glass vessels such as bowls.

Perhaps the most intricate technique of the Roman era was glass cutting, as seen in cage, or reticulated, cups.

The Disch Cantharus, a late 3rd- or early 4th-century Roman cage cup, has a glass outer "cage" connected to the inner vessel by discreet bridges.

Making glass today

Modern glass-blowing requires a pre-heated blowpipe to be dipped into molten glass so that a quantity of the glass can be gathered on its end. The molten glass is then shaped roughly on a flat surface, or marver, which simultaneously cools the outer surface of the glass. This "gather" of glass is then inflated to create a bubble. For larger vessels, additional quantities of glass may have to be gathered on top of the initial bubble so it can be blown to the correct size.

Once the glass-blower has realized the rough form of the vessel, they usually break it from the blowpipe at a thin, weakened section for further working. The usual way to create a temporary support for the vessel while it is being completed is to apply a pontil, or punty – a solid metal rod with molten glass on the tip that is attached to the bottom of the object. When removed, this often leaves a ring-shaped scar, or pontil mark, on the glass.

Other tools that are now used for crafting blown glass include blocks, paddles, and jacks. These resemble large pairs of tweezers and are used to elongate and manipulate the hot glass, and to create decorative flourishes by pincering it.

Cultural recognition

From tableware to technology, glass is now a ubiquitous product in our daily lives. The importance of glass-blowing was recognized by UNESCO in 2023, when it listed two practices – ancient Syrian glass-blowing and handmade glass shaping and decorating in several European countries – on its definitive list of Intangible Cultural Heritage. It also registered the craft of glass-blowing to be in urgent need of safeguarding.

Although glass-making is now overwhelmingly a large industrial process, UNESCO's recognition helps to underscore the highly specialized knowledge and skill required to perfect the ancient technique, and the myriad artisanal workshops in which it was perfected. ∎

A glass-blower, remember, breathes life into a vessel, giving it shape and form and sometimes beauty.
Daphne du Maurier
The Glass-Blowers, 1963

The Portland Vase, which is now on display in the British Museum, London, is so named because it was once owned by the Duke of Portland, a British aristocrat.

OPEN, IT STRETCHES; CLOSED, IT ROLLS UP

PAPER

IN CONTEXT

FOCUS
A new writing material makes recording and sharing ideas easier

FIELD
Material design, book design, craftmanship and artisanal techniques

BEFORE
25,000–10,000 BCE Early humans use bone, ivory, and bark as surfaces for mark-making materials.

***c*.4000 BCE** In Mesopotamia, the Sumerians, Babylonians, and Assyrians develop cuneiform script, which is impressed onto wet clay using a stylus.

AFTER
1844 Canadian inventor Charles Fenerty and German inventor Friedrich Gottlob Keller independently develop processes for pulping wood fibres, which leads to a shift from rag-based paper to wood-based paper production.

The innovation that enabled humans to spread words and ideas beyond their own communities was the use of lightweight, durable, portable materials as writing surfaces. The first portable written documents were made on clay tablets; later writing surfaces included bark, animal skins, and sheets made from leaves or plant fibres. The invention that sparked mass communication, though, was paper. Today, even in the digital age, paper is still used everywhere in communication, education, and documentation.

See also: Written communication 34–41 ▪ Movable type and early graphic design 70–77

Cai Lun

Cai Lun (Ts'ai Lun) is believed to have been born around 50 CE in Guiyang – present-day Leiyang – during the Eastern Han Dynasty (25–220 CE). He served at the Imperial court as a chamberlain, messenger, and counsellor, but he is best known to history for his pivotal role in the development of papermaking.

According to legend, Cai was inspired by watching wasps collect and chew up wood to build their nests. Around 105 CE, he improved the composition of paper by adding materials such as bark, hemp, fishing nets, and old rags, thus making it more robust and versatile. Cai also refined the papermaking process: boiling the ingredients to a pulp, which was pounded, stirred in water, and sieved through reed mats before being drained, dried, and bleached. This process would spread through China and then to the rest of the world.

Cai Lun died in 121 CE, either by suicide or in custody, allegedly following political intrigue and accusations of corruption. In east Asia he is revered as the Chinese god of papermaking.

Early writing materials

The word "paper" has its roots in the Latin papyrus. This was the writing material used in ancient Egypt as far back as the fourth millennium BCE. It was made from the fibrous pith of *Cyperus papyrus*, also known as Nile grass. While papyrus was adopted by Mediterranean civilizations, including the ancient Greek and Roman empires, by the first centuries BCE and CE it had largely been supplanted by parchment and vellum, which were both prepared from animal skins. This shift was partly due to the fragility of papyrus; it was not pliable enough to fold without cracking, and so it was commonly rolled into scrolls. In addition, the papyrus plant, mainly cultivated in the Nile Delta, had been excessively harvested, pushing it towards extinction.

In most parts of the world, the book, or codex, format began to replace the scroll almost as soon as it was introduced. Early Christian and Islamic writers fashioned codices from folded sheets of parchment, including sacred texts such as the Bible and sections of the Qur'an. The design was influenced by the form of wax tablets, another early writing surface that was constructed from wood covered with a layer of wax and bound in pairs (diptychs) using strips of leather. In Asia, the scroll remained standard for far longer. In Mesoamerica, meanwhile, a paper-like surface called amatl, made from bark, was used to create manuscripts; a concertina style of folding was favoured by the Mayans and Aztecs.

The influence of paper

Paper – along with the compass, gunpowder, and printing – is known as one of the Four Great Inventions of China. Its origins can be traced to around 200 BCE, during the Han dynasty. Paper was produced from plant fibres, mixed with water, then pressed and dried into thin sheets, in a process developed by Imperial court official Cai Lun. Paper production was a manual craft, with each sheet being formed (or laid) one at a time by skilled workers.

The use of paper revolutionized the recording and spread of information, as paper was much lighter and more affordable than animal hide. It was also portable, »

This Latin Bible from 1407 is richly illustrated with illuminated letters and other decorations. The condensed letter shapes and abbreviations used in the text were devices that helped to save space on the costly parchment.

Origami

One of the most striking uses of paper is in the Japanese art of origami ("folding paper"). The first use of folded paper shapes was in Shinto religious ceremonies; a poem by Ihara Saikaku, dating from 1680, describes the use of origami butterflies during weddings. From the Heian period (794–1185), paper-folding became one of the skills practised in the Japanese court in the etiquette for wrapping gifts.

By the Edo period (1603–1868), origami had become a recreation. Shapes were based on forms such as flowers and birds, and included the classic crane design still made today.

Origami is still a pastime, but it also has applications in engineering, from making lighter drinks cans to fitting medical devices in the body and packing components for the James Webb space telescope.

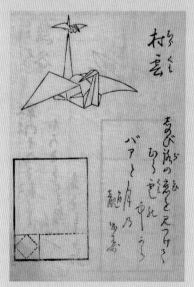

This guide to making two linked origami cranes is from the first known technical book on origami, published in 1798.

Manufacturing paper

Records show **the first paper mills** were established in Morocco and in Muslim Spain in the **12th century**.

Papermaking begins at Fabriano, Italy in **1264**. Fabriano still makes **high-quality art paper** today; it also supplies paper for **Euro bank notes**.

Johannes Gutenberg builds the first printing press using **movable type** on paper in **1440**, **sparking a revolution** in publishing.

French **mechanical engineer** Nicholas-Louis Robert invents the **first papermaking machine in 1798**.

The International Association of Hand Papermakers and Paper Artists (IAPMA), **the world-leading association** for handmade paper artists, is established in Düren, Germany in **1986**.

flexible, easy to store, and provided a sizable and consistent writing surface. The manufacturing process was easy to replicate on a large scale, which led to a rapid spread across China, promoting learning and literacy, and supporting the imperial administration.

By the 6th century, paper was so prevalent in China that it was used both as a writing material and for personal hygiene – although there was a discernible difference in quality. In 589 CE, the Chinese scholar and official Yan Zhitui remarked: "Paper on which there are quotations or commentaries from Five Classics or the names of sages, I dare not use for toilet purposes."

During the Tang dynasty (618–907), paper was first used to create bags for preserving the flavour of tea, while the Song dynasty (960–1279) witnessed the introduction of paper currency – banknotes – issued by the government. Paper was primarily composed of hemp, mulberry, and ramie (*Boehmeria nivea*) fibres, and was often smoothed with wax to provide a polished surface for writing. Silk borders were sometimes added to reinforce the top and bottom edges.

Pulp fiction

In 19th-century Europe and North America, the availability of cheap wood-pulp paper led to an explosion in mass-market literature. In the UK, the rise in literacy created a vast new market for "penny dreadfuls": stories originally of 8–16 pages costing one penny. From the 1860s, these were joined by US "dime novels" and "story papers". Adults and children devoured these tales of crime, horror, adventure, and romance. By 1895, more than 1 million boys' periodicals were sold every week in the UK, where the sensational subjects caused great concern among leaders of society.

In the US, "pulp" magazines appeared in the 1890s; by 1907 the first, *Argosy*, had half a million readers. Their popularity was eclipsed by television in the 1950s, but they had a lasting impact: not only did authors such as Isaac Asimov and H.P. Lovecraft gain a cult following, but the provocative, vivid cover art would influence advertising and even fine art.

The magazine *Black Mask* featured "hard-boiled" crime stories; some, such as *The Maltese Falcon*, became world-famous.

Paper was also commonly dyed yellow using the juice extracted from the bark of the Amur cork tree (*Phellodendron amurense*). This not only served a decorative purpose but was also an insect repellent.

A rich tradition of reading developed, with scholars amassing huge collections of scrolls to show their erudition and importance. Alongside this format, a version of the codex emerged from the 9th century onwards. Early folded-leaf pamphlets evolved into an improved "butterfly binding", where folded pages were pasted together at the seam. Eventually, a "wrapped back binding" emerged, which was held together at the spine by screws. By the Tang dynasty, China led the world in book production, boasting library collections three times larger than of any other nation.

Paper became central to every facet of Chinese culture, encompassing poetry, painting and calligraphy, as well as packaging, economics, and rituals. As an example, during the Yuan dynasty (1271–1368), Marco Polo, the Venetian merchant and the first well-documented European in China, observed the practice of burning paper effigies as part of funeral rites.

The spread of knowledge

By the 7th century, papermaking had reached Korea and Japan. At first, due to its cost, paper was reserved for ceremonial purposes. It was made popular by monks and in Japan gave rise to origami, the art of paper-folding. In the 8th century, papermaking spread from China to the Islamic world. This was the catalyst for a flourishing of knowledge and culture, enabling the circulation and preservation of literary works. In Baghdad, it

Fill your paper with the breathings of your heart...
William Wordsworth
Letter to his wife, Mary,
29 April, 1812

led to the inauguration of the House of Wisdom, which attracted scholars from all over the Muslim world, triggering the Golden Age of translation and intellectual advancement.

By the 11th century, paper had reached Europe via Baghdad – for which reason it was initially known by the Byzantine name *bagdatikos*. In the 13th century, papermaking was further refined in Europe by using water-powered mills to speed up production. The introduction of the mechanical printing press in the mid-15th century vastly increased the demand for paper. Public and private libraries were able to build their own collections, and for the first time in over a thousand years they overtook the imperial libraries of China.

Industrializaton in the 19th century significantly reduced production costs. The invention of the Fourdrinier machine in Europe – patented in 1806 by British entrepreneur Henry Fourdrinier – enabled mass production of paper rolls. Today, most production relies on machinery, but handmade paper survives as a specialized craft and a canvas for artistic expression. ∎

INVENTIO

ENLIGH

1000–1900

AND
NMENT

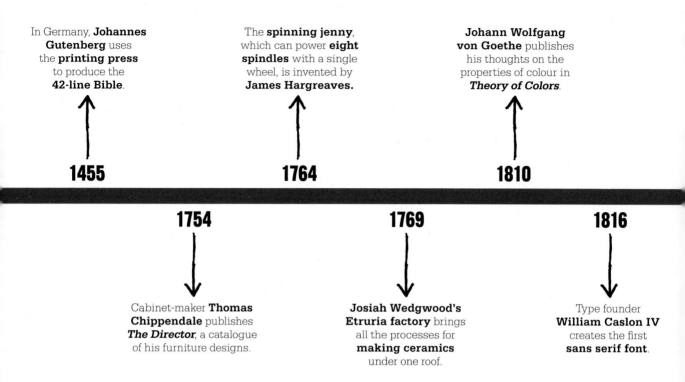

In Germany, **Johannes Gutenberg** uses the **printing press** to produce the **42-line Bible**.

1455

The **spinning jenny**, which can power **eight spindles** with a single wheel, is invented by **James Hargreaves.**

1764

Johann Wolfgang von Goethe publishes his thoughts on the properties of colour in *Theory of Colors*.

1810

1754

Cabinet-maker **Thomas Chippendale** publishes *The Director*, a catalogue of his furniture designs.

1769

Josiah Wedgwood's Etruria factory brings all the processes for **making ceramics** under one roof.

1816

Type founder **William Caslon IV** creates the first **sans serif font**.

I n medieval Europe, the church controlled visual culture and it was in the monasteries that what might be termed "proto-design" was produced by monks with craft skills. Objects of beauty, ingenuity, and virtuosity – stained glass, illuminated manuscripts, and soaring cathedrals that took centuries to build – were intended to aid unquestioning veneration. In their aim and purpose, they were radically different from "design" as we know it today.

However, the mid-15th century ushered in an era of change with the invention of the printing press and the spread of literacy, which transformed communication. More dramatic change occurred later in the period, when initial moves towards organizing labour to produce goods *en masse* were

combined with a series of mechanical innovations that completely revolutionized the British textile industry.

Industrial impact
In late 17th century, the process of urbanization accelerated in tandem with early industrialization based around the exploitation of coalfields and iron ore deposits, and society began to be restructured with the emergence of expanding working and professional classes. The development of steam engines in the late 18th and early 19th centuries further accelerated and expanded these processes. While upper echelons of society – royalty, the aristocracy, and the high clergy – viewed themselves as being God's chosen servants on earth, the emergent middle class needed to

demonstrate their status through education, professional abilities and the quality and visual appeal of the possessions they could buy.

Classical inspiration
The archaeological discovery of the preserved contents of the buried Roman cities of Herculaneum and Pompeii in the 18th century created a new fascination with the classical world. Interiors were designed with furnishings and patterning emulating what had been revealed. For the upwardly-mobile, owning a terraced townhouse equipped with classically-ornamented fine furniture and tableware bought from respectable makers reflected progress and good taste.

Classicism also inspired urban intellectuals to develop methods of enquiry derived from those used by

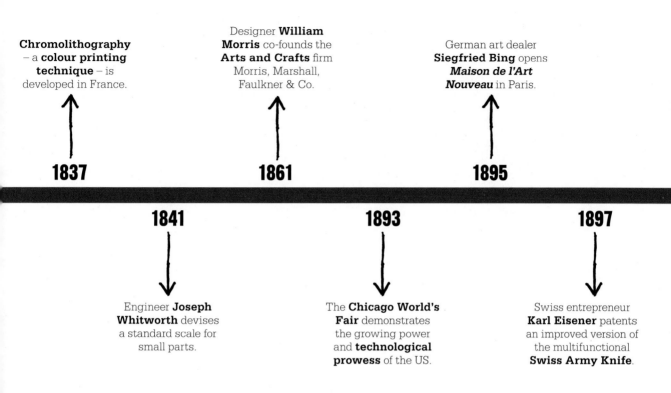

Chromolithography – a **colour printing technique** – is developed in France.

1837

Designer **William Morris** co-founds the **Arts and Crafts** firm Morris, Marshall, Faulkner & Co.

1861

German art dealer **Siegfried Bing** opens *Maison de l'Art Nouveau* in Paris.

1895

1841

Engineer **Joseph Whitworth** devises a standard scale for small parts.

1893

The **Chicago World's Fair** demonstrates the growing power and **technological prowess** of the US.

1897

Swiss entrepreneur **Karl Eisener** patents an improved version of the multifunctional **Swiss Army Knife**.

---

ancient Greek philosophers. In Glasgow – a burgeoning mercantile city in Scotland, trading in cotton and tobacco – Adam Smith applied this logic to investigate the causes of economic growth. He reasoned that growth was brought about through a combination of clear laws fairly applied, allied with minimal tax and regulation to encourage entrepreneurship. Smith's thinking would prove highly influential. For design, one implication was that objects and products of many styles could be produced, and succeed or fail on the market's whim.

Quality control

In the 19th century, liberal ideas advocating minimal regulation allowed industrial entrepreneurs to do as they saw fit. There was little or no control over the quality of what was produced: designed objects would succeed or fail according to the whims of fashion and the marketplace. There was no such thing as a professional "designer" – instead manufacturers used artistically-inclined employees to produce sketch designs and ideas for decoration.

In an attempt to improve the standard of mass-produced goods, the British government set up Government Schools of Design to train designers for work in industry. Typically, they received a basic artistic training and also technical drawing skills, learning by copying. Nonetheless, those who considered themselves to be better educated in aesthetic matters often were appalled by what they viewed as the poor taste of the nouveau riche, who appeared to favour acquiring the more ostentatious of items as means of attempting to gain enhanced social status.

"Good" design

These matters came into focus at the 1851 Great Exhibition, where it was possible to compare British and overseas-made goods. In the Exhibition's wake, theories of what might constitute "good" design emerged. It usually meant design that showed stylistic restraint and appeared coherent, in line with a preference for abstract, flat ornamentation derived from patterning in West Asia, as collated by Owen Jones in *The Grammar of Ornament*. National romanticism provided another strand, drawing upon British history – as reflected in the Gothic Revival and in the Arts and Crafts movement. ∎

ALL TRADES HAVE GAINED BY DIVISION OF LABOUR
EARLY MASS PRODUCTION

IN CONTEXT

FOCUS
Items with standard sizes and specifications can be produced faster

FIELD
Product design, industrial design

BEFORE
4000 BCE The earliest known water wheel is used. It is thought to be the first machine to turn a natural force into mechanical energy.

AFTER
1769 The first steam engine capable of powering a machine is patented by Scottish engineer James Watt. His design improved an earlier invention by Thomas Newcomen in 1711.

1770 English inventor James Hargreaves patents a machine for spinning wool, called the spinning jenny. The machine used a single wheel to spin eight strands of yarn at once.

The concept of mass production is usually associated with the period following the early steam age at the beginning of the 19th century and, even more so, with the highly efficient US system of manufacture that dominated during the 20th century. However, elements of mass production – such as standardization, the division of labour into relatively simple repetitive tasks, and the assembly of parts – were evident in manufacturing much earlier.

In the ancient world, primitive forms of mass production can arguably be seen in the making of bricks, roofing tiles, storage vessels, coins, and *gladii* (Roman metal daggers). However, these comparatively simple items lacked the complexity and refinement that is generally associated with the concept of modern mass production.

Standardization

Principles resembling those of modern mass production were first applied in the making of military equipment. Standardization – the concept of making varied objects similar by setting standard sizes, shapes, or materials – was ideal for supporting warfare. Making weaponry and uniforms in standard shapes and sizes improved the efficiency of production, maintained a flow

Demand surges for cast metal items so forges must be more productive.

→

Items that are **similar** in **size and shape** can be made in the same mould.

↓

Standard shapes and sizes enable items to be mass produced.

←

Casting items in the same mould means **many items** can be made very quickly.

See also: Standardizing pottery 48–49 ▪ Mass-produced ceramics 92–93 ▪ Interchangeable parts 106–07 ▪ Industrial design 146–47

The division of labour at Venice's Arsenale Nuovo is clearly seen in this 18th-century painting. Workers in the foreground create separate elements for the galleys in the background.

of supplies to front lines, and helped to create order and discipline in troops through unified aesthetics.

In China, during the Song dynasty (960–1279), an early version of mass production appears to have been applied to make armour and weapons. Different sizes of otherwise standard components were produced in batches, suitable for use by different heights and weights of warrior, and, most likely, these elements were assembled prior to distribution and use.

Specialist craftspeople

During the 14th century, a sophisticated production method was set up to build galley ships by the Arsenale Nuovo of Venice, Italy. The process of constructing these large, masted vessels was broken down into separate tasks – for example, building the masts and framing, cladding the hulls, and making the rigging – and workers became specialists in particular areas of shipbuilding.

The throughput was phenomenal. The vast site – on a par with a large modern factory – could accommodate as many as 100 vessels at different stages of construction, and the Arsenale employed around 16,000 workers in iron founding, joinery, rope-making, assembly, and outfitting.

This clear, efficient organization of labour into specialisms was to become common in shipbuilding and in other industries – such as ceramics – in later centuries. ▪

Armour for Song dynasty warriors, as depicted by this pottery figure, was manufactured in a small, medium, and large size.

Production during the Song dynasty

In the early years of the 11th century, China's iron industry expanded rapidly. By 1078 it was producing 113,000 tonnes (125,000 US tons) per year. Water wheels were used to power bellows for the furnaces that produced the molten ore. The major consumer of iron at the time was the army, which required a constant supply of armour and weaponry. Arsenals employed around 40,000 workers, who churned out an estimated 17,000 iron arrowheads and 23,000 gunpowder packages every day.

By the 13th century, another form of mass production was in use – mechanized rope-making. Belts attached to a water wheel turned multiple spinning heads at once, which twisted strands of fibre together to make lengths of rope much faster than any human. The process was not unlike the methods used today. Later, a similar method was used to speed production in the making of silk, which was a prized material and an important export commodity.

A REFLECTION OF ALLAH'S PERFECT ORDER

ISLAMIC GEOMETRIC PATTERNS

IN CONTEXT

FOCUS
Creating impact using repetitive shapes

FIELD
Textile design, interior design, architecture

BEFORE
7th–8th centuries CE Early Islamic geometric patterns begin to emerge, influenced by Persian, Roman, and Byzantine traditions.

AFTER
1643 The Taj Mahal, commissioned by Mughal emperor Shah Jahan, is completed. The white marble mausoleum is considered the crowning glory of Islamic art in India.

1895 British architect George Aitchison completes work on Leighton House, London. Its Arab Hall features carved windows and Turkish tiles.

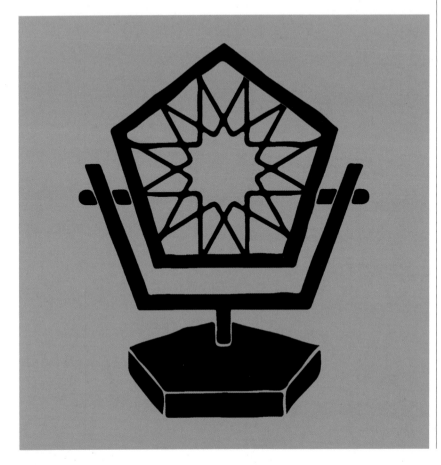

F aith-inspired creativity has influenced design over the ages. A striking example of this can be found in Islamic geometric patterns, renowned for their intricate beauty and mathematical precision, which flowered especially in the 13th and 14th centuries. Islam originated early in the 7th century CE in the Arabian Peninsula, when Muhammad received from Allah the revelations contained in the Qur'an. The new religion spread rapidly through West Asia, North Africa, and parts of Europe.

Islam did not allow the depiction of living creatures in religious contexts, so early Islamic artists

See also: Woodblock textile printing 78–79 ▪ Mass-produced ceramics 92–93 ▪ The Arts and Crafts movement 112–19

Pattern variations

Islamic geometric patterns, whether used in carpets, ceramics, or on the domes of mosques, are usually built from combinations of repeated circles and squares. The pattern elements may be interlaced or overlapped to create a multitude of different designs. The other primary decorative features associated with Islam are arabesque and calligraphy, and all three are frequently used together. Shown here are some patterns that have stood out over time for their popularity and widespread recognition.

Arabesque patterns are characterized by flowing, interlacing lines and floral motifs, often with vine-like structures.

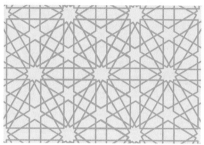

Girih patterns involve complex geometric tessellations featuring stars and polygons, creating the illusion of infinite repetition.

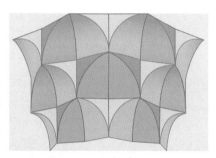

Muqarnas, or stalactite vaulting, consists of three-dimensional geometric designs resembling honeycomb structures.

Eight-pointed star patterns feature intersecting squares and triangles and symbolize light and guidance.

Interlacing patterns involve the weaving or interlocking of shapes, whose repetition adds complexity and a sense of infinity.

and craftsmen embraced simplicity in geometric design as a means of symbolizing the unity and infinity of Allah. Basic shapes, such as circles and squares, were used for spiritual significance. The circle, with its absence of corners and continuous form, was a symbol of unity and perfection, reflecting the notion of Allah's oneness. With no beginning or end, the circle symbolizes the eternal nature of the divine. The square, with its cornered structural form, was used to represent the earthly realm and the material world. In Islamic patterns, squares are often transformed into more complex designs, conveying order and

balance in the divine creation. Some of the very first examples of geometric design in Islamic architecture can be seen in the Great Mosque of Kairouan, Tunisia (836 CE), while the Mosque of Ibn Tulun, in Cairo (876–79 CE), displays good early examples of such patterns being interlinked.

Increased complexity

As the culture of Islam evolved, so did the sophistication and intricacy of geometric designs, calligraphy, and arabesque patterns as a form of artistic expression. These patterns flourished across the world of Islamic art and architecture, adorning mosques, palaces, »

When we look at nature, we find a reflection of Allah's perfect order … in the shapes of flora and fauna, in geological structure, in a cell's shape.
Nashwah Akhtar
"Islamic Geometry: A Reflection of His Perfect Order", 2019

manuscripts, carpets, ceramics, leatherwork, and woodwork to visually honour the Islamic belief in the unity and unending nature of Allah. The various Islamic empires and dynasties developed their own styles, and these evolved over time.

Cultural exchange

The Islamic world was located at the crossroads of Africa, Asia, and Europe, and had an abundance of spices, textiles, ceramics, and precious metals. Merchants and empires embraced opportunities for trade and developed extensive networks that fostered cross-cultural interactions. This exchange of goods, ideas, and technologies had a huge influence on shaping a rich and diverse cultural heritage. This included the reciprocity of artistic ideas, some of which were incorporated into Islamic patterns.

Islamic scholars also had a major influence on the fields of design and architecture. For example, Ibn al-Haytham was an Arab mathematician, astronomer, and physicist of the 10th–11th centuries who made significant contributions to the principles of optics. Around the same time, Persian polymath Omar Khayyam contributed to the understanding of mathematics equations and was able to calculate the duration of the solar year with remarkable accuracy. The enlightenment revealed by such men provided artists with a deeper understanding of geometric relationships – and, with the ruler and compass as tools, this helped them to create perfectly symmetrical designs.

New and more intricate designs appeared during the time of the Seljuk Empire (1037–1194). For

example, the Tomb Towers of Kharaqan, Iran (1067–93), near Qazvin, Iran, feature more complex six-, eight-, and 12-point patterns. By the late 11th and early 12th centuries, architects had found ways to integrate structural and even more complex decorative elements. At this time, the heptagon makes its first appearance – in the Great Mosque of Isfahan, Iran. In the 13th and 14th centuries, the Nasrid dynasty created the glorious Alhambra in Spain.

Sufism, a mystical dimension of Islam, flourished from the 13th century onwards through the teachings of mystics such as Rumi,

The 10th-century dome above the *maqsura* of Córdoba's Great Mosque in Spain is supported by crisscrossing arches and decorated with a tiled sunburst radiating from a small star.

Islamic craftsmen turned geometry into an art form because pictures of people were not allowed in holy places.
Alex Bellos
The Guardian, 2015

a celebrated Sufi mystic and poet. Sufism evolved into a prominent contemplative practice within Islam, emphasizing spiritual closeness to Allah through introspection, devotion, and love. Sufi practitioners sought to experience the divine through contemplation, and Sufi artists had a great influence on developing intricate geometric designs as a visual aid for meditation and spiritual reflection.

The Ottoman Empire

The 14th–16th centuries marked a dynamic period in the evolution of Islam. The Ottoman Empire, which emerged in present-day Türkiye, adopted the legacy of the Islamic Golden Age (622–1258). It reached its zenith in the 16th century under Kanuni Suleiman (Suleiman the Magnificent), extending its influence deep into central Europe and across West Asia. The most important Ottoman architect of this period was Mimar Sinan, who designed more than 300 major structures, including the masterpiece of the Selimiye Mosque, Edirne (1568–74), whose domes, doors, and portals are richly decorated with geometrical figures.

The Safavid dynasty emerged in Persia in 1501 and produced its own design style. This can be seen in the complex brick and tile patterning at Isfahan's Ali-Qapu palace (1598) and the later Hakim Mosque (1656–62).

Beyond decoration

From the 7th century onwards, artisans realized the architectural patterns of the great Islamic monuments through a variety of techniques and materials, depending on what was available at the time and what was desired. From the Alhambra's palaces to the Topkapi Palace in Istanbul, Türkiye, and from the Great Mosque of Córdoba, Spain, to the Taj Mahal in Agra, India, there are thousands of examples of beautiful, decoration. There are vibrantly coloured ceramic tiles, wooden panels and screens, stucco, and plaster moulded into intricate shapes. There are carved and inlaid walls, ceilings, and floors made of marble and stone, with calligraphic inscriptions, exemplary brickwork, and intricate metalwork, including grilles and screens for doors and windows.

However, Islamic geometric patterns are not only decorative; they invite contemplation and reflection, encouraging the viewer to engage with the order and transcendence embedded in the designs, and fostering a sense of connection with the divine.

Contemporary artists continue to adapt these ancient principles through innovative approaches to create new expressions of Islamic art. This evolution showcases the enduring relevance of Islamic geometric patterns in a modern context and stands as a testament to the rich artistic and spiritual heritage of Islamic civilization. ∎

The Alhambra

Built in Granada, Spain, the Alhambra is one of the most famous examples of Islamic architecture. The ruling Nasrid dynasty of the Emirate of Granada first commissioned the palace and fortress complex in 1238, and it was massively expanded during the following century, when it became a self-contained city. Its name means "red castle" in Arabic, likely derived from the reddish colour of its outer walls. The Alhambra is renowned for its intricate architecture, with geometric patterns meticulously crafted in tilework, stucco, and wood, showcasing a symphony of interlacing lines, polygons, and stars. These patterns adorn walls, ceilings, and courtyards, creating a harmonious visual experience. Many *muqarnas* further enhance the depth and complexity of the patterns. After the fall of the emirate to Catholic forces in the Reconquista of 1492, the Spanish monarchy seized the Alhambra and used it as a royal palace.

The blind arch in the Alhambra's Mirador de Daraxa has *muqarnas* and intricate patterns set in tiles above two mullioned windows.

GIVE ME TWENTY-SIX SOLDIERS OF LEAD AND I WILL CONQUER THE WORLD

MOVABLE TYPE AND EARLY GRAPHIC DESIGN

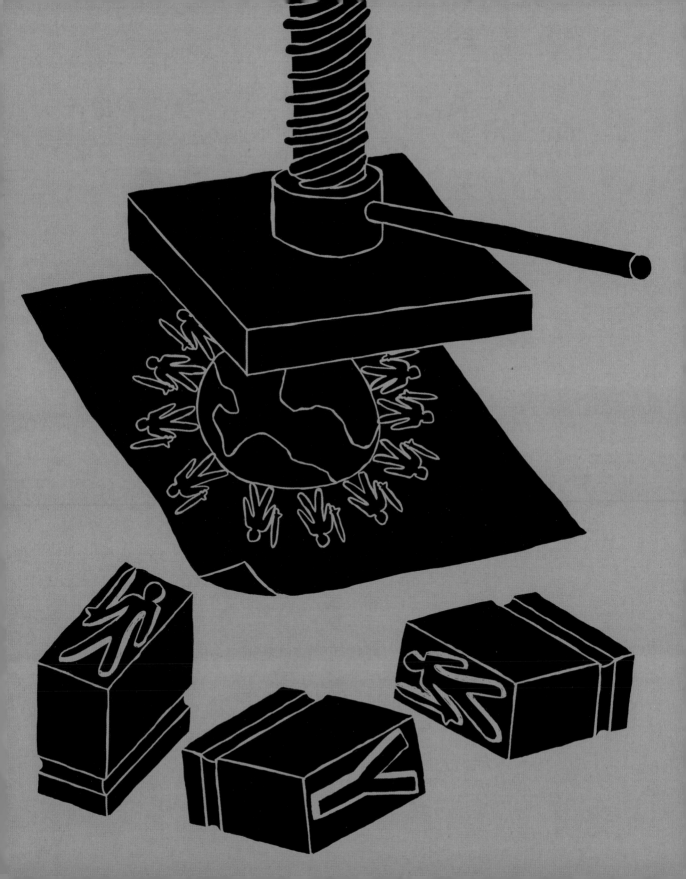

IN CONTEXT

FOCUS
Movable type and the printing press help to spread knowledge

FIELD
Typography, graphic design, communication

BEFORE
***c.* 500 CE** Monks in writing rooms known as scriptoria copy out religious texts by hand.

868 CE The oldest, dated printed book in existence, the Buddhist manual *Diamond Sutra*, is produced in China using woodblock printing.

AFTER
1917 During the Bolshevik Revolution, poster art designed by Russian Constructivists becomes a tool for propaganda.

1960s Designers including Paul Rand, Saul Bass, and Lester Beall use Modernist principles to create visual identities for corporate clients.

Printing was the technology at the heart of the earliest graphic design, and it remains a key part of its expression today. The process allowed texts and ideas to become available to all – not just to royalty, the clergy, and the aristocracy – thereby facilitating the spread of knowledge all over the world.

Movable type was in use in East Asia as early as the mid-11th century. When this technology appeared in Europe in the 1450s, it was as a result of the efforts of German craftsman Johannes Gutenberg, who developed the printing press.

Calligraphy and woodblock

Typography and printing have always gone hand in hand, and it is possible to trace the evolution of type – from handwritten scripts, to digital formats – by looking at the historical conditions in which it was created and the prevailing technology of the era.

In the Western world, early books and documents existed because of the painstaking calligraphic work of monastic scribes, who wrote and copied

Knowledge began freely replicating and quickly assumed a life of its own.
George Dyson
US science historian, on the invention of the printing press

text on parchment with ink and a quill. These handwritten pages – often featuring elaborate illuminated capitals, intricate borders, and delicate illustrations – were then bound into volumes or pasted together as scrolls. Time-consuming and laborious to produce, these documents and illuminated manuscripts were available only to the select few who could afford them.

The ability to print multiple copies of a text can be traced back to the 9th century, when Chinese artisans began carving entire pages of text – sometimes

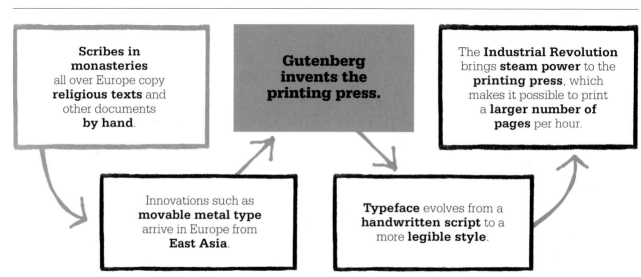

Scribes in monasteries all over Europe copy **religious texts** and other documents **by hand**.

Innovations such as **movable metal type** arrive in Europe from **East Asia**.

Gutenberg invents the printing press.

Typeface evolves from a **handwritten script** to a more **legible style**.

The **Industrial Revolution** brings **steam power** to the **printing press**, which makes it possible to print a **larger number of pages** per hour.

See also: Written communication 34–41 ▪ Paper 56–59 ▪ Woodblock textile printing 78–79 ▪ Sans serif fonts 102–03 ▪ Political messaging 164–69 ▪ Design for social change 180–81

Movable type first emerged in the 13th century, but it was between 1800 and 1875 that printing really came of age, with continual technological innovations accelerating the process to 50 times faster than what was possible on a Gutenberg-style press.

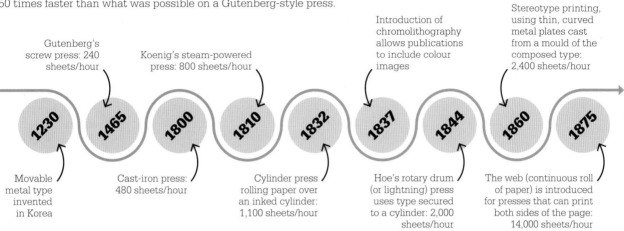

Gutenberg's screw press: 240 sheets/hour

Koenig's steam-powered press: 800 sheets/hour

Introduction of chromolithography allows publications to include colour images

Stereotype printing, using thin, curved metal plates cast from a mould of the composed type: 2,400 sheets/hour

1230   1465   1800   1810   1832   1837   1844   1860   1875

Movable metal type invented in Korea

Cast-iron press: 480 sheets/hour

Cylinder press rolling paper over an inked cylinder: 1,100 sheets/hour

Hoe's rotary drum (or lightning) press uses type secured to a cylinder: 2,000 sheets/hour

The web (continuous roll of paper) is introduced for presses that can print both sides of the page: 14,000 sheets/hour

accompanied by illustrations – on woodblocks. These would then be printed on sheets of paper, and the sheets combined end to end to form scrolls. Paper money and playing cards were also woodblock-printed. Unlike handwritten manuscripts, this process could produce multiple identical copies of a single text; however, it was still slow and labour-intensive.

Early movable type
The concept of movable type – that is, a system that uses one piece of type to represent each character – was first developed by East Asian cultures. Its earliest iteration occurred around the 1040s thanks to a Chinese alchemist named Pi Sheng. He created individual characters from a mixture of clay and glue, and used them to compose texts on an iron plate coated with a blend of resin, wax, and paper ash. Heating this plate, then

letting it cool, baked and solidified the type. Once the inked impression had been printed, the type could be removed and reused simply by reheating the plate.

Although Pi Sheng had discovered a method critical to the manufacture, assembly, and recovery of reusable type, his technique did not replace the

popular handcut woodblock method in Asia, partly because the thousands of characters used in pictographic languages – more than 50,000 glyphs in Chinese, and in excess of 24,000 in Korean – made setting and re-filing the separate character blocks difficult. As a result, movable type was not initially adopted in its original birthplace.

Wood and metal type
Around 1297, Chinese Yuan dynasty official Wang Zhen developed movable wooden type. Carving it was still a time-consuming process, but this was a more durable option than Pi Sheng's earlier clay type.

An even sturdier product – movable metal type – was introduced in 13th-century »

Movable wooden type was used by Wang Zhen to print official county records. He organized and stored types according to a rhyming scheme.

Korea, during the Goryeo dynasty. Around the 1230s, the Korean government funded the casting of metal type to print official and legal documents; these were followed by Buddhist scriptures, the *Four Books and Five Classics* of Confucianism, and texts on medicine, history, and astronomy. In 1403, King Taejong ordered the first complete set of 100,000 pieces of type to be cast in bronze.

The world's oldest existing book printed with movable metal type is *Jikji* (1377). In 2001, this Korean anthology of Buddhist teachings was registered in the UNESCO Memory of the World Programme to honour its importance in print history.

Gutenberg's revolution

Innovations in typesetting and printing spread across West Asia and North Africa and into Europe, slowly displacing the scribes writing by hand in monastic libraries.

A small number of woodblock broadsides and books were produced in Europe, but the true revolution in communication occurred when movable type

Typography is the craft of endowing human language with a durable visual form.
Robert Bringhurst
The Elements of Typographic Style, 2008

and the printing press arrived, courtesy of Johannes Gutenberg, around the mid-15th century.

Combining several discoveries and inventions, Gutenberg's printing press was based on the traditional screw press that had long been used to produce wine and olive oil. The machine allowed printers to arrange individual metal letters in a frame to form different words and lines of type; these would then be secured with quoins (wedges) so they worked as a single unit called a lockup. After printing multiple copies efficiently,

economically, and quickly, the characters were released from the lockups and stored for use on the next job.

In 1455, Gutenberg started to print bibles using this press and movable metal type. It is believed that his Mainz workshop produced about 180 copies – most were on paper but some were on vellum, or animal skin – and they became known as the 42-line bibles because of the number of lines on each page.

The notion of typography as a separate discipline with its own specific advantages – increased legibility, for example – was years away. Gutenberg's Blackletter font, which was also known as Gothic, Fraktur, or Old English, closely resembled the handwriting of the monks: it was black, heavy, and visually dense, with little differentiation between letterforms.

Evolving typefaces

Around the 1460s, the heavy Gothic fonts started to fall out of favour and were replaced by Humanist typefaces. Also known as Venetian or Antiqua, these were based on the Carolingian Minuscule handwriting style that was already popular in Renaissance Italy. Although Humanist alphabets maintained some visual references to handwritten letterforms, they looked nothing like Gutenberg's Blackletter typeface: they were more delicate and far easier to read.

Humanist typefaces, including Jenson and Centaur, remain reliable text choices for book and magazine designers to this day. While they might appear a little old-fashioned

The Korean book *Jikji* is a collection of Buddhist writings. The sole surviving copy of the second volume of the book is kept at the National Library of France, in Paris.

This 1863 etching by French artist Auguste Ledoux shows the interior of Johannes Gutenberg's printing house, where the German printer examines a printed page with his assistants.

to the modern eye, these typefaces are attractive and legible – a useful combination, especially when typesetting lengthy passages.

The next historic category of type styles emerged between the late 1400s and early 1700s. They came to be known as Old Style or Garalde, a word that combined the names of two prominent figures in the industry: 16th-century French engraver and punchcutter Claude Garamond and Venetian printer Aldus Manutius. With its even stroke width and fine proportions, the type showed just how much progress had been made in the field of precision metalwork.

Punchcutting – that is, making individual letterforms from metal by hand – was a highly skilled craft requiring years of training to master. Each character in the alphabet had to be cut and cast in every desired size and style (roman, bold, italic) of the typeface. It was a labour-intensive, time-consuming

process, and even experienced punchcutters produced just one or two letterforms per day.

Garalde typefaces such as Garamond, Bembo, and Caslon are supremely legible classics that are still widely used today.

Transitional styles

Starting in the late 17th century, the Age of Enlightenment was a period of enormous fervour in

Europe, with mechanical and technical improvements propelling typographic experimentation and development into high gear.

In 1692, King Louis XIV of France established a committee at the Académie des Sciences to produce a new typeface for exclusive use in government and official documents. Known as Romain du Roi (literally, "the king's roman") and first used in »

Johannes Gutenberg

Born in Mainz, in modern-day Germany, around the end of the 14th century, Johannes Gutenberg brought movable type, the printing press, and mass-produced printed matter to Europe and the Western world.

Among Gutenberg's innovations were a quick-melting, fast-cooling metal alloy used to create durable, reusable type; a high-viscosity oil-based ink that adhered well to metal type and transferred cleanly to substrates on press; and

a printing press that applied the necessary firm, even pressure to the printing plates.

Gutenberg's method involved arranging typeset pages on a matrix (or frame), inking them, then securing the matrix onto the screw press and lowering it to make an impression on the paper. The process was labour-intensive but generated pages faster than woodblock printing.

In 1465, Gutenberg was granted an annual stipend by the Archbishop of Mainz in recognition of his achievements. He died in 1468.

> Having been an
> early admirer of the
> beauty of letters,
> I became insensibly
> desirous of contributing
> to the perfection of them.
> **John Baskerville,** 1758

1702, this typeface design was the result of a strictly rational, mathematical approach. Royal typographer Jacques Jaugeon mapped out each letter on a square grid with a ruler and compass to achieve the most pleasing geometrical proportions.

Punchcutter Philippe Grandjean crafted the individual letterforms, which were then engraved on copper plates.

With an almost vertical axis and a notable weight difference between thin and thick strokes, Romain du Roi is considered the first Transitional typeface – that is, typefaces that sit between Old Style and Modern, with calligraphic elements replaced by a more structured, refined approach.

The Transitional classification also includes the precise alphabets created by William Caslon and John Baskerville – styles that later informed the Modern type families produced by Giambattista Bodoni in Italy and Firmin Didot in France.

Industrial presses

Printing technology advanced at an exponential rate after the start of the Industrial Revolution in Britain, from roughly 1760.

Around 1800, British politician Charles Mahon, third Earl Stanhope, developed the first printing press made entirely out of cast iron. Operated by hand via a system of levers, the Stanhope press was a vast improvement over earlier versions, which contained wooden components liable to break from repeated use and from the heavy pressure needed to ink pages properly. As well as being able to withstand hard use, the metal press could churn out pages at more than twice the rate of its forerunners: 480 pages per hour versus Gutenberg's 200.

German inventor Friedrich Koenig took Mahon's concept even further in 1812, when he developed the steam-powered double-cylinder press, which could produce in excess of 1,000 printed pages per hour. *The Times* of London, UK, was the first newspaper to use the Koenig press, starting with its issue

The individual components of letterforms are named after parts of the human body: lobes, ears, spines, eyes, legs, and shoulders. Early Humanist fonts echoed the movements of the human hand across a page. Over time, the forms of the Latin alphabet developed in tandem with innovations in printing presses and type. In the early 1800s, higher contrast in the letter strokes became possible thanks to new, stronger metal alloys, leading to Modern typefaces such as Didot and Bodoni, with their bold main strokes and hair-thin serifs.

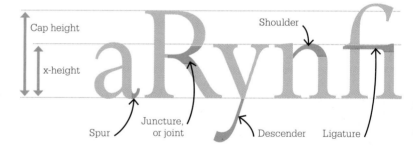

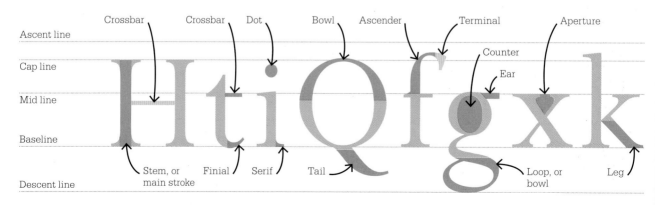

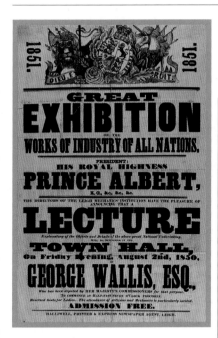

of 29 November 1814. Fearing that his workforce might revolt against the introduction of a machine that made them redundant, *Times* editor John Walter secretly purchased and set up two Koenig presses in a separate building.

A modern aesthetic

Typefounder William Caslon IV produced the first sans serif font, English Two Line Sans-Surryphs, in 1816. There was some resistance at first: the public's loathing of the stripped-down letterforms was such that early sans serifs became known as "grotesques". However, with mechanization powering the transition from maker culture to consumer culture, sans serif fonts found a receptive audience among manufacturers keen to advertise their products with new bold and eye-catching typefaces.

Richard March Hoe's type-revolving press, patented in 1847, came with as many as 10 cylinders, each of which was capable of printing 2,000 sheets per hour.

This 1851 poster advertising the Great Exhibition of London commands attention through its bold combination of serif and sans serif fonts.

Continuous advances in printing technologies helped companies to promote their products far and wide. Developed in the 1830s but coming into widespread use around 1860, chromolithography is a printing method that sees oil-based coloured inks applied to porous blocks of limestone. The new process made it possible for designers to layer as many as 30 different colours, each requiring its own stone, into a single image. The resulting richly hued artwork was instrumental in advertising – and driving sales for – the new consumer products flooding the Victorian marketplace.

Unstoppable progress

In 1870, American engineer Richard March Hoe invented the perfecting press, which further increased the speed of the process by simultaneously printing on both sides of the page. Other innovations included the introduction of the web – a large roll of paper that fed continuously through the press – and the folding machine, which folded and cut individual sheets into signatures (groups of pages) on press. What was once a painstaking and slow process driven at every step by human hands had become a rapid-fire, machine-based industry producing millions of pages every year.

The birth of graphic design as an independent profession followed soon after, with printed matter branching out from its original main purpose – the spread of information – to become a commercial medium for persuading people to buy things. However, selling products was not the only reason behind the emergence of graphic design: by the start of the 20th century, the discipline had become an indispensable tool in spreading messages of revolution and political reform in Europe.

Just as modern movements redefined the role of the artist in society, design came to be seen as a platform for the graphic symbols of reform. Print became the vehicle that carried political movements along. ∎

TEN CYLINDER TYPE-REVOLVING PRINTING MACHINE.

WEAR A WORK OF ART
WOODBLOCK TEXTILE PRINTING

IN CONTEXT

FOCUS
Adding patterns to textiles

FIELD
Textile design, interior design, fashion design

BEFORE
*c.***2500** BCE Woodblock printing originates in China.

*c.***1390** CE In *Il Libro dell'Arte*, Cennino Cennini's woodblock patterns show how to "imitate whatever style of silk cloth you wish, either leaves or animals."

AFTER
1790 In Europe and the US, mechanized roller printing produces printed fabrics at a lower cost and begins to supplant older techniques.

1805 The Scottish town of Paisley starts to produce its own Indian-influenced textiles.

1952 The All India Handicrafts Board is set up to advise the Indian government on textile development programmes.

W oodblock printing is an ancient practice. On an expanse of cloth, such as cotton or silk that has been pre-washed and dried in the sun, a wooden block, carved with an intricate pattern and coated with dye, is lined up and pressed down.

The process is thought to have originated in China around 2500 BCE and spread to India; the earliest fragments of Indian-made block printed textiles date to the 9th century BCE. India's woodblock art form reached a peak during the Mughal Empire of 1526–1858,

I unwittingly began to pluck at the fruit and flowers, the artificers having copied the beauties of nature with such surprising truth and accuracy.
Emperor Jahangir
Memoirs of the Emperor Jahangir, c.1620

when the patronage of the royal household helped to nurture the skills of its practitioners. The Indian printmakers' knowledge of natural dyes, such as madder and indigo, and mordants – substances that combine with dye to fix its colour to fabric – allowed for great vibrancy in their printed cottons. New styles emerged, inspired by the diverse flora of the region as well as European botanical drawings, and included intricate floral motifs of which the Mughal emperors were particularly fond.

The print process
A pattern is carved onto wooden blocks, typically made of teak, sycamore, or pear. The blocks are dipped in dye and applied, section by section, to the length of fabric. Working by eye, the printmaker's experience means that the join between one block and the next is almost invisible, with any tiny imperfections adding character and value. Once this is dry, the printing process is repeated using another block carved with different elements of the pattern.

Three techniques are commonly used to create block prints: direct, resist, and discharge printing. For

See also: Early textiles 24–29 ▪ Manufacturing textiles 84–91 ▪ Dawn of synthetic fabrics 194–95

A printmaker in Rajasthan, India uses a traditional carved woodblock to apply the first layer of a repeat-pattern print. The fabrics are prized for their quality and precise craftsmanship.

direct printing, the fabric is bleached, dyed, and then printed. In resist printing, areas of the fabric are protected with substances like mud or wax while the fabric is submerged in dye. In discharge printing, chemicals are used to remove the colour from selected areas of dyed fabric; these areas may be left white, or printed over again. Often the outlines and details of a pattern are printed first, and the blocked colour is applied afterwards, using different stamps.

A spread in popularity

By the 17th century the East India Company was exporting fabric from India to Europe, where consumers were enthralled by the quality of the prints and the vibrant patterns. The most popular patterns were copied and reproduced; one well-known example is Paisley, now associated with the eponymous town in Scotland, but its distinctive teardrop motif is actually Persian in origin. Known as the *boteh* or *buta*, it references flora as well as the cypress tree, a Zoroastrian symbol of long life.

Modern prints

Faster, mechanized methods of printing have now overtaken the slow process of block printing, but some practitioners mix old and new, using traditional methods with synthetic dyes. Recently, a period of decline in the industry until the mid-20th century has been followed by a resurgence of interest in the art form – encouraged by national boards, nongovernmental organizations, and commercial projects. ▪

Regional differences

Indian woodblock printing encompasses a wide array of styles and patterns. The variations in technique and imagery are tied to different regions and distinct cultural identities. Their designs may have been adapted to suit different audiences and commercial opportunities, but the techniques used to create them have been passed down over centuries – groups such as the Chhipas and Khatris have been producing printed textiles since the 16th century.

Regional differences in pattern may denote particular local groups. The *Dabu* mud-resist printing in Deesa, for example, includes motifs and colours that relate to local communities. Some patterns include religious iconography or script for ritual purposes, such as *Varak* printing from Jaipur, which uses gold or silver leaf and can be seen in temples. Regional prints may also reference the local flora and fauna: Machilipatnam block prints are known for the complex botanical drawings popularized as chintz.

Machilipatnam block prints are a unique printed form of *kalamkari*, meaning pen-drawn. The designs often feature floral patterns, animals, and geometric forms.

OSTENTATIOUS DISPLAY
BAROQUE FURNITURE DESIGNS

Furniture, particularly that which is expensive and well-crafted, has long been a symbol of power, economic status, and cultural superiority. This was particularly evident in 17th- and 18th-century Europe, where the upper classes sought to spend their earnings from investments in colonial trading companies on high-status products.

In terms of magnificence, the furniture commissioned in France during this period is in a class of its own. The use of rare and expensive materials, along with the highest level of craftsmanship to create intricate designs inspired by nature became a hallmark of Baroque furniture. Furniture-makers such as André-Charles Boulle and Charles Cressent created ornate armoires and cabinets with distinctive bulging fronts, enhancing their works with intricate marquetry and gold adornments that demonstrated their remarkable craftsmanship. The Manufacture Royale des Gobelins, which had once created magnificent tapestries for French royal interiors, expanded its expertise to include the crafting of luxurious furniture.

Royal opulence

The results could be seen in all their glory in the salons of Vaux-le-Vicomte and Versailles, two châteaux located outside Paris. These palaces incorporated long promenades through which visiting dignitaries were escorted – the intention being that by the time they reached the king's chamber, they would feel suitably diminished, having witnessed the enormous power and importance of the king and his nation. One of the most

This side table from c.1685 is an exquisite example of Baroque craftsmanship. Its design is based on one by artist and designer Charles Le Brun for the Hall of Mirrors at the palace of Versailles. It encapsulates the grandeur of the Baroque period.

See also: Design catalogues 82–83 ▪ Art Nouveau 132–33 ▪ Catalan Modernism 134–35 ▪ Material-led furniture design 186–87 ▪ Flat-pack furniture 228–29

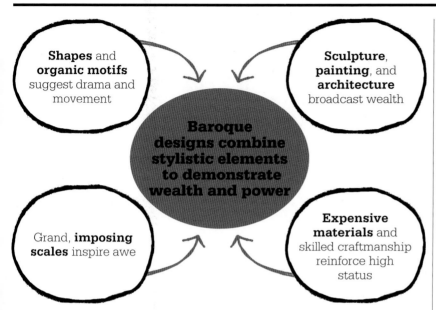

Shapes and **organic motifs** suggest drama and movement

Sculpture, **painting**, and **architecture** broadcast wealth

Baroque designs combine stylistic elements to demonstrate wealth and power

Grand, **imposing scales** inspire awe

Expensive materials and skilled craftmanship reinforce high status

and mirror frames, and Gerrit Jensen, known for his intricate "seaweed" marquetry, contributed significantly to the Baroque furniture of English stately homes. These cabinet-makers helped to introduce French styles into English homes. The work produced in Britain came to be particularly admired for its superior craftsmanship in wood. Oak, the preferred local material, was often supplemented with a diverse variety of tropical hardwoods, reflecting Britain's expanding empire and burgeoning international trade.

The splendour of Baroque furniture helped to establish France's reputation as the world leader in the production of luxury goods. With time, however, the heavy, lavish tastes of Baroque furniture evolved into a lighter, more playful variant known as Rococo, while in Britain, a more restrained style of furniture associated with the cabinet-maker Thomas Chippendale came to predominate. ▪

striking examples was at Versailles, where the Hall of Mirrors contained items of furniture fashioned from solid silver. They were quite literally the wealth of a nation presented as side-tables and chairs.

Compared to these opulent French palaces, the great houses of the English Baroque were more modest affairs. Among the most lavish examples are Castle Howard in Yorkshire and Blenheim Palace in Oxfordshire – both celebrated for their fine furnishings housed within grand, if somewhat more liveable spaces. Prominent cabinet-makers such as John Pelletier, renowned for his gilded furniture

Baroque as a cultural phenomenon

The Trevi Fountain in Rome, Italy, was designed by Nicola Salvi and Giuseppe Pannini, and completed in 1762.

Baroque art and design first emerged in 16th-century Italy, and has become synonymous with wealth and status. This is in part due to the Roman Catholic Church's promotion of grand architecture, aimed at asserting its ongoing importance following the Reformation.

Applicable at every scale – from grand palaces to tiny items of jewellery – the Baroque encompassed all of the arts and crafts. Baroque furniture was usually classical in proportion, but heavily embellished with ornamentation and gilding.

The growth of an aspirational working and middle class in the wake of the Industrial Revolution led to the style's re-emergence in popular culture. It can be found in the decoration of pubs, music halls, theatres, ballrooms, and even the parade banners carried by trade unionists. More recently, this style has become a global phenomenon. It can now be found in casinos in Macau and on international cruise ships – venues that are a far cry from the religious settings where the Baroque first originated.

A LARGE COLLECTION OF THE MOST ELEGANT AND USEFUL DESIGNS
DESIGN CATALOGUES

IN CONTEXT

FOCUS
Illustrated books from which customers select and customize their goods

FIELD
Communication design, interior design, furniture

BEFORE
1667 The first recorded catalogues in England, listing seeds, are distributed by gardener William Lucas. They are quickly imitated by other gardeners and nurserymen.

AFTER
1759–63 London furniture-makers Mayhew and Ince publish *The Universal System of Household Furniture* to compete with Chippendale.

1861 Draper and entrepreneur Pryce Pryce-Jones establishes the first modern mail order company in Newtown, Wales, selling woollen goods via catalogue. By 1880, he has 100,000 UK customers.

I n 1754, English cabinet-maker Thomas Chippendale published and circulated an illustrated book of furniture designs that customers could commission from his business. *The Gentleman and Cabinet Maker's Director* – which was released in editions until 1763 – profoundly influenced furniture styles; but as the first comprehensive trade catalogue, its format had a much broader impact on commerce and design.

Today, most products are not only uniform and mass-produced, but also listed in extensive,

detailed, and easily searchable online catalogues. They can be ordered from vast distances and, if necessary, returned. This is a far cry from 18th-century England, where customers shopped in person for bespoke items – from clothes to ceramics to chairs – or paid artisans to make them to their specifications.

Democratizing design
Unlike later catalogues, the first edition of Chippendale's *Director* both enabled the client to choose furniture and – by providing measurements and beautifully detailed engravings – allowed any cabinet-maker to reproduce its designs. While around 50 of the 308 subscribers to the first edition of the *Director* were aristocrats interested in buying furniture, the majority were cabinet-makers, who wished to copy its pieces.

The *Director* advertised its furniture in the styles fashionable with Chippendale's London clients: Gothic; Chinoiserie, a Western take

This elegant armchair was commissioned from Thomas Chippendale by the actor David Garrick and his wife Eva Marie, as part of a suite of furniture for their home.

See also: Baroque furniture designs 80–81 ▪ Design Reform movement 110-11 ▪ Visual merchandizing and retail design 124–31 ▪ G Plan design 226-27 ▪ Flat-pack furniture 228–29 ▪ Customization 310–11

New designers like **Thomas Chippendale** struggle to establish themselves in **London's competitive** furniture-making industry.

Chippendale creates his catalogue the *Director* to **promote his designs** to rich clients.

The *Director* becomes popular with other designers, who **imitate** and **adapt** Chippendale's **designs**.

Chippendale's work becomes **well known**, leading to **royal commissions** and important clients from overseas.

The *Director* was a brilliant early example of branding.

---

on Chinese motifs; and "Modern" (Rococo), a contemporary French style. These had rarely been seen outside high-society metropolitan settings, but the *Director* allowed woodworkers anywhere to apply these styles to their work. Across the UK, Europe, and North America, artisans made their own versions of Chippendale designs for decades to come.

Enduring legacy

Chippendale used modern methods of printing and distribution to build the reputation of his business, accelerating the spread of ideas and influences. The *Director* helped to satisfy the needs of a growing population and to create a mass market for furniture that was more standardized and easier to produce. As industrial manufacturing continued to develop in the 19th century, so too did manufacturers' catalogues, and many types of retailers began to issue them. Bolstered by photography, the printed catalogue went on to flourish throughout the 20th century, and into the Internet era. Today, most catalogues have effectively transformed into e-commerce platforms. ▪

Thomas Chippendale

Furniture designer Thomas Chippendale was born into a family of joiners and woodworkers in the Yorkshire village of Otley, UK, in 1718. He moved from Yorkshire to London, where he established a workshop and showroom in 1753. Chippendale's *Director* propelled him to international fame. Catherine the Great and Louis XVI both owned French editions, and Chippendale designs were imitated from Philadelphia to Hamburg.

Prolific and influential, Chippendale was commissioned by royals and aristocrats to furnish their homes, yet his business struggled with costs. After his death in 1779 from tuberculosis, his children did not inherit great wealth, although his son continued the business into the 19th century. Chippendale remains the most famous British furniture designer, and his name is a byword for an Anglicized style of Rococo furniture.

Key works

1766 Nostell Priory, Yorkshire
1767 Harewood House, Yorkshire

FABRIC CREATED WITH SPEED AND PERFECTION

MANUFACTURING TEXTILES

IN CONTEXT

FOCUS
Mass-producing textiles

FIELD
Textile design, fashion design, industrial design

BEFORE
c. **500–1000 CE** The first spinning wheel, or *charkha*, is invented in India. It speeds up the spinning process by using a wheel to turn the spindle and draw the fibres into a thread.

1764 James Hargreaves invents the spinning jenny, which can power eight spindles with a single wheel.

AFTER
1804 Joseph-Marie Jacquard patents a punch-card system to programme woven patterns for a loom.

1891 British inventor James Northrop patents a fully automated power loom, which is named for him and first manufactured in the US.

Weaving entails stretching strong warp (vertical) yarns across a frame, and passing perpendicular weft yarns under and over them using a device called a shuttle. It is a labour-intensive process, and for centuries inventors experimented with machines to reduce both time and manpower involved in making woven fabric. The most significant innovation came in 1769, when British business owner Richard Arkwright developed the spinning frame and effectively mechanized textile production. Although originally designed to be horse-powered, the device was soon modified to be powered by water wheels and became known as the "water frame".

Desirable textiles

By the time Arkwright patented his invention, textile products had been in use for millennia, serving both functional and decorative purposes – from shelter, to display of status. Textiles were also used as currency, especially on the Silk Road trading routes linking Europe to East Asia, and in certain regions of West and Central Africa.

Textile designs were influenced by the indigenous fibre-producing plants and animals, as well as the spinning and weaving techniques developed, dye sources available, and patterns reflecting local tastes and traditions. India, for example, which combined a climate suitable for the cultivation of mulberry trees and cotton plants with generations

The mechanized spinning process led to round-the-clock production. The textile factory's windows in Joseph Wright's *Arkwright's Cotton Mills* (1782) are illuminated for the night shift.

of skilled workers, was renowned for its silk and cotton production. Indian textiles – printed calicoes, cotton muslins, chintzes with vivid patterns of flora and fauna, and high-quality woven silks – dominated international markets from at least the 15th century.

In the early 18th century, British cloth production focused on wool, linen, and a coarse fabric called fustian, which combines stronger linen and weaker cotton threads. Global trade brought other textiles, valued for the properties of different fibres, as well as the rarity and perceived exoticism of their designs.

The economic value of textiles and their difficult production methods drove early industrialists

See also: Early textiles 24–29 ▪ Woodblock textile printing 78–79 ▪ Dawn of synthetic fabrics 194–95 ▪ Safety fabrics 244–47

> A child can produce as much as would … ten grown up persons.
> **Ralph Mather**
> *An Impartial Representation of the Case of the Poor Cotton Spinners in Lancashire, 1780*

wanting to cut their costs to look for potential innovations. Engineers tried to build machines to replicate foreign production methods and so reduce the reliance on imports. Designers also spurred innovation as they sought to copy foreign cloths.

Production methods

Textile making was time- and labour-intensive at almost every stage of production. First, the raw source material – for example, sheep and silkworms, or cotton and flax plants – had to be reared or grown. Next came the processing – whether the dew- or water-based retting (controlled degradation, almost rotting) of coarse flax stems, which took up to two weeks, the shearing of wool from sheep, or the laborious removal of seeds from cotton fibres.

Once the fibres had been extracted and cleaned, most of them had to be worked into a strong, continuous thread – and this was another time-consuming process. The exception was silk, which is spun into long lengths by silkworms as they make their cocoons.

Although the spinning wheel had been invented in the 1st millennium CE, the basic technology behind it had not progressed in any meaningful way from the original Indian *charkha*, and spinning was still slow. Next came the weaving process – but first the yarn might need to be dyed, whether creating plain or patterned fabrics. Finally, the finished cloth could be dyed or decorated with a printed pattern.

The delicate silk worn by the lady in this 1750 portrait by Thomas Hudson came from India. Import costs meant that only the upper class could afford these exotic fabrics.

The first textile factories were built in the Italian region of Piedmont from as early as 1678. They mechanized a process of spinning silk known as "throwing", in which silk fibres are twisted to produce stronger, usable threads. Two machines with multiple spindles »

Richard Arkwright

Born in Lancashire, UK, in 1732, Richard Arkwright was the son of a tailor and one of 13 children. He did not have the money to attend school but was taught to read and write by his cousin. His first profession was as a barber and wig maker, and while travelling for work he became familiar with the spinning and weaving processes.

Seeing the opportunities in textiles, Arkwright started working on a spinning machine, employing clockmaker and engineer John Kay. Their 1769 invention, the water frame, combined other people's ideas and innovations. Creating the wider system in which to use these machines, Arkwright set up cotton mills and pioneered the factory system.

Arkwright was knighted in 1786. By the time of his death six years later, he owned factories in Derbyshire, Staffordshire, Lancashire, and Scotland, and had amassed a personal fortune of £500,000 (which equates to around £200 million today).

on circular frames worked in sequence: first the throwing machine, or *filatoio*, then the *torcitoio*, which doubled the strength by twisting threads together in the other direction. The first such factory in Britain was Lombe's Mill, built between 1717 and 1721 on the River Derwent, Derbyshire, using the knowledge John Lombe had gained spying on the Italian mills.

In early 18th-century Britain, the textile industry relied on small narrow looms, operated by a single weaver, and larger broad looms, around 2 m (6.5 ft) in width, which were operated by a pair of workers. In the broad loom, the first weaver operated the loom and passed the shuttle through, while the second person was responsible for throwing the shuttle back to the first weaver each time.

John Kay, an inventor from Bury, Lancashire, developed a metal version of the reed, the device that separates warp threads for the loom, in about 1720. While travelling around England to sell his product, Kay spotted an opportunity to save labour in the weaving process – effectively making the second weaver's role redundant – by enabling the shuttle to move across the loom with little effort. Patented in 1733 and originally called the wheel shuttle, Kay's invention became known as the flying shuttle for the way it was propelled back to the start of each row.

In France, inventor Jacques de Vaucanson was famous for building fun automata, including a mechanical duck that "ate" grain and "defecated". On the strength of these inventions, he was recruited to apply his skills to weaving, and in 1745 he devised a system by which perforated cards could guide the lifting of individual warp threads according to a pattern. However, he was unable to apply this successfully at scale, something that would not happen until early in the 19th century.

As weaving became faster, demand for thread increased and this became a driver for innovations in the spinning process. The most important of these came in 1764, when British inventor James Hargreaves devised the spinning jenny, which allowed one operator to spin multiple spindles by turning a single wheel. Other inventors continued to experiment to bring further improvements, and their ideas and research informed Arkwright's water frame. Working with (a different) John Kay, a clockmaker from Warrington, Arkwright succeeded thanks to the use of rollers that drew out the cotton fibres, imitating the action of a hand spinner's fingers.

From cottage to factory

In 1771, Arkwright opened the first water-powered cotton-spinning factory in Derbyshire. Cromford Mill was filled with the latest

---

Textile making is **laborious and time-consuming**, using techniques that evolved **slowly over centuries**.

↓

Textiles are valuable **trading commodities**, and fabrics **imported from elsewhere** are seen as **more desirable** than those available from domestic industry.

↓

Many manufacturers **try to replicate** desirable cloths and **develop machines** to make them faster.

↓

New spinning and weaving machines change the nature of textile making and play an important part in the **Industrial Revolution**.

↓

Textiles can be produced more quickly and at lower cost, but the Industrial Revolution has a dehumanizing effect.

By 1812, thousands of Samuel Crompton's spinning mules were in use, driving millions of spindles. Since he did not patent his invention, Crompton received no royalties.

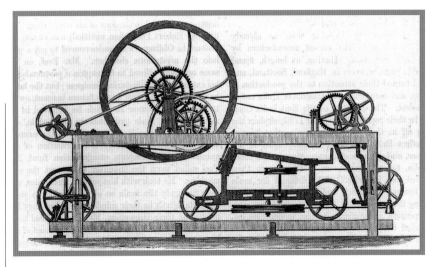

spinning technology and operated by a new kind of workforce. Prior to this, yarns and cloth had been made by individual workers in their own homes. Relationships were built and maintained with travelling merchants who delivered the raw materials and sold the spun thread or woven cloth when the work was done.

Invention follows invention

When mechanization of the fabric-making processes replaced practised techniques passed down through generations, the workers found themselves replaced by machines that could be operated by unskilled labourers, including young children. Invention after invention in the early and middle decades of the 18th century transformed the individual stages of the fibre sourcing, preparing, spinning, and weaving processes, setting the wheels in motion for the factory system, the standardization of tools, parts, and labour, and a highly profitable leap in production.

When Arkwright put his new water-frame technology to use at scale, cotton was his fibre of choice. This was popular with consumers for its easy washing and ability to take dyes for vibrant Indian woodblock prints, as well as for weaving into a fine, diaphanous fabric known as muslin. At the time, production of these textiles was based in India; with European countries unable to manufacture products of the same quality, governments put duties and bans on imports in order to protect their domestic industries.

The earlier Calico Acts of 1700, 1720, and 1721 had made the import, sale, and wearing of cotton fabrics illegal in Britain. However, once Arkwright had acquired the sourcing and technology to produce cotton, he was able to put pressure on the British government to repeal the Calico Acts, and his factories could then begin work spinning huge amounts of cotton.

In 1779, elaborating on the technology used for the spinning jenny and the water frame, Lancashire spinner Samuel Crompton invented the spinning mule, which improved on the

As Arkwright and Whitney were the demi-gods of cotton, so prolific Time will yet bring an inventor to every plant.
Ralph Waldo Emerson
Fortune of the Republic, 1878

process once again and produced the stronger, finer cotton required for weaving muslin.

Power looms

In 1784, British clergyman Edmund Cartwright invented the first mechanical loom, or power loom – a much-needed tool to match the rate at which cotton could now be spun. Having heard of the popular spectacle of the Mechanical Turk chess-playing machine, built by Hungarian inventor Wolfgang von Kempelen in 1770, Cartwright believed that a machine could be made to replicate the complex movements of the weaving process. Although the chess machine was later revealed to be a trick, Cartwright was able to release a crude first mechanical loom in 1784 and made further improvements in the following years.

Before long, mechanical looms were able to produce plain weaves. However, more complex patterned designs, including premium silk textiles, remained the preserve of skilled weavers. Designs would be developed after conversations with merchants, following popular trends, or taking inspiration from imported fabrics. Designers would » then paint the finished designs onto gridded paper for weavers to translate.

Once the design had been plotted, the process of weaving the patterns was also complex. Historically, skilled weavers sang mnemonics to remember patterns, while the operation of a draw loom required an assistant known as a draw boy to sit on top and manually lift the warp threads according to the pattern. The part of a loom known as a semple controlled the pattern; it had to be programmed each time a new design was used. A big step towards the mechanization of pattern weaving came from Philippe Lasalle, a successful designer from Lyon in France. In the late 18th century, he invented a removable semple that could store and transfer a design from one loom to another.

Building on Vaucanson's earlier idea of using perforated cards, it was French weaver and merchant Joseph-Marie Jacquard who finally improved the pattern-weaving system, patenting the Jacquard loom in 1804. Making use of punch cards – where for each corresponding thread there was either a hole or a solid card – its binary system effectively programmed the loom to follow any given pattern. Although rather crude in its early iteration, the Jacquard loom could reliably reproduce complex patterns using a large number of punch cards tied together. Jacquard's textile mechanism is widely considered the precursor of modern computing since its binary method inspired Charles Babbage to draw up plans for his Analytical Engine in 1837.

From France to London

Expensive, specialist textile design had long been concentrated in areas where materials and skilled labour were present. The south of France was home to a skilled silk-

The profits arising from the machinery of Sir Richard Arkwright were so considerable ... that the machinery was employed for the whole four-and-twenty hours.
Sir Robert Peel, 1816

weaving workforce, but religious persecution caused Protestant Huguenots, many of whom were weavers, to flee the country and settle in Spitalfields, east London. Long before the advent of pattern weaving, many talented weavers had emerged from this burgeoning

The weaving loom

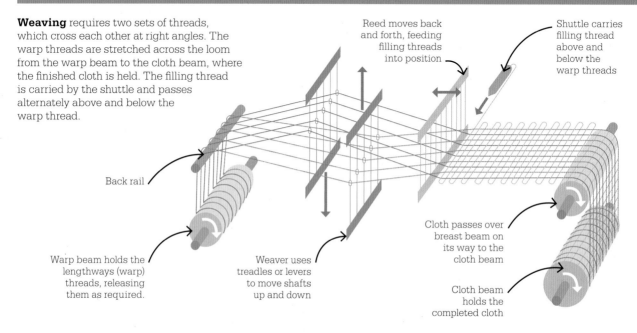

Weaving requires two sets of threads, which cross each other at right angles. The warp threads are stretched across the loom from the warp beam to the cloth beam, where the finished cloth is held. The filling thread is carried by the shuttle and passes alternately above and below the warp thread.

Reed moves back and forth, feeding filling threads into position

Shuttle carries filling thread above and below the warp threads

Back rail

Cloth passes over breast beam on its way to the cloth beam

Warp beam holds the lengthways (warp) threads, releasing them as required.

Weaver uses treadles or levers to move shafts up and down

Cloth beam holds the completed cloth

A woven silk floral design dating from 1740 by Anna Maria Garthwaite, who was renowned for her botanically accurate patterns, is displayed in London's Victoria and Albert Museum.

community of designers and textile makers in the early 18th century. They included James Leman, who left behind an album with almost 100 designs for woven silk, and Anna Maria Garthwaite, who is now celebrated for her skilful designs and meticulous design records in what was a male-dominated industry. A century after Leman and Garthwaite were active, the introduction of Jacquard's loom in weaving communities like east London meant patterns that had previously been the preserve of the rich could be produced cheaply and in large quantities, making them accessible to middle-class consumers.

A craft is lost

While the innovations in textiles democratized access to fashions, the wealth that was gained by industrialists was paired with negative impacts elsewhere. Textile workers lost out especially: skilled, relatively well-paid employment was replaced by monotonous work in hot, dusty, and noisy conditions. Workers' rights were minimal, and children below the age of ten were regularly employed in textile mills. Some workers protested against the new inventions – which they felt were taking their jobs – by breaking machines. The Luddites organized the most effective of these actions in the years 1811–13, but they were put down by force, with many of the participants hanged or transported to Australia.

In the US, the mass production of cotton was fuelled in large part by slave labour. In 1794, American

inventor Eli Whitney had created a device called the cotton gin, which pulled the cotton pods through a small grate to separate the cotton seeds far more quickly. The increase in production and the vastly improved opportunities to amass profits helped perpetuate slavery and the slave trade. Further profits were sought by Europeans in their colonial territories. The export of cheaper textiles from Britain to India – as well as the imposition of tariffs on Indian exports, for example – decimated India's domestic industry.

The Arts and Crafts movement, which started in Britain in the second half of the 19th century and included designers such as William Morris, responded to homogeneity of design and the devaluation of craft by looking back to pre-industrial methods and individual artistry. Today, however, designing for mass production in factories remains the dominant method for the manufacture of textiles – and it has become ever faster and cheaper in the more than 250 years since Arkwright opened his mills. ∎

ARTISTIC PERFECTION ON AN INDUSTRIAL SCALE

MASS-PRODUCED CERAMICS

During the 18th century, the production of ceramics underwent a revolution in Britain. What had been a craft-based activity carried out at home transformed into a fully-fledged industry. This shift was driven by technical innovations and business-minded individuals, and led to the efficient mass-production of ceramics. A network of makers and retailers emerged, creating a demand for these ceramic wares across the country.

In the preceding century, the demand for domestic items had been mostly met by small, local potteries, while luxury goods were imported from East Asia in great numbers. However, after about 1680, the English county of Staffordshire emerged as a centre for domestic pottery production. This was mostly due to its location: Staffordshire had easy access to essential raw materials, such as coal, and local clay beds satisfied the needs of these smaller family-run potteries.

From craft to industry
Between 1720 and 1760 the manufacture of ceramics in Staffordshire expanded rapidly, in part because of new production methods. The adoption of plaster of Paris moulds for casting and pressing ceramic forms meant that production could be carried out by less-skilled workers, and ceramics could be adapted easily to changing fashions and tastes.

However, from around 1760, the production process began to grow in complexity. Strict divisions of labour and specialization emerged at each stage. Skilled roles included throwing, mould-making, glaze-dipping, polishing, engraving, and packing, to name a few. As these processes became more technical,

Jasperware pottery consists of unglazed matte stoneware. This plate includes a typically intricate white relief set against a "Wedgwood Blue" background.

See also: Standardizing pottery 48–49 ▪ Early mass production 64–65 ▪ The Arts and Crafts movement 112–19 ▪ Service design 270–71

they required additional space and specialist tools. As a result, larger manufacturers began to dominate the industry.

In 1769, potter and entrepreneur Josiah Wedgwood opened a ceramics factory, Etruria, outside Stoke-on-Trent, in Staffordshire. His ambition was to open the most modern factory in existence, and he succeeded in doing this by bringing together all the processes necessary for the mass-production of ceramics under one roof. While this approach was not entirely new, Wedgwood's factory distinguished itself by meticulously streamlining and rationalizing every process.

Sited near the newly built Trent and Mersey canal, Etruria benefited from low transportation costs. Its quality-control was meticulously upheld, and almost all the items produced there met the set standards. Wedgwood pioneered a unique approach by integrating the production, marketing, and retailing of his products.

Worldwide fame

Wedgwood made ceramics that were accessible and appealing to the emerging middle class. His sophisticated distribution network meant that he could deliver products to a wide customer base with relative ease. Subsequent generations of manufacturers expanded Wedgwood's range of ceramics to include porcelain and transfer-printed earthenware, establishing Britain's reputation for practical and affordable ceramics throughout the world. ▪

Josiah Wedgwood

Born in 1730 into a family of potters in Staffordshire, Josiah Wedgwood revolutionized the ceramics industry with his innovative production and marketing techniques.

Having founded his company in 1759, he became renowned for his innovative pottery. Wedgwood applied a scientific mind to his work, studying the best temperature required inside a kiln to fire ceramics without causing an accident. He was meticulous about producing the right colours and textures for his ceramics and glazes.

In 1768, having persuaded Queen Charlotte to purchase some of his cream-coloured earthenware and renaming it "Queen's ware", Wedgwood partnered with London merchant Thomas Bentley. Bentley managed the pottery's London showroom, and kept Wedgwood informed of the latest metropolitan trends.

Wedgwood was an ardent abolitionist and is remembered today for his 1787 anti-slavery medallion including the motto: "Am I Not a Man And a Brother?" He died in 1795, his name synonymous with the elegant ceramics he mastered.

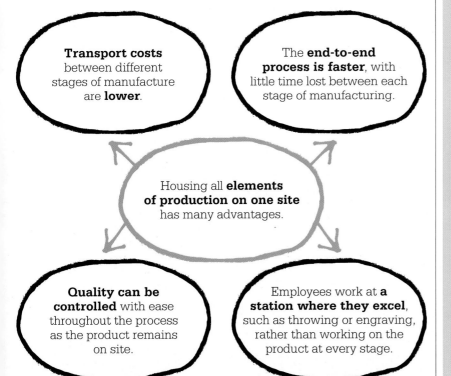

Transport costs between different stages of manufacture are **lower**.

The **end-to-end process is faster**, with little time lost between each stage of manufacturing.

Housing all **elements of production on one site** has many advantages.

Quality can be controlled with ease throughout the process as the product remains on site.

Employees work at **a station where they excel**, such as throwing or engraving, rather than working on the product at every stage.

THE DEEDS OF LIGHT

THEORY OF COLOURS

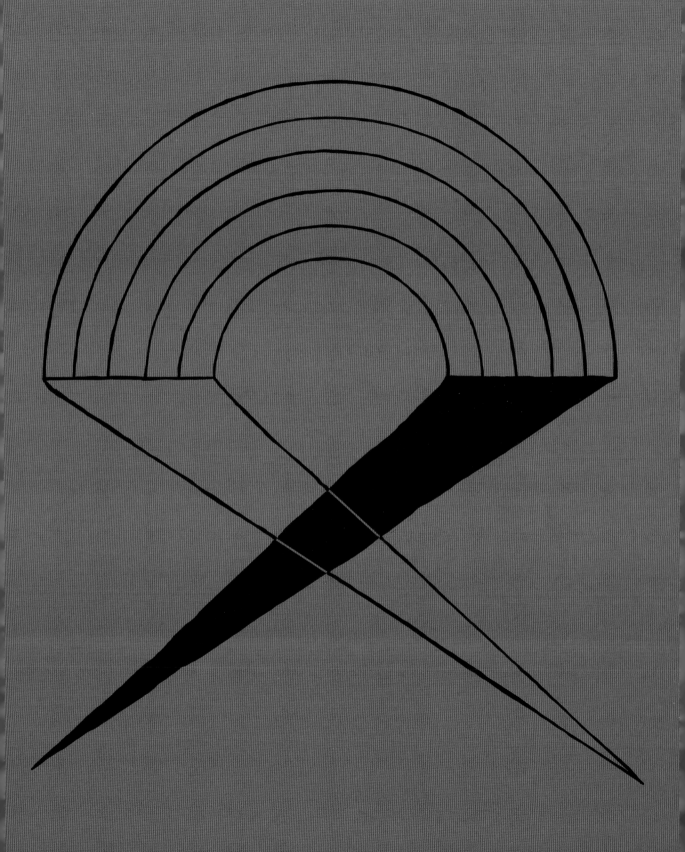

IN CONTEXT

FOCUS
**Understanding colours and
how they work together**

FIELD
**Graphic design, branding,
environmental design**

BEFORE
c. 77–79 CE Pliny the Elder, a
Roman naturalist, categorizes
colours based on the
substances from which they
were derived.

c. 1000 Mathematician and
astronomer Ibn al-Haytham
proposes that light rays enter
the eye from an object.

AFTER
1861 Scottish physicist James
Clerk Maxwell experiments
with colour photography.

1906 The Eagle Printing
Ink company invents the
CMYK colour process with
wet inks in four colours: cyan,
magenta, yellow, and black.

Colour theory is sometimes referred to as the art and science of colour. It is best understood as a framework that is used to describe how colours interact with one another, how they can be combined, and how they evoke emotional and psychological responses. The system that we understand today can be traced largely to the German philosopher and writer Johann Wolfgang von Goethe in the early 19th century.

Alchemy and colour

Early theories of colour were based on speculation rather than experimental observations. For instance, in the fourth century BCE, Aristotle, a philosopher from ancient Greece, suggested that all colours originate from "celestial rays" that embody both light and darkness. He associated each colour with one of the four elements – fire, earth, air, and water.

Similar elemental models persisted through the Medieval period. Alchemists of the time expanded the associations of colour to include the four humours (the fluids thought to influence human behaviour), organs, seasons, and even directions, as part of what they understood as an "integrated universe". The Swiss physician Paracelsus, a medical pioneer of the 16th century, believed that colours were reflections of fundamental qualities in nature and that the power of colour, used in conjunction with music and herbs, had healing powers.

A rational approach

Towards the end of the Middle Ages, these theories began to lose their prestige. The early modern period saw a growing interest in empirical observation and the study of natural phenomena. While mysticism and metaphysics remained popular, these more rational and scientific approaches began to transform how people understood the world. They also laid the groundwork for the Enlightenment in the 18th century.

Italian polymath Leonardo da Vinci was among the first to suggest an alternative to Aristotle's hierarchy of colour, challenging the prevailing ideas of his time. In order to mix the pigments for his painting more

See also: Pigments and colours 20–21 ▪ Visual merchandizing and retail design 124–31 ▪ Camouflage patterns 158–61 ▪ Bauhaus 170–71 ▪ Branding 200–07 ▪ Pantone colours 250–51

effectively, he set out to understand colour better. He noted how colours interacted and gave practical tips for painters: "Black garments make the flesh tints… whiter than they are… while red garments make them pale."

Aristotle had suggested that all colours resulted from the interplay of light and shadow – or mixtures of white and black – but in his *Treatise on Painting* (written in the 1480s and 1490s) da Vinci listed six "simple colours to serve as a foundation" – white, yellow, green, blue, red, and black. At the same time, however, da Vinci continued to associate the colours with the four elements: "yellow for the earth, green for the water, blue for the air, red for fire."

As part of his treatise, da Vinci investigated light as a physical phenomenon. While many believed that colours were qualities inherent in objects, da Vinci recognized that colour perception was influenced by other factors, such as lighting conditions, atmospheric effects, and the properties of the human eye. He

> As the quality of colours is discovered to the eye by the light, it is natural to conclude, that where there is most light, there also the true quality of the colour is to be seen.
> **Leonardo da Vinci**
> *Treatise on Painting*, c.1482–99

Isaac Newton conducts his experiment on light in this 19th-century engraving. He used a prism to refract a ray of light from a hole in the shutters over a window. The light split into the colours of the rainbow.

explored the idea that colours could be understood in terms of the reflection and absorption of light. While philosophers viewed white as the "cause, or the receiver" of colour and black as the absence, da Vinci wrote that both were essential to the painter. In addition to his studies on hue, da Vinci also distinguished between brightness ("value") and colourfulness ("chroma"). Together, these innovative approaches allowed him to reach a far more comprehensive understanding of colour than that in earlier eras.

Scientific breakthrough

The Enlightenment utterly transformed the way people understood the natural world. A breakthrough in the science of colour came in 1672 when English mathematician and physicist Isaac Newton published his first, controversial paper on experiments with prisms. Newton passed a

beam of sunlight through the glass, demonstrating that white light was composed of seven colours, which could be identified and ordered: red, orange, yellow, green, blue, indigo, and violet. Newton was also the first scientist to use the word "spectrum" to describe this range of colours, using a Latin word meaning "apparition" or "spectre".

Newton's research proved that colours were not inherent properties of objects, but rather a result of the interaction between light and matter, overturning Aristotle's theory, still accepted by many scholars at the time. Newton also observed that each colour was "refracted" (or "bent") at different angles that could be measured. »

This provided a quantitative framework for understanding the behaviour of light and colour, moving studies towards a more rigorous, scientific approach. In 1704, Newton documented his findings, including the prism experiment in *Opticks*, his treatise on light. This work is considered by scientists to be one of the most influential scientific books ever written, and it remains a cornerstone of modern physics. In this work, Newton defined three groups of colours – primary, secondary, and tertiary colours – and included the first colour wheel, in which he set the seven colours into a circle of uneven segments.

The colour wheel

Newton's colour wheel provides a rough guide to the concept of "additive" colour mixing, the process by which colours are mixed by adding their respective light spectra together. Newton explained that the resulting colour would be determined by the "number of rays" from each colour's light involved in the mixing. He used this to explain the process of combining different colours of light to create new colours: for example, magenta is made by overlapping red and blue light. He also demonstrated how each colour had a complementary – another colour that produces grey when the two are mixed together. This discovery showed that colour could be deployed rationally to achieve premeditated effects – it is the foundation of all theories of colour harmony known today.

Several artists in the 18th century were inspired by Newton's groundbreaking work, including Joseph Wright of Derby, an English painter known for his dramatic use of light and shadow. Wright held a keen interest in the scientific advancements of his era. His paintings vividly document the shift from alchemy towards a more empirical understanding of the natural world. They also capture the tension between these scientific ideas and the religious values of the period. Wright's paintings often feature scenes illuminated by artificial light sources, such as candles or lamps, which allow him to make use of Newton's theories and explore the interplay of light and colour.

In 1708, German-born printmaker Jakob Christoffel Le Blon used Newton's theory to develop a new printing technique, known as mezzotint. Le Blon created three separate metal plates, each representing a primary colour – yellow, red, and blue. He then used the plates to print an image onto a single sheet of paper. The three original colours combined on the page to produce a wide array of other colours. This technique still underpins colour printing processes today.

Colours and emotions

In the early 19th century, Johann Wolfgang von Goethe posed a challenge to Newton's theories. Goethe conducted his own research into spectral colour using the prism experiment but concluded that colours were a product of the interaction between light and darkness, supporting the ancient theory that colour came from black and white. In his *Theory of Colours*

Colour schemes

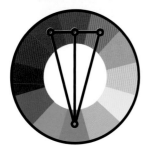

Complementary colours lie opposite each other on the colour wheel, for example red and green. Split complementary refers to a colour scheme that includes one base colour and two colours adjacent to its complement on the colour wheel.

An analogous colour scheme involves any three adjacent colours on the wheel. This scheme is often found in nature, and creates a visually pleasing look. These colours naturally harmonize with each other, providing a sense of cohesion.

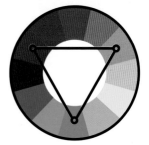

A triadic colour scheme features three colours that are equally spaced around the colour wheel. One colour often dominates, while the other two serve as accents. This scheme creates a palette that is balanced yet vibrant, and is popular in many art forms.

A monochromatic colour scheme has a single base colour that can be adjusted by adding white, black, or grey to create different tints, shades, and tones. It can create a harmonious and balanced look.

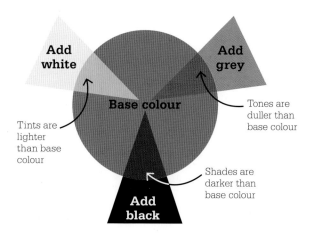

Add white

Add grey

Base colour

Tints are lighter than base colour

Tones are duller than base colour

Shades are darker than base colour

Add black

(1810), Goethe argued that darkness is an integral part of colour, not the absence of light. In particular, Goethe took issue with Newton's insistence that colour was an objective property. He resisted the reduction of colour to a purely physical or chemical phenomenon, instead seeing it as a holistic experience, one that encompasses both the sensory perception and the emotional response it evokes. Although the science behind Goethe's model was later disproved, his general approach to colour remains very influential. His symmetrical colour wheel, divided into six distinct hues – three primary and three secondary – is rooted in this concept of colour being the result of perception.

Unlike Newton's spectrum-based colour diagram, which was derived from a scientific understanding of light, Goethe's arrangement was decided by observation and personal introspection. Each primary colour is paired with a "diametrically opposed" secondary colour – yellow with violet, blue with orange, and magenta with green. This reflects Goethe's theory that colours interact with one another in a

dynamic and harmonious way, which is experienced by the human eye and mind.

These ideas on colour were deeply integrated with Goethe's views on aesthetics – he believed that understanding colour was crucial for anyone interested in visual expression. Goethe's approach resonated with artists who shared his sense of a profound connection between colour and feeling. British painter J.M.W. Turner even paid homage to Goethe by creating a pair of paintings shortly after the English translation of *Theory of Colours* was published in 1840. One painting, titled *Light and Colour*, makes use of the warmer, brighter colours from Goethe's colour wheel; the other, *Shade and Darkness*, contrasts cool and warm colours.

Goethe's legacy

Goethe's principles of colour harmony were further developed by the French chemist Michel Eugène Chevreul. In his role as director of dyeing at the Gobelins tapestry works in Paris, Chevreul published his theory of "simultaneous contrast" in 1839. It explored how the perception of colour depends on

its closeness to another colour that either complements it or stands in contrast to it. His theory was invaluable in revitalizing the vibrancy of the tapestries Chevreul worked on, which had become muted over time. Although this idea had been widely explored by artists, it was Chevreul's scientific approach, combined with the use of Goethe's colour wheel – by this time expanded into 72 colours – that gave the theory credibility.

In 1905, Albert Munsell, a painter and teacher, expanded on Chevreul's theory. He introduced the classifications of "chroma" ("colour intensity") and "value" ("lightness") to construct a three-dimensional model of colour, which Munsell represented as a sphere.

The artist's palette

Goethe's idea that seeing is "coloured" continued to inform European painting. In late 19th-century France, artists shared a common interest in achieving psychological effects through the "scientific" manipulation of colour. While striving to convey the intensely sun-soaked brilliance of the Provençal landscape, Post-Impressionist painter »

Light and darkness, brightness and obscurity… light and its absence, are necessary to the production of colour.
Johann Wolfgang von Goethe
Theory of Colours, 1810

Vincent van Gogh's oil-painting *Farmhouse in Provence* (1888) presents a rural scene in France. It showcases van Gogh's use of colour to express his emotional response to his surroundings.

Vincent van Gogh stated: "There is no blue without yellow and without orange," suggesting that colours could only ever be understood in relation to one another. Van Gogh's assertion that he had "tried to express the terrible passions of the human heart by means of red and green" served as a catalyst for artists seeking to harness the ability of colour to both express and symbolize emotion.

In the early 20th century, further advances in the development of a "chromatic language" were made by artists and designers associated with the Bauhaus in Weimar, Germany. A key figure among them was the Swiss designer Johannes Itten, whose writings blend speculation with an empirical study of colour design principles. Itten shared Goethe's belief that colour has the power to rouse emotions. He assigned colours with qualities such as "warm" and "cool", and also grouped colours into seasons. His system is still used in art and design today and has found applications in various fields, such as home decoration and hairdressing. Over time, the language of colour has matured into a vocabulary that is as practical as it is poetic.

The psychology of colour

Goethe's exploration of colour and mood played a key role in the emergence of colour psychology. His colour wheel is notably accompanied by evocative terms, like "beautiful" and "noble" that convey the emotional qualities of each colour. Goethe proposed that colours evoke specific sensory responses, and that these responses are deeply tied to human experiences and cultural contexts. For example, he associated blue with calmness and melancholy, while yellow was linked to warmth and joy.

Building on Goethe's early insights, in the 20th-century psychologists such as Carl Jung developed an understanding of how colour affects human perception and behaviour. Jung integrated colour symbolism into his system of "analytical psychology", proposing that certain colours evoke universal archetypes within the human psyche. "Colours are the mother tongue of the subconscious," he wrote, "They express the main psychic functions of man." Jung proposed a theory that classified psychological personality types

Additive and subtractive colour theory

Additive colour theory explains how different colours are produced by combining varying amounts of red, green, and blue light. For example, yellow is made from green and red light. All three colours combine to form white.

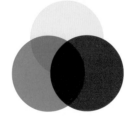

Subtractive colour theory explains how visible colours can be produced by absorbing certain wavelengths from white light using cyan, magenta, and yellow pigments. All three colours combine to form black.

in relation to four distinct energies: fiery red, cool blue, earth green, and sunshine yellow. These colours were arranged in a grid, with axes representing introversion / extroversion and thinking / feeling.

Colour in education

Goethe's theory of colour was also put to practical use in education and art therapy. According to Rudolf Steiner, an Austrian philosopher, esotericist, and educationalist, individuals consist of intricate networks of physical, spiritual, and emotional aspects, all interconnected with the natural world. Steiner taught that a harmonious balance could be achieved through the use of colour and music in education. He advocated the use of specific colours in educational environments to support students' cognitive and emotional well-being. For instance, warm colours such as yellow and orange were believed to promote creativity and enthusiasm, while cool colours like blue and green fostered focus and concentration. Steiner's theories continue to be applied in art therapy, where working

He who wants to become a master of colour must see, feel, and experience each individual colour in its many endless combinations with all other colours.
Johannes Itten
The Elements of Colour, 1961

Jung's personality types correspond to four colours: cool blue is cautious and thoughtful; earth green is caring and stable; sunshine yellow is fun and dynamic; fiery red is confident and action-driven. Each colour leans towards either introversion or extroversion, and feeling or thinking.

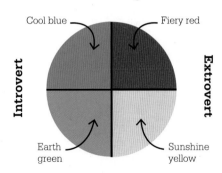

creatively with colour allows individuals to express and explore their emotions in a non-verbal way.

A tool in business

In the 21st century, colour theory has established itself as an essential tool in the business world. Market research has underscored the important role that colour plays in determining what customers buy and how they are attracted to different products.

Colour plays an important role in branding. For example, it is no coincidence that popular fast-food companies such as McDonald's have red and yellow logos, as these colours are believed to stimulate appetite. Other colours, such as Coca-Cola red, Facebook blue, and Barbie pink, have become contemporary cultural icons. These colours not only make it easy to recognize these products, but they also contribute to the creation of new symbolic meanings in our collective subconscious through a process that is known as "associative learning".

Colour psychology also applies to other fields, such as medical therapy, sports, and even game design. Businesses recognize

that the quality of the work environment influences their employees' productivity and performance. Similarly, hospitals and prisons acknowledge the influence that colours have on the mental health of patients and prisoners. Paint, clothing, and cosmetic companies offer ranges with the therapeutic aspects of colour in mind.

Today, it is widely acknowledged that colour affects our emotions and mood. While certain colours have been identified as triggering specific emotional or physical reactions, it is important to note that the same colours can have both positive and negative connotations, and the perception of these colours can differ from person to person. While some associations are shared universally, it is understood that there are noticeable differences between cultures and that colours change in significance at points through human history. The influence of colour on individuals also varies based on factors such as age, gender, and context.

There is no exact, universal theory of colour, but as Goethe once aptly noted: "Grey is the colour of all theory." ∎

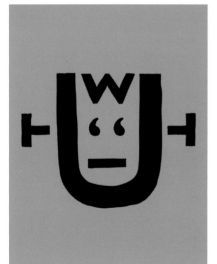

TYPOGRAPHIC MONSTROSITIES!!!
SANS SERIF FONTS

IN CONTEXT

FOCUS
Advertising and communication

FIELD
Typography

BEFORE
1440s Johannes Gutenberg's movable-type printing press allows for the mass production of printed materials.

1720s William Caslon I establishes his type foundry in Islington, London.

AFTER
1898 The Berthold Type Foundry releases Akzidenz Grotesk, the first widely used sans serif typeface. Akzidenz, loosely meaning "commercial", indicates its intended use as a typeface for trade printing.

1920s Bauhaus alumni Herbert Bayer and Jan Tschichold play key roles in the development of sans serif typefaces with clean lines and geometric simplicity.

Commonly seen in inscriptions on ancient monuments, the serif is a small stroke added to the ends of Roman letters. As well as being ornamental, the serif serves a functional purpose, forming a link that helps to "bind" letters together as words. In metal type, it creates a fine white space between the main strokes of the letters, which makes the characters easier to read.

Whether carved in stone or printed, most formally drawn letters in the Latin alphabet have taken

The essence of the New Typography is clarity. This puts it into deliberate opposition to the old typography whose aim was 'beauty'.
Jan Tschichold
The New Typography, 1928

inspiration from ornate calligraphy, Roman square capitals, or Gothic blackletter. As a result, for the first three and a half centuries of printing in Europe, serif typefaces were the prevailing style.

Printing developments

In the early 19th century, the Industrial Revolution brought about a profound shift in printing technology. It transformed the processes of type casting (producing individual letters), typesetting, and printing from manual craftsmanship to mechanized operations. The increased speed of the automated press allowed thousands of copies to be printed in the time it previously took to print only a few dozen. The proliferation of printed material had a dramatic impact on literacy.

Businesses could now advertise products and services to wide audiences at relatively low cost. As a result, printers began to distinguish between book printing and commercial printing, known as "jobbing". This new printing required a new aesthetic. The typefaces that had been designed in earlier centuries for long sections

See also: Movable type and early graphic design 70–77 ▪ Political messaging 164–69 ▪ Bauhaus 170–71 ▪ Modernism 188–93

of text appeared inadequate for the demands of the modern medium of advertising, which called for type that was larger, bolder, and more attention-grabbing.

In 1803, the British type founder Robert Thorne was among the first to experiment with a "fat face", a serif typeface with an extremely bold design. A variation of this concept involved eliminating the serifs altogether. William Caslon IV introduced this idea in 1816, creating a letter form without serifs characterized by an even stroke weight that followed the proportions of classical Roman capitals.

Probably influenced by the contemporary fascination with ancient Egyptian architecture and art, Caslon dubbed his typeface "Egyptian". Detractors labelled it "grotesque", finding the style malformed and monstrous, while others referred to it as "gothic".

A stylish couple leans against large sans serif letters spelling *été* (French for "summer") in this 1925 poster capturing the sleek elegance of the Art Deco era.

It was English type founder Vincent Figgins who, in 1832, first coined the term "sans serif" (from the French *sans*, meaning "without").

The new style was adopted in both Europe and the US, and by the mid-19th century it was found everywhere – from posters and shop signs, to brochures and newspaper headlines. However, it was mainly used for titles and, occasionally, captions.

A modern face

The use of sans serif exploded in earnest in the early 20th century, with the emergence of Modernism. This movement, inspired by industrial machinery and mass production, brought about a shift from ornate styles to typefaces emphasizing uniformity. Several of the most widely recognized sans serif typefaces emerged during this period, including Futura, which is characterized by its geometric simplicity, and Helvetica, known as a neo-grotesque. Both played a significant role in shaping the visual landscape of modern design. ▪

William Caslon IV

Born in 1780, William Caslon IV was the great-grandson of English type designer William Caslon I, founder of the Caslon Type Foundry and developer of the eponymous typeface.

In 1807, Caslon IV took over the running of his father's firm, and in 1816 he released the first commercially produced sans serif typeface. Originally called Two Lines English Egyptian (and now commonly known as Caslon Egyptian), this was an upper-case only typeface. The "two lines" referred to the typeface's body size, which equates to about 28 points. In one of the foundry's specimen books, Caslon's simple, bold letterforms were shown in the example text "W CASLON JUNR LETTERFOUNDER".

The font was favoured by several printers. One of them was Richard Taylor, who published scientific and academic titles from his premises in Red Lion Court off London's Fleet Street. There today, outside no 2, a plaque honours Caslon – who died in 1869 – and his typeface.

I SEEK ANTIQUITY NOT NOVELTY

HISTORICISM AND NEO-GOTHIC

IN CONTEXT

FOCUS
Reviving the past

FIELD
**Product design,
architecture**

BEFORE
18th century French
Enlightenment philosophers
Montesquieu and Voltaire
study ancient cultures and
classical civilizations.

1764 German art historian
Johann Joachim Winckelmann
publishes the influential book
History of the Art of Antiquity.

AFTER
1919 The Bauhaus school is
founded in Germany. "Truth
to materials" – one of its central
tenets – is traceable to Pugin's
thinking about honest design.

1935–37 German architect
Albert Speer appropriates
Classicism for his Zeppelinfeld,
built for the Nazi Party Rally
Grounds outside Nuremberg.

From around the mid-18th century, Britain witnessed a strong current of historical mindedness. This heightened consciousness of the past – termed "Historicism" – was important for architecture and design because it led to a number of historical revivals, including the significant Neo-Gothic style.

Some architects provided clients with a choice of plans that drew on different revival styles – so, the same municipal town hall could be imagined in either a Neoclassical or Neo-Egyptian style.

Pugin's *Contrasts*
A central figure within the Neo-Gothic movement was British architect and writer Augustus Pugin, who fervently believed that design had social, moral, and national responsibilities.

Like many of his peers, Pugin was alarmed by the rapid rate of social, cultural, and technological change affecting Britain at that time. Indeed, he perceived the society in which he lived to have morally failed.

In his 1836 book *Contrasts*, Pugin compared different types of contemporary buildings with similar ones from the Middle Ages. The approach was highly visual. One illustrated plate contrasted an elegant medieval almshouse

The clock tower of London's Palace of Westminster – which houses the bell known as Big Ben – was designed by Pugin in Gothic Revival style, with heavy ornamentation and tall spires.

See also: Mass-produced ceramics 92–93 ▪ The Arts and Crafts movement 112–19 ▪ Catalan Modernism 134–35 ▪ Deutscher Werkbund 162 ▪ National Romanticism 163 ▪ Bauhaus 170–71

with a contemporary prison; another showed a squalid late-Georgian inn crammed in among a row of terraced houses, whereas the medieval equivalent featured generous bow windows and an inviting beer cellar. Pugin's message was clear: if design and architecture are a reflection of the society in which they are produced, then modern life is bad, and medieval life is good.

Art and social values

Although Pugin's views largely centred on style, the fundamental concerns he raised also affected the social and political spheres.

British art historian John Ruskin shared Pugin's views. He explored the relationship between art and labour, criticizing the factory model as dehumanizing. Conversely, he believed that the irregularity and variety of the Gothic style favoured the individuality of the artisan, who was able to express his creative freedom and find artistic fulfilment through his work. Ruskin believed that this sense of fulfilment – and,

The Historicist revival

styles that became popular during the Victorian era were usually informed by contemporary archaeological discoveries.

Romanesque
Buildings with rounded arches and turrets echoed the architecture of the Roman Empire.

Neoclassicism
Popular from the mid-18th century, this style looked back to ancient Greece and Rome.

Scots Baronial
This Caledonian interpretation of the Middle Ages resulted in castle-like mansions and turreted buildings.

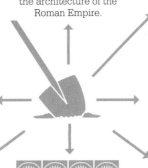

Italianate
Loggias, belvederes, cupolas, and overhanging eaves were inspired by the country villas of medieval Italy.

Neo-Gothic
Inspired by medieval religious buildings with lancet windows, this style also influenced furniture.

Neo-Egyptian
This style drew on motifs linked to ancient Egypt. Later, it inspired makers of Art Deco jewellery.

Renaissance
In furniture, features of this style included marble-top tables, fluted legs, and scroll motifs.

potentially, even pleasure in workmanship – meant the work itself could be considered good.

By drawing a link between the conditions in which design and architecture were produced and the moral value attached to that work,

Ruskin and Pugin were taking aim at industrial capitalism and the poor working conditions that many people endured in the 19th century. These values would later inform the work of William Morris and the Arts and Crafts movement. ∎

Morality and design

Augustus Pugin, who converted to Catholicism in 1834, associated the late medieval period with a mythical pre-Reformation time of true values and architectural forms serving the Christian faith. He perceived Gothic art – the style of that bygone era – as morally superior to the "pagan" styles popular in Britain in his time, especially Neoclassicism, and believed that adopting it would help rebuild Britain as a Gothic Catholic Christendom.

Stylistic disorder was a symptom of social disorder for Pugin. He objected to the "cheap deceptions of magnificence" – that is, making poor-quality materials appear expensive – that tempted the lower classes. These design shams were mostly related to mass-production methods. They ranged from casting, which removed variety, to casing, or the addition of an illusion to conceal an object's construction, such as the use of wooden veneers.

This bread plate was designed by Pugin around 1850. On the rim is a maxim in Gothic-style lettering about not wasting food, adding a moralizing and educational touch.

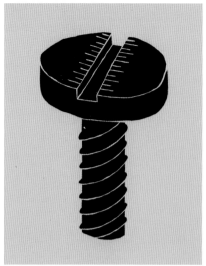

STRICTLY DEFINED DIMENSIONS
INTERCHANGEABLE PARTS

During the early 18th century, artisans working in precision crafts such as clock-making discovered the advantages of creating components in standard sizes. This not only ensured accuracy but allowed users to replace parts quickly. Weapons manufacturers were among the first to benefit from this innovation, as the development of interchangeable parts meant that equipment could be swiftly repaired and returned to use.

Using identical patterns made it easy to create similar castings. Templates could also be used to replicate shapes in wood and metal. However, achieving consistency in the assembly of items posed a greater challenge. In the mid-19th century, an

---

Parts are **made individually** and shaved down to size **by hand** to fit each weapon – this is **labour-intensive and inefficient**.

↓

Parts made to **precise measurements** are **designed to fit the weapon perfectly**.

↓

Weapons and their parts can be **accurately sized** and made to the **same measurements**.

↓

Small parts can be **mass-produced** for any weapon of that model, making production **quicker and more efficient**.

See also: Early mass production 64–65 ▪ Mass-produced ceramics 92–93 ▪ Multifunctional tools 136–37 ▪ Industrial design 146–47 ▪ Ford Model T 154–55 ▪ Planned obsolescence 176–77 ▪ Making things better 286–87

Sir Joseph Whitworth

Born in Stockport, England, in 1803, Joseph Whitworth was the son of a clergyman. From an early age, he showed a talent for engineering. Working as an apprentice at his uncle's cotton mill, he noticed that machinery frequently broke down due to ill-fitting components.

Whitworth went on to work for London engineer Henry Maudslay, making precision machine tools. Following service with other mechanics and engineers, he moved to Manchester in 1833. There, Whitworth started his own business, producing high-quality lathes and other machine tools.

Whitworth worked to tolerances of a thousandth of an inch (the "thou"), which necessitated unprecedented accuracy. By the 1850s, he was a well-known name, serving as the President of the Institution of Engineers and becoming a noted philanthropist, particularly in supporting education in engineering.

Appointed a Baronet in 1869, Whitworth died in 1887. The Whitworth Scale for the measurement of fastenings remains a British Standard to this day.

entrepreneurial engineer from Manchester, Joseph Whitworth, developed a standardized unit of measure for the sizes and the pitches of the threads used in drills, screws, and bolts. Whitworth had a keen eye for precision, and had earlier devised a method to check the absolute flatness of metal surfaces. The Whitworth Scale, introduced in 1841, remains a British Standard measurement for fastenings.

Military innovation

Whitworth gained national recognition during the Crimean War (1853–56), when he developed a highly effective rifle. At the same time, the Royal Navy used Whitworth's techniques to build rapidly a large fleet of gunboats. While the hulls were relatively simple to construct in British shipyards, the production of reliable steam engines for 120 vessels within just 90 days posed a greater challenge. The solution was to dismantle two existing engines and to send each individual part to a

workshop or foundry where they were copied multiple times. This ensured that enough identical engine parts were delivered to enable the gunboat fleet to be built and deployed on schedule.

Precision engineering

In steam-powered machines, components expand at varying rates. This makes it crucial to calculate meticulously the tolerance – the amount a part can acceptably expand or contract – for each item. The emergence of more sophisticated measuring tools, such as adjustable calipers, along with a

growing knowledge of metallurgy, allowed engineers to make highly accurate measurements, and paved the way for enhanced precision in manufacturing.

Despite being the first industrial nation, Britain began to fall behind other countries in the later 19th century, due in part to its laissez-faire approach to industry, which led to insufficient investment. However, in the US, production methods were revolutionized with the emergence of the "American system of manufacture". This system mandated the inclusion of written tolerances in design drawings, ensuring that every manufactured part could be installed without adjustment or replaced with an identical one. This principle of interchangeability paved the way for the mass-manufacturing we know today. ▪

Joseph Whitworth presented a number of his machines, including the radial drilling machine pictured here, at the 1862 International Exhibition in London, UK.

THE INTERSECTION OF IMAGE, WORD, NUMBER, ART
VISUALIZING DATA

When a deadly outbreak of cholera first struck England in late 1831, the prevailing (non-science-based) theory in the medical community was that the disease spread via toxic, foul-smelling air – or "miasma in the atmosphere" – caused by sewage and rotting matter.

A second epidemic of the disease struck in 1848–49; by the time a third wave hit London's Soho in 1853–54, British anaesthetist and pioneering epidemiologist Dr John Snow set out to prove his suspicions that cholera was transmitted not through the air, but via contaminated water.

The task of the designer is to give visual access to... the revelation of the complex.
Edward R. Tufte
The Visual Display of Quantitative Information, 2001

This contradicted all established theories at the time, and Snow had a difficult task convincing medical peers and public officials that the deaths would not stop until the real method of transmission was identified and dealt with.

Charting data
In 1854, Snow generated a map of Soho where he indicated the district's 11 water pumps by crosses, and cholera deaths by dots. Examining the scatter graph over the surface of the map, it became visibly obvious that cholera occurred almost entirely among those who lived near (and drank from) the water pump on the corner of Broad and Cambridge streets. Armed with this visual representation of epidemic data, Snow managed to convince the Board of Guardians, which was in charge of welfare and relief for the local population, to remove the handle of the contaminated pump to take it out of service.

A similar approach to making statistical numbers come alive was used a few years later by British nurse, statistician, and reformer Florence Nightingale. During the Crimean War, she was horrified

See also: Movable type and early graphic design 70–77 ▪ Information design 144–45 ▪ Bauhaus 170–71

Nightingale's Rose Diagram shows how many British soldiers died of their wounds (red), infectious diseases (blue), and other causes (black) every month from April 1854 to March 1856.

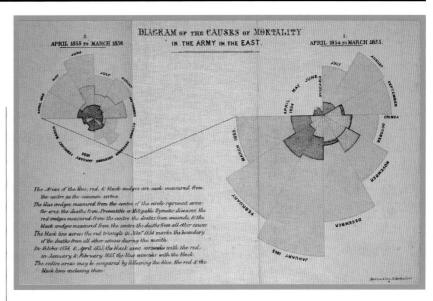

to observe that more soldiers died of transmissible infections in the hospital than from battlefield wounds. In 1858 Nightingale gathered mortality data on contagious disease, wounds, and other causes of death and used line graphs, scatter plots, and other graphic devices to display the information. Her best-known graphic, the so-called "Nightingale's Rose Diagram", used a visualization called a polar-area diagram to summarize complex statistics simply and persuasively, using colour for emphasis.

Modern-day usage

Illustrating medical statistics in a clear and effective manner continues to be of vital importance, as demonstrated during the Covid-19 pandemic. Starting in 2020, the UK Health Security Agency and other public health agencies around the world began publishing data about the pandemic. Easy-to-read charts displayed the numbers of infections, hospitalizations, and deaths, alongside population percentages of vaccinated individuals and other relevant data – all in graphic form. By breaking the information down into colour-coded regional maps and time-series, bar, and pie charts, a reader could see the most pertinent statistics at a glance.

Data visualization contributed to understanding the true nature of Covid-19. In addition, tracking national and global trends helped bring the pandemic under control, by offering solutions that may have been less clear when presented in grey columns of numbers. ▪

Presenting information

In 1644, Dutch cartographer Michael van Langren drew what is considered the first statistical graph. As royal cosmographer and mathematician to King Philip IV of Spain, he used a simple drawing with estimates of the longitude between the city of Toledo, in Spain, and Rome, Italy, to prove that there were better, more accurate ways to calculate this coordinate.

By introducing the line graph, bar chart, pie chart, and circle graph in 1786, Scottish engineer William Playfair created an easily understood universal language useful to science and commerce alike and permanently changed the way we look at data.

Data visualization enables a reader to see numbers or facts as real, vivid information by revealing what would otherwise remain invisible: making a downward trend in sales suddenly clear; spotting a disparity in income in adjoining neighbourhoods; or noticing which bird populations have declined over a certain period of time.

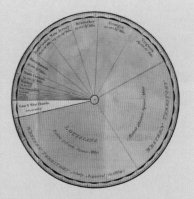

William Playfair's pie chart of US states, territories, and provinces (as they were in 1805) gives a clear visual representation of their relative sizes.

THE DECORATION OF UTILITY
DESIGN REFORM MOVEMENT

IN CONTEXT

FOCUS
Decoration is secondary to form

FIELD
Product design, textile design, interior design, architecture

BEFORE
1836 The Parliamentary Select Committee on Arts reports on the poor quality of British design.

1837 The first Government School of Design opens in London. In 1896, it becomes the Royal College of Art.

AFTER
1860s–1910s The Arts and Crafts movement promotes handmade goods, traditional craftsmanship, and a return to simpler designs.

1918–1939 The inter-war period sees the development of the Modernist design and art movement.

By the 1830s, the Industrial Revolution had begun to transform Britain. The rapid expansion of industry helped to create a new middle class that was keen to spend its earnings on the many household products – such as furniture, pottery, and ornaments – that were now available.

However, not everyone was satisfied with these products. There was concern that mass production had resulted in lowering standards, especially when British goods were compared to those from Europe. At the same time, there was a reaction against the excessive use of ornamentation and colour, and the indiscriminate mixing of styles and patterns that had become the norm in design.

Raising design standards

The advocates of the Design Reform movement included the civil servant and designer Henry Cole, the artist Richard Redgrave, and the architect and theorist Owen Jones. All three were closely involved in the Government Schools of Design initiative: a state-sponsored network of schools across Britain, founded in 1837 with the aim of raising the design standards of manufactured goods.

They championed a "balance between beauty and utility", and stressed the importance of designs that could be readily mass produced. With the support of Queen Victoria's husband, Prince Albert, they developed a set of

This mahogany armchair (c.1867–70) was designed by Owen Jones for a wealthy department store owner. Like much of his work, it incorporates elements from non-Western art.

See also: The Arts and Crafts movement 112–19 ▪ Art Nouveau 132–33 ▪ Deutscher Werkbund 162 ▪ Bauhaus 170–71 ▪ Modernism 188–93 ▪ G Plan design 226–27

Jones's book includes examples of art and design from different eras, such as these columns and capitals from ancient Egypt.

The Grammar of Ornament

Owen Jones was a key figure in Design Reform, who helped to formulate the principles of pattern and ornament that formed the teaching framework at the Government Schools of Design.

In 1856, he expanded on these principles in *The Grammar of Ornament*, a global and historical design source book that sought to identify the common principles of design throughout history.

Jones illustrated examples of ornament from a diverse range of historical and geographical sources, looking especially to Islamic decoration for inspiration. He argued that ornament should be "based upon an observation of the principles which regulate the arrangement of form in nature". Jones set out 37 general principles derived from these examples. His book helped to pioneer modern colour theory and Jones's theories on flat patterning, geometry, and abstraction still influence designers today.

formal guidelines for modern design. There were three basic principles: firstly, decoration should be secondary to form; secondly, form should be dictated by function and materials; and thirdly, design should draw from historical English and non-Western ornament, as well as plant and animal sources that could be distilled into simple geometric motifs. Students were encouraged to study and rework patterns from non-Western cultures, and to examine nature in order to understand how natural forms could be adapted rather than simply copied.

Industrial design is born

In 1856, Jones expanded on these principles in his seminal design source book, *The Grammar of Ornament*. He sought to develop a modern style, and his patterns, which were often based on linear tessellations, became a major influence in the design of textiles and wallpaper. Owen's ideas were taken forward by his protégé and Government School graduate,

Christopher Dresser. From the late 1850s, Dresser developed a design methodology that was visually and industrially radical, and designed a range of household items, such as vases, jugs, and teapots, that were functional yet beautiful. In doing so, he pioneered "industrial design", creating affordable, well-designed pieces that could be mass produced. Although the Design Reform movement only had limited success in refining the styles bought by Victorian consumers, it paved the way for other designers in the late 19th and early 20th centuries, including the Werkbund and Bauhaus in Germany. ▪

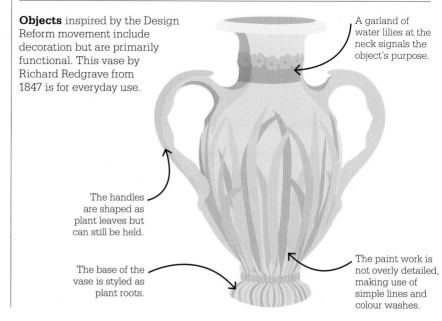

Objects inspired by the Design Reform movement include decoration but are primarily functional. This vase by Richard Redgrave from 1847 is for everyday use.

A garland of water lilies at the neck signals the object's purpose.

The handles are shaped as plant leaves but can still be held.

The base of the vase is styled as plant roots.

The paint work is not overly detailed, making use of simple lines and colour washes.

A JOY FOR THE MAKER AND THE USER

THE ARTS AND CRAFTS MOVEMENT

IN CONTEXT

FOCUS
Reviving craftsmanship

FIELD
Architecture, design, metalwork, and crafts

BEFORE
1836 Augustus Pugin, co-designer of the Palace of Westminster, advocates the importance of craftsmanship and tradition in architecture.

1853 John Ruskin argues that only a return to craftsmanship can reverse the moral collapse caused by industrial practices.

AFTER
1919 German architect Walter Gropius founds the Bauhaus art school, which emphasizes the importance of function.

Mid-1920s Influenced by Ruskin and William Morris, Japanese philosopher Yanagi Sōetsu founds the *Mingei* movement, which seeks to preserve traditional crafts.

The Arts and Crafts movement emerged in Britain around the 1860s, and it became the country's dominant force in design for about half a century. The movement extended its influence globally, flourishing in Europe and North America between 1880 and 1920.

Inspired by the ideas of British figures such as historian Thomas Carlyle, art critic John Ruskin, and designer William Morris, the movement was a response to the perceived decline of decorative arts as a result of industrialization. Those involved advocated a return to craftsmanship, a strong relation between maker and materials, and access to the arts for all as a means of enhancing people's lives.

Rather than being a clearly defined style, Arts and Crafts was an approach to the process of making and an ideology for a way of living. This resulted in a disparate output, with some works featuring rich ornamentation and others displaying a stark simplicity.

In addition, the movement was simultaneously conservative and radical. On the one hand, it valued traditional methods of

Have nothing in your house that you do not know to be useful, or believe to be beautiful.
William Morris

craftsmanship and romanticized the Middle Ages as an era of moral integrity. On the other, it promoted alternative ways of living and working, and many of its practitioners embraced the notion of "the simple life" in the English countryside.

William Morris's influence

The guiding principles of the Arts and Crafts movement grew out of ideas that William Morris had developed in the 1850s as part of the Birmingham Set – a group of students at the University of Oxford who combined a love of

---

William Morris

Born in 1834 in London, UK, William Morris was a hugely influential designer who developed the aesthetic and social vision of the Arts and Crafts movement.

As a student, Morris was heavily affected by historian Thomas Carlyle's championing of medieval values and by art critic John Ruskin's rejection of industrial manufacturing in favour of a return to craftsmanship. Expanding on these ideas, Morris advocated honest functional design, the use of natural forms in pattern, and the importance of creative manual work. He put

these principles into practice at Morris, Marshall, Faulkner & Co, the firm he co-founded in 1861.

In 1883, Morris joined the socialist Democratic Federation party; however, his views grew increasingly radical, and a year later he became a founding member of the Socialist League, which called for a global proletarian revolution. Morris died in 1896.

Key works

1882 *Hopes and Fears for Art: Five Lectures*

See also: Manufacturing textiles 84–91 ▪ Historicism and Neo-Gothic 104–05 ▪ Aestheticism 120–21 ▪ Art pottery 122–23 ▪ Art Nouveau 132–33 ▪ Bauhaus 170–71 ▪ Art Deco 184–85

The Pimpernel wallpaper, designed by William Morris in 1876, features swirling leaves and flowers. It hangs in Kelmscott House, London, where Morris lived from 1879 to 1896.

what they saw as the chivalric and pre-capitalist values of the Middle Ages with a commitment to social reform.

In 1859, Morris began to put these ideas into practice in Red House, his new dwelling in Bexleyheath, London. This had been built for him by British architect Philip Webb, while Morris designed the interior furnishings.

In 1861, as a direct result of the experience of designing for Red House, Morris and his friends founded the firm Morris, Marshall, Faulkner & Co. They described themselves as "fine art workmen" and aimed to reform British attitudes to production. The firm produced mainly domestic items – furniture, textiles, wallpaper, and metalwork – that quickly became popular. It also obtained lucrative commissions to design stained glass for ecclesiastical buildings. In 1875, Morris took complete control of the firm and renamed it Morris & Co.

The Art Workers Guild

By the 1880s, a new generation of makers and designers had taken up the Arts and Crafts ideals, establishing many associations and craft communities. These included the Art Workers Guild, a discussion group set up in 1884 by a group of young architects and designers with the aim of breaking down the barriers between the fine and applied arts, and raising the status of »

The Arts and Crafts movement emerges to revive craftsmanship as a reaction to industrialization.

A **strong social conscience** leads to experiments with **alternative ways of living**, such as craft communities.

The Arts and Crafts approach influences **all aspects of design –** from **architecture** and landscaping, to **jewellery** and fashion.

Poorly made products flood the market, leading to the **public losing confidence** in handcrafted items.

The movement **declines**, but ideas about making **good design** available to all and **protecting the environment** still resonate.

Female artists

The Arts and Crafts movement coincided with important social advancements for women, such as the Married Women's Property Acts of 1870 and 1882, the expansion of art-school training for women, and the agitation for female suffrage. In addition, the movement itself was notable for the professional opportunities it offered female artisans. Some developed successful careers in collaboration with family members – for example, Georgie Gaskin, who made jewellery with her husband Arthur, and Margaret Macdonald, who worked alongside her husband Charles Rennie Mackintosh on a series of interiors. Female entrepreneurs who established themselves in their own right include garden designer Gertrude Jekyll and artist Phoebe Traquair, who created jewellery, embroideries, and murals.

Female designers and makers flourished in the US, too: of the 160 artisans whose work was exhibited at the first American Arts and Crafts Exhibition in 1897, half were women.

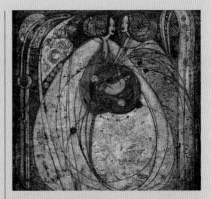

Heart of the Rose, a gesso panel by Margaret Macdonald, was first shown at Turin's International Exhibition of Modern Decorative Art in 1902.

designers and craftsmen. Although it was based in London, it involved individuals from all over Britain.

It soon became clear that the established art world did not consider the decorative arts important enough to warrant an exhibition. Therefore, in 1887, in order to bring members' work to the public's attention, a group of designers created an offshoot of the Guild, called the Arts and Crafts Exhibition Society. It was the first time the term "arts and crafts" had been used, and in doing so, the movement found its name.

In 1888, the Exhibition Society held its first show in London. It was enormously successful in popularizing arts and crafts, and the society went on to hold another ten exhibitions between 1889 and 1916.

Social awareness

The thoughtfulness of the Arts and Crafts movement appealed particularly to those with a social conscience and a dislike of materialism and consumerism. Many of those involved took a keen interest in education, driven by the belief that the lives of the working classes would be improved by their becoming better educated and more culturally aware.

Architect, designer, and social reformer Charles Robert Ashbee was particularly influential in this respect. In 1888, he founded the Guild and School of Handicraft in the slums of London's East End. A craft cooperative working with local men to design and manufacture items in wood, metal, and leather, the guild embodied many of the Arts and Crafts ideas: it was modelled on the medieval guilds; it was intended to give

If art is not recognized in the humblest object, the arts cannot be in a sound condition.
Walter Crane
Of the Revival of Design and Handicraft, 1893

working men satisfaction in their craftsmanship; and it was an experiment in new communal ways of working and living.

In 1902, inspired by the idea of a simple country life, Ashbee moved about 50 craftsmen and their families from London to the Cotswold town of Chipping Campden in Gloucestershire to begin an experimental community. However, the guild did not prosper there, and it was liquidated in 1908.

In 1884, social reformer Eglantyne Louisa Jebb founded the Home Arts and Industries Association. Her aim was to encourage the working classes to take up handicrafts – not for profit but to provide leisure activities and improve their taste and sense of moral worth. By 1889, Home Arts had 450 classes, 1,000 teachers, and 5,000 students, and it was almost as influential as the Art Workers Guild in the development of the Arts and Crafts movement in Britain, especially in rural areas.

A mainstream movement

By 1890, Arts and Crafts studios and workshops were active in many parts of England, and the movement was also beginning to make a strong impact in Scotland. A number of high-end department stores, including Liberty in London, began selling Arts and Crafts items, from fabrics to pieces of furniture. Magazines also promoted the work of Arts and Crafts designers and architects, who then became household names.

By the end of the 19th century, Arts and Crafts was the dominant style in Britain, touching every facet of design – from architecture and landscaping, to interior decoration and fashion.

Buildings and gardens

Many of the key players in the Arts and Crafts movement – including Philip Webb, William Lethaby, and Charles Voysey – were trained in architecture. They set out to reform this discipline with an approach that focused on simplicity of form and construction, and good-quality vernacular materials, such as stone, brick, wood, and thatch. They also embraced appropriate techniques to create work that reflected both the local environment and the needs of the users.

Comparison of principles	
Mainstream aesthetic	**Arts and Crafts**
Ornate and elaborate designs that prioritize aesthetics over functionality	A focus on practicality and usability, with function a key principle
Emphasis on excess, intricate details, and opulent embellishments	Honest expression of materials and craftsmanship
Often features exuberant floral imagery and Oriental motifs such as pagodas and exotic birds	Uses nature-inspired motifs, but with a more restrained and geometric approach
Dark, heavy colours and rich, contrasting patterns	Earthy and muted colour palettes, emphasizing natural tones
Mass-produced goods as a result of technological advances and industrialization	An emphasis on the importance of skilled craftsmanship and the dignity of labour, with an appreciation of handmade goods
Social status and wealth often showcased through richly ostentatious designs	A desire to make design available to all

Belief in the importance of the connection between a building and its setting meant that in Britain the Arts and Crafts movement had a lasting impact on garden design. During the Victorian era, gardens had been another medium for displaying an owner's wealth, and they were characterized by exotic plant species and brightly coloured geometric designs. By contrast, Arts and Crafts gardeners, such as Irish-born William Robinson, promoted the use of native species and natural planting, drawing inspiration from indigenous hedgerows and meadows.

One of the most influential partnerships of the Arts and Crafts movement was that between the architect Edwin Lutyens and the garden designer Gertrude Jekyll. They worked together on the design of the house and gardens for Jekyll's home Munstead Wood, near Godalming in Surrey. Jekyll went on to provide designs for some 400 gardens, often in collaboration with Lutyens. Her work was characterized by a subtle painterly approach, radiant colours, and borders of hardy flowers.

Interior design

Most Arts and Crafts designers worked across a wide range of different disciplines – such as architecture, furniture, and wall »

Hestercombe Gardens, in Somerset, was designed by Edward Lutyens and Gertrude Jekyll in 1904. The plantings and stone paths of the sunken Great Plat enhance the view of the house.

decoration – in an effort to create a "total" harmonious interior. They often took inspiration from plant forms used in a natural way. In addition, they wanted materials to be used honestly, so that anyone could tell just by looking at an object how it was made and what it was made from, and the details of construction – such as hammer marks on metal work – were often left exposed as a reminder that the piece had been made by hand.

Clothes and jewellery

The all-embracing Arts and Crafts approach also included ideas about fashion. Proponents rejected the elaborate early Victorian clothes for women, with their unnatural silhouette based on tight corseting and heavy, voluminous crinolines. Instead, they advocated "rational dress" – simple clothes that did not require any tightly laced undergarments and followed the body's natural shape.

Arts and Crafts women wore dresses made from soft, light materials – such as fine cotton or silk, or from a coarse, unbleached linen known as Holland – perhaps embellished with hand embroidery.

This ornate pendant, with delicate silver flowers and foliage set with cabochon gems, shows how designers Georgie and Arthur Gaskin drew inspiration from nature.

Their clothes lacked a defined waist and were often based on romanticized medieval styles.

Extravagant jewellery designs – often inspired by contemporary archaeological discoveries and featuring diamonds and exotic materials such as ivory and coral – were regarded as ostentatious and rejected. Instead, Arts and Crafts designers found inspiration in natural forms, and used enamels and semi-precious stones, often in a rounded cabochon cut, to suggest an organic quality.

American Craftsman style

In North America, as in Britain, the Arts and Crafts movement was the aesthetic counterpart of a drive to improve society through social reform. Its ideals were reinterpreted in a variety of ways, and the style of architecture, interior design, and decorative arts in the period from about 1910 to 1925 is generally known as American Craftsman.

A key figure in the US movement was furniture manufacturer, designer, and publisher Gustav Stickley. His furniture reflected his ideals of simplicity, honesty in construction, and truth to materials. In 1901, Stickley started to publish *The Craftsman* magazine, which became an important vehicle for promoting the Arts and Crafts philosophy and was a great influence on the development of American Craftsman architecture. The magazine's pages included architectural plans for homes characterized by open-floor plans and the use of both natural and innovative materials. An excellent

Garden cities

Arts and Crafts ideas informed the garden city movement of the early 20th century. This was inspired by urban planner Ebenezer Howard, who saw it as a means to tackle issues of housing and labour as more people moved to the towns. Capturing the benefits of the countryside and the city, while avoiding their drawbacks, garden cities were meant to be self-sufficient, with equal priority given to housing, industry, shops, and amenities.

Laid out in 1903 by architects Barry Parker and Raymond Unwin, Letchworth, in Hertfordshire, was the first garden city. Parker and Unwin shared Howard's belief that the working class deserved better housing. They were influenced by the ideas of William Morris, particularly his emphasis on making good design accessible to all. As a result, Letchworth was designed and built to high-quality standards, although the architects ignored Howard's symmetrical design and replaced it with a more organic design, in line with their Arts and Crafts principles.

Letchworth's Spirella Building housed a corset factory. It was designed with the wellbeing of its workers in mind, with a library, exercise spaces, and showers.

An oak table by Gustav Stickley distils the designer's beliefs in simple, sturdy construction principles. It had an optional leather cover and was sold as a "library table" via his catalogue.

example of American Craftsman style architecture, albeit on a rather grand scale, is Castle in the Clouds, designed by J. Williams Beal in 1913–14. Standing in the Ossipee Mountains of New Hampshire, this 16-room mansion combines oak timbers, locally mined pink granite, and other natural materials with then-modern construction methods such as concrete pouring and the use of steel beams.

Frank Lloyd Wright and the architects of the Prairie School (1890s–1916) were also keen to develop an indigenous North American style of architecture in line with the Arts and Crafts movement. Most common in the Midwest of the United States, this look is characterized by dramatic horizontal lines with long flat roofs; open, flowing interiors; and rows of tiny windows arranged to give the illusion of a glass wall. The Robie House in Chicago, Illinois, is perhaps Wright's most famous Prairie-style design.

Diverging fortunes

By the early 20th century, Arts and Crafts designs were being copied to make mass-produced items in factories using industrial methods. At the same time, a proliferation of handmade products of variable quality led to a loss of public confidence in handcrafted items.

The events organized by the Arts and Crafts Exhibition Society ceased to make a profit in the 1910s, and the progressive impetus of the movement began to lose momentum. Under the control of older artists, the Society rejected

a commercial role and collaboration with manufacturers, withdrawing into a purist celebration of the handmade. The situation then deteriorated further during World War I, which closed many of the small workshops that had formed the backbone of the Arts and Crafts movement.

Although Arts and Crafts stagnated in Britain, artisanal workshops across continental Europe continued to develop the

To be complete, we must live in all the tenses – past, future as well as present.
Ernest Gimson
Architect and designer,
May 1916

movement's ideas, innovating in the design field and forging alliances with industry. The Deutscher Werkbund (German Association of Craftsmen), founded in 1907 as a partnership between designers and manufacturers, became a key element in the development of modern architecture and industrial design, particularly through the Bauhaus School of Design. In Britain, however, the Arts and Crafts movement failed to change and was superseded.

The Arts and Crafts movement exercised a strong influence on the arts in Europe until the 1930s, when it was displaced by Modernism. Nevertheless, the movement continued to inspire craftspeople, designers, and town planners long afterwards. Indeed, many modern ideas about protecting the natural world from the ravages of industrialization, achieving a healthy work–life balance, and making good-quality design accessible to everyone have roots in the Arts and Crafts movement. ∎

NOTHING IS REALLY BEAUTIFUL UNLESS IT IS USELESS
AESTHETICISM

IN CONTEXT

FOCUS
Beauty in objects

FIELD
Interior design, product design, art

BEFORE
1856 Christopher Dresser contributes a botanical plate of leaves and flowers to Owen Jones's celebrated publication *The Grammar of Ornament*.

1858 The Anglo-Japanese Treaty of Amity and Commerce leads to a flood of Japanese culture into Britain.

AFTER
1907–08 Austrian painter Gustav Klimt completes *The Kiss*. His work displays decorative and symbolic characteristics associated with the Aesthetic movement.

1951 The Labour organizers of the Festival of Britain seek to celebrate the beauty of everyday objects.

The British Aesthetic movement, which was active from around 1860 to 1900, believed in the supremacy of beauty over utility. To some extent, Aestheticism was a reaction to the perceived ugliness of industrialization, and to the social moralizing of the Arts and Crafts movement. For many of its proponents – including avant-garde British designers Edward William Godwin and Christopher Dresser, writer Oscar Wilde, and American artist James McNeill Whistler – Aestheticism offered a different approach, celebrating design that was beautiful but had no deeper

I look upon all my work as Art Work. A building is to me as a picture to a painter or a poem to a poet.
E.W. Godwin

meaning, and valuing "art for art's sake". It was individualistic, nonconformist, bohemian, romantic, and hedonistic. In direct opposition to William Morris's egalitarian approach to design's social purpose, the mainly upper- and middle-class Aestheticists held the view that culture was for elite groups in fashionable society – and certainly not for everyone.

Motifs and influences
The designs that emerged out of Aestheticism represented a move away from the heavy, dark ornamentation associated with the Victorian era, towards lighter, simpler, more elegant shapes. Although the movement was stylistically diverse, it relied on a number of recurring motifs, such as the lily, the sunflower, and the peacock feather.

One of the greatest surviving examples of Aesthetic interior design is the Peacock Room, which was designed by Whistler for a wealthy British patron in the mid-1870s. It was intended to function as a dining room to showcase a collection of Chinese blue-and-white porcelain, but Whistler's design went much further. He

See also: Baroque furniture designs 80–81 ▪ The Arts and Crafts movement 112–19 ▪ Art Nouveau 132–33 ▪ Bauhaus 170–71 ▪ Art Deco 184–85 ▪ Modernism 188–93

The extravagant Peacock Room was poorly received by Whistler's patron, Frederick Leyland, who balked at the cost. Whistler was paid only half of the agreed compensation for his work.

created a radically different type of interior, infused with the colours of blue, green, and gold to reflect the beauty of the peacock, and borrowing elements from the arts of East Asia, particularly Japan.

Like his friend Whistler, E.W. Godwin had a deep admiration for Japanese art. His elegantly linear furniture designs fused traditional British styles with Asian influences. The Godwin Sideboard, made in 1867–70, is an innovative example of this Anglo-Japanese style, combining functional aspects – such as adjustable shelves and easy-to-clean hard surfaces – with a modern sensibility in the shape of simple, linear elements.

Beauty and business

Godwin's work is close stylistically to another figure associated with Aestheticism: Christopher Dresser,

who was also inspired by Japan. However, unlike his contemporaries who elevated beauty above utility, Dresser reconciled aesthetic values with commercial interests.

Considered by some to be the first industrial designer, Dresser also designed a wide range of merchandise – including wallpapers, ceramics, textiles, cast-iron furniture, and carpets – for more

than 30 international firms. His metalwork, in particular, is characterized by a simplicity of form, absence of ornament, meticulous analysis of function, and close attention to the ease of use. Dresser's rejection of handicraft, and his recognition of the benefits of industrialization, mean that he is considered a precursor of the Bauhaus era. ■

The Aesthetic legacy

The stigma surrounding Oscar Wilde and his prosecution for gross indecency in 1895 marked the beginning of the end of the Aesthetic movement. The Irish writer had spearheaded Aestheticism in literature, believing that it should provide beauty for its own sake, without didactic purposes.

Although tainted with scandal, Aestheticism paved the way for the art and design movements of the 20th century. Its ideas and styles inspired

Gustav Klimt and the Viennese Secessionists, while elements of the Aesthetic movement's elevation of beauty feature in Art Nouveau works of Czech painter and illustrator Alphonse Mucha, and French glassmaker and jeweller René Lalique.

In remaking the domestic world of the British middle class, and reconfiguring the relationship between the artist and society, as well as being the link between fine and decorative arts, Aestheticism provided an important step between Victorian historicism and the Modern movement.

A shoal of fish adorns Lalique's Oléron vase of 1927. His joyous decoration of everyday objects reveals the influence of Aestheticism.

BEAUTY OF FORM AND TENDER COLORATIONS
ART POTTERY

IN CONTEXT

FOCUS
**The artistic merits
of pottery**

FIELD
Product design

BEFORE
1851 The Great Exhibition
of Art and Industry, in London,
UK, provokes a reaction
against mass-produced wares.

1854 Japan opens its borders
to facilitate trading deals with
the West.

AFTER
1861 William Morris and
partners establish Morris,
Marshall, Faulkner & Co, a
furnishing and applied-arts
manufacturer and retailer,
bringing Arts and Crafts
items to a mass audience.

1925 Paris, France, hosts
the International Exhibition
of Modern Decorative and
Industrial Arts, which signals
the arrival of the Art Deco
movement.

A rising in part as a reaction
to the mass-produced
ceramics of the first half
of the 19th century, art pottery
made the craftsperson – the potter
or decorator – the central creator
of a work, and the object an
expression of their artistic vision.
Stylistic schools of thought that
emerged from the 1860s, such as
the Arts and Crafts movement
in Britain, played a key role in
encouraging the handmade
aspect of ceramic production.

Art pottery includes items
crafted by individual artists and
small workshops, as well as objects

Our first avowed end is to
do our utmost to produce a
beautiful and artistic ware
which can be utilized.
Harold Rathbone
**"The Industrial Aims of the
Della Robbia Pottery", 1896**

made by large, well-established
factories, many of which added
studio-made wares to their more
commercial output. One of the
first British firms to do this was
the Doulton pottery in London,
which was known for its sanitary
wares. Acknowledging the rising
popularity of art pottery, in 1871
factory owner Henry Doulton
forged a relationship with the
nearby Lambeth School of Art,
creating opportunities for young
artists to work in a growing studio.

Art pottery viewed ceramics
as decorative pieces that could
be used in an interior setting to
create a stylistically coherent whole
alongside furniture, metalwork,
paintings, and sculptures. Interior
decorating manuals, such as
Charles Locke Eastlake's *Hints
on Household Taste* (1869),
recommended the integration
of simple ceramics – including
antique and second-hand pieces –
into domestic settings.

Cultural influences
Sources of inspiration for Victorian
art potters ranged from the Italian
Renaissance to North African and
Eastern cultures. The simplicity of
Japanese forms, in particular, tied

See also: Mass-produced ceramics 92–93 ▪ The Arts and Crafts movement 112–19 ▪ Art Nouveau 132–33 ▪ Deutscher Werkbund 162 ▪ Art Deco 184–85

in neatly to the new focus on pared-back and well-made products. The stoneware made in Seto throughout the Early Modern period (1603–1868), in which glazes were applied in a free-form fashion, appealed to the new taste for abstracted ornament, especially in France.

Japonism – a catch-all term for the influence of Japanese aesthetics – was reflected in most national art pottery movements. In the US, for example, the Rookwood Pottery, founded in 1880 by Maria Longworth Storer, produced wares with Japanese glazes and imagery, including naturalistic applied animals and flowers.

Other potters were heavily influenced by the ceramic arts of West Asia and North Africa. London-born William De Morgan, who began his career by painting blank tiles, plates, and dishes, strove to perfect the use of a metallic, iridescent glaze known as lustre, a technique that originated in the 9th century in Mesopotamia, before spreading to Egypt and Persia.

The Della Robbia Pottery was set up by artist Harold Rathbone and sculptor Conrad Dressler in 1894 in Birkenhead, near Liverpool, UK. It found inspiration closer to home, in the output of the Italian family of sculptors of the same name, who produced work in glazed terracotta in 15th- and 16th-century Florence. ▪

This William De Morgan plate decorated with dragons and stylized flowers reflects the artist's interest in the Persian style.

Théodore Deck

A key figure in French art pottery, Théodore Deck was born in Alsace in 1823. He trained as a chemist and sculptor, and he set up his first pottery studio in 1856.

Deck was determined to recreate the surface effects of the ceramics of West Asia and North Africa, particularly those found on Iznik pottery made in Türkiye between the 15th and 17th centuries. These effects included glazes of bright turquoises, reds, and greens – all colours that were not in mainstream use in French ceramics at the time. Deck's re-creations of these styles became wildly popular, and his pottery items were sought after and highly prized by both private individuals and public museums.

In 1887, in recognition of his contribution to ceramic production, Deck was made art director at the Manufacture de Sèvres, which had been the main maker of ceramics in France since the 18th century. He maintained his own independent studio alongside his work at the manufactory. Deck died in Sèvres in 1891.

EXCITE
THE MIND, AND THE HAND WILL REACH FOR THE
POCKET
VISUAL MERCHANDISING

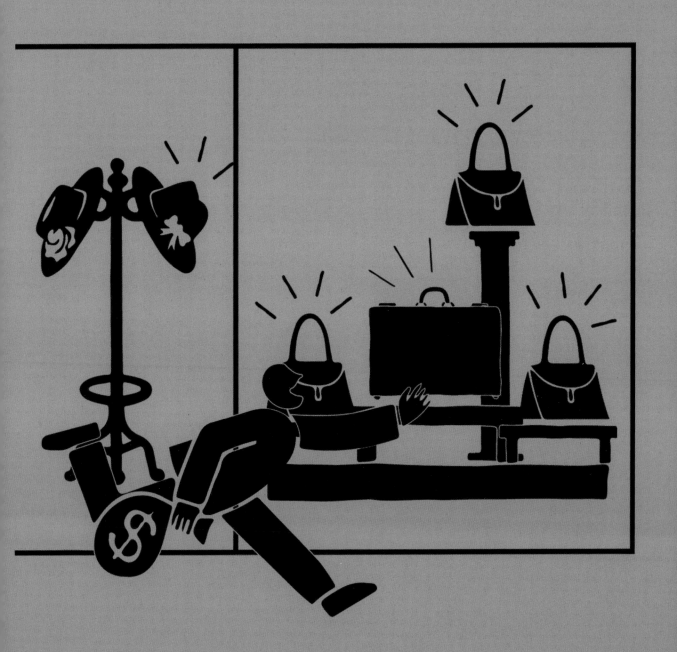

IN CONTEXT

FOCUS
Visual displays in shops

FIELD
Communication design

BEFORE
Early 18th century Shops begin to fit glazed windows, and display products in the window area.

1771 The Colisée, the first shopping arcade in Paris, is opened. However, customers find the location too remote, and it closes within two years.

AFTER
1922 The Country Club Plaza, the first shopping mall established in the US, is opened in Kansas City.

1995 Online book store Amazon is launched.

2009 The world's largest department store, Shinsegae Centum City, opens in Busan, South Korea.

Every time we visit a shop or a stall, we encounter visual merchandising: goods displayed attractively to entice us to buy them. This sales technique has probably existed for as long as goods have been sold; think of the ancient Greek agora, where people came to browse and socialize as well as to buy produce.

The simplest forms of visual merchandising include displays of fruit and vegetables on a market stall, or the spices and textiles in a Middle Eastern souk or bazaar. The Industrial Revolution saw an explosion in global trade, with the development of steam-powered international rail and shipping networks allowing commodities to be moved around the world in unprecedented quantities, as well as an increase in money and leisure among the populations of Europe and North America. This led to the creation of carefully designed shop layouts, window displays, and – in recent decades – websites and apps. As a result, visual merchandising has evolved into a specialism that enables companies to shape the consumer experience with great precision.

The first shopping arcades

Until relatively recently, city streets were not pleasant places to be. Horse-drawn traffic produced dirt and smells. Rapid urban growth in the 18th and 19th centuries made matters worse. It was therefore necessary to provide safe, clean, comfortable spaces in which consumers could enjoy browsing at leisure.

In Paris, a very successful solution was the insertion of roofed-in shopping arcades – or passages – through urban blocks, connecting parallel streets. Shoppers would be dropped off by carriage at one or other entrance. The Passage du Caire in Paris, named to evoke a sense of an eastern bazaar, was the first successful arcade, opened in 1798. In London, meanwhile, the first example was the Burlington Arcade of 1819.

The arcades' clean, polished floors allowed customers to promenade and browse without getting their clothes dirtied. Of greater significance, though, was the use of large, industrially-produced plate-glass windows, secured by factory-made frames

The ambience at Le Bon Marché in 1872 was grand and luxurious thanks to its light-filled space, elegant frontages, and ornate interior design.

Le Bon Marché

The first department store in Paris was established in 1852, when fabric merchant Aristide Boucicaut and his wife took over a shop named *Le Bon Marché* ("The Good Deal"), which sold textiles and novelty items. They transformed the shop into a "cathedral" of modern commerce, in which fashion, accessories, and designer homewares were presented beside art and cultural exhibits.

By the mid-1860s the store's success called for larger premises. The owners engaged architects Louis-Auguste Boileau and Alexandre Laplanche, who created a complex with iron framework and glazed cupolas over atria, through which rose grand stairways connecting the departments. Some of the interior work was carried out by Gustav Eiffel, who later created the Eiffel Tower.

Work began in 1869 and was completed in 1905. After a serious fire in the 1920s, the store was rebuilt in the Art Deco style and reopened in 1923. *Le Bon Marché* is still welcoming shoppers today.

See also: Art Nouveau 132–33 ▪ Chicago World Fair 138–39 ▪ Branding 200–07
▪ The online user experience 294–99

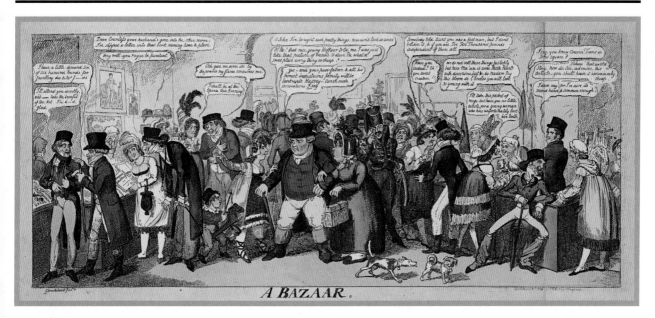

A BAZAAR.

Soho Bazaar This satirical image by George Cruikshank (1792–1878) captures the bustle of the bazaar, showing patrons not only inspecting the lavish displays but also taking the chance to see and be seen.

formed from slender cast iron components, for the fronts of shops and skylights in the roofs of arcades. The method for making blown plate glass had first been discovered in France in the mid-17th century and was industrialized in the 18th century. This innovation in display techniques led to the expression faire du lèche-vitrines – "to lick the windows" – becoming the commonly used French phrase for window-shopping.

The rise of the bazaar
Another development during the early 19th century was the shopping bazaar – a name borrowed from the Persian word for a market, which reflected the fascination with eastern cultures that arose in the late 18th and early 19th centuries. Beginning with the Soho Bazaar, established in London in 1816, the bazaar was a kind-of market hall: an open-plan space, often on multiple levels and containing many counters, leased to different retailers and selling particular categories of item – notably decorative goods. The term "bazaar" lent a sense of the exotic, and sometimes street frontages and interior decoration reflected the styles of the Near East.

The layouts allowed customers to circulate and browse freely. In addition to goods for sale, bazaars hosted entertainments and exhibitions, including menageries of animals, and exhibitions of art or scientific wonders and curiosities. Most famous of these exhibits was the collection of waxworks first displayed by Madame Tussaud at the Royal London Bazaar in Gray's Inn Road and then, from 1835, at the Baker Steet Bazaar.

These developments helped to change shopping into a leisure activity rather than a necessity.

Department stores
The third innovation – and the one that would become most successful during the 20th century – was the department store. This was a large shop under single ownership »

His creation provided a new religion; the churches, deserted little by little by a faltering faith, had been replaced by this bazaar...
Émile Zola
Au Bonheur des Dames (*The Ladies' Paradise*), 1883

containing various separate sales rooms, each retailing a particular category of goods. An early example was Debenham's in London, which dated from 1778 and sold furs, haberdashery, jewellery, ornaments, perfumes, millinery, and dresses. In terms of organization, the department store concept had an advantage of scale, as operators could buy and sell in bulk while shoppers could hopefully find most of the items that they wanted under one roof. In these stores, the focus was inward: sales areas were arranged with displays around their perimeters, drawing customers in and deeply immersing them in the retail experience, while elegantly uniformed and obliging sales staff helped to encourage retail therapy.

One model for the new, large-scale retail space was not a shopping area at all but the "Great Exhibition" held in London's Hyde Park in 1851. The Exhibition was housed inside a giant temporary building created from cast iron and glass. Within were three storeys with open balconies around a soaring central atrium, which enabled spectacular vistas across

the displays. The open planning also allowed attendees to see and be seen. Although the goods shown were not for sale, the layout of the structure, popularly known as the Crystal Palace, provided a prototype for the next generation of much larger department stores.

All of the new shopping spaces – arcades, bazaars, and department stores – brought in a wider range of customers than traditional shops. They emerged during a period of great social transformation. Industrialization and urbanization had led to the expansion of the middleclasses, who were tempted through advertising and peer pressure to spend their salaries on aspirational symbols of enhanced social status. Often, the aim was to imitate the taste of the established upper class – but whereas the aristocracy's grand attire and splendid interiors had been hand-crafted, the same styles could now be quite accurately imitated using industrial processes.

Advertising also played an increasingly crucial role in retail. Newspapers contained pages of seductive offers, while billboards and signage proliferated on the gables of buildings, and the retail premises themselves were adorned outside and in with inducements to make purchases.

The owners of the new retail spaces particularly sought to attract women. Hitherto, it had been considered unsafe and unseemly for females to go out in public unaccompanied, but

> I sold from the windows more goods … than paid journeymen's wages and the expenses of housekeeping.
> **Francis Place**
> **Cambridge University Press, 1972**

department stores in particular made efforts to promote themselves as providing welcoming, safe, and respectable environments where it was possible to browse or socialize alone or with friends. In addition, they employed many female sales staff. This era also saw the emergence of cafés and women's lavatories, which helped to make the shopping experience more pleasant and comfortable for female patrons.

The allure of the boutique

At the opposite extreme from the department store was the boutique: a small shop selling high-fashion clothing or accessories. This was another innovation that arose in Paris, when in 1895 an established retailer, Maison Bing, decided as an experiment to open a boutique, separate from its main store, which it named L'Art Nouveau. The entrance was flanked with giant cast iron vases containing sunflowers, symbolizing youth and beauty, while the interior décor and advertising featured stalks and tendrils with exaggerated whiplash forms. Not only did L'Art Nouveau become the favoured haunt of Paris's bright young things, but it gave rise to the Art Nouveau style.

The entrance of L'Art Nouveau
at its opening in 1895. The boutique also had glass windows designed by Henri de Toulouse-Lautrec and Louis Comfort Tiffany, that complemented the Japanese and modern art sold inside the store.

Much later, in 1950s and 1960s London, modern speciality fashion boutiques would take on many forms. In addition, unlike the department stores, boutiques could be regularly redecorated to reflect the latest trends. Shops such as Bazaar, run by designer Mary Quant, Biba, established by Polish-born designer Barbara Hulanicki, and "psychedelic boutique" Granny Takes A Trip established "swinging London" as the centre of the fashion world.

Window displays

The French term *faire du lèche-vitrines* suggests how desire was provoked by the seductive displays of goods. From the early 19th century, window-shopping became a leisure activity enjoyed not just by potential customers but also by people who could only dream of buying the luxuries on display.

A window shopper from the early 20th century gazes longingly at a display in a fashion boutique. Many people enjoy "retail therapy" – the sensory pleasure of browsing and the reward of purchasing treats.

From the beginning, shop owners capitalized on the use of large front windows to entice customers. A visitor to London in 1786 described a window display of "silks, chintzes or muslins" draped in long folds to show how they would hang as part of a woman's dress. Displays were also embellished with life-sized mannequins of human forms wearing the clothes on sale, and other goods arranged in settings that would show them off or help customers imagine how they might be used. One of the most striking examples was created by luxury London food store Fortnum & Mason; having won a gold medal in the Great Exhibition at the Crystal Palace, they reproduced their winning display of the "fruits of the earth" in their shop window.

During the 20th century, window dressing became increasingly sophisticated and eminent artists were commissioned to create displays. In New York, luxury department store Bonwit Teller, on Fifth Avenue, employed surrealist Salvador Dalí, only to find that his 1939 displays featuring »

Harry Gordon Selfridge

Born in Ripon, Wisconsin in 1858, Selfridge began his retail career as a stock boy in Chicago department store Marshall Field. Over the next 25 years, he worked his way up to become a junior partner.

In 1906, on a holiday to London, he noted that there were no department stores like those in the US or Paris, so he invested £400,000 in creating one. He built it at the unfashionable west end of Oxford Street – but his advertising was so successful that policemen had to hold back the crowds on the opening day. The store opened to the sound of trumpets.

Selfridge's was the first London store to employ a window dresser. Inside, Selfridge had the merchandise displayed within reach of the customers; he also made the store a safe public space for women to socialize and shop.

The political and economic conditions in the 1930s resulted in Selfridge losing control of the business in 1941. He died in 1947, but the retail experience that he created has influenced the character of stores around the world.

Mannequins

Mannequins are life-sized, human-shaped forms used to display clothes and textiles. They were first created for dressmakers and milliners in the 15th century, but their use became more widespread with the Industrial Revolution. The models, made from papier-mâché or wax, were so realistic that some shops had to cover their windows for modesty while changing the mannequins' outfits.

As well as their outfits, the forms of the mannequins themselves – especially female forms – have changed with the demands of fashion. For example, models from the 1950s had curves like the figure of film star Marilyn Monroe, while in the 1990s the shapes were much slimmer. Recently, there have been concerns that the use of very slim shapes might adversely affect body image in susceptible people. In 2007, Spain enacted a law banning the use of mannequins smaller than a US size 6. Today, many mannequins are still tall and slim, but some retailers have begun using more "inclusive" models that reflect different body sizes.

scantily-clad mannequins and depicting "the Narcissus complex" were not welcomed by the public. The store toned down the displays; Dalí, in a rage, tried to remove the bathtub that formed part of one scene, and – together with the bath – crashed through the window pane. Other artists who would subsequently work for Bonwit Teller included Jasper Johns and Andy Warhol.

In London, Selfridge's department store on London's Oxford Street had become world-famous for its window displays. Opened in 1909, the store had the longest window facade ever seen in the UK at that time, and the displays formed an integral part of the "theatre" of the retail experience. To this day, the revelation of new window displays at Selfridge's is a significant event in the London retail scene.

Different retail experiences from famous department stores, such as Macy's in New York or GUM in Moscow, were provided in the shopping malls that spread from the US across the world from the 1940s onwards. The biggest and most glamorous examples nowadays are in the Middle East and South-East Asia, where shopping has become the prime leisure activity. In these contexts, any conventional architectural expression is usually subordinate to the primacy of brand identities, the facades of the stores within acting as giant billboards for famous fashion names.

Interior layouts

In 18th-century shops, the shop floor was a place where the shopkeeper and customer would discuss possible purchases, while much of the merchandise was kept

Store layout

Retailers use different ways to draw customers in and guide them around a store, so that they see a range of products as well as the items they intended to buy. This diagram shows a typical layout with areas of interest.

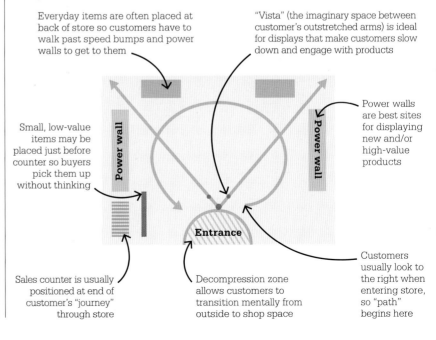

Everyday items are often placed at back of store so customers have to walk past speed bumps and power walls to get to them

"Vista" (the imaginary space between customer's outstretched arms) is ideal for displays that make customers slow down and engage with products

Small, low-value items may be placed just before counter so buyers pick them up without thinking

Power wall

Power wall

Power walls are best sites for displaying new and/or high-value products

Entrance

Sales counter is usually positioned at end of customer's "journey" through store

Decompression zone allows customers to transition mentally from outside to shop space

Customers usually look to the right when entering store, so "path" begins here

An Apple store in Tokyo, Japan. Apple uses clean, minimalist layouts and bright, soft lighting to reflect the brand's identity. Staff demonstrations and advice help customers to make the most of their purchases.

in a back room and brought out only when needed. By contrast, the department stores of the late 19th and early 20th centuries put a wide range of products on display, and used factors such as colour, lighting, and décor to give visitors multi-sensory experiences, whether or not they were there to buy.

Selfridge's in London was designed from the outset to create such an atmosphere. Harry Gordon Selfridge, the founder, imported ideas from the US to make shopping a pleasure and an adventure rather than just a practical activity. Patrons were welcome to browse as well as buy. Merchandise was put within their reach, so they could touch and examine it at their leisure. Soft lighting accented particular items on display. Daringly, the highly profitable perfume and cosmetics counters – seen as part of a lady's personal care – were moved to the front of the store. As well as styling the interior, Selfridge put on scientific and educational displays to attract visitors. He even exhibited the aeroplane in which French aviator Louis Blériot had just made the first cross-Channel flight, thus attracting more than 150,000 viewers.

During the early 20th century, American retailers began applying psychological techniques to encourage customers to buy. Studies of cognitive and emotional factors in customers' behaviour led to the development of "wayfinding" measures to draw customers into a retail space and then guide them

around it. Such measures include designing the path through the store so customers can find necessities quickly, for example in DIY stores – or, conversely, to get them to linger at display points showing off the latest or most appealing products. Display stands provide points of excitement, while clear spaces allow customers to relax and look more closely at particular items.

As with the store facade, branding can play a vital role in drawing customers in and getting them to engage with the products; Apple's stores are an effective example, with the Apple logo displayed prominently both on the storefront and on every device that is put out on display.

The influence of the Internet

From the 1990s onwards, the rise of internet shopping has meant that the "store" has escaped its physical boundaries and is now everywhere. Retailers' websites bring shopping right into customers' homes. The website's landing page is the "shop

entrance", where customers are welcomed. The page might have glamorous images or a slide gallery of products being used in particular settings. There might also be a button taking customers to new or featured items. Products may be grouped for impact, and the site can be designed to lead customers to items associated with the product they wanted to buy. Finally, some sites have a "just before you go" selection of items to tempt shoppers before they check out. ∎

There's different shopping in Paris than there is at a bazaar in Istanbul, but they're all wonderful.
Iris Apfel
Elle magazine, 2015

ELABORATE, INTRICATE, AND WHIMSICAL, LIKE NATURE ITSELF
ART NOUVEAU

Art Nouveau is often seen as the first self-consciously international modern art movement. The style spread across Europe and the US from epicentres in Brussels, Paris, and Munich, and it was applied to disciplines ranging from architecture to jewellery.

The movement went by different names in different countries – for example, Belle Époque in France, Jugendstil in Germany, and Vienna Secession in Austria. Each country developed its own distinct attributes, but they all shared broadly similar traits: a sense of dynamism and movement, often expressed through the characteristic whiplash lines, sinuous curves and flowing organic shapes, asymmetry, and the use of modern materials.

Natural forms
Like the Arts and Crafts movement, Art Nouveau took its inspiration from nature. However, while Arts and Crafts designers generally used flowers and other natural elements in a realistic way, Art Nouveau practitioners used elongated and distorted plant forms, with delicate tendrils and swirling lines to add a sense of movement.

Another shared feature is that both movements often depict young women with classical drapery and flowing hair, but in Art Nouveau, their bodies are generally sensuous and exotic – even erotic. Also, while Arts and Crafts designers advocated the honest use of materials, Art Nouveau designers were happy to disguise materials in order to add to the richness of effect.

Classic examples of Art Nouveau style include the ornate poster designs of Alphonse Mucha; the erotic, richly decorated paintings of Gustav Klimt; the seductive drawings of Aubrey

Art Nouveau is the art of the feminine, of the sensual, of the emotional.
Louis Comfort Tiffany

See also: The Arts and Crafts movement 112–19 ▪ Aestheticism 120–21 ▪ Art pottery 122–23 ▪ Deutscher Werkbund 162 ▪ Natural luxury 174 ▪ Modernism 188–93

The Guimard-designed entrance to Porte Dauphine station, on the Paris Métro, has a fan-shaped glass canopy resembling a dragonfly and sinuous floral motifs on the side panels.

Beardsley; the luxurious glass and jewellery of René Lalique; the curvaceous architecture of Victor Horta and Paul Hankar; and the Paris Métro station entrances designed by Hector Guimard.

Two 1893 buildings erected in Brussels – Hôtel Tassel by Horta, and Hankar House by Hankar – were among the first Art Nouveau designs to attract international attention. They both featured the wrought-iron decoration and curling, stylized floral patterns that became the signature of the movement. They were accompanied by a wave of decorative arts in the new style.

Rise and fall

The style was further popularized in 1895, when German art dealer Siegfried Bing opened Maison de l'Art Nouveau in Paris. The gallery, which featured interiors by Belgian architect Henry van de Velde and stained-glass windows by Louis Comfort Tiffany, displayed ceramics, prints, furniture, and other works by Art Nouveau designers. Then, in 1900, the Paris Exposition Universelle provided an international showcase for the movement – and prompted a worldwide craze.

Ultimately, the style's popularity was short-lived. Many Art Nouveau designers used decoration lavishly, which resulted in accusations of extravagance. In the years leading up to World War I, Art Nouveau was replaced by Modernism, which emphasized function over form and the elimination of unnecessary ornament. ▪

Aubrey Beardsley

Born in Brighton, UK, in 1872, illustrator Aubrey Beardsley made a significant contribution to the development of Art Nouveau style. He was influenced by Pre-Raphaelite painter Edward Burne-Jones, who encouraged him to enrol at art school, and by a visit to Paris in 1892, during which he discovered the poster art of Henri de Toulouse-Lautrec and the aesthetic of Japanese woodcuts.

Beardsley's illustrations were produced as black-and-white line block prints, which allowed his work to be easily reproduced and widely circulated. *The Peacock Skirt*, which Beardsley created in 1893 to illustrate Oscar Wilde's play *Salome*, is a superb example. His style was elegant and sophisticated, with flowing, sinuous lines; however, his drawings were also subversive, irreverent, provocative, and frequently obscene. This contradiction made him one of the most controversial artists of the time.

In 1898, at the age of 25, Beardsley died of tuberculosis in Menton, in the south of France.

THE STRAIGHT LINE BELONGS TO MEN, THE CURVED ONE TO GOD

CATALAN MODERNISM

IN CONTEXT

FOCUS
Building Catalan identity through art, design, and architecture

FIELD
Architecture, art, furniture design, stained glass, ceramics, metal work

BEFORE
1850s Catalonia grows wealthy. The *Renaixença* seeks to establish a national identity, separate from Castilian Spain.

1872 *Entretiens sur l'architecture*, by French architect Eugène Viollet-le-Duc calls for "a new architecture" free of the past.

AFTER
1930s Catalan surrealists, such as the artist Salvador Dalí and writer Josep Vicenç Foix, create radical new art forms.

1938 Francisco Franco seizes power in Spain. Catalan identity is repressed.

Modernisme was an artistic and cultural movement that emerged in Catalonia, a region in northeast Spain, during the late 19th century. It built on the popular revivalist movement known as the *Renaixença* – the Catalan for "renaissance" or "rebirth" – which sought to reinvigorate Catalan culture and develop distinct local forms of art and design. Strongly associated with the Art Nouveau style, Modernisme shared its use of asymmetry, dynamic shapes, and vibrant colours. It was a radical movement, which rejected traditional values and attempted to use art to change society.

Lavish and ornate

Like Art Nouveau movements elsewhere, Modernisme drew inspiration from the British Arts

The *Palau Música Catalana* – "Palace of Catalan Music" – designed by architect Lluís Domènech i Montaner, is a lavishly decorated concert hall with a stained-glass canopy.

See also: The Arts and Crafts movement 112–19 ▪ National romanticism 163 ▪ Futurism 175 ▪ Modernism 188–93

> **Modernisme celebrates the cultural identity of Catalonia, distinguishing it from that of Spain.**

It uses a mixture of **bold, bright colours**.

It is highly **ornamental** with shapes inspired by nature.

It references Catalan **history, folklore, and crafts**.

Antoni Gaudí

Born in Catalonia in 1852, Antoni Gaudí trained as a teacher before going on to study at the Barcelona Higher School of Architecture, where he graduated in 1878. Gaudí was influenced by John Ruskin and the Arts and Crafts movement, as well as traditional Islamic-Hispanic art and Gothic architecture.

By 1900, Gaudí had developed his own highly personal style, integrating crafts such as ceramics, stained glass, and wrought ironwork into his architecture. Using his extensive study of geometry, Gaudí incorporated innovative arches and curves into his buildings, which were then encrusted with rich, organic decoration.

His most famous building is perhaps the Sagrada Família church, which Gaudí worked on for 40 years, and which remained unfinished at his death in 1926. It is scheduled for completion in 2026 under architect Jordi Faulí i Oller.

Key works

1883–present Sagrada Família
1906 Casa Batlló
1912 Casa Milà
1914 Park Güell

---

and Crafts movement and Gothic Revival. It was characterized by elements derived from history, and a dramatic use of ornamentation, with motifs inspired by nature and rural life – all deeply rooted in Catalan tradition. Bright colours, the use of ceramic tiles, Arabic patterns and decorations, and surprising, dynamic forms helped to give an overall impression of colour and flamboyance.

Catalonia's wealthy industrialists enthusiastically embraced Modernisme, commissioning houses, churches, parks, factories, and apartment buildings in Barcelona and elsewhere. Architects, painters, sculptors, and craftsmen were given financial support that allowed them to unleash their imaginations and create work that was distinctive and spectacular.

Defining a city
Although Modernisme encompassed all artistic disciplines, it found its fullest development in architecture. The best-known of the architects is perhaps Antoni Gaudí, whose Casa Batlló (1906) includes flowing stonework, asymmetrical carving, and stained glass. Other important architects included Josep Puig i Cadafalch, whose Casa Amatller (1900) has a facade adorned with ceramics shaped into fruits and flowers, and Lluís Domènech i Montaner, a prominent politician and director of the Barcelona School of Architecture, who designed the Hospital Sant Pau (1902). This complex of buildings – many of them reminiscent of Islamic architecture – includes pavilions decorated with mosaics of bright red, yellow, and green that span across their ceilings. The close collaboration of these architects with some of the best craftsmen of the time created a legacy of extraordinary buildings that has helped to transform Barcelona into one of the most distinctive cities in Europe.

A more conservative version of Catalan nationalism became dominant from around 1910 and Modernisme fell out of favour. However, the enduring mark that the movement left on Barcelona in particular is reflected in the fact that seven buildings by Gaudí and two by Domènech have been given World Heritage site status for their outstanding architectural value. ▪

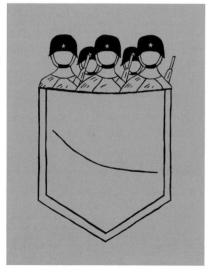

ONE-MAN ARMY THAT FITS IN YOUR POCKET
MULTIFUNCTIONAL TOOLS

IN CONTEXT

FOCUS
One small tool with many functions

FIELD
Product design, industrial design

BEFORE
201–300 BCE Small tools are made that facilitate several tasks, usually with a focus on cutting and eating food.

1889 The Swiss Army introduces a new rifle, which requires a screwdriver to disassemble it for cleaning and maintenance.

AFTER
1983 Tim Leatherman introduces the Pocket Survival Tool, a multi-tool based on pliers rather than a knife.

2009 The oscillating multi-tool is launched, with a range of attachments for various DIY tasks – from sanding to cutting and sawing.

A multifunctional tool is a hand-held instrument that incorporates several functions in a single unit. Romans had multifunctional tools in the 2nd century that unfolded to reveal a fork, spatula, pick, spike, and knife.

From the late 18th century, cutlery makers in Sheffield, UK, produced so-called sportsmen's knives. These multi-tools featured blades and other handy gadgets – a corkscrew, reamer, gimlet, hoof-pick, and more – folding out from

The Swiss Army Knife comes in various sizes, with a wide array of tool options. Many of the fold-out "blades" serve several different functions.

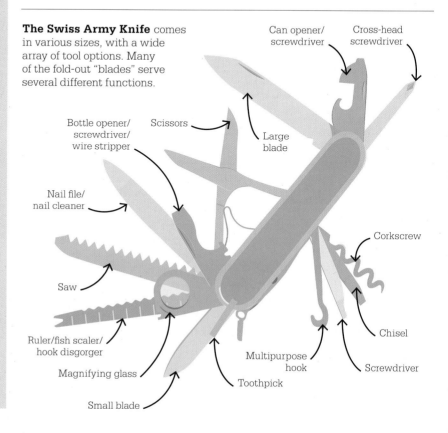

Can opener/ screwdriver

Cross-head screwdriver

Bottle opener/ screwdriver/ wire stripper

Scissors

Large blade

Nail file/ nail cleaner

Corkscrew

Saw

Chisel

Ruler/fish scaler/ hook disgorger

Multipurpose hook

Screwdriver

Magnifying glass

Toothpick

Small blade

See also: Tools and weapons 18–19 ▪ Tools for cooking and eating 30–31 ▪ Built to last 242–43 ▪ Ergonomics 278–85 ▪ Making things better 286–87

both the top and underside of the handle. Aimed at wealthy clients, these tools were often made with fine materials such as mother of pearl, tortoiseshell, and silver. Knives of this kind were displayed at the Great Exhibition in 1851, and in the same year, American author Herman Melville described one in his epic novel *Moby Dick*.

The Swiss Army Knife

The best-known multifunctional tool is probably the Swiss Army Knife, which dates from the 1890s. It was originally designed for the use of all soldiers in the Swiss Army, who needed a pocket-sized tool that could open tinned food, as well as a screwdriver to maintain their standard-issue service rifles.

The first consignment was produced in 1891 by a German manufacturer because no Swiss companies had the necessary production capacity. Known as the Modell 1890, the knife featured a blade, reamer, can opener, and screwdriver, and the handle was made of a dark wood.

The most multifunctional penknife is the Swiss Army Giant Knife 2007, which contains 87 tools and offers 141 different functions.
Guinness Book of Records 2007

Later that year, Karl Elsener, the owner of a Swiss surgical-equipment company (renamed Victorinox in 1921), also began to produce the Modell 1890 and supply the army. A second Swiss company, later known as Wenger, launched a similar product in 1893 and shared the army contract from 1908 to 2005, when Victorinox acquired Wenger. It was Elsener, however, who developed the knife that is ubiquitous today.

In 1897, Elsener secured a patent for an improved version of the Modell 1890. The upgrade featured a new spring mechanism, which allowed tools to be mounted on both sides of the handle. The knife – which Elsener called the Schweizer Offiziers und Sportmesser ("Swiss Officers' and Sports Knife") – was lighter and more compact than the Modell 1890. Elsener sold this directly to the public. The following year, he introduced the red grip with its white cross logo, which was based on the Swiss coat of arms.

A multi-purpose name

During World War II, Elsener's knives gained global prominence when they attracted the attention of American soldiers. Unable to pronounce the German name, the Americans simply called them Swiss army knives. Since then, that adopted name has become a metaphor for usefulness and adaptability, and the knife itself has become a design icon that has inspired other multifunctional tools. ▪

Karl Elsener

A Swiss cutler, inventor, and entrepreneur, Karl Elsener was born in Schwyz, Switzerland, in 1860. He trained as a knife-maker before opening a factory of his own in Ibach in 1884, and began to produce surgical instruments.

Disappointed that knives for the Swiss army were in fact commissioned from a German manufacturer, in 1891 Elsener put his factory to work making the knives with the aim of gaining the contract himself. However, he was unable to compete with the German firm on cost, and by 1896 his company was on the brink of bankruptcy.

Elsener was saved from ruin when he developed and patented an improved version of the knife in 1897; this was the first Swiss Army Knife. Although this new tool was not commissioned by the army, it proved popular with both army officers and civilians.

Elsener died in 1918, but his company Victorinox still makes the knives to this day.

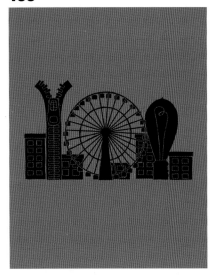

THE MOST MAGNIFICENT RESUME OF THE WORLD'S WORK AND THOUGHT
CHICAGO WORLD FAIR

Following the success of the 1851 Great Exhibition in London, large cultural and industrial exhibitions happened increasingly frequently. Hosting one was a sign of national strength, and having the most admired pavilion a point of pride.

By the late 19th century, the US had begun to challenge the cultural and industrial dominance of Europe. The first major American exhibition, in Philadelphia in 1876, was a disappointment. However, the Chicago World's Fair of 1893 – also known as the World's Columbian Exhibition – proved to be a major success, and became a symbol of the US's growing power and technological prowess. It was the largest and most attended exhibition of its time, drawing visitors from around the globe.

American dominance

Chicago, with its diverse population and strategic location at the intersection of key rail and sea routes, was the ideal host city for the event. The fair's central feature, located in Jackson Park, was a group of white-painted domed pavilions designed in a Beaux Arts-inflected neoclassical idiom by architect Daniel Burnham and others. These pavilions, surrounded by landscaped gardens with water features, were collectively known as the "White City".

The style and arrangement of the White City closely mirrored the main buildings and spaces around Capitol Hill in Washington, D.C. This was no accident. The design of the exhibition was meant to reflect the ideals and dominance of American culture. While the fair was ostensibly a celebration of the 400th anniversary of Christopher Columbus's landing in the Americas, its real purpose

I was dazed at the marvelous variety of odd, instructive, and beautiful articles on exhibition.
A. B. Humphrey
26 June, 1893

See also: Design Reform movement 110–11 ▪ The Arts and Crafts movement 112–19 ▪ Art Nouveau 132–33 ▪ Industrial design 146–47

A bird's-eye view of the Chicago World's Fair shows how it combined water features, landscaped gardens, and exhibition spaces to present a strikingly modern vision of the US.

was to demonstrate American pre-eminence in engineering, science, and the fine arts.

Culture of exclusion

The fair reflected the dominant culture in US at the time, which was primarily white and masculine. Despite lobbying from African-American groups, the organizers refused to include non-white contributions in the White City area. Instead, these were located in a separate area of the fair, which also contained a series of ethnographic displays featuring peoples from around the world, who were variously presented as "exotic" or "savage".

However, the fair also showcased distinctly modern designs. The progressive Chicago architect Louis Sullivan designed the Transportation Building to resemble a modern American railroad station, with his distinct style of naturalistic decoration liberally applied upon its facade. Ornamental glassmaker Louis Comfort Tiffany created a chapel, the windows of which showcased his company's fine craftsmanship. The state of Idaho's pavilion was rustic in appearance and furnished in the Arts and Crafts manner.

Alongside the scientific, engineering, and decorative arts exhibits, the Chicago World's Fair included a vast amusement park, featuring the first Ferris wheel. This formula of blending education and entertainment proved such a resounding success that it was repeated at most subsequent great exhibitions – including the 1933 Chicago World's Fair, which celebrated the city's centennial. Altogether, 27 million visitors attended the 1893 fair and a substantial profit was recorded. ▪

Inventions of the fair

Since the first Great Exhibition in London in 1851, world fairs have served as platforms for scientists, engineers, and manufacturers to display an array of novel inventions. The 1893 fair in Chicago was no exception.

The most prominent attraction was a huge rotating wheel, standing 80 m (264 ft) in diameter, engineered by Gale Ferris Jnr. The wheel could carry up to 2,160 spectators at a time, offering them panoramic views of the city as it slowly revolved. Ferris envisaged the wheel as Chicago's answer to the Eiffel Tower, which had been the highlight of the 1889 Exposition Universelle in Paris.

At the opposite end of the scale, US inventor Whitcomb Judson exhibited the first zipper at the fair, which he promoted as the "Universal Fastener". In the years since 1893, Ferris wheels have remained a firm favourite at amusement parks, and zippers have found countless applications.

The original Ferris wheel had 36 cars, and each one could accommodate up to 60 passengers. The wheel took 20 minutes to make two revolutions.

THE AGE OF INDU

1900–1950

STRY

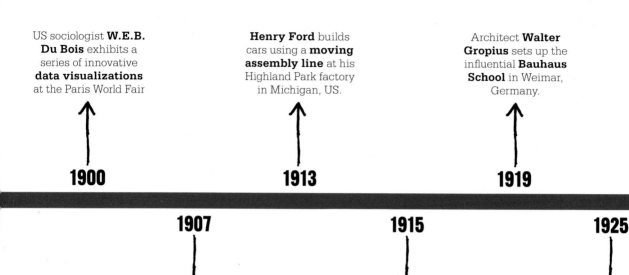

US sociologist **W.E.B. Du Bois** exhibits a series of innovative **data visualizations** at the Paris World Fair

1900

Henry Ford builds cars using a **moving assembly line** at his Highland Park factory in Michigan, US.

1913

Architect **Walter Gropius** sets up the influential **Bauhaus School** in Weimar, Germany.

1919

1907

Belgian chemist **Leo Baekeland** creates **Bakelite** – the first synthetic **plastic**.

1915

The **French Army** sets up a **camouflage unit** to disguise military movements and materials.

1925

In **Paris**, the *Exposition Internationale des Arts Décoratifs et Industriels Modernes* showcases **Art Deco**.

The mechanization of many manufacturing industries during the 19th century meant that – in countries that had embraced industrialization – the world in 1900 appeared to be a very different place from that of even 50 years before. Industrialists such as Henry Ford continued to innovate to increase the speed and efficiency of the manufacturing process, while a new generation of "industrial designers" came to the fore, adapting their designs and creating products that were suitable for mass-production in factory settings.

In Austria-Hungary and in Germany the Vienna Secession – founded in 1897 – and the Deutscher Werkbund (1907) were formed to encourage better cooperation between art and industry and, in this aim, they had considerable success. A leading light in the Werkbund was the architect and designer Peter Behrens, who was commissioned by the German electrical goods maker Allemagne Elektrizität Gesellschaft (A.E.G.) to devise a complete identity for the company and the electric goods that it produced. This was an early and highly successful example of corporate branding, which lent coherent aesthetic forms to objects of the new electric age.

Post-war Modernism

Germany emerged from the catastrophe of World War I as a republic and Russia had turned to communism. In both instances, a desire for a fresh start encouraged avant-garde thinking – it being argued by art, architecture, and design radicals that new visual cultures would be needed for a new, technologically-driven era. In reality, the post-revolutionary Russian economy contracted, which limited the possibility of imposing what was termed the "constructivist" aesthetic and its strange, abstract forms across so large a nation.

In Germany, meanwhile, a new, experimental approach to art and design education was pioneered at the Bauhaus school in Weimar, which became a hotbed of innovative aesthetic and constructional developments.

Collectively, the Bauhaus, Vienna Secession and other groups, such as L'Esprit Nouveau in France and De Stijl in The Netherlands, came to constitute

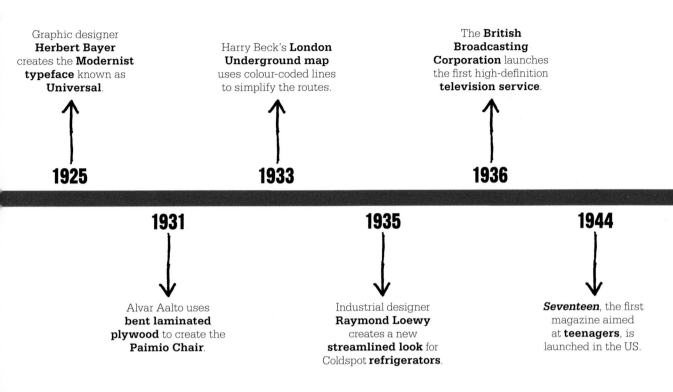

Graphic designer **Herbert Bayer** creates the **Modernist typeface** known as **Universal**.

Harry Beck's **London Underground map** uses colour-coded lines to simplify the routes.

The **British Broadcasting Corporation** launches the first high-definition **television service**.

1925

1933

1936

1931

1935

1944

Alvar Aalto uses **bent laminated plywood** to create the **Paimio Chair**.

Industrial designer **Raymond Loewy** creates a new **streamlined look** for Coldspot **refrigerators**.

Seventeen, the first magazine aimed at **teenagers**, is launched in the US.

the emergent Modern Movement, or Modernism. For its followers, this was more than merely a matter of aesthetics. There was also a moral dimension, that involved allying art, design, and architecture to cultural and political reform. These ideas, however, tended to sound better as rhetoric than to realize in actuality.

Material developments

New materials developed during the early 20th century, such as plastic and bent plywood, were particularly suited to the apparent simplicity of the Modernist aesthetic. Alvar Aalto and Charles and Ray Eames were among the designers to explore the possibilities that they offered. Among their creations were a number of distinctive chairs and

other furniture pieces that have become modern design classics.

The first synthetic fibres were also created during this period. Nylon (1935), polyester (1941), and the acrylic fibre Orion (1950) opened up new possibilties in the design of fashion and textiles.

Economic issues

The Wall Street Crash of 1929 and the Great Depression that followed had a particularly bad effect on Germany, which had been economically and politically unstable since the end of World War I. The election of the National Socialist party of Adolf Hitler in 1933 meant the imposition of stylistic traditionalism and so, fearing persecution, its avant-garde – including many members of the Bauhaus – fled overseas.

In the US, meanwhile, design entrepreneurs offered their services to struggling manufacturers who hoped that novel-looking styling might stimulate consumption and renewed growth. Advancing technology and the quest for speed popularized a streamlined aesthetic, which was widely, if superficially, applied. The concept of "dynamic obsolescence", was devised by Alfred P. Sloan Jr of General Motors in 1924, and involved making design tweaks an annual event. This, he hoped would encourage car owners to invest in a new vehicle and stimulate demand for new models.

This turbulent era drew to a close in 1939 with the outbreak of World War II, which diverted design and industry from commerce to supporting the war effort. ∎

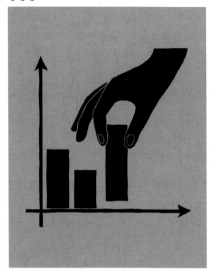

I PUT FACTS INTO CHARTS
INFORMATION DESIGN

The use of data to tell stories is rooted in history and sociology. At the 1900 Paris Exposition, W.E.B. Du Bois and his team of Atlanta University alumni presented a social study to highlight the achievements of Black Americans against a difficult background of racism and discrimination. The display included about 60 richly coloured charts and other statistical graphs.

A colourful chart illustrating a data set allows viewers to see in an instant what the numbers have been saying all along. Information design is the tool that translates raw data into a more accessible visual form. To communicate effectively, it draws upon graphic design, user experience design, and cognitive psychology.

While data visualization presents raw data on its own, allowing users to draw their own conclusions, information design is subjective in nature. It tells a story by displaying data in a logical manner, illustrating relationships between data points through a hierarchical arrangement of content.

Visual layers and chartjunk

In the 20th century, information design grew into a rich language revealing the beauty of information. An early example is the 1953 *World Geo-Graphic Atlas*, designed by Austrian-American artist Herbert Bayer to mark the 25th anniversary of the Container Corporation of America. Bayer's innovative thinking about the broader communicative possibilities of an atlas led him to introduce layers that featured a huge amount of diverse information – from flora and fauna, to commercial and census statistics – over traditional topographical maps.

In the 1970s, British graphic designer Nigel Holmes introduced inforgraphics to a wide readership

The greatest value of a picture is when it forces us to notice what we never expected to see.
John Tukey
Exploratory Data Analysis, 1977

See also: Visualizing data 108–09 ∎ Bauhaus 170–71 ∎ The online user experience 294–99

through his work in the map and chart department of *Time* magazine. Holmes preferred to call his work "explanation graphics", describing it as a mixture of words and pictures combined together so that one cannot be understood without the other.

Holmes's visually integrated – and, at times, irreverent – approach had its critics, including American statistician Edward Tufte. In 1982, in *The Visual Display of Quantitative Information*, the first of his many titles on the importance of clarity when presenting visual information, Tufte warned designers to beware of what he called "chartjunk" – data dressed up in ornamental ways that add little to a reader's understanding.

Computer visualization

The advent of the computer age has made ever-increasing volumes of data available – health statistics, financial information, housing trends, and more – pushing the field of data visualization into the common design culture.

In 2008, the *New York Times* used IBM-developed technology to launch its Visualization Lab, which allowed readers to explore in depth the data provided by the newspaper's editors and use it to make their own charts, graphs, and maps. In addition, the *New York Times* also published innovative information designs illustrating everything from how fire spread through Notre Dame cathedral in Paris in 2019, to "before" and "after" versions of Saray Street, in the southern Turkish city of Antakya, following a massive earthquake. ∎

In his diagrammatic tube map of 1933, Harry Beck showed how the colour-coded London Underground routes intersected, rather than the geographical locations of stations.

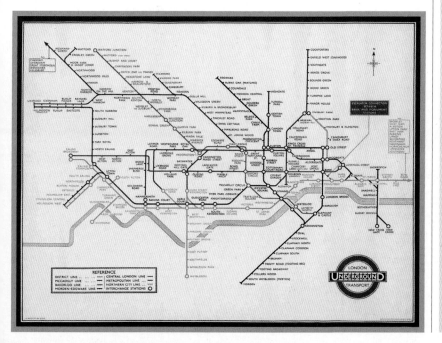

W.E.B. Du Bois

Born in Great Barrington, Massachusetts, in 1868, W.E.B. Du Bois was a Harvard University history graduate. In 1895, he became the first Black American to be awarded a Harvard PhD. Best known for his 1903 book *The Souls of Black Folk*, Du Bois was also one of the founders of the National Association for the Advancement of Colored People (NAACP) in 1909.

Du Bois was one of the earliest proponents of using data visualization to illuminate a difficult truth. He focused on highlighting the oppression of Black Americans by gathering and collating information on their lives "within the Veil".

As a professor in the 1930s and 1940s, Du Bois established and taught in the sociology programme at Atlanta University in Georgia, which is now recognized as the first school of American sociology. He died in Ghana, where he had lived for several years, in 1963.

Key works

1899 *The Philadelphia Negro: A Social Study*
1903 *The Souls of Black Folks*

THE LOVELIEST CURVE I KNOW IS THE SALES CURVE
INDUSTRIAL DESIGN

Prior to the First Industrial Revolution, the manufacture of products was reliant on skilled craftspeople. In the late 19th and early 20th centuries, the so-called Second Industrial Revolution brought a global shift to machine-driven mass production.

The discipline of industrial design emerged in response to this seismic change. Forced to make their creations suitable for the new type of production, designers also applied a modern aesthetic to functional, everyday objects. Raymond Loewy's famous quote "Ugliness does not sell" encapsulates this philosophy.

As the impact of industrial design grew, designers perfected the art of applying both creative flair and technical expertise to their processes. This resulted in a renewed dynamism in the design of everything from chairs and lamps, to coffee makers and radios.

A toothbrush is 28 grams of matter ... made to get rid of scraps of meat from between the teeth. Every gram of matter must provide its service as best it can.
Philippe Starck
Le Monde, 1994

Iconic designs
Many manufacturing companies hired forward-thinking designers to develop new products. In the process, the firms came to be closely associated with the people who ran their design departments.

Swedish-born Ivar Jepson worked for the Florida-based small-appliances company Sunbeam. His Mixmaster, the first electric food mixer, was released in 1930 and soon became a staple in many American homes. Featuring two detachable beaters and a range of attachments – such as a slicer and a juice extractor – it saved time, money, and effort in the kitchen.

Sunbeam also commissioned appliances from Italian-American designer Alfonso Iannelli. His T-9 electric toaster, launched at the

See also: Written communication 34–41 ▪ Transport and portability 32–33 ▪ Early mass production 64–65 ▪ Branding 200–07 ▪ Ergonomics 278–85

1939 New York World's Fair, became so iconic that it took centre-stage on the cover of a 1948 issue of *The Saturday Evening Post*, painted by American artist Norman Rockwell.

Like many mid-century designers, Iannelli was influenced by the Bauhaus principle that form should follow function. This philosophy continued to resonate throughout the 20th century, shaping the ideas of, among others, Dieter Rams, head of design at the German company Braun from the 1960s until 1997.

Wartime applications

For centuries, war has been central to innovation in fields ranging from medicine to technology. As weaponry grew more intricate, requiring precise user operation, industrial designers took a greater interest in the interactions between humans and machines – and in the burgeoning discipline of ergonomics.

An example of ergonomic design in the military field is the German MG 42 machine gun, launched in

The Polaroid model 95, designed by American inventor Edwin Land, was the first commercially available camera to deliver instant prints.

1942. Simple to use and reliable in battle, it was also easy to mass manufacture. This highly successful weapon is still in production today.

Everyday functionality

Industrial design has shaped many aspects of daily life, as well as of cultural history. The 1948 arrival of the Polaroid camera allowed users to document their lives with more spontaneity than ever before, while the launch of home video players in the 1970s provided a new way to watch films and television programmes – and created a new mass market for recorded material.

In the 21st century, industrial designers continue in their aims to create innovative products that are aesthetically pleasing, functional, and easy to operate. ▪

The Sony Walkman cassette player, launched in 1979, was the first portable music player to allow individuals to listen to their choice of music on the go.

Raymond Loewy

Often called "the father of industrial design", Raymond Loewy was born in Paris, France, in 1893 and moved to the US in 1919. He became an American citizen in 1938.

Loewy's pioneering work had an enduring impact in the arena of industrial design. His legacy includes the creation in 1955 of the distinctive Coca-Cola contour bottle, with its curvy, ergonomic shape and eye-catching white logo.

Celebrated for landmark automotive designs, Loewy worked for the Studebaker company for more than 20 years, leading a team that designed the Starlight Coupe (1947) and the Avanti (1962), among others. He also designed the Greyhound Scenicruiser bus, which has become a classic symbol of North American travel, and contributed to the distinctive livery of the US presidential plane Air Force One.

Loewy's work remains a testament to the importance of usability, elegance, and timelessness in industrial design. He died in Monaco in 1986, aged 92.

FINE ART
FOR 39 CENTS
PLASTIC

Oil and gas resources are **exploited for fuel**.

By-products include organic compounds with **limited value as fuel**.

Chemists use these by-products to **create polymers**.

Polymers form the basis of the synthetic plastics industry.

Plastic is the workhorse of the modern economy – it is practically impossible for the vast majority of the world's population to avoid using it on a daily basis. The innovation in materials that came about with the invention of plastic has affected nearly every aspect of life.

The world's first synthetic plastic, Bakelite, was created in 1907 by Belgian chemist Leo Baekeland. Formed out of a chemical reaction between two organic compounds – phenol and formaldehyde – Bakelite quickly became popular because of its special qualities: it can be moulded and hardened into any shape; it does not conduct electricity; and it is resistant to heat. For more than three decades after its discovery, it was unchallenged as a synthetic alternative to traditional materials

Leo Baekeland

Born near Ghent, Belgium, in 1863, Leo Baekeland was a chemist and inventor whose work laid the foundation for the plastics industry. Having emigrated to the US in 1889, he worked as a consultant chemist and, four years later, invented Velox – the first commercially successful photographic paper. Thanks to the success of Nepera, the chemical company he founded to market Velox, he established his own laboratory in the early 1900s.

Baekeland set out to explore other promising areas for chemical research and began to experiment with synthetic resins. His work with phenol and formaldehyde led him to the groundbreaking invention of Bakelite in 1907. Baekeland's creation earned him recognition as a pioneer in the field of materials science and engineering, and he was appointed a professor at Columbia University, New York City. In 1939, he sold the General Bakelite Company, which he had established three decades earlier, to US chemicals giant Union Carbide. From then until his death in 1944, Baekeland lived as a recluse.

See also: Tools for cooking and eating 30–31 ▪ Early mass production 64–65 ▪ Safety fabrics 244–47 ▪ Eco design 258–65 ▪ Sustainable materials 302–07

Thanks to plastics, countless lives have been saved in the health sector … and safe food storage has been revolutionized.
Erik Solheim
UN Environment Programme, 2018

This 800 series telephone of the 1960s has a casing made of ABS plastic, which is strong, light, scratch resistant, and less brittle than its Bakelite forerunner.

such as wood, stone, or metal. Radios were encased in Bakelite, which was used to make a vast range of other items, from kitchenware and light switches, to buttons and toys. By 1944, global production was about 178,000 tonnes (196,000 US tons).

The material lent itself to design creativity, and its non-conductivity meant it was ideal for insulating electrical equipment. It spawned a new genre of design. For example, the GPO's model 162 dial telephone, which was introduced in the UK in 1929, is encased in a pyramid of shiny black Bakelite. Models in red, ivory, and green were introduced later. The material had limitations, however, being brittle, impossible to reshape once hardened, relatively heavy, and only available in a limited range of colours.

A polymer revolution

The creation of a synthetic plastic marked the beginning of a material revolution for the chemical industry, which had historically concentrated on manufacturing cloth dyes and explosives. Bakelite's commercial success inspired the industry to research and develop polymer chemistry. This in turn led to the creation of diverse types of synthetic plastic with varied properties during the 1930s.

In 1933, British chemists Eric Fawcett and Reginald Gibson accidentally discovered the polymer polyethylene while conducting research at ICI's facility in Northwich, UK. Large-scale production began at the DuPont and Union Carbide factories in the US during World War II. While experimenting with polyethylene waste, Earl Tupper, a DuPont employee, discovered that he could make non-breakable, lightweight cups, plates, and containers with it. He set up his own company and, in 1947, designed a range of polyethylene kitchenware. These products – which came to be known as Tupperware – were flexible, durable, chemically resistant, and described by *House Beautiful* magazine as able to "withstand almost anything". Tupperware introduced a range of airtight household products that revolutionized food storage and preservation through its unique "burping seal", which Tupper patented in 1949. Tupperware remains popular: its containers keep food fresher for longer and contribute to the convenience of modern domestic life.

PET (polyethylene terephthalate), a derivative of polyethylene, became one of the staples of » plastic manufacture after going into production in the early 1950s. Strong and lightweight, this material was ideal for making many products. It can be blow-moulded to make bottles and other containers, stretched to create food packaging, or spun to produce durable, detergent-resistant fabrics such as Dacron and Terylene, which were used for bedding, clothing, and curtains.

Contemporary designers have used PET in creative projects, including coverings for solar panels that give them the appearance of stained glass – by Dutch designer Marjan van Aubel – and decorative drapes from Dutch architects Beyond Space. PET is also readily recyclable, with US furniture company Emeco's 111 Navy chair – made from around 170 recycled bottles – now a design classic.

Functional diversity

Another plastic that made its debut in the 1950s was polypropylene, whose properties included being very tough but semi-flexible,

translucent, and heat resistant. Designers have used it to make tools, car parts, and furniture – including the Panton Chair (1967). Based on Danish designer Verner Panton's earlier S Chair, it is made from a single piece of injection-moulded polypropylene, curved to fit the body.

Chemists of the post-war period produced other varieties of plastic, each with their own advantages. For example, PVC is resistant to light, chemicals, and corrosion and is commonly used in the manufacture of pipes, gutters, and window frames. Polyurethane is a flexible yet supportive material used in mattresses and upholstery. Lycra, another polyurethane product, can be stretched repeatedly without suffering damage. Polystyrene, with its light weight and low thermal conductivity, is used for insulating buildings and hot food, as well as packaging fragile items.

These new materials offered an enhanced functionality and durability that opened up new possibilities for creative design.

> About 430 million tons of plastic are produced annually, according to the United Nations. [The] amount is set to triple by 2060.
> **Leslie Kaufman**
> **Bloomberg News, 2023**

Plastic became an integral part of daily life and played a pivotal role in the rise of consumer culture.

Mass manufacture of plastic goods allowed for the creation of affordable and disposable products, aligning with the growing demand for convenience and accessibility. Its light weight made it an ideal material for packaging, reducing transportation costs and energy consumption. In healthcare, sterile and disposable plastic items became standard, contributing to advances in medical hygiene.

The plastics industry is now global. Plastic materials and products have become significant components of international trade. Countries with advanced manufacturing capabilities export plastic goods, contributing to economic growth.

Beyond its utilitarian uses, plastic has found its way into art and cultural expression. Artists and designers have embraced it

Hermit crabs increasingly use plastic waste – rather than discarded mollusc shells – for protection. Millions of tonnes of plastic end up in the world's oceans every year.

for its versatility, and it has been used to create installations that reflect the aesthetic of the modern era. Increasingly, these include recycled disposable plastic items as a way to highlight the problems created by single-use plastic.

Disposal problems

Although plastics have delivered undeniable benefits, they have come at a substantial environmental cost. Plastic pollution began to be a problem in the world's oceans as early as the 1960s. The durability that makes plastic products so useful also means they persist in the environment for years beyond their useful lives. Improper disposal and inadequate recycling infrastructure have led to insidious levels of plastic pollution via rivers and landfill to our oceans and landscapes. Plastic waste can take anywhere from 20 to 500 years to decompose – and even then, it never fully disappears: the pieces just get smaller and smaller.

At the demand of consumer culture, the widespread use of single-use plastics in bags, bottles, and packaging has become a defining legacy of the 20th century.

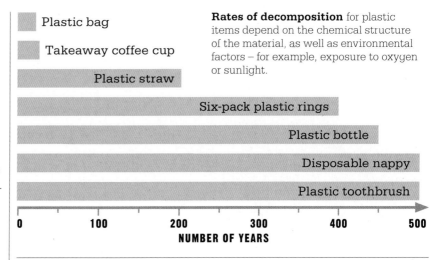

Plastic bag

Takeaway coffee cup

Plastic straw

Six-pack plastic rings

Plastic bottle

Disposable nappy

Plastic toothbrush

0   100   200   300   400   500
NUMBER OF YEARS

Rates of decomposition for plastic items depend on the chemical structure of the material, as well as environmental factors – for example, exposure to oxygen or sunlight.

The convenience of these disposable items, coupled with a lack of awareness about their environmental consequences, has contributed to a global waste crisis, well documented in the 2021–22 *Waste Age* exhibition at London's Design Museum. Landfill sites are overflowing with non-biodegradable plastics, and marine ecosystems are suffocating due to plastic debris.

Sustainable solutions

The production of plastics is closely linked to the petrochemical industry. About 99 per cent of plastics are derived from fossil fuels, primarily oil and natural gas. The extraction, refining, and processing of these resources contributes 3.4 per cent of global greenhouse-gas emissions. Efforts to address the environmental impact of plastic are shifting global industry towards the development of more sustainable practices. Biodegradable plastics and innovations in recycling technologies to create more sustainable consumption and production systems are starting to emerge. ■

The Ellen MacArthur Foundation

Committed to creating a circular economy, in which waste and pollution are eliminated and nature is regenerated, the Ellen MacArthur Foundation advocates an economic system that delivers better outcomes for people and the environment, and considers every stage of a product's journey – before and after it reaches the customer.

Advancing a circular economy for plastics involves recycling, reusing, and minimizing waste, fostering sustainability and environmental responsibility in both production and consumption. This approach is vital to stop plastic pollution and also offers strong economic, social, and climate benefits. By 2040, according to the foundation, a circular economy has the potential to reduce the annual volume of plastics entering our oceans by 80 per cent, reduce greenhouse-gas emissions by 25 per cent, generate savings of $200 billion per year, and create 700,000 additional jobs.

Ellen MacArthur is a British yachtswoman who has twice broken the record for the fastest solo circumnavigation of the globe.

ANY COLOUR, SO LONG AS IT IS BLACK

FORD MODEL T

IN CONTEXT

FOCUS
**A motor vehicle
for the masses**

FIELD
**Automotive engineering,
industrial design, product
design, manufacturing**

BEFORE
1888 The first petrol-driven
car – the Benz Patent-
Motorwagen developed
by Karl Benz – goes on sale.

1901 Ransom E. Olds mass-
manufactures the Curved
Dash Oldsmobile, and patents
the assembly line process
used to produce it. It is the
US's first mass-produced car.

AFTER
1938 The Volkswagen Beetle,
a mass-produced economy
car, is launched in Germany.

2010 Nissan's Leaf is the
first all-electric family car
to be produced by a major
manufacturer.

The first modern cars were developed during the 1880s and 1890s – by mechanical engineer Karl Benz in Mannheim, Germany, and by bicycle-making brothers Charles and Frank Duryea in Massachusetts, US. However, these early vehicles were luxury purchases that were only available to the wealthy. The car that brought motoring to the masses was the Ford Model T.

Henry Ford established the Ford Motor Company in 1903 and launched his first car, the Model A, that same year. Over the next few years, Ford worked on perfecting his vision of a reliable, affordable car that was simple to maintain and that could cope with the dirt roads of the rural US. This was realized in the Model T, which went into small-scale production in October 1908.

Practical and popular
The Model T came in a range of colours and body styles, all built on the same chassis. The engine could run on fuels that were commonly used in rural areas, such as petrol, ethanol, or kerosene, which was used for tractors. The car could also double as a portable engine – to power a threshing machine or a water pump, for example.

Like other cars at this time, the Model T was originally hand-assembled. In the first month, the factory produced just 11 cars. By 1910, Ford had produced 12,000 Model Ts and was struggling to keep up with demand. He

This 1912 British poster for the Ford Model T highlights the vehicle's affordability and reliability, promoting the car as suitable for any use.

See also: Early mass production 64–65 ▪ Interchangeable parts 106–07 ▪ Industrial design 146–47 ▪ Planned obsolescence 176–77

The Highland Park Ford Plant in Michigan was the first to feature a moving assembly line, with workers assigned to specific tasks.

Henry Ford

Born on a farm in Michigan, US, in 1863, Henry Ford moved to Detroit aged 16 to train as a machinist. In 1891, he began working as an engineer at Edison Electric, experimenting with petrol engines in his spare time. After some unsuccessful business ventures, he started the Ford Motor Company in 1903 and launched the Model T in 1908.

In an effort to satisfy the overwhelming demand for the Model T, Ford introduced new mass-production methods, including large factories, standardized interchangeable parts, and, in 1913, moving assembly lines. In 1914, to ensure a stable, motivated, and committed workforce, he raised his employees' pay from $2.34 to $5 a day, split between a wage and a bonus; in 1926, he reduced the working week to five days.

Ford was a pioneer and an innovator. He revolutionized the car industry, and more than any other individual, he was responsible for the profound way the car shaped the 20th century. He died in Dearborn, Michigan, in 1947.

responded by opening a new factory and putting a new moving assembly line in place. In 1914, black became the standard colour, partly because it was the fastest-drying paint at the time.

Affordable transport

Ford's new production method cut the build time for a Model T from 12.5 hours to 93 minutes. This led to a dramatic increase in output and substantially lower production costs, which allowed Ford to reduce the price of a Model T from $825 – the price of a hand-built car in 1908 – to $360 for a mass-produced vehicle in 1916. By 1925, as many as two million Model Ts were produced each day, and the price fell further, to just $260.

The lower prices brought car ownership within reach of millions of people for the first time. Ford also opened factories in other countries, making the Model T the first global car.

Prized for its low cost, durability, versatility, and ease of maintenance, the Model T was a huge success: more than 15 million were made in total. However, in the mid-1920s, other manufacturers began to sell more stylish cars, and the Model T was soon seen as old-fashioned. Sales dropped, and production of the Model T ended in 1927. ▪

Any man holding down
a steady job should,
if he so wished,
be able to have
his own car.
Henry Ford

THE POWER TO UNITE PEOPLE

SPORTS BRANDING

Besides the feel-good factor associated with playing or watching a sport, the challenge of competition, and the drive to reach new personal bests, sport is also big business.

Football, tennis, and golf tournaments are watched by millions around the world. Team branding – first introduced to help players identify their teammates on the pitch – now also helps to bring fans together to support their common cause. Demand for merchandising creates opportunities for sponsorship – of individual athletes, entire teams, or the sporting event itself.

From football to Formula 1
One of the earliest examples of sports branding dates from the late 1850s. Rules devised by Sheffield Football Club included a law that each player should have a red and a navy cap – "one colour to be worn by each side during play". Caps soon evolved into standardized football kits with team colours and a logo creating a visual identity that fans could recognize. In 1975, another British football team, Leeds United, began selling replica kits to its fans, and a new industry was born.

The commercialization of sports through branding has elevated the prominence of several disciplines.

The Olympic rings logo, created in 1913, was first used on posters and flags for the 1920 Games in Antwerp, Belgium. The planned 1916 games had been cancelled due to World War I.

Nike doesn't want to make products for everyone, they want to make products for champions.
Simon Sinek
Huffington Post, **2010**

Basketball superstars like Michael Jordan and LeBron James have transcended the court to become powerful brand ambassadors, endorsing and advertising food and drink companies, as well as sportswear brands – in return for large sponsorship deals. The distinctive logo, merchandise, and global outreach of the National Basketball Association (NBA) have propelled basketball into a significant cultural phenomenon.

Formula 1 motor racing teams such as Ferrari and Mercedes have cultivated high-performance aesthetics and a luxury image, creating a global appeal that is amplified by high-profile sponsorships. Every part of their drivers' kit – from helmet to shoes – bears a sponsor's name, as does every part of the cars they drive.

Sporting logos

Branding has transformed sports into a global spectacle, turning athletes and teams into marketable entities, expanding fan bases, and creating enduring commercial success for companies such as Adidas, Puma, and Nike. The Nike Swoosh logo, created by US graphics student Carolyn Davidson, is a simple yet dynamic tick mark. It is immediately associated with Nike's commitment to performance, innovation, and the spirit of its "Just Do It" slogan.

The Olympic Games also boast an instantly identifiable visual brand. The five different-coloured, interlocking Olympic rings, created

Nike adopted its Swoosh logo in 1971. It was inspired by the Greek goddess of victory – after whom the company is named.

by French educator Pierre de Coubertin, represent the inhabited continents and the unity of sports. Branding for the Games now goes much further, including typefaces, mascots, and signage designed to capture the imagination of sports fans across the globe. ▪

Adi Dassler

The founder of the German sportswear company Adidas, Adolf "Adi" Dassler was born in the German state of Bavaria in 1900. Originally working as a cobbler, in 1924 he and his older brother Rudolf set up a shoe factory specializing in sports footwear. His inventive designs included studded football boots, as well as spiked track shoes that were famously worn by US sprinter Jesse Owens at the 1936 Olympic Games in Berlin.

After World War II, the two brothers fell out and dissolved the firm. In 1948, Adi founded Adidas, while Rudolf went on to establish rival sportswear firm Puma.

Adidas soon became Europe's largest manufacturer of sportswear; today it is also the second-largest in the world, after Nike. The distinctive three-stripe logo and an emphasis on cutting-edge technology have become synonymous with the brand. Adi Dassler died in 1978, having played a pivotal role in shaping the design of sportswear with his commitment to performance-driven products that look good.

INVISIBLE TO THE ENEMY

CAMOUFLAGE PATTERNS

IN CONTEXT

FOCUS
**The evolution and
significance of camouflage**

FIELD
**Textile design, fashion
design, industrial design,
graphic design, visual arts**

BEFORE
1890s Researchers look for
ways to translate camouflage
in nature into techniques that
can be used by the military.

1910s Pablo Picasso and
Georges Braque pioneer the art
movement Cubism, which later
influences military camouflage.

AFTER
1980s Camouflage designs
become fashionable, often in
highly impractical colours.

2004 The US Army introduces
a digital Universal Camouflage
Pattern designed for use in
multiple terrains.

C amouflage is the art
of hiding or disguising
people or equipment by
making them blend in with their
background. Inspired by strategies
for survival in the animal world,
today camouflage is particularly
important in military settings.

From the earliest times, people
have used basic camouflage
techniques. Prehistoric hunters
used charcoal or pigment to paint
their faces and bodies and wore
animal skins and antlers to get
as close as possible to their prey
without being detected.

There are also ancient accounts
of camouflage being used to conceal
ships, with Mediterranean pirates

See also: Pigments and colours 20–21 ▪ Islamic geometric patterns 66–69 ▪ Theory of colours 94–101 ▪ Youth culture 230–33 ▪ Smart materials 314–17

Animal camouflage

In the natural world, animals use a number of different tactics to reduce their visibility. Some use colour to blend into their surroundings, while others conceal themselves by donning twigs, shells, or other materials to match their background. Others may disguise themselves as another object to guard against predators – for example, the wings of some moths are shaped like crumpled, dead leaves. Disruptive patterns – such as spots, stripes, or other non-repeating markings – are an important feature, since they help to break up the animal's outline. They may also create an effect known as "motion dazzle" to confuse predators. For example, in a herd of zebra, the boldly contrasting stripes reduce the predator's ability to estimate the speed and direction of their prey.

In a military setting, these strategies translate into uniforms in colours or patterns that match the environment in which they are deployed, and the use of dazzle camouflage to break up the outline of World War II battleships.

A leafy seadragon is perfectly camouflaged against a background of seaweed thanks to the long, leaf-like appendages on its body.

painting their vessels blue-grey, and Julius Caesar deploying bluish-green reconnaissance boats that matched the colour of the sea to gather intelligence during the Gallic Wars of 58–50 BCE.

Learning from nature

Animal camouflage became a topic of research in the mid-19th century. In his 1890 book *The Colours of Animals*, British zoologist Edward Poulton described different types of camouflage. They included coloration that allows an animal to blend into the background, and mimicry, where the animal can disguise itself as another object.

In 1892, British zoologist Frank Beddard identified a further form of camouflage: countershading. An example of this is a fish with a dark top surface and a lighter underside. This makes the fish harder to see when viewed from above – as it merges into the seabed – or from below, as it blends in with the sky.

American artist Abbott Thayer was one of the first to describe disruptive patterning, a technique that is used to break up an object's outlines. Although Thayer saw that these camouflage techniques might have military applications, he was not successful in getting them adopted.

Military khaki

Before the 1800s, most armies dressed their soldiers in brightly coloured uniforms – like the British red coats – that were designed to accentuate their visibility. This was

We must believe that these tints are of service to these birds and insects in preserving them from danger.
Charles Darwin
On the Origin of Species, 1859

believed to improve the morale of the troops and to intimidate the enemy. It also made it easier for soldiers to recognize each other in hand-to-hand combat. However, the early 19th century saw the increased range and accuracy of the rifle replacing the musket, and personal concealment in battle became an essential consideration.

During the Napoleonic Wars (1803–15), two British Army rifle regiments that served as marksmen discarded their scarlet tunics in favour of less conspicuous green jackets. Green jackets were also worn by rifle units throughout the American Civil War (1861–65).

In 1848, the Corps of Guides, a British Indian Army regiment led by Lieutenant William Hodson, became the first to adopt khaki uniforms. *Khaki* means "soil coloured" in Urdu, and it was thought that the muted, drab hue would help to make the troops "invisible in a land of dust". Other regiments followed suit, and by the Second Boer War (1899–1902), khaki uniforms were in use throughout the British Army. »

Other major powers followed the British example: the US adopted "olive drab" (khaki), Italy *grigio-verde* (grey-green), and Germany *Feldgrau* (field grey). By the time World War I broke out, only the French army continued to dress in conspicuous uniforms of blue jackets and red trousers; faced with high casualty rates on the Western Front, these were quickly replaced by greyish-blue clothing.

Camouflaging equipment

World War I introduced a new element in warfare: aerial reconnaissance. This meant that troops, weaponry, and buildings could now be seen from above.

In 1915, the French Army created the world's first dedicated camouflage unit under the artist Lucien-Victor Guirand de Scévola. Members of this innovative unit were known as *camoufleurs*, derived from a Parisian slang term meaning "to disguise". Many of them were theatre set designers and artists – including Cubist luminaries Georges Braque and André Mare. They created the first camouflage patterns and used them to hide military material

---

Scientists ponder the reason for **colours in the animal kingdom**.	→	**Armies** around the world begin using **muted tones for uniforms**.

Experiments are carried out on the **camouflage of military vehicles**.	←	**Artists** help to develop what are today considered **camouflage patterns**.

↓

Camouflage becomes a fashion staple.

---

and movements from the enemy. Initially, the *camoufleurs* painted vehicles and weaponry in patterns designed to blend into the landscape, and they attempted to disguise buildings with leaf-covered netting and painted tarpaulins. As World War I progressed, their techniques became increasingly complex: for example, they used decoy pâpier-maché heads to draw the fire of

snipers, and disguised observation posts as trees. Other armies soon set up their own camouflage units.

The French and British armies also experimented with limited use of hand-painted camouflage clothing for specialists such as snipers, but there was no mass production of camouflage material for uniforms. In 1917, Germany began using what is thought to be the earliest printed camouflage fabric – a lozenge design, made up of irregularly shaped polygons in different colours – which was used to cover aircraft. In 1918, Germany also pioneered the first standardized camouflage design for personal use in the form of a disruptive splinter pattern known as Buntfarbenanstrich 1918, which was used on steel helmets.

Dazzle ships

Camouflage spread to the seas, too. The British had already tried – and failed – to conceal their warships by painting them in tones of blue to match the sky and the sea. In 1917, British artist Norman Wilkinson

---

André Mare

Born in Normandy, France, in 1885, André Mare studied art and design in Paris, where he became part of the Cubist avant-garde movement, alongside his childhood friend Fernand Léger, Robert Delaunay, and Marcel Duchamp. In 1912, Mare was responsible for the interiors of the Maison Cubiste, a collaborative installation designed to display Cubist art.

During World War I, Mare joined the newly formed French Camouflage Unit. Working alongside other artists, he led the development of camouflage techniques in a military setting. He applied the principles of disruptive coloration, using forms derived from Cubism, to deceive the eye by breaking up the shape of weaponry. His *Cubisme et Camouflage, 1914–1918* is a series of illustrated notebooks based on his wartime experiences.

Mare pursued a highly successful career as a designer after the war, and he was one of the founders of the Art Deco movement. He died in 1932.

developed the alternative technique of dazzle camouflage, which involved painting warships with bold stripes, swirls, and zigzag patterns. The aim was not to make the ship less visible but to break up its shape, thereby making it more difficult for German U-boats to calculate its size, speed, and distance accurately. Other Allied navies also adopted this strategy of optical trickery, though its effectiveness was never proven.

World War II

The camouflage techniques developed in World War I were expanded upon during the second global conflict. All sides used camouflage, particularly to defend themselves from aerial attacks.

For the first time, camouflage uniforms were also worn on a large scale, albeit often only by specialist units, while most Allied soldiers continued to wear plain, single-coloured fatigues. From 1942, British paratroopers and Royal Marine commandos wore a coverall jacket called the Denison smock. It featured one of the most influential camouflage patterns, known as Brushstroke, with broad, mop-like

Camouflage is no mystery and no joke. It is a matter of life and death – of victory or defeat.
Roland Penrose
The Home Guard Manual of Camouflage, 1941

swathes of colour that became one of the most influential camouflage designs. In 1944–45, the same pattern was used on clothing issued to the infantry in Europe and to tank crews. Brushstroke was also the basis for the Tiger Stripe pattern, which was used in the Vietnam War.

The first widespread use of camouflage by the US Army dates back to 1942, with the introduction of dappled-green jungle camouflage in the Pacific arena. US soldiers also used face camouflage creams and helmet nets.

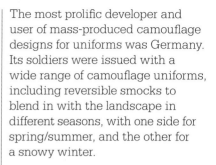

The most prolific developer and user of mass-produced camouflage designs for uniforms was Germany. Its soldiers were issued with a wide range of camouflage uniforms, including reversible smocks to blend in with the landscape in different seasons, with one side for spring/summer, and the other for a snowy winter.

Post-war developments

In the 1960s, the British developed Disruptive Pattern Material (DPM), which could be printed in different colours to suit different types of terrain – whether desert, woodland, or snowy slopes. The British Armed Forces switched to the Multi-Terrain Pattern (MTP) in 2010, but DPM remains one of the world's most widely copied designs. Another influential design came from Germany in the 1970s. Flecktarn ("mottled camouflage") is a disruptive five-colour pattern that was developed for use in woodland. Similar designs have been adopted by Austria, Ukraine, and China.

Attempts to design a pattern to suit all environments have so far been unsuccessful. However, digitally designed pixellated motifs have solved the problem of making a pattern that works both at close range and at a distance. The goals now are to develop "smart" camouflage that is capable of changing to match the surrounding environment; camouflage that can elude infrared, thermal, and hyperspectral imaging cameras; and materials that can bend light waves to make objects or people invisible. ∎

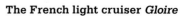
The French light cruiser *Gloire* sails in the Mediterranean in 1944. From the hull to the turrets, it is painted with the bold, geometric lines typical of dazzle camouflage.

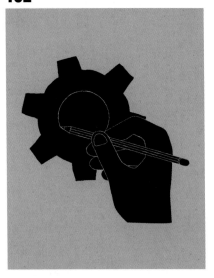

THE COOPERATION OF ART, INDUSTRY, AND CRAFTS
DEUTSCHER WERKBUND

IN CONTEXT

FOCUS
Bringing manufacturers and designers together

FIELD
Architecture, industrial design, applied arts, furniture design

BEFORE
1896 The first edition of *Jugend* is published, which inspires the Jugendstil movement, a German variant of Art Nouveau.

1905 Hermann Muthesius pens *The English House*, spreading the ideas of the English Arts and Crafts movement in Germany.

AFTER
1949 The Deutscher Werkbund is revived, fostering links between design and industry in post-war Germany.

1950s–60s Sleek Mid-century Modern designs are strongly influenced by the Werkbund.

F ounded in Munich in 1907 by the German architect Hermann Muthesius, the Deutscher Werkbund ("German Work Federation") was a collective of artists, architects, designers, and industrialists. The Werkbund focused on unifying traditional crafts and skills with mass production. It was not in itself a creative movement, but rather a state-sponsored initiative whose aim was to improve Germany's economic position in the world by forging partnerships between product manufacturers and designers.

Nurturing new ideas
The establishment of the Deutscher Werkbund was pivotal to design history and the development of modern architecture. Many of the techniques and ideas behind the broader modernist movement were presented at the first Werkbund exhibition in 1914. It was at the Werkbund that designer Walter Gropius developed the founding principles of the Bauhaus school. By 1929, the Werkbund had grown into an alliance of almost 3,000 craftspeople and industrialists, but it was forced to disband after the Nazis came to power in 1933. ■

Exhibitions – such as the event held in Basel, Switzerland, advertised by this poster from 1917 – were an opportunity to promote the work of artists linked to the Deutscher Werkbund.

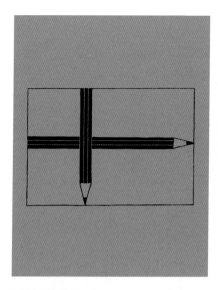

WE MUST BE FINNS
NATIONAL ROMANTICISM

IN CONTEXT

FOCUS
Embracing national identity through design

FIELD
Architecture, furniture design, interior design, decorative arts

BEFORE
1888 Antoni Gaudí's Palau Güell is completed in Barcelona. His Art Nouveau style of architecture influences National Romanticism.

1892 Construction begins on Copenhagen City Hall. The design features symbols inspired by local animals and plantlife.

AFTER
1919 Walter Gropius writes the Bauhaus manifesto, championing more simplistic, Modernist design thinking.

1925 The Art Deco movement – featuring a cleaner, simpler style – gains prominence at the International Expo in Paris.

During the late 19th century, nationalist ideas spread rapidly across Europe, fostering the belief that a state should be built around a people and their common language, culture, religion, and customs. These ideas influenced the art, architecture, and design of the era, especially in Scandinavia, where a style known as National Romanticism emerged in the 1900s.

Inspired by tradition

In an effort to evoke national pride, artists, designers, and architects drew inspiration from traditional local crafts and building techniques. They adopted ornate motifs rooted in national folklore in their work, and often depicted plants and flowers that grew locally. This National Romantic style was used in many public buildings, including Gustaf Nyström's Museum of Art in Turku, Finland (1904), and Lars Israel Wahlman's Engelbrekt Church in Stockholm, Sweden (1914). Some of the themes that defined Art Nouveau – such as

Stockholm City Hall with its 106 m (348 ft) tower was built using traditional North European brick construction techniques. The tower includes three crowns from the Swedish coat of arms.

the emphasis on organic forms – were pertinent to National Romanticism, and these design features were incorporated in the architecture of buildings such as Eliel Saarinen's Helsinki Central Station (1919) and Ragnar Östberg's Stockholm City Hall (1923). Many of these buildings include ornate design features, such as doors, window frames, and even drainpipes with folkloric motifs. ∎

See also: The Arts and Crafts movement 112–19 ▪ Art Nouveau 132–33 ▪ Catalan Modernism 134–35 ▪ Bauhaus 170–71 ▪ Modernism 188–93

THEY PULL THE WIRES WHICH CONTROL THE PUBLIC MIND

POLITICAL MESSAGING

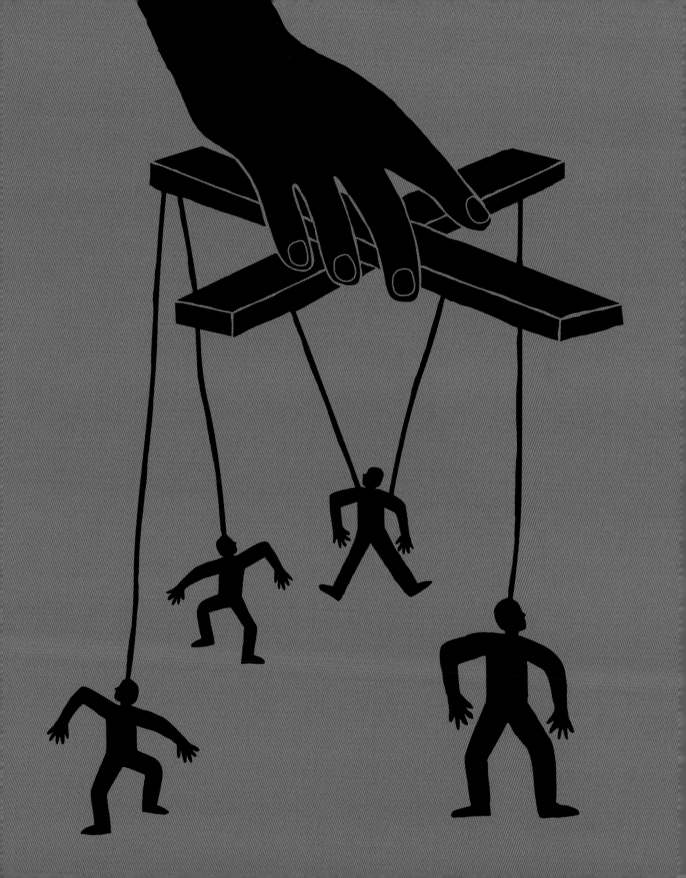

IN CONTEXT

FOCUS
**Communication design
can influence thoughts
and actions**

FIELD
Graphic design

BEFORE
1450s Johannes Gutenberg
invents the printing press with
movable type, which increases
the spread of ideas through
printed materials.

1870s French typesetter Jules
Chéret creates artful posters
that help to establish the new
communication format.

AFTER
1960s Emory Douglas designs
posters for the Black Panther
Party, a powerful voice during
the Civil Rights era in the US.

2024 OpenAI add watermarks
to their image-generated
content to make it easier
to distinguish AI-generated
images from real photographs.

At the beginning of the 20th
century, design became
integral to the spread of
messages of revolution and political
reform in Europe and the US. Design
had long been used to sell products,
but a new Modernist idea that
designers had a moral duty to drive
social and political progress began
to spread. Graphic posters featuring
strong, clear political messages, and
products bearing easily identifiable
emblems, were used to promote
political parties, recruit soldiers,
and disseminate ideas to the
general public. Political messaging
and its more manipulative version,
propaganda, became a powerful
tool during periods of war and
in times of peace.

World War I messaging

The outbreak of World War I
necessitated advertising campaigns
in many countries to encourage
fundraising, recruitment to military
operations, and a push for volunteers
in supporting industries. Political
messaging at this time was often
communicated through posters:
some cheery and hopeful that were
used to spur on production; and
others that took a defiant tone to
rally the population against enemy

Posters from the Soviet Union used
bold colours and simple, impactful designs.
This example from 1929 depicts a worker
with a flag, emblazoned with Lenin's
silhouette, breaking free from chains.

forces. In the US alone, around
20 million posters – nearly 1 for
every 4 citizens – were churned
out in little more than two years.

The inter-war years saw
passionate art movements such
as De Stijl, Constructivism,
Dada, Futurism, Surrealism,
and Modernism rise in response
to growing political tensions across
Europe. Propaganda – which is used

See also: Theory of colours 94–101 ▪ Information design 144–45 ▪ National romanticism 163 ▪ Futurism 175 ▪ Modernism 188–93 ▪ Youth culture 230–33

to manipulate popular opinion and often contains biased or misleading information – increased around this time, and artists and designers called for a modern and sometimes revolutionary vision of the future.

The art of seduction

In the 1920s and 1930s, economies crashed, revolutions took place, and political extremists such as Benito Mussolini in Italy and Adolf Hitler in Germany began to gain political influence. The populations of these countries were seduced with dynamic visual narratives and iconography that quickly became familiar and easily recognizable as belonging to particular political parties. These parties adopted techniques that were once the exclusive purview of industries and corporations to create graphic identities and spread their version of information across all forms of media. Traditional formats such as posters, newspapers, film, and advertising were all used. They saturated the media with the images and words of a heroic leader, identified an enemy to vilify, and promoted their messages consistently and often.

Design was also used in other ways to convey political messages at this time. The built environment, mundane household products, and even clothing were infused with the political identities of the ruling party. Large-scale spectacles such as rallies and marches, cultural events such as opera and museum exhibitions, and flags, sculptures, and facades on public buildings made sure that the ruling party's messages were distributed widely.

Soviet Union propaganda

The 1917 Bolshevik Revolution that led to the formation of the Soviet Union (now Russia) had been driven in part by printed propaganda whose visuals were influenced by the emergent literary and artistic avant-garde movements. Posters, magazines, books, and exhibits featured iconography and bold typography. Designed by artists and photographers including »

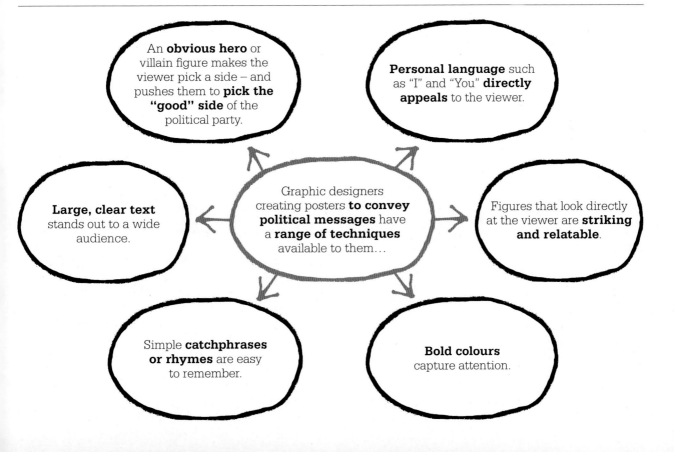

An **obvious hero** or villain figure makes the viewer pick a side – and pushes them to **pick the "good" side** of the political party.

Personal language such as "I" and "You" **directly appeals** to the viewer.

Graphic designers creating posters **to convey political messages** have a **range of techniques** available to them…

Large, clear text stands out to a wide audience.

Figures that look directly at the viewer are **striking and relatable**.

Simple **catchphrases or rhymes** are easy to remember.

Bold colours capture attention.

> The conscious and intelligent manipulation of the organized habits and opinions of the masses is an important element in democratic society.
> **Edward Bernays**
> *Propaganda*, 1928

El Lissitzky, Aleksandr Rodchenko, Varvara Stepanova, and Vladimir Tatlin, these works contained minimal text to communicate with a largely illiterate population. Films were also key to Soviet propaganda, by conveying information that was disguised as mass entertainment.

One characteristic element of Soviet propaganda was photomontage – the combination or adjustment of photographs. This was a new way to manipulate and transform otherwise ordinary images to produce alternative messages and through photomontage the truth could be skilfully blended with fantasy. Joseph Stalin, as leader of the Soviet Union, had images of himself pasted into photographs of his popular predecessor Vladimir Lenin to insinuate that they were close friends and political peers. He also had purged leaders and bureaucrats removed from old photographs, as if they had never existed. For example, when Nikolai Yezhov, an eminent secret police official, fell from favour in 1938, censors deleted him from every photograph, including one image that showed Yezhov with Stalin.

Referencing past empires

Around the same time as the Bolshevik Revolution, Benito Mussolini began his rise to power in Italy. His ideology included an aesthetic plan that was carefully aligned with the visuals of a revolution. The messaging of his party, the National Fascist party, featured a jumble of Futurist style with symbols derived from ancient Rome, and images of his own likeness – a domed head, distinctive jutting chin, and sharply down-turned mouth. The Roman *fascio* – a bundle of rods with a projecting axe blade, carried by a *lictor* (Roman officer) – became a symbol of authority in Fascist Italy. It appeared in both literal and abstract form on posters, monuments, and building facades. Sharp-edged typefaces with hard right angles expressed velocity and progress in the mode of the Futurists, and the classic Roman alphabet was replaced by stencil-based letterforms.

A systematic approach

Where the Fascist approach to branding had been eclectic and varied, the messaging of the National Socialist party (more commonly known as the Nazi party) that emerged in Germany during the 1930s had a tightly prescribed visual language.

Adolf Hitler found Mussolini's comprehensive approach to propaganda inspiring and took it even further in a rigidly directed way. Published in 1936, the Nazi's official brand manual *Organisationbuch der NSDAP* specified exhaustive brand

Indoctrinating the young

Targeting the young was a common strategy employed by 20th-century political parties. Malleable young minds could be filled with messages that soon crystallized as accepted truth.

In Italy, Fascist youth organizations, such as the Opera Nazionale Balilla (ONB) hosted a range of children's activities, including sporting events, cultural activities, and military training. Young people were specifically targeted with propaganda through magazines and textbooks illustrated with Fascist images. Educational certificates were also decorated with Fascist emblems such as the imperial eagle, stylized daggers, and silhouettes of Mussolini.

Political messaging for children extended to clothing design too. Young Fascists were encouraged to wear uniforms festooned with regalia designed to appeal to their age group, such as badges and insignia that proclaimed to the world their support of the party.

ONB uniforms mimicked the uniforms worn by adult Fascists. Girls wore white shirts with the ONB logo while boys wore black shirts.

One of the most recognizable political posters ever published is James Montgomery Flagg's *I Want You for the U.S. Army*. Instead of hiring a model, Flagg used his own face for Uncle Sam.

supportive audience and heroic shots of Hitler that were taken from below eye-level to make him seem godlike and monumental.

World War II and beyond

Once again, designers during World War II created posters to generate public support for the war effort, stir up patriotism, demonize the enemy, and lift public spirits during a time of death and deprivation. Political posters shared the spotlight with other media, particularly radio and print. Most were printed using the new mass-production technique of photo-offset, that enabled the use of photography in posters. This technique, developed in the Soviet Union during the 1920s, became as common in political messaging and propaganda around the world as illustration had been before it.

Later, during the socially and politically turbulent 1960s, graphic design played a critical role in the anti-war, civil rights, feminist, and environmental movements as posters and publications demanded justice and social change. Raw, confrontational messages – this time from activist groups as well as political leaders – demanded a different future, and communicated a refusal to continue with the status quo. The messaging appealed to a restless audience hungry for change, but was also used by opponent groups to stir up retaliation. Political messaging continues today through radio, television, and online campaigns, and propaganda is evolving with advances in AI technology. ∎

standards for everything from publications to the design and furnishing of worker's housing blocks. With iconography that included arrows, lightning bolts, swords, and eagles, as well as the swastika, Nazi branding used bold swashes of red along with solid heavy blacks to aggressively convey their political might.

Graphic design was not the only branding tool employed by the Nazis; public spectacle became a means of propaganda as well. Realizing that grand pageantry would influence the masses, the party leadership staged huge rallies of more than 30,000 soldiers stepping in formation for up to five hours. The public were intimidated by, and in awe of, the sheer size and volume of such events.

Cinema became an agent of propaganda as well: Leni Riefenstahl's *Triumph of the Will* (1934) is considered one of the best examples of film propaganda ever produced. It used innovative techniques including frequent close-ups of the fervently

James Montgomery Flagg

Born in New York, US, in 1877, James Montgomery Flagg was a prolific cartoonist and illustrator. His work was first published in the children's magazine *St. Nicholas* when Flagg was 12 years old. He later studied at the Art Students League in New York City between 1894 and 1898, before attending art schools in France and the UK. By the 1900s Flagg was well known as an illustrator, having had his work published in various magazines, journals, and books. However, his most famous creation, *I Want You for the U.S. Army*, was a recruitment poster for the US government. It featured Uncle Sam, a popular symbol of the US, pointing directly to the viewer and was reused during World War II. Flagg made 46 political posters for the US government between 1917 and 1919, alongside his other work. He died in New York in 1960.

Key works

1917 *I Want You for the U.S. Army*
1917 *Wake Up, America!*
c.1935 *Your Forests – Your Fault – Your Loss*

ART INTO INDUSTRY
BAUHAUS

F ounded in Weimar, Germany, in 1919 by architect Walter Gropius, the Staatliches Bauhaus – known as the Bauhaus – was a radical art school. Its aim was to reimagine the material world by unifying crafts and the fine arts. Gropius set out his intention for the school in its manifesto, writing, "Architects, sculptors, painters – we all must return to craftsmanship!" He also stated that "There is no essential difference between the artist and the artisan." The school initiated a movement that was pivotal to contemporary thinking of art, design, and architecture.

New standards
Known for its "form follows function" approach, the school's students and teachers walked the line between art and craft, setting new benchmarks for what was considered good design. They challenged the limits of metal and woodwork, glass, textiles, and art practices, and they embraced new technological innovations. They

The Bauhaus brought together **three distinct fields** to create a movement that reflected the **unity of all art forms**.

Artists were encouraged to **explore the craft** of their work and **embrace the workshop**.

Designers were to consider **all elements** of their work, including the **artistry of functional objects**.

Technology was to be used to make **mass production easier** and the products **more accessible**.

See also: The Arts and Crafts movement 112–19 ▪ Deutscher Werkbund 162 ▪ Design for social change 180–81 ▪ Mid-century Modern 216–21

This elegant teapot was created by sculptor Marianne Brandt, whose metalwork centred around everyday items. It features simplified shapes that are characteristic of Bauhaus designs.

regarded mass production as an opportunity to create design that was accessible to the masses.

Although the Bauhaus proclaimed gender equality, the reality was often different. Women tended to be directed towards practices that were traditionally women's crafts, such as textiles and weaving. One of them was Anni Albers – widely recognized as the foremost textile designer of the 20th century – who led the weaving workshop at the school from 1931–32. According to her own testimony, she was discouraged from attending the glass workshop. Despite this, Albers' wall hangings and, later, her printed works used experimental patterns and graphic compositions in keeping with the functionality and clean lines that the Bauhaus championed.

Forced closure

The Bauhaus came to prominence in an era of immense global change, and had to adapt to the tumultuous political landscapes of interwar Europe. In 1925, the school moved from Weimar to Dessau, and then onto Berlin in 1932. In April 1933 pressure from the Nazi regime forced the director Ludwig Mies van der Rohe to close the Bauhaus. The Nazis condemned artists of the school such as Paul Klee and Wassily Kandinsky, as "degenerate" and treated the institution as a breeding ground for communist ideology. Former students and teachers of the Bauhaus including Otti Berger, Friedl Dicker-Brandeis, and Richard Grune were murdered during the Holocaust.

The Bauhaus legacy

Some Bauhaus luminaries including Marcel Breuer, Anni Albers, and her husband Josef Albers escaped to the US. They continued their work, laying the groundwork for later art and design movements such as Mid-century Modern and Internationalism.

Gropius and Mies van der Rohe also migrated and continued their work. Today, they are considered pioneers of architecture, and their visionary influence, together with the legacy of the Bauhaus, has shaped the modern world. ▪

Walter Gropius

Born in Berlin, Germany, in 1883, Gropius studied architecture at technical institutes in Munich (1903–04) and Berlin (1905–07). He became a member of the Deutscher Werkbund in 1907. The following year, he began working for architect and industrial designer Peter Behrens, alongside Ludwig Mies van der Rohe and Le Corbusier. Gropius started his own architecture firm in 1910, working on factory and office buildings, and shared his approach in *The Development of Industrial Buildings* (1913).

Following World War I, Gropius was appointed master of Grand-Ducal Saxon School of Arts and Crafts in Weimar, and transformed it into the Bauhaus in 1919. He remained its Director until 1928. Gropius fled Nazi Germany in 1934, travelling to Italy and the UK, before arriving in the US in 1937. He died in 1969, in Boston, US, aged 86.

Key works

1925–26 Bauhaus Dessau School Building
1937 Gropius House
1949–50 Harvard Graduate Center

THE ART OF ARRANGEMENT

STREETSCAPE

IN CONTEXT

FOCUS
The visual and functional elements that shape urban streets

FIELD
Urban design, city planning, architecture

BEFORE
618–907 In Tang Dynasty China, planned cities feature straight, orderly streets.

1600s Grand ceremonial streets become a sign of power and order during the Baroque period in Europe.

AFTER
2000s Smart city technologies, such as traffic management systems, LED street lighting, and sensor-based infrastructure are introduced.

2019 The "15-Minute City" concept gains attention, promoting neighbourhoods in which residents can access services and amenities within a 15-minute walk or bike ride.

The term "streetscape" is used to describe the overall look and feel of a street. It includes much of what a passer-by sees in the street – from buildings and trees to railings and benches.

Street furniture is a fundamental component of the streetscape. It encompasses a variety of objects found in public spaces. These include objects connected with transport, such as bike racks and bus shelters; public services, such as water fountains; and communication, such as signs and postboxes. Communities have created street furniture throughout history, and while some objects

The street should **prioritize the movement** of people and vehicles.

Every element should meet **high standards** of design and manufacture.

Space should be **organized by function**, not proportion or symmetry.

The design of the urban environment and streetscape should **enrich people's lives**.

Buildings should be easy to use and **simple to navigate**.

Streets and street furniture should be **purposefully planned** before they are built.

Beauty should be sought in all things.

See also: Hospitality design 178–79 ▪ Design for social change 180–81 ▪ Urban design 248–49 ▪ Eco design 258–65 ▪ The Internet of Things 300–01 ▪ Artificial Intelligence 313

This historic photograph of Tunbridge Wells, UK, includes features typical of a streetscape, such as ornamental trees, decorative railings, and space for people to socialize.

become obsolete – horse troughs, for instance – they are replaced with modern counterparts that cater to current needs, such as charging stations for electric vehicles.

Urban visions

In the early 20th century, British design reformers set out to improve the appearance of the country's streets. Frank Pick, head of the London transport network, aimed to achieve this through well-designed stations with attractive signage and branding. Pick's objective was to transform the street into a work of art. Art historian Nikolaus Pevsner and architect Gordon Cullen shared this scenographic approach. They thought of the urban landscape as a painting or urban scenery, and the principles they developed – which later became known as Townscape – were informed by Pevsner's research on 18th-century landscape gardening. Their approach was based on the simple idea that planning should serve the views it creates. Cullen believed the city should be an environment for a complete human being, who "demands the drama that can be released all around him from floor, sky, buildings, trees… by the art of arrangement."

Today, it is understood that a well-designed streetscape should be inclusive, sustainable, connected, and equitable. Streets have users with diverse needs, speeds, abilities, and desires. There is greater awareness and appreciation of the importance of open-air public space and streetscapes that are truly shared. While it can be difficult for designers to accommodate all needs – people with visual impairments, for example, are often poorly served in environments designed for cyclists – there are nonetheless wide-ranging benefits when the streetscape serves multiple users. ▪

The Garden City movement

The importance of integrating green spaces into towns and cities has been recognized for more than a century. Ebenezer Howard's Garden City movement, founded in 1899, grew out of dissatisfaction with the overcrowding and disease found in British cities. It was conceived as a progressive union between town and countryside, with the positive aspects of town life – jobs, transport and infrastructure – combined with those of the countryside – space, fresh air and access to nature. As an alternative model of urban planning, it became hugely influential, and examples can be found in the US, Japan, Brazil, Israel, Singapore, and South Africa. Although Garden Cities were later criticized for destroying the countryside, as well as their inefficient use of land, the movement still exists. Today, it aims to integrate green spaces into urban areas and infrastructure, for example, through the use of rooftop gardens or community gardens.

A bird's-eye view of the Garden City of Teutoburgia in Herne, Germany, showcases its blend of urban living and lush greenery.

A TREE BATHED IN LIGHT
NATURAL LUXURY

Jewellery and "objet d'art" inspired by organic forms such as flora, fauna, and the female body became the pinnacle of luxury in the early 20th century. One outstanding designer of the period was French jeweller René Lalique who experimented with a mix of glass, precious metals, semi-precious stones, mother-of-pearl, and enamel to bring his nature-inspired visions to life.

Lalique's approach was starkly different from that of other jewellery designers of the time who worked exclusively with precious stones and metals that were chosen for their high value. Instead, Lalique chose materials for their unique characteristics such as their colour or how the material interacted with light. Lalique's elegant, material-led designs became synonymous with quality and luxury.

Simplifying designs
The 1920s saw an era of economic growth, which allowed arts and culture to thrive. Lalique and his contemporaries – who included Irish architect and furniture designer Eileen Gray, French metalworker Edgar Brandt, and the jewellery and luxury goods house Cartier – embraced simplicity in their designs, in line with the emerging Art Deco aesthetics.

With this pared-back style, designers increasingly emphasized the beauty and richness of natural materials such as marble, glass, enamel, leather, metal, and wood. Lalique worked almost entirely with glass during this period and founded the Verrerie d'Alsace glassworks in France to facilitate production of his designs. ∎

The car mascot, Victoire (1928), by René Lalique features an Art Deco style head made of glass. It was designed to be illuminated so that light spreads over the figure's wind-blown hair.

See also: Art pottery 122–23 ▪ Art Nouveau 132–33 ▪ Art Deco 184–85 ▪ Material-led furniture design 186–87

THE BEAUTY OF SPEED

FUTURISM

A key artistic and social movement of the early 20th century, Futurism was founded by Italian poet Filippo Tommaso Marinetti with his 1909 manifesto. The movement celebrated what Futurists saw as the growing victory of technology over nature. Fragmented forms were used to depict youth, speed, and violence through cars, airplanes, and industrial environments. The designs evoked modern urban life and Futurists aspired not only to create cultural change, but a complete annihilation of the past.

Finding a style

Futurism did not immediately emerge with a distinctive style. Its visual identity was largely influenced by Cubism, although Futurism was more varied and eclectic in its expressions. Futurist graphic designers explored bold colours, geometric shapes, and unconventional typography, while futurist architects such as Antonio Sant'Elia created designs that

Futurist graphic design featured on magazines and book covers of the time. The Italian current affairs magazine *La Rivista*, released in 1935, featured industrial tools alongside a geometric representation of the Italian flag.

heavily featured straight lines. In his *Manifesto of Futurist Architecture* in 1914, Sant'Elia advocated architecture that was dynamic, monumental in size, and evoked speed, although few of his designs were ever realized. ■

See also: Art Nouveau 132–33 ▪ Bauhaus 170–71 ▪ Design for social change 180–81 ▪ Youth culture 230–33

A WORLD OF EXPIRATION DATES

PLANNED OBSOLESCENCE

IN CONTEXT

FOCUS
Limiting the lifespan of products to increase sales

FIELD
Product design

BEFORE
Mid-19th century The technological advancements made during the Industrial Revolution lead to mechanized mass production.

1921 Osram founds the Internationale Glühlampen Preisvereinigung cartel to protect the interests of light bulb manufacturers.

AFTER
2015 France becomes the first country in the world to make planned-obsolescence practices punishable by law.

2023 The European Commission proposes a "right to repair" rule: manufacturers of electronic products would be legally obliged to make their items easier to repair.

The controversial practice of designing products with a deliberately limited lifespan is known as planned obsolescence. This term is often credited to Bernard London, a Russian-American real-estate broker who argued in a 1932 essay that this business strategy could stimulate the post-Depression economy in the US.

While disposability makes a selling point of the single-use nature of some products – hygiene items such as latex gloves, medical masks, and contact lenses, for example – planned obsolescence is applied rather more covertly. Most people have experienced it first hand with their household electronics and personal devices. Planned obsolescence is the reason why smart phones start to perform less well a couple of years after purchase; it is also the reason why, despite technology constantly advancing, the lifespans of many household appliances have not significantly improved.

Early examples

Although it might appear counter-intuitive to the end user, the practice of rendering a product purposefully unusable or obsolete within a specific time frame makes perfect sense from the perspective of manufacturers, who regard it as a way to generate sales.

One of the earliest examples of planned obsolescence appeared in 1924, a time when the US automotive market was at a point of almost complete saturation. In desperate need of an uplift in sales,

A General Motors poster from the 1930s advertises the "refinements and improvements" that have been applied to their latest automobiles.

See also: Plastic 148–53 ▪ Branding 200–07 ▪ Built to last 242–43 ▪ Eco design 258–65 ▪ Computer gaming 272–75 ▪ Making things better 286–87

Types of obsolescence

Planned obsolescence is generally simplified as intentionally designing a product to fail after a certain number of uses or a period of time. There are a number of strategic variations of the concept, each with their own tactical tools, strategies, and implications. Some of the most common versions include:

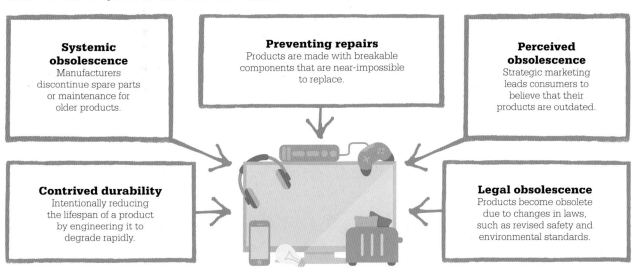

Systemic obsolescence
Manufacturers discontinue spare parts or maintenance for older products.

Preventing repairs
Products are made with breakable components that are near-impossible to replace.

Perceived obsolescence
Strategic marketing leads consumers to believe that their products are outdated.

Contrived durability
Intentionally reducing the lifespan of a product by engineering it to degrade rapidly.

Legal obsolescence
Products become obsolete due to changes in laws, such as revised safety and environmental standards.

General Motors executive Alfred P. Sloan Jr formulated a daring, new marketing strategy. The company would introduce annual design changes to make car owners believe that their vehicle had become out of date, therefore stimulating demand for newer models. Sloan called this policy "dynamic obsolescence".

Another exercise in planned obsolescence started in January 1925, when global manufacturers of incandescent light bulbs – including the German company Osram, Philips from the Netherlands, and General Electric in the US – formed the Phoebus Cartel. In addition to establishing market share and pricing strategies, the members of the cartel secretly agreed to reduce the average light bulb's lifespan from 2,500 hours to 1,000 hours in an effort to boost sales.

Although the Phoebus Cartel was dissolved at the outbreak of World War II, the 1,000-hour light bulb was its enduring legacy – until the introduction of energy-efficient fluorescent and LED bulbs, which last for 15,000–50,000 hours.

Stoking demand
In the mid-1950s, US industrial designer Brooks Stevens promoted a form of planned obsolescence that relied on constantly stoking demand for a product by regularly releasing updated, sleeker, faster, and more innovative models. Modern technology companies can attribute much of their continued growth to this concept. Indeed, corporations such as Apple, Samsung, and Tesla have all been accused of using planned obsolescence practices to create the demand required to sustain their businesses.

Planned obsolescence is now a key driving force in the modern economy, but its use remains controversial, and its ethics are complex. It is also a major contributor to the negative environmental impacts associated with mass manufacture. ▪

Instilling in the buyer the desire to own something a little newer, a little better, a little sooner than is necessary.
Brooks Stevens

PUT IN ONE CONTROVERSIAL ITEM. IT MAKES PEOPLE TALK
HOSPITALITY DESIGN

IN CONTEXT

FOCUS
A new kind of interior

FIELD
Interior design

BEFORE
1898 Swiss hotelier César Ritz is the first to install a bathroom in every guest room at his Hôtel Ritz in Paris.

1920 Prohibition, a ban on the production and sale of alcohol, comes into effect in the US, leading to the creation of illicit drinking dens known as speakeasies.

AFTER
1929 British architect Oswald Milne transforms the lobby of Claridge's Hotel, in London's Mayfair, using Art Deco style.

1984 US entrepreneurs Ian Schrager and Steve Rubell open Morgans, the world's first boutique hotel, on New York's Madison Avenue.

A type of interior design that focuses on commercial spaces, hospitality design is most closely associated with hotels, restaurants, bars, and clubs, although it also extends to fitness venues, spas, and even airports.

The aim of hospitality design is to elevate a functional space by creating a particular style or mood, while maximizing financial gain.

New demand
The early 20th century brought significant societal changes in the US and Europe. Life was faster thanks to mass communication, and social liberation resulted in large numbers of women going out to eat and socialize. The Roaring Twenties were famous for their wild parties and excesses, which even Prohibition could not curb.

The emergence of train, car, and – eventually – plane travel, along with an increase in people's disposable income and holiday leave, led to a demand for new accommodation options – and more of them.

Hotel empires
US businessman Conrad Hilton bought his first hotel in 1919. The Mobley in Cisco, Texas, was a popular lodging for workers at a nearby oil field. Capitalizing on the Texas oil boom, Hilton continued to buy lodgings, slowly building a property empire that became a chain of hotels.

The first hotel to bear the Hilton name was also the first to be built from scratch. Designed by the architectural firm Lang and Witchell, the Dallas Hilton opened in 1925. The 14-storey U-shaped brick building was innovative for stacking its services, including laundry chutes and lifts, along the

A poet could write volumes about diners, because they're so beautiful. They're brightly lit, with chrome and booths and Naugahyde and great waitresses.
David Lynch
Food & Wine, 2012

See also: Industrial design 146–47 ▪ Promoting travel 182–83 ▪ Material-led furniture design 186–87 ▪ Branding 200–07 ▪ Mid-Century Modern 216–21 ▪ Lighting design 222–23 ▪ Corporate identity 234–35

The airy lobby of New York's Waldorf Astoria hotel, bought by Conrad Hilton in 1949, is a quintessential expression of Art Deco style.

This lively period also saw the professionalization of the interior design industry, largely thanks to the efforts of Dorothy Draper, who designed many iconic hospitality venues from the 1930s to the 1960s.

Food and drink

Many of the restaurants, cafés, and bars that opened during this time to cater for a newly mobile population opted into the new design trend, too. Dining interiors were influenced by their location, clientele, and the type of food or drink served. For example, in the US in the 1920s, new kinds of casual eateries – such as cafeterias, tearooms, and drive-ins – blossomed, along with speakeasies and underground bars. Meanwhile existing establishments, like the classic diner, acquired a new machine-age aesthetic inspired by the locomotive. ▪

western facade, which faced the hot setting sun, while most of the guest rooms faced east, to avoid the searing Texas heat.

Where Hilton led, other entrepreneurs followed, with competing chains such as Sheraton (established in 1937), Marriott (1957), and Hyatt (1957) amassing large numbers of hotels under their brands. While the decor of the grand hotels from the late 19th century was inspired by castles and palaces, chain hotels tended to have uniform interiors so that guests would feel at home in any one of their hundreds of branches.

Besides chain hotels, the boom in the hospitality industry also led to the transformation of old hotels and the opening of new establishments with interiors drawn from a variety of styles – from Art Nouveau to Bauhaus.

Dorothy Draper

One of the most influential interior decorators of the 20th century, Dorothy Draper (née Tuckerman) was born in 1889 into a wealthy family in Orange County, New York State.

Despite having no formal training or experience other than decorating her own home, in 1925 Dorothy Draper set up an interior design business and remained at the helm until her retirement in 1960. Among her clients were many high-end establishments, such as Arrowhead Springs Hotel in San Bernardino, California (1938–39), the Mayflower Hotel in Washington, DC (1941), and Palácio Quitandinha in Petrópolis, Brazil (1942–44).

Draper embraced all decorative styles, liberally borrowing from any period or place; in doing so, she created her own style, which she called Modern Baroque. Rejecting any kind of reductivism or minimalism, she combined colours and patterns in a riot of exuberance that became known as the "Draper Touch". By the time she died, in 1969, Draper had become a household name.

THE LIQUIDATION OF ART
DESIGN FOR SOCIAL CHANGE

IN CONTEXT

FOCUS
Creative output with a social purpose

FIELD
Graphic design, product design, architecture

BEFORE
1907 A group of German artists and designers form the Deutscher Werkbund, which aims to apply industrial techniques to traditional crafts.

1917 The Russian Revolution begins. It leads to the birth of the Soviet Union, where art becomes propaganda.

AFTER
1960s Artists Jan Kubíček and Vladislav Mirvald spearhead the Constructivist movement in Czechoslovakia.

1979 US artist Barbara Kruger develops her signature text-based works, inspired by Alexander Rodchenko's Constructivist style.

Emerging as a pivotal theme in the creative industry in the early 20th century, design for social change is an approach to art and design that addresses – and intends to solve – social, political, or economic issues. In the majority of cases, design for social change rejects aesthetics for aesthetics' sake, focusing instead on the impact of a designed image, product, or building on the individuals and societies that will experience it.

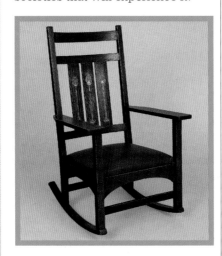

In this Mission-style rocking chair made by Harvey Ellis in 1903, the only nods to decoration are the copper and bronze inlays on the back slats.

Examples of a socially focused approach to art and design can be recognized as early as the Arts and Crafts movement of the late 19th century. Emerging as a response to the dehumanizing effects of industrialization, this movement countered the heartlessness of mass production by championing craftsmanship and the design of objects that were simultaneously aesthetically pleasing and highly functional.

Bauhaus influence
In 1919, the Berlin-born architect Walter Gropius founded the Bauhaus School with the primary objective of unifying art, craft, and technology in order to inspire the creation of more functional and accessible design solutions.

The Bauhaus approach centred around improving the living conditions of the masses. A celebrated example of this type of social design is the Weissenhof Estate in the German city of Stuttgart, which was built in 1927 and overseen by pioneering Bauhaus architect Ludwig Mies van der Rohe. Created as a response to the pressing housing shortage in Germany following

See also: The Arts and Crafts movement 112–19 ▪ Deutscher Werkbund 162 ▪ Political messaging 164–69 ▪ Bauhaus 170–71 ▪ Branding 200–07

I reduced painting to its logical conclusion and exhibited three canvases: red, blue and yellow. I affirmed: it's all over.
Alexander Rodchenko
On his monochromatic works of 1921

World War I, the estate embodied principles of accessibility and functionality throughout its 21 buildings, which were designed by several European architects, including Le Corbusier, Victor Bourgeois, and Peter Behrens.

Soviet Constructivism

Designing for social change was also key to the development of the newly formed Soviet Union. Constructivism had started to emerge during the years of the Russian Revolution, but it came of age in the 1920s and 1930s, with its design approach reflecting the Soviet government's vision for a more egalitarian society.

Constructivists rejected the emotional and aesthetic aspects of art, stressing the importance of function. The socially useful imagery, products, and architecture that they produced mirrored the

increasingly industrial landscape and upheld Communist values by fusing them with the rituals of everyday life.

Among those advocating purpose-driven art and design was Alexander Rodchenko. At the 1925 Paris World Fair, he presented an installation called *Workers' Club*. It consisted of wooden furniture elements – among them, a reading table and a chess-playing station – illustrating a model space where the working classes could pursue educational and leisure activities.

Other notable examples of Constructivist design include El Lissitzky's propaganda materials and Varvara Stepanova's textiles, whose bold, geometric shapes, limited colour palette, and emphasis on functionality over decoration marked a radical departure from earlier nature-inspired designs. The language of abstract forms typical of Alexandra Ekster's experimental art has also come to define the Constructivist movement. ▪

Soviet architect Alexey Shchusev's 1929 sketch for a government complex in the Uzbek city of Samarkand features cubes, cylindrical towers, and other typically Constructivist elements.

Alexander Rodchenko

Born in Saint Petersburg, in the Russian Empire, in 1891, Alexander Rodchenko was a key figure in the Russian avant-garde and a founding member of the Constructivist movement. He began his artistic training in 1910 at the Kazan Art School, where he met textile designer Varvara Stepanova, who later became his wife. In 1914, he joined Moscow's Stroganov Academy, renowned for its decorative and applied arts programme.

Celebrated for his bold compositions, in 1921 Rodchenko contributed three monochromatic canvases (*Pure Red Colour*, *Pure Yellow Colour*, and *Pure Blue Colour*) to the 5x5=25 exhibition of abstract art in Moscow. He then declared that the works he had submitted represented the death of painting.

Rodchenko's work included book covers, posters, and advertisements. His influence is notably present in the work of contemporary artists such as Barbara Kruger, whose style has been appropriated by 21st-century youth culture brands like Supreme. Rodchenko died in 1956.

SPEED, SAFETY, AND CONVENIENCE
PROMOTING TRAVEL

IN CONTEXT

FOCUS
Vehicles designed to offer comfort in compact spaces

FIELD
Transport design, industrial design

BEFORE
1830 The world's first inter-city passenger railway is opened. Steam-powered trains travel on the line between the cities of Liverpool and Manchester in the UK.

AFTER
1964 The Shinkansen, commonly known as the bullet train, is launched in Japan. Travelling between Tokyo and Osaka, it is the world's first high-speed train.

1990s To improve their sustainability, planes start to use lightweight materials. Carbon fibre is used to construct the fuselage, and a light aluminium-lithium alloy replaces aluminium parts.

Before the early 20th century, train travel provided fairly unpleasant journeys with wagon-style seating, chuffing exhausts, grinding sounds, and frequent derailments. As rail technology improved, the perception that train travel was dangerous persisted. The railway industry had rising costs and an image problem that needed to be solved to attract passengers.

Leaps in engineering lead to **faster, safer trains** with **greater capacity** for customers...

... but train travel's image as unsafe, uncomfortable and dirty means people need to be **encouraged to use** rail services.

Train carriages are **redesigned** inside and out to make rail travel **more comfortable and appealing**.

Eye-catching branding and posters that suggest **glamour and sophistication** tempt customers onto the trains.

Trains become a popular and luxurious way to travel.

See also: Transport and portability 32–33 ▪ Ford Model T 154–55 ▪ Streamlining 196–99 ▪ Branding 200–07 ▪ Corporate identity 234–35

A brand new look

To attract wealthier customers, trains had to be carefully designed and presented as a respectable mode of transport. Locomotives were made more elegant: their boilers were clad in smooth casings; domes and chimneys were trimmed in brass and copper; and railway companies added their liveries.

Pullman company posters in 1927 used stylized graphics and fashions of the time to present their service from London, UK to Vichy, France as a luxurious way to travel.

The design of carriages developed from compartments of eight or twelve seats depending on the class, to coaches with side corridors and concertina-like connections that gave everyone access to toilet facilities and the restaurant car. *Compagnie Internationale des Wagons-Lits* launched a network of luxury trains, including the Orient Express, while Pullman cars with opulent saloons were introduced in Europe and the US.

By the 1930s, diesel- and electric-powered trains began to appear. General Motors produced elegant locomotives with slanted and curved bonnets, and their designer, Leland A. Knickerbocker, devised a range of striking liveries. Air-conditioned observation cars enabled passengers to enjoy the passing landscape, and some had sleeping compartments with couchette berths.

Air travel takes off

By the 1950s, for those who were affluent but time poor, air travel became more enticing. Once again, design was used to convince potential passengers that a new mode of travel was both safe and respectable. Each airline commissioned a unique visual identity – and this branding was present from the planning of the journey in travel brochures through to the design of tickets, airport signage, and branded counters. Inside the plane cabin, the environment was carefully styled by industrial and interior designers in the modernist aesthetic of the time.

As the popularity of air travel grew, railways tried to compete. A new generation of high-speed trains emulated planes for aerodynamic reasons, and the design of coach interiors also began to resemble plane cabins. Rows of high-backed seats with luggage racks above became the standard whether travelling by air or rail. ▪

Textile designs for transport

In the 1920s, Frank Pick of London Transport saw an opportunity to influence public taste. He employed modern artists to design posters promoting travel and hired the architect Charles Holden to design elegant new stations, with lighting, signage, and advertising all carefully integrated into the plans.

Pick also hired the acclaimed Modernist textile designers Marion Dorn and Enid Marx to design upholstery for buses, trams, and tube trains. Both designers realized that strong, saturated colours would shine through surface dirt and so their initial upholstery used contrasting red, black, and green. The colours were woven in a durable woollen fabric, known as moquette, and bright, repetitive patterns were ideal to enliven vehicle interiors. Their work proved highly influential and echoes of their approaches can still be discerned in the upholstery of British public transport today.

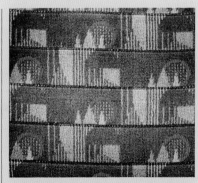

Moquette covers are still used on public transport in London. This print features a geometric pattern of abstract, but still recognizable, London landmarks.

A SPIRIT, AN ATTITUDE

ART DECO

IN CONTEXT

FOCUS
A blend of tradition and geometry

FIELD
Architecture, furniture design, graphic design

BEFORE
1914 The Art Nouveau style, which had a formative influence on Art Deco style, starts to decline in popularity as World War I begins.

AFTER
1976 The Chrysler Building in New York City, US is declared a National Historic Landmark. The skyscraper's architecture is widely considered the epitome of Art Deco design.

2018 The bay area in South Mumbai, India is recognized as a UNESCO World Heritage site for its Art Deco buildings. The architecture has been described as Indo-Deco.

The 1925 *Exposition Internationale des Arts Décoratifs et Industriels Modernes* – also known as the Paris Exposition – was a grand showcase of decorative arts and established the Art Deco style. Featuring geometric shapes and clean lines, Art Deco became popular across Europe and the US, and spread east to Japan, China, and India where it was blended with local design styles to create a mix of old and new.

A sign of prosperity
In 1926, Japan's consumer boom created a fashion for European luxury goods and American culture. Prince Yasuhiko, son of Emperor Hirohito, had attended the Paris Exposition, and invited designers Henri Rapin and René Lalique to design a new Art Deco mansion in Tokyo. Soon, new passenger ships with Art Deco interiors, and Art Deco hotels, department stores, and cinemas were built in Tokyo, Yokohama, Osaka, and Kobe.

Many Japanese Art Deco buildings and ships were destroyed during World War II or by earthquakes. The Hikawa Maru, a 1930s passenger liner with stylish Art Deco saloons, is a rare survivor and is preserved as a reminder of the style's influence in Japan.

Cosmopolitan designs
Shanghai, China's largest port, also experienced a great expansion and economic boom in the inter-war era. Already a highly cosmopolitan

The Cathay Theatre in Shanghai, China, built in 1932, was one of the first cinemas to be built in the city. It features typical Art Deco geometric shapes and sleek vertical lines.

See also: Historicism and Neo-Gothic 104–05 ▪ The Arts and Crafts movement 112–19 ▪ Art Nouveau 132–33 ▪ Modernism 188–93 ▪ Urban design 248–49

László Hudec

Born in Banská Bystrica, Austria-Hungary (now Slovakia) in 1893, László Hudec studied architecture at Budapest University, and graduated in 1914. He served in the Austro-Hungarian army during World War I, but in 1916 he was captured by Russian forces and taken to Siberia as a prisoner of war. In 1918, while he was being transported as a prisoner, Hudec managed to escape and made his way to the Russia-China border on foot. Hudec used forged documents to cross the border into China and from there he travelled to Shanghai.

Hudec found employment at R.A. Curry, an American architecture firm in Shanghai, and subsequently established his own practice in 1925. During the next 15 years, Hudec was responsible for many of Shanghai's finest Art Deco buildings, including the city's first skyscraper in 1931.

In 1947, Hudec moved to Italy and then to the US in 1950, where he worked in the Architecture faculty of the University of California. In 1958, Hudec died of a heart attack during an earthquake.

city, a large number of Eastern Europeans settled there bringing with them avant garde ideas about architecture and design.

During the mid-1920s, the businessman Victor Sassoon commissioned Shanghai-based architects Palmer & Turner to design the Cathay Hotel. Completed in 1929, it was the city's first major Art Deco building and the first of several new luxury hotels to be built there. Subsequently, more Art Deco buildings appeared including ballrooms, department stores, cinemas, and apartment blocks. One prominent example is the 20-storey Park Hotel which was completed in 1934. It was built to a design by architect László Hudec, who sought to make it resemble a New York skyscraper.

New style for a new district

In the port city of Mumbai, India, an architectural revolution also took place. Scottish architect John Begg had co-founded the Indian Institute of Architects in 1917, nurturing the first generation of Indian-trained

practitioners who, in the mid-1930s, designed nearly all of the buildings in the new bay area of the city. Their Art Deco cinemas, apartment blocks, and commercial buildings were notable for having modern curved corners, projecting concrete balconies, sunshades, fluting, and fins. In the 1940s, Maharajah Umaid Singh, employed Polish artist Stefan Norblin to create

interiors for a new palace in Jodhpur. Norblin painted Art Deco murals and chose lush furnishings in the style, creating grand, modern spaces that contrasted with the palace's traditional exterior.

The Art Deco designs found in the major cities of Japan, China, and India were reflective of the prosperous, outward-looking culture that the style inspired. ▪

Art Deco buildings often feature several key traits that make them stand out from other buildings. Some have straight lines and geometric shapes while later examples are streamlined. Visual interest is created with stylized engravings and sculptures.

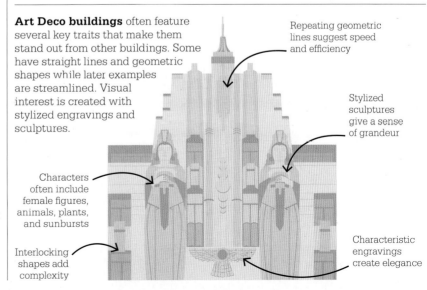

Repeating geometric lines suggest speed and efficiency

Stylized sculptures give a sense of grandeur

Characters often include female figures, animals, plants, and sunbursts

Characteristic engravings create elegance

Interlocking shapes add complexity

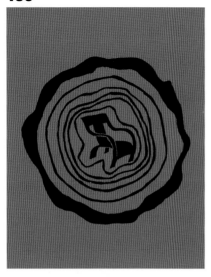

EXPERIMENTS IN WOOD
MATERIAL-LED FURNITURE DESIGN

IN CONTEXT

FOCUS
Manipulating materials into aesthetic furniture

FIELD
Furniture design, product design, architecture

BEFORE
1919 The Bauhaus school is founded in Germany. Its slogan "art into industry" encourages some of its members to experiment with materials and technology.

1925 Marcel Breuer creates his "Wassily" armchair, which is based around a tubular steel frame.

AFTER
1965 Danish designer Verner Panton develops his stacking chair, using plastic rather than wood or steel.

1985 The "SingSingSing" armchair by Japanese designer Shiro Kuramata is based around a folded sheet of steel.

The superior lightness, stability, and malleability of bent plywood has had a huge impact on furniture design. It is made from thin layers – or "plies" – of wood veneer that are glued together with the grain of each layer placed in alternating directions for additional strength.

Applying heat and pressure allows plywood to be manipulated into complex shapes that can be used in furniture.

Early pioneers of plywood furniture from the 19th century included German-Austrian cabinet maker Michael Thonet, who designed a bentwood chair in 1870.

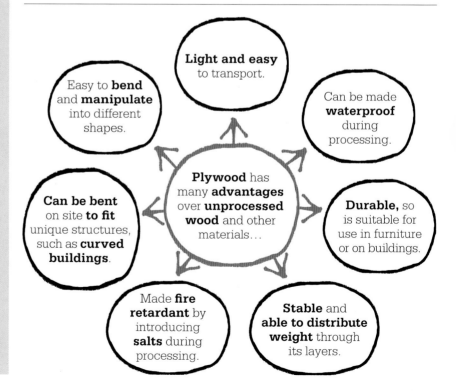

Easy to **bend** and **manipulate** into different shapes.

Light and easy to transport.

Can be made **waterproof** during processing.

Plywood has many **advantages** over **unprocessed wood** and other materials…

Can be bent on site **to fit** unique structures, such as **curved buildings**.

Durable, so is suitable for use in furniture or on buildings.

Made **fire retardant** by introducing **salts** during processing.

Stable and **able to distribute weight** through its layers.

See also: Bauhaus 170–71 ▪ Mid-century Modern 216–21 ▪ G Plan design 226–27 ▪ Flat-pack furniture 228–29 ▪ Eco design 258–65

The "small Paimio", also known as Armchair 42, was designed by Alvar Aalto in 1932 for use at a sanatorium. Its seat and back are formed from a single piece of plywood.

Two US furniture makers also experimented with the material: Isaac Cole created a one-piece plywood chair in c. 1873, and George Gardner presented his bent plywood furniture at the Centennial Exposition in Philadelphia in 1876. However, it was in the 1930s – with industrial production and inventions such as the hot press and veneer rotary cutter – that plywood furniture began to be made in its modern form.

Plywood innovation

Finnish architect and designer Alvar Aalto began to experiment with bent laminated plywood in the late 1920s, working alongside his wife, architect Aino Aalto. Their first chair consisted of a bent plywood seat with a metal frame, but by the time they developed the Paimio chair in 1931–32, they had

increased the strength of plywood to such an extent that the Paimio's legs and armrests could be made from plywood too. Armchair 406, produced in 1939, was the first to have a cantilevered design that combined plywood with linen belt-webbing. These designs revealed the huge potential of bent plywood.

The Bauhaus school's wood workshop was another important site for experiments with bent plywood, with Bauhaus founder Walter Gropius heading the carpentry workshop in the early years. After the school was closed by the Nazis in 1933, its furniture

designer Marcel Breuer found exile in London, where he produced a number of plywood pieces, including his short chair and armchair, both released in 1936.

Modernist masterpieces

In the US, Charles and Ray Eames began working with plywood, after Charles collaborated with Finnish architect Eero Saarinen on a group of award-winning wooden furniture designs in 1940. Following this, the Eames built a machine to bend and laminate wood in their apartment. A moulded plywood sculpture by Ray Eames from 1943 shows how the material could be pressed into three-dimensional shapes. In 1946, the Eames designed the LCM (Lounge Chair Metal), using two moulded-plywood panels to form the seat and back, supported by a chromium-plated frame. This is one of several moulded-plywood chairs made by the Eames that are classics of Mid-century Modern design; another is the Eames lounge chair (1956), one of the most recognizable chairs of the period. ▪

Alvar Aalto

Born in Kuortane, Finland, in 1898, Alvar Aalto was a Finnish architect and designer, and a key figure of Mid-century Modern design. He studied architecture at the Helsinki University of Technology, before setting up his own office in 1923. He worked largely in Finland but also completed a number of significant projects overseas. Aalto was attracted to the modernist style, incorporating organic forms and prioritizing the use of wood in his works. In collaboration with his first wife, architect Aino Aalto, he worked on projects such as the

Paimio Sanatorium (1933) and the Aalto house (1936), for which he designed not only the structure of the building, but also its interiors, furniture, lighting, and glassware. This collaboration also produced innovations in furniture design, including the Paimio chair. In 1976, Aalto died at the age of 78 in Helsinki, Finland.

Key works

1932 Model 60 stacking stool
1932 Paimio chair
1939 Armchair 406

FORM
FOLLOWS
FUNCTION

MODERNISM

IN CONTEXT

FOCUS
**Using design to make
the world a better place**

FIELD
**Graphic design, product
design, architecture,
interior design**

BEFORE
1919 Architect Walter Gropius
founds the Bauhaus design
school in Weimar, Germany.

1929 Ludwig Mies van der
Rohe's German pavilion for
the International Exposition
in Barcelona features a free
plan and a floating roof.

AFTER
1948–49 US architect Philip
Johnson pioneers the use of
glass in architecture in the
Glass House, his home in
New Canaan, Connecticut.

1965 Construction begins on
the Brutalist Barbican Estate in
the City district of London, UK.

A product is designed to do a job or solve a problem **effectively** and **efficiently**.

The **function** of the object is more **important** than its looks.

The **object's purpose** may determine **elements of the design**, such as the materials from which it is made, and **its shape**.

Form follows function.

The Modernist movement was founded on a progressive ideology that aimed to sweep away the old world order and introduce a new society informed by the latest scientific and technological discoveries.

The movement took its first steps in the late 19th century, but it gathered momentum after World War I, taking hold as a way to re-imagine society after years of violent destruction. It looked towards redressing the wrongs of the world by redesigning the most basic elements of life – housing, furniture, and domestic goods.

Modernism dominated architecture and design between the 1930s and the 1960s, but its impact was also felt across the creative arts – from literature and painting, to music and cinema – and in fields such as philosophy and psychoanalysis.

During this time, several influential European architects and designers – among them, Bauhaus directors Walter Gropius and Ludwig Mies van der Rohe, as well as Italian architect Lina Bo Bardi – chose to escape oppressive governments in their own countries and moved to the US, South America, and Australia. This Modernist migration

Le Corbusier

Born in Switzerland in 1887, Charles-Édouard Jeanneret moved to Paris aged 30 and adopted the name Le Corbusier in 1920. In his 1923 book *Towards a New Architecture*, he rejected past styles and non-structural decoration, arguing for a machine-age, functionalist approach using reinforced concrete and steel. He also proposed new ways of building cities, with tower blocks served by multi-lane highways.

Before World War II, Le Corbusier built mainly individual houses with clean lines, geometric forms, and bare facades. After the war, he put his communal-housing ideas into practice with the Unité d'Habitation (1947–52) in Marseille, France, a self-contained city in rough concrete.

Le Corbusier died in 1965. Although he is criticized for inspiring soulless tower blocks, as many as 17 of his projects in seven countries are designated UNESCO World Heritage Sites.

Key works

1950–55 Notre-Dame du Haut, Ronchamp, France
1951–56 Chandigarh, India

See also: Movable type and early graphic design 70–77 ▪ Sans serif fonts 102–03 ▪ The Arts and Crafts movement 112–19 ▪ Bauhaus 170–71 ▪ Futurism 175 ▪ Mid-century Modern 216–21

helped what had been until then a largely European movement become an international style.

Interwar idealism

The roots of the Modernist movement can be traced back to the Bauhaus, the German art school that operated between 1919 and 1933, when the advent of the Nazi regime forced it to close down.

Bauhaus-trained architects shared an idealistic aim: to address post-war housing shortages and rebuild Europe. Many designed socially conscious mass housing schemes, although not all of them came to fruition. In Germany, Ernst May's New Frankfurt, a large-scale settlement built between 1928 and 1930, featured high-standard residential blocks with

De La Warr Pavilion is a Modernist waterfront cultural centre in Bexhill-on-Sea, UK. It was built in 1935 by architects Erich Mendelsohn and Serge Chermayeff.

airy apartments, green areas, and community facilities such as schools, theatres, and playgrounds.

Architect J.J.P. Oud's De Kiefhoek estate (1928–30), in Rotterdam, The Netherlands, comprised about 300 two-storey, three-bedroom houses. The development, built for working-class families, included a church and facilities such as playgrounds, shops, and a boiler room.

New materials, new forms

Modernists embraced reinforced concrete, steel, and other innovative materials. These, along with advances in engineering, led to new architectural forms that were no longer dependent on thick, load-bearing walls. The results were buildings with glass facades, flat roofs, and uninterrupted windows, such as Villa Savoye, which was built between 1928 and 1931 in Poissy, north-west of Paris, by Le Corbusier and his cousin Pierre Jeanneret.

Space and light and order. Those are things that men need just as much as they need bread or a place to sleep.
Le Corbusier

The designs of Finnish architect Alvar Aalto also favoured new technologies and the spirit of Modernism but did not adhere to the material constraints of high Modernism, instead embracing the use of timber. Surrounded by the timber of Finnish forests, Aalto believed that natural materials could bring warmth and humanism to forms that were »

rationally and structurally modern, such as in his Paimio Sanatorium building, completed in 1933.

Interior design

Le Corbusier believed that a house was a "machine for living in" – that is, a tool where functionality outweighs decoration. He was inspired by the pure pragmatism of modern engineering, arguing that the results of this process tend to be quite beautiful. Indeed, this era is also known as the machine age, with industrial designers like American Henry Dreyfuss creating items designed to improve modern life in the home, whether clocks, toasters, or vacuum cleaners. As in architecture, the design aesthetic of the machine age favoured steel and anything mechanical.

The ideal of the functional home also fuelled innovations in the field of furniture, and designers experimented with materials such as bent steel and bent plywood. Irish architect and furniture designer Eileen Gray was one of the first to develop furniture using bent tubular stainless steel. Her E-1027 side table was designed to serve her guests tea at her own house while standing rather than bending down to a low table, making it truly functional.

Alvar Aalto and his wife Aino spent five years experimenting with the bending of wood. This led to the development of several design classics of the 1930s, including the cantilevered Model 31 armchair and L-leg stool.

Graphic design and De Stijl

Modernism changed graphic design and typography from decorative styles that filled every available space to a more spare, structured approach. Designers adhered to a grid, used blocks of colour, sans serif fonts, and significant amounts of negative or white space to accentuate the focus on visual clarity.

The Modernist approach is evident in designs that emerged from the Bauhaus printing workshop, led by Austrian graphic designer Herbert Bayer. Features of the Bauhaus graphic style include minimalist layouts, geometric compositions, and limited colour palettes. After the Bauhaus moved to Dessau in 1925, Bayer developed the Universal typeface, a simple, clear sans serif font with no embellishment and no capital letters, which were deemed unnecessary.

Modernist graphic designers were also influenced by the Dutch De Stijl group founded in 1917. The group – which counted among its members painters Theo van Doesburg and Piet Mondrian, and architects J.J.P. Oud and Gerrit Rietveld – favoured simplicity and abstraction, reducing elements to pure geometric forms and primary colours. These ideals reflected their utopian vision of a modern era of order and harmony. Examples of De Stijl graphics can be seen in the De Stijl journal and in Theo van Doesburg's De Stijl typeface, based on the geometry of the square.

> The future projects light, the past only clouds.
> **Eileen Gray**

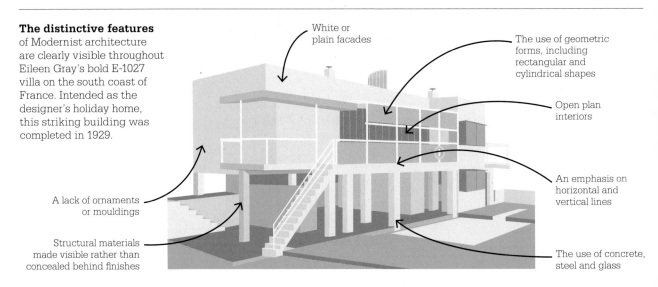

The distinctive features of Modernist architecture are clearly visible throughout Eileen Gray's bold E-1027 villa on the south coast of France. Intended as the designer's holiday home, this striking building was completed in 1929.

White or plain facades

The use of geometric forms, including rectangular and cylindrical shapes

Open plan interiors

An emphasis on horizontal and vertical lines

A lack of ornaments or mouldings

Structural materials made visible rather than concealed behind finishes

The use of concrete, steel and glass

The Model 41 armchair, also known as Paimio, is one of a series of furniture designs created by Alvar Aalto in the early 1930s using bent plywood.

Beyond Modernism

Emerging in the 1950s, Brutalism was a new architectural style that took the concrete and geometric shapes of Modernism one step further. Brutalism – whose name comes from *béton brut*, French for "raw concrete" – is marked by the abundant use of poured, unfinished concrete creating a monolithic appearance. Brutalist buildings have an imposing, and heavy-looking aesthetic, with repeated shapes formed through prefabricated elements or with windows that are typically small.

Often used for high- or mid-rise buildings, hospitals, and universities, Brutalism can be found across Europe, including the UK; in the Soviet Union and other communist countries of the time such as Yugoslavia, Czechoslovakia, and Bulgaria; and further afield. Famous examples include the Unité d'Habitation de Marseille, conceived in 1920 and completed in 1952 by Le Corbusier; and Litchfield Towers, three concrete edifices for student accommodation at the University of Pittsburgh, Pennsylvania, in the US, designed by Deeter & Ritchey (1963).

Mid-century Modern

In the late 20th century, Modernism and, especially, Brutalism were criticized for a lack of consideration of site and climate, and for being responsible for a number of drab housing estates. However, in the 21st century, these old buildings have been embraced again, and what was considered ugly is now celebrated. In architecture, interior design, furniture, and graphic design, what is now referred to as Mid-century Modern remains popular today. This term embraces clean lines and functionality, as well as the new materials, furniture, and products that date from the Modernist period of 1933–65. ∎

La Pyramide building, designed by Italian architect Rinaldo Olivieri and built 1968–73, was one of the first high-rises in Abidjan, Côte d'Ivoire.

African Modernism

The influence of Modernism in Africa started in the mid-1940s, when British architects Maxwell Fry and Jane Drew brought the style to the British colonies of Ghana, Nigeria, Gambia, and Sierra Leone. The style proliferated thanks to the work of invited architects from Britain, Europe, the US, and the African diaspora collaborating on projects with local architects.

As the continent went through a process of decolonization – with 32 African countries claiming independence between 1957 and 1966 – Modernist buildings took on a symbolic role as markers of a burgeoning national identity.

Although Modernist constructions in Africa are largely public buildings – such as government centres, banks, conference halls, and universities – there are also apartment blocks, water towers, and mosques created in the style. Many of these buildings lean towards Brutalism, with blocky geometries and the extensive use of concrete.

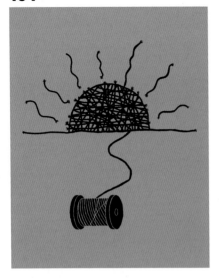

A NEW WORD AND A NEW MATERIAL
DAWN OF SYNTHETIC FABRICS

Although their production often involves extensive processing and treatment, natural textiles still originate from an animal or plant source. Synthetic, or artificial, fibres, on the other hand, are created in a chemistry lab.

Early synthetics aimed to replicate the look and feel of natural fibres. This quest began in the 1850s, when an infectious disease targeting silkworm colonies spread across France, affecting the country's production of silk. The economic impact was so severe that the government tasked chemist Louis Pasteur with finding ways to stop the disease from spreading.

Silk from cellulose
The first rudimentary "artificial silk" was developed in 1855 by Swiss chemist Georges Audemars, who dipped a needle into a solution of mulberry-bark pulp and rubber to create silk-like threads. However, this method was too slow to be commercially viable.

A more effective cellulose-based alternative was developed in 1884 by French chemist Hilaire de Chardonnet. His "Chardonnet silk" was created using sulphuric acid and copies of silkworm spinnerets made from glass. Unfortunately, it was highly flammable, and was soon removed from the market.

Research into synthetic textiles continued into the 20th century. It was partly driven by the need

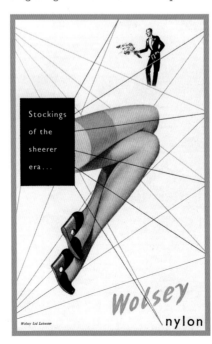

Stockings of the sheerer era...

Wolsey

nylon

Wolsey Ltd Leicester

Nylon stockings were launched at the 1939 New York World's Fair. They proved so popular that riots broke out in 1945–46, when they returned to the shops after a wartime hiatus.

See also: Early textiles 24–29 ▪ Manufacturing textiles 84–91 ▪ Natural luxury 174 ▪ Safety fabrics 244–47 ▪ Eco design 258–65

In over four thousand years, textiles have seen only three basic developments. Nylon is a fourth.
Fortune magazine, 1938

to find alternatives, should natural materials be in short supply, but also by a desire to "improve" natural fabrics – making them stronger, more durable, or more elastic.

A new material

The first wholly synthetic fibre was created in 1935 by US chemist Wallace Carothers at DuPont. Carothers was researching polymers, materials made of long chains of repeating molecules. He managed to synthesize a viscous stretchy substance from which he could draw out strong silk-like filaments of polyamide 6-6 – nylon – that stretched the length of the lab's hallways.

More synthetics arrived in the decades that followed: in 1941, British chemists John Rex Whinfield and James Tennant Dickson created polyester; and in 1950, DuPont developed the first commercially successful acrylic fibre, Orlon. Later innovations in

The rise of low-cost "fast fashion" during the 1990s was directly linked to the popularity of easy-care clothing made from synthetic fabrics.

synthetics have led to great leaps in performance textiles, such as those used for sportswear. For example, the extra stretch offered by spandex allows unrestricted movement, and moisture-wicking technology – in which sweat droplets are drawn out rather than being absorbed into the fabric – greatly increases comfort during physical activity.

Other desirable technical properties include water repellency and resistance to stains, bacteria, and abrasion. Attractive qualities such as these have encouraged consumers to open their wardrobe doors to synthetic fabrics – and polyester is now the most widely used clothing fibre in the world.

Eco-friendly alternatives

Synthetic fabrics are a significant source of global pollution: they are made from oil, using energy-intensive processes, and they take a long time to decompose in landfill. However, the continued popularity of properties linked to synthetics is encouraging designers to explore sustainable alternatives made from recycled or bio-based sources. ∎

Wallace Carothers

Born in Burlington, Iowa, in 1896, Wallace Hume Carothers attributed his great interest in science to a series of books by chemist Robert Kennedy Duncan.

At the age of 19, Carothers enrolled at Missouri's Tarkio College, intending to study English literature. After switching to chemistry, his aptitude soon became clear, and Carothers was asked to take charge of the university's chemistry department even though still a student himself. After obtaining a Master's degree and PhD at the University of Illinois, Carothers moved to Harvard in 1926 to teach organic chemistry.

Carothers's reputation as an original thinker resulted in an approach from chemical giant DuPont – along with an invitation to lead its experimental department in Wilmington, Delaware. He initially turned down the post, fearing that his fragile mental health would prove an obstacle, but eventually accepted in 1928. In 1937, two years after inventing nylon, Carothers died by suicide without knowing the impact of his work.

DYNAMIC FUNCTIONALISM

STREAMLINING

IN CONTEXT

FOCUS
Aerodynamic design can be applied to mass-market products

FIELD
Vehicle design, product design

BEFORE
1899 Camille Jenatzy sets a new land-speed record with his streamlined vehicle, *La Jamais Contente*.

1920s Developments in steel technology enables curving shapes to be more easily fabricated at many scales. Even passenger ships were built with rounded superstructures.

AFTER
1953 General Motors develops the Firebird I, the first of a series of prototype cars inspired by contemporary fighter aircrafts. They include features such as tail fins that serve no practical use.

Streamlining, defined as the process of shaping an object for efficient movement through a liquid or gas, has had a major influence on design in the 20th century. Although it is often associated with the 1930s, when designers used it to give products a futuristic appeal, its roots lie in the late 19th century. This was a period of remarkable advancements in science and engineering, including breakthroughs in hydrodynamics that enhanced the efficiency of ship hulls, and aeronautics that enabled the first powered flights.

Both ship hulls and aircraft fuselages face resistance as they move, and this increases

See also: Ford Model T 154–55 ▪ Planned obsolescence 176–77 ▪ Promoting travel 182–83 ▪ Making things better 286–87

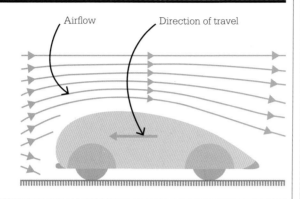

Airflow   Direction of travel

A "teardrop" shape, rounded at the front with a tapering rear, minimizes resistance when travelling at speed. Cars and other vehicles of the 1930s and 1940s often echoed this form, despite few reaching speeds that could fully benefit from it.

massively with speed. Engineers discovered that the "teardrop" shape, which is characterized by a rounded front and a tapered, pointed rear, minimizes this resistance and drag. This knowledge was put to effective military use during World War I, influencing the design of warship and submarine hulls, aircraft fuselages, and the torpedoes and bombs that were deployed.

Speed-inspired design

During the inter-war period, the pursuit of speed and the thrill of breaking records captured the imagination of designers and architects. The Swiss-French modernist architect Le Corbusier was captivated by the functionalism of Fiat's new concrete-framed car factory in Turin, which had a racing track on the roof for testing new vehicles. His German contemporary, Erich Mendelsohn, sought to encapsulate the essence of speed in his commercial building designs, generating a sense of exhilaration at the point of purchase.

In the 1920s, Mendelsohn travelled to the US aboard the liner, Columbus. Its curved forms and ribbon windows left a lasting impression on him, and inspired his

designs for the cinemas, department stores, and corporate headquarters that were later built in Berlin and elsewhere. In France, a similar aesthetic characterized by horizontally elongated forms came to be known as "moderne".

An economic lifeline

The Great Depression of the 1930s presented American businesses with a challenge: how to stimulate demand in a struggling economy? They were also faced with another predicament – their products were so well-made that there was little need for frequent replacements.

In response to this, Raymond Loewy, a French industrial designer who had emigrated to the US in 1919, proposed a novel solution. Loewy's idea was to restyle these products, creating designs so compelling that those who could afford it would be enticed to purchase the latest models. His theory was put to the test with his successful redesign of Coldspot refrigerators, which he transformed into sleek, curvaceous forms.

Loewy even created an "Evolution Chart of Design" to illustrate how various goods would progressively adopt streamlined »

Streamlining in architecture

Erich Mendelsohn, born in present-day Poland in 1887, was a German architect who gained recognition for his radical 1917 design for the Einstein Tower in Potsdam, Germany. The tower's curvilinear forms were intended for poured concrete construction, but as this technology was unfamiliar, brick was used with stucco dressing to lend Mendelsohn's desired fluid shapes.

Mendelsohn became famous for his streamlined department stores, cinemas, and office blocks. His style incorporated cylindrical and cuboid forms, and exaggerated horizontals. In 1933, he fled Nazi Germany to Britain, where, together with Russian-British architect Serge Chermayeff, he designed the De La Warr Pavilion at Bexhill-on-Sea. This striking example of modernist architecture featured expansive metal-framed windows and wide terraces. Mendelsohn moved the US in 1941, and remained there until his death in 1953.

The Einstein tower formed a key part of a science park dedicated to investigate physicist Albert Einstein's theories.

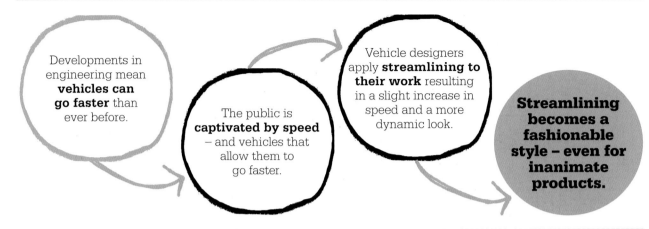

Developments in engineering mean **vehicles can go faster** than ever before.

The public is **captivated by speed** – and vehicles that allow them to go faster.

Vehicle designers apply **streamlining to their work** resulting in a slight increase in speed and a more dynamic look.

Streamlining becomes a fashionable style – even for inanimate products.

forms in the future. This suggested that consumers who wanted to keep up with the latest in styles would need to make new purchases annually. This approach arguably marked the beginning of the throw-away consumer culture.

Form over function?

Following his success with refrigerators, Raymond Loewy was hired by the Pennsylvania Railroad to streamline their express locomotives used to haul prestige trains, such as the 20th Century Limited, which connected New York and Washington, D.C. The railroad's publicists were delighted at the dynamic new image Loewy created. The engineers, however, pointed out that the extra layer of steel not only made the locomotives heavier and less efficient, but also made it more difficult for depot staff to access vital mechanical parts.

By the late 1930s, Loewy was only the most prominent member of a group of American industrial designers who shared his approach – other notable figures included Henry Dreyfuss, the designer of the "Model 150" Hoover vacuum cleaner, and Walter Dorwin Teague, who designed a series of highly successful cameras for Kodak. While the designs they produced were undoubtedly popular with the public, critics argued that these men were not specialists, and lacked the in-depth professional knowledge of engineers and architects. These designers, claimed the critics, were merely creating new casings for objects whose fundamental forms had been designed and engineered by more specialized experts.

As the economy began to recover in the late 1930s, the concept of streamlining became unavoidable. People could live in a streamline moderne villa, decorated with streamlined patterns on its wallpaper, carpets, and curtains, that was furnished with streamlined seating, tables, and lights. Outside the home, they could drive a streamlined car to a streamlined movie theatre, then eat in a streamlined diner. Indeed, the emergence of fast food was itself another manifestation of the desire to streamline everyday life. Even the process of digestion was not immune to this trend, with the latest pharmaceuticals claiming to "streamline" this natural process.

Other examples of streamlining were equally absurd. In Denmark, where bacon is a major export, the co-operative farming industry claimed to have bred a streamlined pig. And when a chrome, teardrop-shaped, streamline pencil sharpener – a stationary object with no need at all for aerodynamics – went on sale, critics of the streamlined style felt their scepticism was justified.

PRESENTING **THE COMET**

NEW STREAMLINED AIR-CONDITIONED TRAIN

The New York New Haven and Hartford RAILROAD CO.

TO OPERATE IN REGULAR SERVICE *between* BOSTON *and* PROVIDENCE

This advertising poster for the New York, New Haven and Hartford Railroad from 1935 features the Comet, a diesel-electric streamliner. It was encased in varnished aluminium.

The Mercedes-Benz 540K Streamliner, was a one-off built in 1938 for a race between Berlin and Rome. It was designed to optimize aerodynamic performance for long-distance driving at high speeds.

Despite such criticism, by the late 1940s, streamlining had become a popular and effective strategy to make products stand out and succeed in the market. This was epitomized in 1949, when Raymond Loewy featured on the cover of *Time* magazine with the caption "He Streamlines the Sales Curve."

A new generation

For the most part, the vehicles of the 1930s rarely hit speeds sufficient for streamlined bodywork to lend any significant advantage. By the 1960s, however, a new generation of faster cars, trains, jet planes, and spacecraft were being developed that genuinely required streamlined designs.

The Boeing 707 jetliner and the Japanese Shinkansen bullet train epitomized this new era. Although each was very different in terms of underlying engineering, they both adopted similar external shapes out of necessity – their bulbous nose cones were vital for minimizing drag and turbulence.

Engineers used wind tunnels to test vehicle designs, using plumes of smoke to reveal turbulence and eddies. This research helped to improve the speed and overall efficiency of vehicles. However, this focus on aerodynamics led to a convergence in designs, possibly resulting in less distinctive marques than those of earlier years.

In recent years, streamlined artefacts from the mid-20th century have become coveted items for collectors. These items are valued not just for their aesthetic appeal, but also for what they represent – a time of technological optimism and progress. They reflect an era when vast liners powered across the oceans, express trains first exceeded speeds of 100 mph, jetliners shrank the world, and rockets shot out into space. ∎

Paul Jaray

Paul Jaray was born in Vienna in 1889. He studied engineering in his home city, before moving to Friedrichshafen, in Germany. There, he designed seaplanes and Zeppelin airships, and developed a wind tunnel to test and improve the aerodynamic profiles of his fuselage designs.

In 1922, Jaray applied these principles when designing a car that reduced wind resistance. This was so successful that it prompted him to shift his focus to road vehicles. In 1927, he co-founded a design studio in Zürich, Switzerland, aiming to produce designs for car bodywork. His radical concepts, however, failed to impress traditionally minded car makers.

Jaray found success with the Czechoslovak car maker Tatra, which put his streamlined bodywork design into production in 1936. With its unique bodywork, three headlights, and luxury interior, the T87 was a critical success. His stylish vehicle inspired Ferdinand Porsche's design for the Volkswagen Beetle and many post-war car designs. He died in 1974.

DESIGN IS THE SILENT AMBASSADOR OF YOUR BRAND

BRANDING

More than just a logo, a brand encompasses the holistic perception that people have of a company, product, or service – from its values and reputation, to the emotional connection with its consumers. Branding is the process of creating and managing this perception through elements such as product design, visual identity, messaging, and customer experience.

Creating a strong brand requires investment to nurture the relationship with the audience, engender loyalty, and maintain relevance in the marketplace. Authenticity and consistency are also key – a brand that promotes its commitment to sustainability but is found to engage in environmentally harmful practices may lose its reputational value.

Brand equity is established when there is a close correlation between the image a company sets out to create and the way that message is received by its audience. High brand equity means that consumers are more likely to choose a certain brand over another because of the perceived benefits they associate with it.

Products, like people, have personalities, and they can make them or break them in the marketplace.
David Ogilvy
Ogilvy on Advertising, 1983

Such is the case with Coca-Cola. The ubiquitous red can with the white logo is instantly recognizable, and the product has become a byword for quality cola in the minds of consumers.

Historic origins

The birth of sophisticated branding can be traced to the late 1940s, when industry in many countries was switching from wartime to peacetime production in the aftermath of World War II. Coca-Cola was one of many businesses that sought to build its position in the market by vigorous advertising, and it understood the value of creating a strong brand.

Brands had existed long before the 1940s. The term itself derives from the practice of branding livestock – that is, marking them with a hot iron to identify the owner. The brand was often a single letter or a combination of letters – a shorthand for the farmer's name. A farmer with a

The practice of branding cattle to indicate ownership is thought to have been in use in Egypt as early as 2700 BCE. Ancient Egyptians also branded the people that they enslaved.

See also: Corporate identity 234–35 ▪ Visual merchandising and retail design 124–31 ▪ Sports branding 156–57 ▪ Dawn of television 208–11 ▪ Exit through the gift shop 288–89

reputation for quality would find that his brand became sought after at market.

Another precursor of branding is the heraldic device, which emerged in the Middle Ages. Before literacy became widespread, images such as crests, shields, and banners coalesced into a symbolic language that represented a country's armies and noble families, as well as themes such as allegiance, craftsmanship, and quality.

Echoing this style, professional associations of craftsmen and merchants known as "guilds" developed their own industry emblems, such as identifying hallmarks, watermarks, and seals. These symbols denoted adherence to specific quality standards. Guilds enforced rules on who could bear their insignia, and guild members were held accountable to laws and regulations.

Mass production

Prior to the Industrial Revolution, customers might ask a shopkeeper for Scotch whisky, French lace, or

Family crests, such as this of Hugh Campbell and Henrietta Stewart at Cawdor Castle, Scotland (1672), were an early form of branding, long before companies began to market products.

other products identified only by their geographic origins. However, with the dawn of mass production in the second half of the 18th century, producers realized that they needed to distinguish their goods from those of their competitors. Having a distinctive visual identity – a logo or symbol to appear alongside the company name – became essential for recognition; it made it easier for consumers to remember and request a certain

item in the shops, and it strengthened the link between the company and the product.

Early logos often echoed heraldic principles. In 1787, British tea company Twinings devised an upper-case wordmark beneath a lion crest, based on the founding family's coat of arms. Twinings' logo has remained in continuous use ever since.

Other companies followed the tradition of the trade guilds, using visual signs and symbols to create a clear connection with the services or products sold – such as a horseshoe for a blacksmith, or a key for a locksmith.

Standardized packaging

By the 1850s, the trade of manufactured goods started to go beyond regional distribution, which created new challenges »

Brand identity

Intangible assets: emotional connection, reputation, values

Aims: loyalty, ubiquity, differentiation

Tangible assets: visual identity, messaging, product design, customer experience

Tools: investment, marketing, customer research

and opportunities. Until then, retailers had traded in loose dry, fresh, and cured goods, weighing and packaging them in store on demand. With wider distribution, it became easier for traders to supply pre-packaged parcels, jars, and tins of standard sizes and weights.

Standardized sizes allowed manufacturers to set their own pricing strategy, rather than leaving it to the retailer, which gave them more control. The uniformity of packaged products meant that retailers could hold more stock, and they took advantage of this by offering multiple brands in each category. The relationship between retailers and customers shifted: while stores could no longer provide the same level of personal service, they now offered more choice.

Forging a visual identity
In order to compete on the shelf, a product's visual identity had to work harder than ever. Chromolithography, a new colour printing technique patented in 1837, allowed manufacturers to print directly on to tin and paper to help their products stand out. Bovril, Cadbury, Rowntree, and

Your brand is what people say about you when you are not in the room.
Jeff Bezos
Founder of Amazon

Oxo were among the first dry goods manufacturers to adopt branded packaging.

At first, it was difficult for factory-produced packaged items to compete against familiar, local products – and this led early marketeers to use "brand personality" to build trust. Logos for companies such as the British chain of pharmacies Boots (1883) and Coca-Cola (1887) used cursive Spencerian script to suggest a founder's signature, which implied a personal assurance of quality. Other companies used mascots to soften the brand image and inject human warmth. For example, US cereal manufacturer Quaker Oats (1877) relied on the figure of a 17th-century Quaker man to signal honesty and integrity, while French tyre company Michelin (1894) created the jolly humanoid character Bibendum out of white tyres.

Packaging also provided a canvas for advertising messages and brand promises: "absolutely pure", claimed Cadbury in 1892, while Bovril promoted itself as "powerful and invigorating" in 1894. Coca-Cola, meanwhile, promised to "revive and sustain", positioning itself as a tonic and therefore different from other soft drinks.

Manufacturers have used human and animal motifs, bright colours, and imaginative typography on packaging to create instantly recognizable and memorable brands.

As branding became increasingly sophisticated, companies started to demand legal protection against their logos being copied or faked. In 1862, the British Parliament introduced the Trade Marks Registration Act; evolved from guild patents, it made it a criminal offence to imitate another brand.

The more comprehensive Merchandise Marks Act followed in 1875. Manufacturers could now register their logos, signatures, and other identifying devices at the UK Patent Office. The first-ever trademark to be registered, on 1 January 1876, was the logo of the Bass Brewery, based in Burton-upon-Trent, UK. It featured a simple red triangle, which still appears on beer bottles and cans.

The psychology of branding
In 1900, the American advertising agency J. Walter Thompson (JWT) published a house advertisement explaining to potential clients the importance of having a strong brand. It stated that

consumers buy into a company and its values, rather than simply purchasing a product.

During this period, advertising agencies gradually changed from being intermediaries between companies and publications with advertising space to sell, to providing a more comprehensive service that included writing and design. To persuade companies to buy these services, the agencies conducted research into why consumers bought certain brands so that they could tailor their messaging to reinforce or change behaviour. These studies resulted in many social, anthropological, and psychological insights that still apply to brand strategy.

American theorist Edward Bernays was particularly instrumental in shaping the idea that purchasing could be influenced through psychology. In the 1920s he drew on the ideas of his uncle, founder of psychoanalysis Sigmund Freud, to harness the power of creating emotional associations between products and certain symbols or ideas. For instance, in his Torches of Freedom campaign, he associated Lucky Strike cigarettes with the idea of women's liberation, linking smoking to notions of independence.

Bernays also understood that drawing on scientific authority and third-party endorsements could increase consumer trust. A notable example is his campaign promoting bacon as a breakfast food, associating it with the idea of a hearty morning meal. To achieve this, Bernays persuaded a doctor

to endorse a large breakfast as a healthier option than a lighter one. He then gathered responses from 5,000 more doctors and sent their support to the media. Soon, headlines on American newspapers claimed that "4,500 physicians advocate heavy breakfasts for better health", often citing bacon and eggs as the perfect example.

The rise of mass media

By the 1940s, advertising agencies knew how to imbue a brand with personality traits – whether fun and youthfulness, or luxury and glamour. They understood that you could create appeal by tapping into people's desires, aspirations, fears, and insecurities, and they recognized the value of market research and consumer studies.

The social, economic, and technological changes that followed World War II laid the groundwork for a new type of consumer–brand relationship. The key factors in this transition were the widespread adoption of radio and the emergence of television. These platforms

> Get closer than ever to your customers. So close that you tell them what they need well before they realize it themselves.
> **Steve Jobs**
> **Co-founder of Apple**

enabled brands to reach a much wider audience and develop impactful advertising campaigns across multiple touchpoints. Jingles, catchphrases, and visual storytelling became integral parts of a product's promotion, while consistency across different kinds of media helped to foster familiarity.

The 1940s also marked the formalization of brand identity systems. Companies published »

Edouard Manet's 1882 painting
A Bar at the Folies-Bergère shows a range of alcoholic drinks on the counter, including two bottles of Bass beer, identifiable by the red triangular logo.

extensive brand guidelines and corporate identity manuals, which advised designers and printers on how to correctly apply branding across different formats, media, and territories. This helped to shift visual communication from an intuitive practice to a strategic one with strict requirements.

Brand consultancy

As brands became more prominent in consumer lives, the goal was no longer just to sell a product, but to create a loyal customer base that identified with the brand's values and aspirations. Brand-consulting agencies grew quickly on the back of emerging fields like consumer behaviour and corporate identity, to help companies build their brands at home and abroad.

Walter Landor, founder of San Francisco-based brand consultancy Landor Associates, was among the influential voices of the mid-20th century. He introduced the concept of "branding the total product", which focused on the entire customer experience – from product design and packaging, to marketing strategies. Landor, who believed that a brand should evoke emotions and

Marketing teams use brand touchpoint wheels to show all the ways people come into contact with a company and its products – with a view to reinforcing its brand.

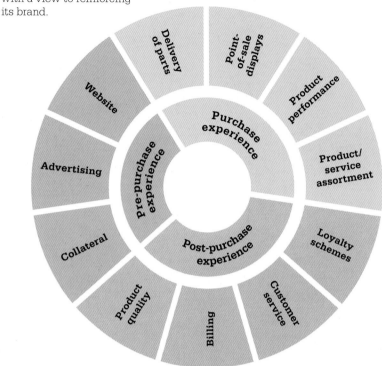

forge a strong bond with consumers, emphasized the importance of simplicity, functionality, and an understanding of cultural nuances. Based on insights gleaned from

consumer research, brand designers like Landor sought to give products brand personalities. Marlboro cigarettes, for example, were associated with ruggedness and independence, while Coca-Cola was not just a fizzy drink – it was happiness, joy, and freedom in a bottle. Advertising was used to support these messages. Coke's successful "Hilltop" campaign (1971) featured young people of many races and nationalities singing about love and harmony, each holding a bottle of the product. "Holidays are coming" (1995) featured a convoy of brightly lit trucks driving through snow to deliver the product and complete the festive season.

Brand experience

Since the 1980s, brand owners have sought to actively shape how

Ethics

Conscious of the fact that successful branding can influence behaviour, many designers refuse to work with companies that sell products that are harmful to human health, promote discrimination, or disregard the environment.

For others, design is a form of activism. A "citizen designer" is a professional who actively engages in socially responsible practices by only using their design skills to contribute positively to society. This

movement, spearheaded by graphic designer Ken Garland, emerged in the 1960s as part of a backlash against consumerism.

Garland's 1964 manifesto *First Things First*, co-signed by 21 British designers, was a plea for creatives to use their skills for "worthwhile purposes" and for "more useful and more lasting forms of communication". The document continues to find relevance among new generations of designers – the latest version was published in 2020 and attracted more than 1,700 signatures.

consumers engage with their brand beyond the purchase. They emphasize that the product is only a part of what their brand represents. Brand environments, such as Disneyland or Apple's flagship stores, reinforce brand values through the spaces where consumers interact with the brands, and in the service they provide.

Advertising has also moved away from focusing solely on products to sell a holistic brand experience. Wieden+Kennedy's "Just Do It" campaign for Nike, which debuted in 1987, focuses on athletes and inspirational stories, using the company's swoosh logo as a central element; and McDonald's 2023 "Raise Your Arches" campaign (Leo Burnett Worldwide) does not show the fast-food company's logo until the very last scene.

The significance of brand image has grown so much that it is considered as vital as, if not more important, than product innovation. The relationship between the product, marketing, and branding has become so intertwined that it is impossible to separate an object from its brand image.

The message of this 1950s advert – that Coke is wholesome, delicious, and refreshing – clearly targets women shoppers. The white-on-red branding is ever-present in Coca-Cola advertising.

The Guinness "Surfer" advert, created by British director Jonathan Glazer, was shot in black and white in Hawaii. The Irish stout beer does not appear until the final shot.

Brands act as a kind of language, signalling our status, aspiration, and personal values to others. Opting for a Chanel fragrance might signal refined taste, a love of sophisticated designs, and a desire for understated luxury; while sporting Gucci sunglasses might suggest a flair for avant-garde fashion, a love for statement pieces, and a desire to stand out.

Branding in the digital age
In the 21st century, digital media provide a valuable mechanism that allows brands to connect directly with their audiences, as the Internet and social media provide numerous opportunities for customer engagement and interaction. In contemporary branding, there has been a movement towards flexible systems and immersive "brand worlds" – fostering a dialogue between brands and consumers. This shift has made branding more dynamic, and it is increasingly focused on crafting meaningful experiences that embody brand values.

At the same time, consumers expect authenticity, social and environmental awareness, and a sense of personal connection from the brands they endorse. Companies like Patagonia have excelled by weaving social causes into their identities, striking a chord with conscientious consumers.

There is growing investment in sustainable packaging and corporate social responsibility. Certification programmes that assess a firm's social impact, such as B Corp, continue to grow, leading to a generation of new brands founded on a commitment to balancing profit with purpose. ∎

AUTOMATED DAYDREAMING

DAWN OF TELEVISION

IN CONTEXT

FOCUS
Design for a small, black and white screen

FIELD
Graphic design, set design

BEFORE
1898 The film *Our New General Servant* is the first British film to use intertitles – frames of text shown between film sequences.

1941 The first paid TV advertisement is shown in the US. The advertisement, for Bulova watches, features an animation of a clock imposed on a map of the country.

AFTER
1966 Systems Resources Corporation in the US devises the first "chyron", a character generator for displaying text overlaid across the base of the screen on live TV programmes.

The emergence of television (TV) in the early 20th century gave companies and even national corporations a new opportunity to engage and inform mass audiences. Design, and especially graphic design, would play a major part in the new "televisual language" – but it took some time before television companies learned how to exploit the full potential for graphics and other visuals.

The first TV systems
The development of systems to transmit and receive images had been under way since the late 19th century, and the word "television"

See also: Branding 200–07 ▪ Lighting design 222–23 ▪ Computer gaming 272–75 ▪ The online user experience 294–99

was coined in 1900 by Russian scientist Constantin Perskyi. Then, in 1923, Scottish inventor John Logie Baird devised the first complete television system, based on a mechanical process for transmitting images.

Baird carried out the first public display of TV transmission on 26 January 1926, when he showed images of human faces at the Royal Institution in London. In 1928, he set up his own TV company, and the following year helped to establish companies in Germany and France. Meanwhile, American, Japanese, and Russian inventors developed variations of his system. In 1927 Bell Telephone Laboratories in the US created the first system that included synchronized sound. These mechanical systems were superseded by electronic TV in the 1930s, when the first public TV channels emerged.

Television transmission in Europe and Russia was interrupted by World War II, after which mass TV viewing spread across the world. In 1936, the BBC inaugurated the world's first high-definition TV service, transmitting black and white images at a resolution of 405 lines. From a design perspective, black and white TV had similar requirements to black and white film in that images needed to have sharply defined contrast to enhance their legibility. This meant, for example, that any text shown had to be in large, bold lettering, illustrations needed simple, distinct shapes and minimal detail, and the presenters of TV programmes even had to wear thick make-up in shades of white, grey, and black. The poor quality of some receivers (TV sets) was also an issue; images had to »

Studio D at the BBC's Lime Grove, Shepherd's Bush, London during the first broadcast in 1950. The studio broadcast a variety of programmes, notably current affairs.

William Golden

Born in New York in 1911, Golden worked designing newspaper advertising in Los Angeles, then returned to New York to work for the lifestyle publisher Condé Nast. In 1937 he joined the Columbia Broadcasting System (CBS), America's leading radio broadcaster and from 1941 a television company too. In 1940, he became Art Director.

As TV grew into a mass medium after World War II, TV channels came to need a distinctive visual identity. CBS president Frank Stanton felt that the existing static logo was not effective, so in 1951, Golden designed the famous "eye". The circle enclosing an eye, with the brand name in the "pupil", suggested both the act of viewing and a globe, indicating wide scope of content. Animated and static forms of the logo were used for all CBS publicity.

Golden died in 1959, aged 48, but the US National Society of Art Directors posthumously awarded him the title Art Director of the Year in 1960.

Key works

1951 "Eye" station ident and logo for CBS TV channel

be filmed or positioned with the focus at the centre, because some TV screens would lose focus at the edges or even cut off part of the image.

Designing for TV

Building on expertise from the Hollywood film industry and Broadway theatre, studio set design came to be an important, although usually unsung, specialism. There were two main approaches; one comprised naturalistic designs, which sought to reflect real scenes, however contrived, and the other was "abstracted", designed to engender an atmosphere or feeling rather than a recognizable scene. A related category was the design of settings for variety and game shows, which took inspiration from those of Hollywood musicals.

New techniques allowed elements of programmes to be made to appear more dynamic. For example, a rostrum camera – a TV camera mounted on a moving platform – could be used to zoom in or out, or pan across to give a sense of movement. For filming action shots, TV borrowed knowledge from the film industry by using a

> I always say film is art, theatre is life and television is furniture.
> **Kenny Leon**

TV camera mounted on a cart called a dolly to enable the smooth tracking of moving subjects.

Text and graphics

Initially, graphic elements for TV programmes, such as titles, captions, artworks, and credits, followed the styles used in films and print media. It was not until the 1950s that graphic design came to be seen as a discipline separate from studio set design or promotion and marketing.

The first notable specialist graphic designer for TV was William Golden, art director for the US TV channel CBS; he used

graphics to define the channel's identity, most strikingly by creating a distinctive "eye" logo. Another pioneer was Saul Bass, a designer for Hollywood movies, who devised the first "kinetic" title sequences, in which text and moving images were integrated to set the mood of the film – most notably for Alfred Hitchcock's film *Vertigo*.released in 1958. The influence of Bass's work led to the creation of title sequences that became an integral part of the programme – one striking example being the original *Star Trek* series, first aired in 1966, which featured an animation of the spaceship USS *Enterprise* flying through the stars, with moving text credits and a voice-over by star William Shatner.

In the UK, meanwhile, the BBC first employed a full-time graphic designer in 1954, but it was another 10 years before it had its own graphic design department.

Within TV programmes, text and graphics started to play an ever larger role in conveying information and creating visual narratives. In sports and news broadcasts, the chyron – a strip of text that rolled across the

Images and music

In the "silent" era of cinema, from the mid-1890s to the early 1930s, film sound tracks were performed live by musicians in each venue, just like in theatres and music halls. The biggest and grandest "picture palaces" had orchestras with conductors, while in modest backstreet venues, a pianist played the accompanying music, often using their imagination to evoke the emotions suggested by the screen imagery. Comedy, tragedy, romance, fear, and

suspense could all be enhanced by suitable compositions. Thereafter, radio and television companies employed studio orchestras to play signature tunes and incidental music during live broadcasts. Even today, the BBC has over 400 professional musicians. Television viewers have become so used to the presence of incidental music that they perhaps take it for granted but, just as in the early days of cinema, it remains vital for the communication of feelings, making broadcasts seem more convincingly life-like.

Inside a New York movie theatre in 1925, a live band and pianist below the screen supply the "sound track" to the drama and comedy.

Different types of design/designers that are needed to make good TV

Set designers create the stage and background "set" where filming takes place. They need to consider how colour and texture will appear on screen.

Lighting designers are responsible for making sure the set and camera shots are well lit. Different types of lighting can be used to provide the right ambience.

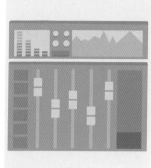

Sound designers capture and edit dialogue and other sound that is recorded in a programme. They also shape the mood of a programme via music and sound effects.

Graphic designers make title sequences, end credits, and other graphic elements. They have to match the style of the show and generate interest from the viewer.

base of the screen – was used to give up-to-the-minute news. Visual elements such as charts and artworks could also be animated, for example in news bulletins or educational programmes. In the UK, the BBC even set up a dedicated graphics unit to create visuals for the programmes that it broadcast for Open University courses.

Another important strand of programming was TV for children. These programmes gave extra scope for creativity, with cartoons and stop-motion animations as well as films and live programmes. In some instances, such as the US *Sesame Street*, puppetry, animated images, and text were combined to amuse or educate young viewers.

Brand identities
An increasingly important element was the use of sound and images for TV channel logos, or "idents". These take various forms. Between programmes, the channel might show an animated text or graphic

with a distinctive sound or short burst of music; some idents can be elaborate mini-films, as seen on the British TV channels BBC2 and Channel 4. Within programmes, idents might appear as a static logo at the corner of the screen, as with the elegant calligraphic logo for Qatari TV channel Al-Jazeera. For some channels, the ident is part of an overall look that establishes the brand identity in print and on the internet as well as on TV.

Computer design and CGI
The first forays into computer-generated imagery (CGI) occurred in the 1940s and 1950s, with the technique notably being used in Alfred Hitchcock's film *Vertigo* (1958). Since then, CGI has come into play more and more in TV programmes as well as movies; uses include generating intricately realized settings and landscapes for historical dramas or science fiction, and creating animated visuals to enhance the viewing of sports and games. In addition, computers are

used to generate lettering for titles, credits, and other text elements.

Today, TV images form part of a constant 24-hour feed of news, drama and other programmes, transmitted by satellite and over the internet as well as on terrestrial TV channels. The graphics used need to be eye-catching and engaging to make particular programmes stand out in this constant stream of content. They also need to be effective across a range of devices, from wide-screen televisions to tablets and even smartphones.

The future may see graphic design elements initially developed for TV being adapted to shape interactive programmes and virtual reality experiences. Whatever form they take, the need for visuals to inform and entertain viewers will be just as strong as it was back in 1926, when John Logie Baird first transmitted images of human faces to a viewing public and brought the TV age into being. ∎

THE
CONSUM
1950–2000

ER AGE

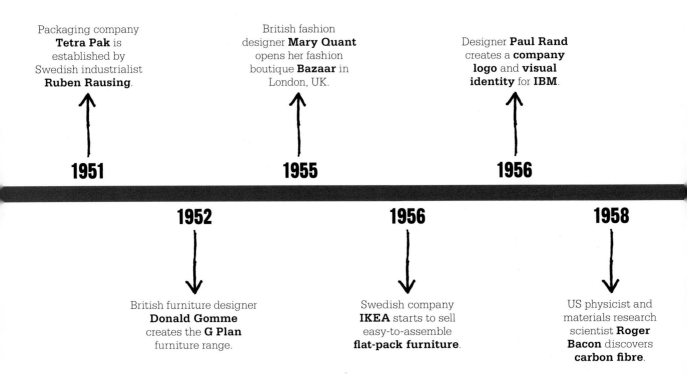

Packaging company **Tetra Pak** is established by Swedish industrialist **Ruben Rausing**.

British fashion designer **Mary Quant** opens her fashion boutique **Bazaar** in London, UK.

Designer **Paul Rand** creates a **company logo** and **visual identity** for IBM.

1951

1955

1956

1952

1956

1958

British furniture designer **Donald Gomme** creates the **G Plan** furniture range.

Swedish company **IKEA** starts to sell easy-to-assemble **flat-pack furniture**.

US physicist and materials research scientist **Roger Bacon** discovers **carbon fibre**.

At the end or World War II, Europe was badly damaged physically and economically, and the US was the emergent Western superpower. There, pent-up demand due to wartime restrictions could now be sated. Demobbed soldiers returned home and started families, causing a "baby boom". Some 15 years later, the coming of age of this wave of youth would give rise to distinct fashion and music cultures upon which commercial businesses and designers would capitalize.

Ideological rivalry between the US and the USSR led post-war US governments to invest in West Germany, Italy, and Japan to help them rebuild and keep them from joining the communist bloc. They became major exporters of goods, notable for their Modern design.

Bauhaus influence
The 1930s had seen a great exodus of the European avant garde in art, design, and architecture to New York. Several leading members of the Bauhaus crossed the Atlantic to begin new lives in the US. By the 1950s, many of them were teaching in American art and architecture colleges. Modernism became the mainstream design language of the post-war period, associated in the US with slick efficiency. In an era of scientific advancement with the advent of jet- and space travel, futuristic aesthetics appeared highly appropriate and were widely applied. The displacement of Modernist creative practitioners from Europe's dictatorships also meant that this approach came to be promoted as the aesthetic of freedom and democracy.

By contrast, in the controlled culture of Stalin's Soviet Union, realism and neoclassicism were the only officially permitted styles. Although many were persuaded of Modernism's supposed democratic virtues, this tenuous argument, ignored the fact that, beyond looking up-to-date, clean-lined forms might be used in support of any belief system. Nonetheless, in the 1950s, new US design ranging from shiny glass-clad corporate headquarters, luxury Hilton hotels, and airport terminals, to furniture, fabrics, and ornaments, reflected Modernist influence.

In 1949, the architecture and design "power couple" Charles and Ray Eames completed their house at Pacific Palisades, California. Filled with scatter cushions, comfort-giving consumer goods,

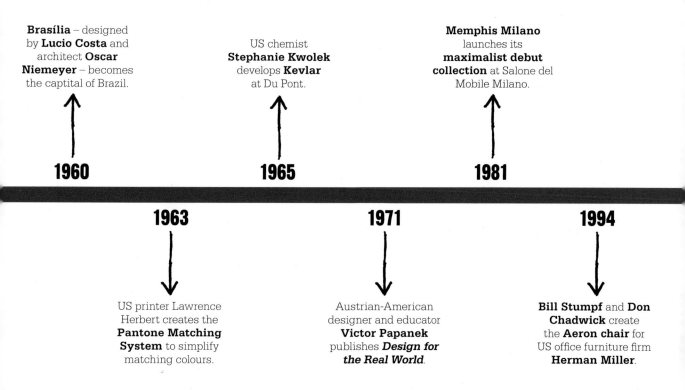

Brasília – designed by **Lucio Costa** and architect **Oscar Niemeyer** – becomes the captital of Brazil.

US chemist **Stephanie Kwolek** develops **Kevlar** at Du Pont.

Memphis Milano launches its **maximalist debut collection** at Salone del Mobile Milano.

1960

1965

1981

1963

1971

1994

US printer Lawrence Herbert creates the **Pantone Matching System** to simplify matching colours.

Austrian-American designer and educator **Victor Papanek** publishes ***Design for the Real World***.

Bill Stumpf and **Don Chadwick** create the **Aeron chair** for US office furniture firm **Herman Miller**.

---

objets d'art, and knick-knacks, it was a distinctly maximalist take on Modernism, with the open-plan living space providing plenty of room to display their acquisitions.

Postmodern consumerism
Modernism in the US appealed primarily to members of an opinion-forming elite, but items of many styles were produced in great quantities. The futuristic was often juxtaposed with the traditional: contemporary Eames chairs were complemented with Baroque-style electroliers and Rococo wallpaper to produce opulent effects, with something to please everyone.

In the 1960s, cultural critics began to apply ideas derived from Marxist social theory to analyse and critique consumption habits from the consumer perspective.

Previously, architects and designers had argued that their approaches were superior, but scholarly opinion was becoming more inclined to view consumer choices as a matter of taste, and a reflection of each individual's accumulated educational and cultural capital. In other words, everything a person learned and experienced as they went through life informed their likes and aspirations – and their buying preferences.

As Modernists tended to emphasize the idea of there being universally-understood ideas of what was "good" in terms of design, this new relativism and the multiple styles it encouraged came to be labelled "Postmodern". Thereafter, populist and even kitsch design items began to be re-appraised in Postmodern terms,

while a new generation of serious designers began to produce solutions using symbolic and quotational techniques reminiscent of Pop Art. Early proponents were the American architect Robert Venturi, and the Italian designer Ettore Sottsass, whose "Memphis" furniture resembled items of contemporary sculpture.

It was not until the 1980s that Postmodern design hit the mainstream. In the US and Britain, consumers gained increased spending power and a retail boom ensued. During the 1990s, following the collapse of the Soviet Union, the demise of communism there and in Eastern Europe, and market reforms in China – instituted by its communist leader, Deng Xiaoping – consumerism grew worldwide to become a global pursuit. ■

CLEAN LIVING. CLEAN LINES

MID-CENTURY MODERN

IN CONTEXT

FOCUS
Optimistic functionality

FIELD
Architecture, interiors, and product design

BEFORE
1930s The Streamline Moderne style of architecture emphasizes aerodynamic shapes and clean lines.

1945 *Arts & Architecture* magazine editor John Entenza launches the Case Study House programme in the US, hoping to solve the housing difficulties anticipated after World War II.

AFTER
1981 Founded by Italian architect Ettore Sottsass, the Memphis Milano group debuts its first collection at furniture fair Salone del Mobile Milano. The flamboyant kitsch aesthetics are a reaction to Modernist minimalism.

A student's room of 1952 in Paris's Maison du Mexique is re-created here for the exhibition *Charlotte Perriand: The Modern Life*, held at the Design Museum, London, in 2021.

Mid-century Modern is not a catch-all term for furniture, products, and buildings designed in the middle of the 20th century. Instead, it actually refers to a particular design movement – most prominent in the 1940s, 1950s, and 1960s – that was defined by a unique style and set of principles.

The term gained popularity in 1984, when author Cara Greenberg used it in the title of her book *Mid-century Modern: Furniture of the 1950s*. Within the book, Greenberg brought together numerous examples of designed objects with clean architectural lines, biomorphic forms, boomerang-like curves, and an unprecedented blend of organic and manufactured materials.

Bauhaus influences

Like many 20th-century design philosophies, Mid-century Modern is rooted in the Bauhaus principles of functionalism. While the post-war movement sought to uphold

Charlotte Perriand

One of the pre-eminent architects and designers of the Mid-century Modern movement, Charlotte Perriand was born in 1903 in Paris, France. She enrolled to study furniture design at the École de L'Union Centrale des Arts Décoratifs in 1925.

Perriand soon became known for her innovations in the use of metals, glass, and textiles. In 1927, she took a position working in the studio of Charles-Édouard Jeanneret (later known as Le Corbusier). Although she was subjected to verbal cruelty and sexism under his leadership, she worked with him for ten years. During that time, Perriand designed three celebrated chairs in collaboration with Le Corbusier and Pierre Jeanneret: the LC2 Grand Confort armchair, the B301 reclining chair, and the B306 chaise longue.

Identifying as a communist, Perriand was keen to design low-cost furniture for mass production. Although none of her designs was produced on an industrial scale, her name has become synonymous with Mid-century Modern. She died in Paris in 1999.

basic Modernist values, it was also built on a desire to marry mass-production techniques with furniture and architecture that reflected an optimistic perspective on the future of society.

In architecture and furniture design, Mid-century Modern reflects a pragmatism and simplicity that resonated with the domestic narratives of the post-war era. All around the world – but particularly in the US and Europe – society was being encouraged to focus on a bright future built around the safety of the nuclear family and a departure from the politics and economics of the two world wars. Aesthetically, this meant embracing new technologies and materials while casting aside the ornate traditions of decades gone by. Everything in the home was designed to serve a purpose – whether feeding family members or entertaining – and the products and furniture advertised in the media also encouraged aspirations of a white-picket-fence, middle-class lifestyle.

Global appeal

Although Mid-century Modern is often regarded as a US- and Euro-centric movement, it did, in fact, have a broader appeal. It was adopted all over the world by those who had the means to create beautiful homes and furniture. Latin American architects and designers, for example, developed their own version of this optimistic

Brasília's cathedral, designed by Oscar Niemeyer, was completed in 1970. Enclosed within 16 curving concrete columns, it is a classic example of Modernist architecture.

> You employ stone, wood, and concrete, and with these materials you build houses and palaces … But suddenly you touch my heart … That is Architecture. Art enters in.
> **Le Corbusier**

design language, incorporating local materials, as well as some Mesoamerican influences.

One factor that distinguishes the Latin American style from its US and European counterparts is that in Latin America the work was usually commissioned by individual families rather than by large corporations. With the buildings and their contents held by private estates, many

accolade-worthy projects in Latin America have been kept hidden from view, and the stories behind their designs left untold.

Among the visible examples of Latin American Mid-century Modern are the projects of Brazilian architect Oscar Niemeyer, particularly those in Brasília. Built from 1956 on the orders of then newly elected president Juscelino Kubitschek and inaugurated as the capital of Brazil in 1960, Brasília was meticulously planned. Architect Lúcio Costa designed the city's layout, while Niemeyer designed most of its public buildings, including the presidential residence Alvorada Palace, with its concrete-and-glass facade; Itamaraty Palace – home of the Ministry of Foreign Affairs – with its colonnaded frontage; and Brasília's crown-like cathedral.

Notable for their pared-down aesthetics and undulating lines, Brasília's buildings embody a bright vision for the future, fusing large structures with novel interpretations of traditional forms. »

Niemeyer won international acclaim for his work, and he was invited to join the team of architects designing the headquarters of the United Nations in New York City.

As with Niemeyer, the work of Italian architect and designer Lina Bo Bardi is found mainly in Brazil, where she moved with her husband, Pietro Maria Bardi, in 1946. In 1951, Bo Bardi designed the Casa de Vidro (Glass House) as a family home. Nestled among the treetops of the rainforest outside São Paulo, the building embodies a vision of optimistic utilitarianism. Its floor-to-ceiling windows and open-plan style speak to the ideals of Mid-century Modern, embracing a fusion of organic and manufactured forms and materials. Bo Bardi went on to design the São Paulo Museum of Art (1968) and the city's vast Centro de Lazer Fábrica da Pompéia performance, leisure, and exhibition venue (1977–86).

Functional furniture

The design of Mid-century Modern furniture was powerfully influenced by a minimalist aesthetic from Scandinavia. Danish architect Finn Juhl, for example, is credited with introducing the minimalist

[Design is] an expression of purpose. It may, if it is good enough, later be judged as art.
Charles Eames
Design Q&A with Charles Eames, 1972

The functionalist **Bauhaus movement** champions **stylistic simplicity** in the interwar years.

Designers embrace **new technologies** and **new materials**, marrying them to the values of the **Bauhaus manifesto**.

The resulting designs are defined by clean architectural lines, organic forms, and minimal decoration.

Latin American designers develop their own Modernist language, which includes local and **Mesoamerican influences**.

Danish Modern style to the US in 1951, when the Baker Furniture Company in Michigan began to manufacture his designs.

Simple, functional pieces became the order of the day, thanks to uncluttered designs without any unnecessary decorative features. These items were typically built to a high standard from affordable, natural materials, but designers also experimented with new materials and techniques – such as plastic and moulded plywood – to create pleasingly shaped furniture that was first and foremost designed for comfort.

The Drop Chair, created in 1959 by Danish designer Arne Jacobsen for Copenhagen's original SAS Royal Hotel, is one well-known example. Others include Finnish-American designer Eero Saarinen's Womb Chair (1948) and Tulip Chair (1957), the latter mounted on a pedestal base to do away with the under-seat clutter of traditional chair legs.

These items focus on comfort and functionality while committing to the smooth curves and nature-inspired forms that are defining features of Mid-century Modern furniture. Saarinen arguably took the preoccupation with biomorphism even further, with the Womb Chair, which sees the body's own pre-birth vessel as the epitome of comfort.

Saarinen – who had moved from Finland to the US in 1923 and studied at Michigan's Cranbrook Academy of Art with designers and architects Charles and Ray Eames – is also known as one of the most important architects of the post-war era. His award-winning designs include the passenger terminal at Dulles International Airport in Washington, DC (1962), and the sleek Gateway Arch in St Louis (1965).

Both Saarinen and the Eameses took a multidisciplinary approach to their work that resulted in some of the most revered architecture and furniture designs of the modern era.

Creative experiments

Charles and Ray Eames met at the Cranbrook Academy of Art and married in 1941. Right from the start, their aim was to create multifunctional designs for modern living – and their innovations in design thinking would affect many aspects of life in the US.

In 1942 and 1943, the Eameses began to explore the possibilities offered by new forms of plywood, building on earlier experiments made in collaboration between Charles and Eero Saarinen at Cranbrook. Having secured a contract with the Evans Product Company to produce moulded plywood leg splints for US Navy servicemen wounded during World War II, the Eameses gained valuable experience of mass production, which they applied to making furniture for adults and children.

Their experiments in moulded plywood included a prototype for a wooden chair. Despite many iterations, the chair was unable to bear the stress and strain caused by the weight of the human body and constantly broke – but the

The Japanese influence

Mid-century Modern design is rightly credited with shaping the American way of life, but its influences and origins can be traced back to rituals and residential design ideas long associated with Japan.

Many traditional Japanese dwellings have a refined minimalism that fosters feelings of tranquillity, while evoking a strong sense of being connected to nature. Finding harmony with nature is a central aspect of Zen Buddhism; in design terms, this can be seen in the considered use of natural materials, as well as the large windows and internal gardens often found in Japanese homes. These characteristics were adopted by several Mid-century Modern architects and feature prominently in many buildings of the post-war period.

The marriage of classic Asian design principles with modern functional thinking is also clearly visible in the work of Japanese-American designer Isamu Noguchi, who created furniture, buildings, and ceramics.

experience paved the way for the Eameses to create the chairs for which they are famed.

Success with Fiberglass

In 1947, the Museum of Modern Art in New York announced the International Competition for Low-Cost Furniture Design. Its aim was to promote comfortable, moderately priced furniture suitable for the small apartments that were becoming the norm in the post-war years. The Eameses saw an opportunity to evolve their earlier failure into modular seating units that would serve the varied needs of many. Their Fiberglass Chair, featuring a single moulded shell, won second prize. By 1952, Herman Miller was advertising a complete range of Eames chairs, touting them as being available in configurations to suit all environments.

Introduced in 1956, the Eames Lounge Chair was designed, as stated by Charles, with "the warm, receptive look of a well-used first baseman's mitt" in mind. Initially conceived to bring comfort and support to the body, the lounger and footstool have become known as the pinnacle of Mid-century Modern furniture design.

Both the Fiberglass Chair and the Lounge Chair symbolize everything Mid-century Modern design represents: functionality, optimistic aesthetic language, and the convergence of industry and natural materials. ■

The Eames Lounge Chair, which comes with an ottoman, features a permanently tilted seat with thickly padded leather cushions.

MUSIC FOR THE EYE
LIGHTING DESIGN

IN CONTEXT

FOCUS
**Manipulating lighting
to create ambience**

FIELD
**Architecture, interior
design**

BEFORE
1879 American inventor
Thomas Edison, with the
help of Hiram Maxim and
Lewis Latimer, creates the
first commercially successful
electric light bulb.

AFTER
1962 Nick Holonyak, an
American engineer, invents
the first visible LED bulb,
which emits red light. LED
bulbs capable of producing
other colours of light, such
as yellow and blue, are
developed in the 1970s.

1996 The white LED bulb
is invented by Japanese
engineering company Nichia.
White LEDs become widely
available in 2006.

The magical beauty of
electric lighting has been
used to draw customers
to entertainment venues since
the late 19th century. Theatres,
amusement parks, and fairgrounds
used large numbers of bulbs to
illuminate attractions and excite
imaginations. As technology
improved during the 20th century,
lighting features were increasingly
used in both the architecture and
interiors of new buildings to inspire
awe and create atmosphere.

Lighting buildings
The 1920s saw German architects
experiment with the use of light
in new cinema buildings. In Berlin,
they were flood-lit and outlined
with strips of neon tubing, creating
a dynamic new aesthetic known
as *lichtspiel arkitektur* (light-play

Titania Palast cinema, in Berlin,
Germany was designed in 1928 with
the principle of light-play architecture.
Inside it featured a large dome light
and imposing illuminated arches.

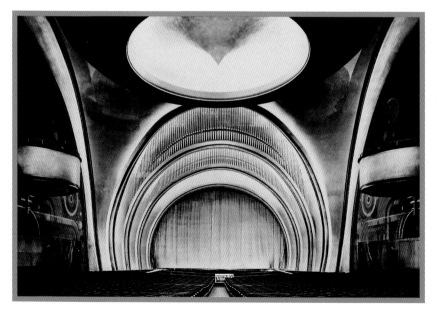

See also: Streetscape 172–73 ■ Hospitality design 178–79 ■ Dawn of television 208–11 ■ Urban design 248–49

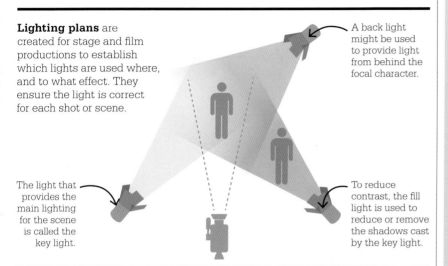

Lighting plans are created for stage and film productions to establish which lights are used where, and to what effect. They ensure the light is correct for each shot or scene.

A back light might be used to provide light from behind the focal character.

The light that provides the main lighting for the scene is called the key light.

To reduce contrast, the fill light is used to reduce or remove the shadows cast by the key light.

architecture). This new design style was adopted by the architects of entertainment venues in Britain. Dreamland cinema in Margate opened in 1935 with a neon-outlined exterior featuring a fin-shaped tower. Its design influenced the cinemas of the Odeon chain.

Inside, most of these buildings were equipped with concealed lighting in coves around the auditorium, which gave an intimate glamour to the decor. Rotating gobo-filters – stencilled coloured discs for projecting patterns or shapes – were placed in front of the thousands of bulbs to suffuse these spaces in constantly changing colours. In foyer and cafe spaces, globe-shaped pendant lights surrounded by frosted glass rings were installed, designed to glow like the planets above cinema-goers' heads.

Drawing a crowd

In the US during the 1930s, the building of the Hoover Dam in Nevada caused thousands of workers to move to the area. Local entrepreneurs, in what was then a village named Las Vegas, spotted opportunities to entertain the workers. Bars, nightclubs, casinos, and brothels appeared there and the owner of an electrical goods store began to make bespoke illuminated signs to adorn their frontages. By the 1950s, Las Vegas was established as a place of leisure where people travelled in increasing numbers. Its main street became a spectacle of fantastic illumination as venues competed to attract punters.

A new type of light

Incandescent, fluorescent, and neon lights in public spaces often need to be replaced, causing ongoing maintenance costs. Since the early-2000s, however, the LED (light-emitting diode) bulb has been a more reliable, energy-saving alternative. The ability to combine LEDs of varying hue and colour temperature, means that exterior and interior spaces can easily be bathed in rainbow colours. Today, LEDs are widely used in architecture and interiors offering opportunities for creativity in illuminating these spaces. ■

Lighting design for cinematography

Lighting is an essential element of cinematography. The black and white film stock used by early film makers at the beginning of the 20th century needed strong contrasts of light and shade for images to register clearly. This led to footage frequently being shot outside in bright daylight. With its temperate, sunny climate and open spaces, California became the epicentre of film making in the US.

For filming indoors, warehouselike studios were built where floodlights and spotlights could be mounted to illuminate film sets. The lighting principles used were similar to those already common in the theatre at the time. For example, impressions of the sky could be created by projecting even lighting onto stretched smooth cloths.

Film studios later came to employ lighting design specialists to realize film directors' visions. Lighting continues to be an important aspect of film effects, and lighting directors are integral to the production of any film.

Lighting technicians on outdoor film sets use portable lights and light reflectors to control the intensity and direction of light.

DROPPED, IT WON'T FALL OVER; OPEN, IT'S HARD TO UPSET
TETRAHEDRON PACKAGING

IN CONTEXT

FOCUS
Using geometric shapes to create packaging

FIELD
Packaging design

BEFORE
1906 The first paper drinks cartons appear in Californian grocery stores.

1915 American John Van Wormer patents Pure-Pak, a gable-top paper bottle that milk producers can add milk into, then seal at the farm.

AFTER
1967 DuPont begins selling milk on the Canadian market in thin, cost-efficient plastic bags. They remain popular in Canada, Israel, and parts of Latin America.

2005 English inventor Martin Myerscough develops a paper pulp-based milk carton inspired by papier mâché.

The tetrahedron is a type of pyramid composed of four triangular sides. It can be folded from a sheet or tube of paper. Swedish company Tetra Pak utilized this geometric property, designing a machine that could package liquids into precise tetrahedron-shaped cartons. The Tetra Pak helped to revolutionize the packaging and distribution of drinks in an era of industrialized food production.

Since prehistoric times, containers such as gourds, ceramic vases, leather pouches, and glass bottles have been used to store, transport, and sell liquids. By the 1920s, most US grocery stores sold milk in paper bottles. These were delivered flat-packed to farms, where they were individually constructed, filled, and sealed. Grocers in much of Europe, meanwhile, sold milk in glass bottles that customers needed to wash and return.

Packaging revolution

Swedish industrialist Ruben Rausing established his company Åkerlund & Rausing in 1929. Focusing initially on packaging for dry goods, his company grew throughout the 1930s. By the 1940s, Rausing was looking to develop an efficient, hygienic, and reliable way of storing milk. In 1944, Erik Wallenberg, a worker at Rausing's laboratory, proposed using tetrahedrons, as they could be continuously folded from a cylinder of paper without wasting material. Meanwhile, Rausing's wife, Elisabeth, had suggested that the packages be sealed with the milk running through the cylinder, so that they could be entirely filled.

This Italian advert for pasteurized milk shows an example of Tetra Pak's classic tetrahedron package. International sales turned the Swedish company into a global success story.

See also: Mass-produced ceramics 92–93 ▪ Industrial design 146–47 ▪ Plastic 148–53 ▪ Ergonomics 278–85 ▪ Sustainable materials 302–07

Ruben Rausing

Industrialist Ruben Rausing was born near Helsingborg, Sweden, in 1895. He studied and worked in Stockholm before receiving a scholarship to study for a masters degree in Economics at Columbia University in New York. There, he saw how US customers browsed the shelves of self-service stores stocked with foods pre-packaged into set units, while European shopkeepers still weighed and measured out products.

Back in Sweden, Rausing co-founded Scandinavia's first packaging company, Åkerlund & Rausing, in 1929. He was determined to develop lightweight containers for drinks to replace heavy glass bottles. In 1944, Åkerlund & Rausing patented the plastic-coated tetrahedron package invented by Erik Wallenberg, and Rausing founded Tetra Pak in 1951. The company's rapid worldwide expansion began in the 1960s, and brought Rausing and his family vast wealth. Rausing died at his estate in Simontorp, Sweden, in 1983, but Tetra Pak has remained the world's biggest packaging company.

This meant the milk would not foam when packaged or be exposed to bacteria in any air left at the top. Over the next eight years, Åkerlund & Rausing developed machines that could heat-seal these tetrahedron packages without burning their contents. By the early 1950s, the company had found a suitable material – a combination of strong paper, aluminium foil to block sunlight and prevent products from degrading, and plastic to hygienically seal in the liquid.

A sealed success

Tetra Pak was established in 1951 as a subsidiary company and went on to transform the packaging industry. In 1952, a local dairy started using its innovative packages. These were around 80 per cent lighter than traditional glass bottles, making them far cheaper to transport.

While the company still produces its tetrahedron packages, its most popular product is the Tetra Brik – a cuboid container that is easier to stack and use.

Tetra Brik, launched in 1963, led Tetra Pak to international success, and since the 1980s, it has been one of the world's largest food packaging companies. Its tetrahedron packages marked a shift away from durable, reusable containers to single-use packaging.

While they save time, labour, freighting space, and fuel, Tetra Paks nonetheless produce significant amounts of waste that needs to be recycled – they are a product of a time when convenience and not sustainability drove innovations in design. ▪

Formation of tetrahedron pack

1: Paper reinforced with layers of plastic and foil is rolled into a continuous tube and liquid is poured in.

Paper is rolled into a tube

The tube is sealed

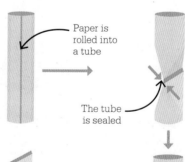

2: With liquid inside, the tube is gripped, and heat sealed. This forms one end of an individual container.

4: The string of sealed containers is cut into individual packs, filled with liquid. Very little material is wasted.

The pack is cut off

A second seal is made

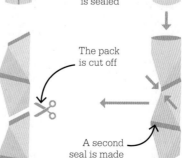

3: The lower part of the tube is then gripped and sealed from the opposite direction, forming a tetrahedron.

A PLAN FOR LIVING
G PLAN DESIGN

Firmly anchored in Mid-century Modern design principles, British furniture range G Plan introduced modern design concepts to the living and dining rooms of the 1950s. It ushered in a new era of quality, craftsmanship, and affordability in the furniture industry.

The range had its roots in E Gomme Ltd, a furniture manufacturing company founded in 1898 by Ebenezer Gomme in

G Plan furniture helped to define the look of 1950s Britain. These examples from 1953 include a drop-leaf dining table and chairs that showcase its modernist-inspired designs.

High Wycombe, Buckinghamshire. Gomme's firm embraced modern furniture-making techniques and went on to develop the concept of the dining-room suite. By 1922, it employed almost 300 people, and it continued to produce furniture until the start of World War II, when the government was forced to restrict the manufacture and sale of furniture through the Utility Furniture Scheme.

A time of hope

The years that followed the end of World War II marked the beginning of a more optimistic era for British designers. In 1951, the Festival of Britain showcased the impressive talent of British designers, helping to boost demand for British products, and the following year, furniture manufacturing restrictions were finally lifted. It was in this context that in 1952 the design director of E Gomme Ltd, Donald Gomme – Ebenezer's grandson – began to develop a new range of furniture that would capture the country's appetite for a contemporary style.

To establish a strong brand, Gomme brought in Doris Gundry from the J Walter Thompson advertising agency. Gundry came

The end of furniture rationing and the UK government's Utility Furniture Scheme created a market thirsty for **modern new designs**.

↓

Families could furnish their homes gradually, and buy **individual G Plan pieces** when finances allowed or through **hire-purchase**.

→

Modular pieces could stand alone or be added to, and items such as **extendable dining tables** suited modern lifestyles.

↓

Magazine adverts showed furniture in homely settings presenting G Plan furniture as an **aspirational lifestyle choice**.

←

Showrooms and exhibitions allowed customers **to touch and try out** G Plan furniture before buying.

↓

G Plan was a plan for living

---

up with the name "G Plan", with the "G" derived from the Gomme surname. The introduction of the G Plan range marked a rejection of Britain's recent utilitarian past: typically made of teak wood, the furniture in the collection made use of more modernist aesthetics, defined by gentle curves, tapered legs, and refined upholstery. It offered a welcome break from the limited, more sombre options of pre-war and wartime Britain.

Affordable elegance
Crucially, the G Plan range offered visual and economic flexibility – it looked good in all types of homes and was affordable. Families could purchase one item of furniture at a time, allowing them to purchase their furnishings at a reasonable cost, while creating their own configurations, tailored to their homes. G Plan was one of the pioneers of modular design for the UK's mass market.

Rather than focus on selling their products through retailers, the team behind G Plan decided to appeal directly to their consumers' imaginations. National advertising campaigns presented their modern furniture designs in settings that were relatable but subtly aspirational. The range was shown to be not only functional and beautiful, but also empowering, enabling people to transform their own homes. ∎

Britain's Utility Furniture Scheme

Following the outbreak of World War II, the British furniture industry faced government restrictions on the use of essential resources, including timber. From September 1942, the "manufacture of civilian furniture" was prohibited without a licence, which would only be granted for the production of utility goods. In 1943, the Board of Trade published a Utility Furniture Scheme catalogue, comprising around 30 household items such as chairs and tables that could be manufactured at low cost.

The Utility Furniture Scheme's main objective was to ensure that furniture was produced in a functional and cost-effective manner and conserved essential materials. A set of design standards was established, and the designs were often characterized by simplicity, with an emphasis on durability and efficiency.

E Gomme Ltd helped the war effort by manufacturing aircraft frames, and only returned to furniture production after the war.

A permit was required to buy furniture as well as for producing it. The utility scheme regulations remained in force until 1949.

UNSCREW THE LEGS
FLAT-PACK FURNITURE

During the mid-20th century, an ingenious new way of selling furniture directly to customers became increasingly popular. The phenomenon of flat-pack furniture – where the item is supplied in kit form with the component parts, screws, and other fastenings accompanied by instructions and sometimes basic tools for assembly – was devised as a way to keep shipping costs down and reduce the likelihood of furniture being damaged in transit. As the furniture is designed in simple parts for self-assembly, the manufacturing process is less complex, and the savings can be passed on to the consumer.

Early experiments with flat-pack furniture began in 1859, when cabinetmaker Michael Thonet created the No 14 chair. It was made from six pieces of wood that were designed to be packed in a flat container and assembled at the other end. Other pioneers of flat-

Up to 36 of Michael Thonet's No 14 chairs could be packed into a 1 cu m (36 cu ft) box, along with all the hardware needed for assembly, which made it easy and economical to export.

pack designs include Australian designer Frederick Ward, who developed a series of furniture kits called "Timber-pack" in 1948 based on the concept of dressmaking patterns. And in the US in 1953, Ohio cabinetmaker Erie J Sauder received the first US patent for ready-to-assemble furniture – for a table designed in 1951 that could be put together at home without the need for glue or fixings.

IKEA embraces flat-pack
While it may not have invented the concept of flat-pack, or even been the first company to sell self-assembly designs in Sweden, the story of flat-pack is dominated by IKEA. The Swedish brand, founded in 1943 by Ingvar Kamprad,

See also: Interchangeable parts 106–07 ▪ Material-led furniture design 186–87 ▪ Mid-century Modern 216–21 ▪ G Plan design 226–27

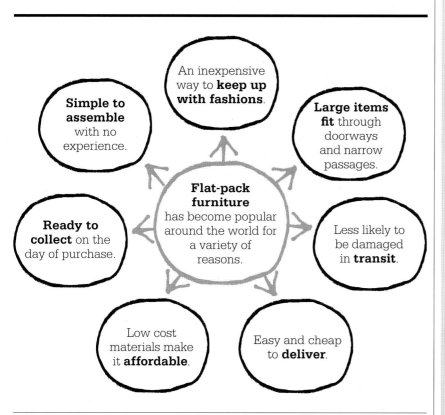

Flat-pack furniture has become popular around the world for a variety of reasons.

- An inexpensive way to **keep up with fashions**.
- **Large items fit** through doorways and narrow passages.
- Less likely to be damaged in **transit**.
- Easy and cheap to **deliver**.
- Low cost materials make it **affordable**.
- **Ready to collect** on the day of purchase.
- **Simple to assemble** with no experience.

originally sold pens and small goods before expanding into mail-order furniture. However, it was the development of a commercial strategy around flat-packs that enabled IKEA to become a global giant in furniture.

Kamprad worked with Ovendals, a supplier of a new table fitting that made assembly easier, and in 1953, IKEA introduced its first self-assembly tables – DELFI, RIGA, and KÖKSA – which could be ordered from the catalogue and assembled at home. Just three years later in 1956, IKEA designer Gillis Lundgren inspired the company's strategic pivot into flat-pack furniture with the creation of the LÖVET table, which had detachable legs and could be put in a flat parcel. The idea that a

customer could go to a store, buy a piece of furniture, take it home that same day or have it delivered, and assemble it themselves was completely new. To customers who were used to waiting weeks or even months for delivery of their furniture, IKEA's innovation was nothing short of revolutionary.

A complex legacy

Since the 1950s, flat-pack furniture has become ubiquitous. The low cost and quality of some pieces has raised concerns that much of it will likely be disposed of in landfill. However, this may be partially offset by the benefits of a lower carbon footprint as a result of using smaller boxes for transport, and easier disassembly allowing more options for recycling. ∎

Gillis Lundgren

Born in Lund, Sweden in 1925, Gillis Lundgren studied at the Malmö Institute of Technology before joining IKEA in 1953 as its fourth employee.

The catalyst for IKEA's move into flat-pack furniture came in 1956 when Lundgren was having trouble fitting a table into his car. He realized that it would be far easier to transport the table if he could just remove the legs during transit and reassemble the table at his destination. Lundgren went on to design more than 200 pieces of furniture for IKEA, including many of the company's most successful products.

One of Lundgren's early designs, the LÖVET table, had a leaf-shaped tabletop made from jacaranda and three detachable legs with brass-covered feet. Another Lundgren design, the BILLY bookcase, remains an IKEA bestseller more than 40 years since its launch in 1979. Lundgren continued to work with IKEA as a consultant after his retirement. He died in 2016 at the age of 86.

My design philosophy has always been ... to create solutions for everyday based on people's needs.
Gillis Lundgren
2012

OPTIMISM, HIGH SPIRITS, AND CONFIDENCE
YOUTH CULTURE

IN CONTEXT

FOCUS
Targeting a new demographic

FIELD
Graphic design, fashion, advertising

BEFORE
1941 The word "teenager" first appears in US magazine *Popular Science*.

1944 *Seventeen*, the first magazine aimed at teenagers, launches in September and sells out in just two days.

AFTER
1965 *Harper's Bazaar* devotes its entire April issue to a celebration of youth culture.

1970 *Soul Train* premieres on US TV. It is seen as the Black counterpart to *American Bandstand*, which appeals to a mostly white audience.

In 1946, a feature in US magazine *Business Week* referred to American teenagers as a "jackpot market". Advertisers suddenly saw an untapped and highly lucrative demographic with a rebellious attitude, a fervent wish to be as different from their parents' generation as possible, and money to spend.

The economic pressures of World War II had drawn large numbers of teenagers into the workforce and provided them with previously unheard-of earning power. At the start of the 1960s, buoyed by babysitting jobs and paper rounds, young people's income was at its highest since

See also: Visual merchandising and retail design 124–31 ▪ Branding 200–07 ▪ Dawn of television 208–11

Advertisers latch onto the **earning power of young people** and start **to promote products** aimed at that demographic.

↓

Youth-targeted TV shows prove a popular way to pitch products to a **young captive audience**.

↓

Gender-specific magazines popularize new masculine and feminine **ideals** for generations of **young consumers**.

↓

Youth culture moves beyond its initial focus, drawing adults into its sphere.

Mary Quant

Legendary British fashion designer Mary Quant was born in London in 1930. After studying art at Goldsmith College, she became an apprentice at milliner Erik Braagaard's shop in Mayfair.

In 1955, Quant opened a boutique called Bazaar on the King's Road in Chelsea. At first, the shop sold outfits bought on the wholesale market, but Quant soon began stocking the racks with her own modern designs. She initiated a gruelling but innovative production cycle: each day's sales at Bazaar paid for fabric to be made up overnight into items for the next day. Her cottage-industry approach meant that Bazaar was continually restocked with brand-new items for truly up-to-the-minute looks. Her super-short skirts and use of new materials such as PVC vinyl fabrics were critical to the development of the Swinging Sixties youth scene. In 1966, Quant introduced a make-up line for young women, featuring bright colours and shiny textures. She remains a powerful influence in fashion even after her death in 2023.

the end of World War II. Youth consumer spending – estimated at more than $9 billion a year in 1958, and increasing to $14 billion by 1965 in the US alone – included mass-produced goods such as fizzy drinks, clothes, records, beauty and grooming products, and cars.

During this period of economic boom, not only did the teenage market enjoy more disposable income and more leisure time than any previous generation, but there were also more of them to sell things to. The millions of babies born in the mid-1940s and early 1950s, at the start of the so-called baby boom, were now well into their teenage years. By 1970, the number of American babyboomers in their teens had reached a peak of 20 million.

The advertising machine
During the 1950s, the advertising industry mastered the language of television. New programme formats emerged – including dance party shows and talent competitions such as *Teen Twirl*, *American Bandstand*, and *TV Teen Club* in the US – all in the service of selling to a seemingly insatiable teenage market.

Traditional print advertising, featuring a lot of text, a serious tone about the benefits of the product, and humdrum photography, was » ditched in favour of an ironic approach, mixed with irreverence and humour, that supported its target audience's wish to be seen as a new, independent generation.

Youth magazines

Seventeen was the first magazine to acknowledge that teenage girls were a unique demographic, with its own set of considerations for designers and writers to address. The publication ushered in a cultural reorientation: its primary message was not service or advice, but consumerism. As such, it was instrumental in introducing girls to a culture of consumption born out of post-war prosperity.

The magazine was an instant hit and played a key role in establishing the taste and behaviour of several generations of teenage girls. Marketeers at the magazine even created a fictional teenager named Teena, compiled from market research data, and sent a booklet entitled *Life with Teena* to major brands, urging them to advertise specifically to this customer.

Advertising both shaped and mirrored youth culture; it drew its cues from its wide, hungry

audience and broadcast them ever further. A 1960 *New York Times* article reported in a survey that the young readers of *Seventeen* had spent nearly $164 million on gifts for family and friends during the previous year.

Gender-based advertising

Marketing aimed at male teenagers initially took a different tack. In the US, there was great social concern

The Five Satins rose to fame in 1956 with the doo-wop song "In the Still of the Night". They were one of the first Black acts to appear on the TV show *American Bandstand*.

coming from parents, religious groups, law enforcement agencies, and the FBI about a lost generation of "juvenile delinquents" that had grown up largely unsupervised in the late 1940s and 1950s – their fathers had died in the war, and their mothers had entered the full-time workforce.

Cosmopolitan's special 1957 issue on youth referred to a "vast, determined band of blue-jeaned storm troopers forcing us to do exactly as they dictate". Tobacco companies harnessed these societal concerns and started to market cigarettes to male teens as being representative of manhood and rebellion, joining manufacturers of jeans, leather jackets, and cars.

Teenage rebels in 1960s Britain splintered into two main factions: mods and rockers. Mods looked sharp in suits and skinny ties, riding around on scooters, and listening to a mix of Motown, ska, and bands such as The Who and Small Faces.

Bobby soxers wearing the ankle-high socks that gave them their name gather to meet their music idol Frank Sinatra in 1945.

American fashion

Youth culture in the US emerged at the beginning of the 20th century, with a leisure-oriented aesthetic for male teenagers – the collegiate, or Ivy League, style. By the 1920s, button-down shirts, chinos, letter sweaters, and cardigans were the norm for stylish young men.

The Great Depression and World War II hit American youth hard, and it was not until the late 1940s and early 1950s that teenagers began to express themselves through clothing once again. Bobby soxer girls wore

twinsets, full circle skirts, and saddle shoes. Their dates either kept to the more conservative college look or adopted a tough-guy greaser aesthetic: leather jackets, Levi's, and white T-shirts, topped with a slicked-back pompadour.

After the British Invasion of the 1960s, an eager population embraced mini skirts, paper and vinyl dresses, brightly coloured unisex fabrics, and hip-hugging bell-bottom jeans. Teenagers tested out new identities through fashion, with new fads arriving at a steady pace.

> You want to hit back at all the old geezers who try to tell us what to do. We're not going to take it.
> **John Braden**
> 18-year-old mod, *c.* 1964

In contrast, rockers rode motorcycles, wore leather jackets, sported greased-back pompadours, and listened to US rock 'n' roll, such as Gene Vincent and Eddie Cochran. The market for the accompanying accoutrements of teenage style was vast and lucrative.

Cultural diversity
In the US, the postwar teen market was predominantly white and middle class. Embedded racism and economic disadvantage made Black teenagers invisible to advertisers – in fact, Black teenagers were not featured in or targeted by mainstream outlets until the mid-1960s, when the growing Black Pride movement created a market for the haircare products that were required to maintain natural Afro styles.

By the end of the 1960s and into the 1970s, TV shows that focused on the experiences of young Black people began to emerge – such as *Soul Train*, *Room 222*, and *What's Happening!!* – and advertisers started to pay more attention to Black youth culture. The soul music boom of the 1960s led to the rise of Motown Industries,

a multimillion-dollar endeavour that included music, movie, TV, and publishing divisions.

Advertising with music
Music also played a vital part in the growing youth culture market: the advent of the 7-inch 45-rpm single and the invention of inexpensive portable record players made music affordable, desirable, and profitable.

In the 1960s, advertisers used popular songs in TV and radio adverts to reach a teen audience that wanted to be seen as hip and cool. A good example is the 1961 "Now It's Pepsi, for Those Who Think Young" campaign, arguably the brand's first foray into youth-targeted advertising. The 1963 "Pepsi Generation" adverts focused as much on selling the product as on creating a desirable lifestyle that showed young people enjoying a number of active pursuits.

Coca-Cola, which had previously promoted its drink using nostalgic scenes of small-town life, quickly jumped on the bandwagon to target the same market. Its 1971 "I'd Like to Buy the World a Coke" campaign featuring a group of young people singing on a hilltop was so popular that the accompanying jingle was re-recorded as a two-minute song – and became a hit in its own right.

Influential attitudes
By the 1960s, the juggernaut of youth culture dominated popular media and reflected the social changes of a turbulent decade: the sexual revolution, the Black Power movement, and the birth of outspoken feminism. Mary

Quant's boutique on London's King's Road offered customers trendsetting fashions that were widely copied elsewhere. British model Twiggy brought her flower-child-meets-waif look to the pages of *Vogue*, along with American heiress – and "youthquaker" – Edie Sedgwick. Rock stars like Jimi Hendrix, the Rolling Stones, and The Beatles also influenced their audiences through fashion and the design of concert posters, album covers, and T-shirts.

Around the mid-1960s, youth culture was also embraced by adults in their 20s and 30s. The consumer-driven lifestyle first marketed to teenagers proved so alluring that even their elders were drawn in. ∎

British model Twiggy became a fashion icon during the Swinging Sixties. She was known for her petite frame, short hairstyle, and large eyes framed by black eyelashes.

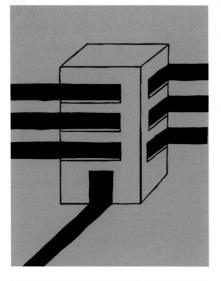

THE GRAPHIC EXTENSION OF A COMPANY

CORPORATE IDENTITY

IN CONTEXT

FOCUS
Building customer loyalty and trust

FIELD
Branding, logo design, visual communication

BEFORE
2000 BCE Craftsmen start to carve mason's marks into tombs and other structures to identify their workshop.

1870s Companies begin to appreciate the importance of logos to differentiate themselves from the competition.

AFTER
1950s–60s Agencies such as the Conran Design Group (established 1957) and Wolff Olins (1965) are set up to focus on developing brand identities.

1990s Cultural organizations, cities, and countries begin to see themselves as brands that require corporate identities to stand out.

As **companies grow** and become multinational, **branding** becomes **more sophisticated**.

After World War I, a **clean, minimal approach** to design and architecture begins to emerge.

Modernism spreads globally, promoting simplicity, consistency, and the use of geometric abstraction to convey meaning.

Organizations adopt a **systematic approach** and introduce **corporate identity manuals** to standardize brand design.

A subset of branding, corporate identity refers to the design components that represent the values, mission, and vision of an organization. It includes the logo, colour palette, typography, and other visual assets, such as photography or illustration.

The discipline began to emerge as a field of graphic design in the early 20th century. As branding and advertising became more sophisticated, businesses seeking to control their public image saw the appeal of a unified visual scheme that could be protected by trademarks and managed with standards and templates.

Behrens and Modernism

One of the first corporate identity systems was designed in 1907 by German architect Peter Behrens for AEG, a prominent Berlin-based producer of electrical equipment. Behrens created a logo and design principles that could be consistently applied across the board – from advertising material and company publications, to packaging and building signage.

In the same year, Behrens co-founded the Deutscher Werkbund, and over the next decade he developed a successful architectural practice focused on progressive design reform. Several of the leading exponents of European Modernism – including Walter Gropius and Le Corbusier – began their careers in Behrens's studio.

Under the broader influence of Modernism, corporate identity systems became widespread in the 1950s. Modernist values – informed by Mies van der Rohe's assertion that "less is more" – were well suited to rapidly growing companies that were beginning to expand internationally. Simplicity helped to ensure consistency across new product lines and regions.

Uniform language

Mid-century designers such as Paul Rand in the US and Yusaku Kamekura in Japan became known for skilfully conveying meaning through geometric abstraction. Rand believed that a distinctive, timeless logo and a well-defined

> If in the business of communication, image is king, the essence of this image, the logo, is the jewel in its crown.
> **Paul Rand**
> *Design, Form, and Chaos*, 1993

visual identity were integral to a company's success, and that design should help to communicate messages effectively, rather than merely being decorative.

Rand's work for IBM (1956–72) is still in use today. After designing a logo to identify and unify the technology company, Rand set about establishing clear guidelines

for typography, the application of colour, and layout formats. The project was directed by the principles of flexibility, versatility, and adaptability, leading to a system of graphic components that could be used in different ways. For example, anchored by the same basic rules, the logo could be applied as a key design element or as a small signature. This resulted in a diverse visual language that was always on brand and appropriate to the content but also allowed space for personality and creative expression across adverts, posters, packaging, and other printed materials.

Through the 1960s, integrated corporate design systems such as the one introduced by Rand at IBM became the norm. The designer's individual, intuitive method was gradually replaced by a rational, systematic approach enforced by corporate identity manuals, or brand guidelines. ▪

Logo types

A lettermark is a distinctive arrangement of letters that incorporates the company's initials or acronym, often simplifying a longer name for easier recognition.

A wordmark is a stylized typographic representation of the brand name. The text is the primary visual element, and it may incorporate a simple visual idea.

A pictorial mark is a graphic symbol or illustration that represents the brand essence without relying on text. These icons can be abstract, figurative, or literal.

In a combination mark, the logo includes both a symbol and a wordmark. Depending on context, the two elements may appear separately.

THE ARRANGEMENT OF THE DESKS WAS SOMEHOW ORGANIC

THE OFFICE LANDSCAPE

IN CONTEXT

FOCUS
Designing a flexible office workspace that encourages collaboration

FIELD
Architecture, interior design, furniture design

BEFORE
1726 The Old Admiralty Building is completed in London. It is widely recognized as the UK's first purpose-built office building.

1945 The end of World War II is followed by a post-war period of rapid economic growth in Germany.

AFTER
2010s The agile workplace, in which employees have no permanently assigned desks, grows in popularity.

2020 Home-working practices introduced during the Covid-19 pandemic, cause companies to rethink their use of office space.

The design concept of Bürolandschaft – German for "office landscape" – originated in West Germany in the early 1950s. Over the next 20 years, it helped to bring about a revolution in office design, championing an organic, open-plan office layout that encouraged communication and collaboration.

In the early 20th century, new technologies allowed firms to build offices away from their factories. Drawing on scientific management theories, companies sought to use these offices as efficiently as possible, with workplaces based around closed-door offices and segregated departmental layouts. Employees were gathered in high densities to maximize productivity.

Rejecting the past

By the 1950s, the West German economy was booming, and designers and managers had time and money to experiment with new ideas about how an office might work. In Hamburg in 1958, brothers

The Action Office suite, designed in the 1960s by Robert Propst for Herman Miller, was a customizable workspace with height-adjustable desks. The use of shelving as partitions gave workers defined areas and a degree of privacy.

See also: Industrial design 146–47 ▪ Hospitality design 178–79 ▪ Flat-pack furniture 228–29 ▪ Ergonomics 278–85

Wolfgang and Eberhard Schnelle founded what would become the Quickborner Team consulting group. Their firm specialized in creating office spaces that rejected the rigid, hierarchical office setup of the past in favour of a more open, collaborative approach.

Building on what they had learned working in their father's furniture studio, the brothers introduced the concept of an office landscape, embracing many of the egalitarian values that were becoming popular in northern Europe. Bürolandschaft was defined by the use of open clusters of desks, room dividers, and strong colours that would disrupt the look of a traditional workspace.

The success of Quickborner's first project, for the German publisher Bertelsmann in 1960, set a new standard for the design of office space in Europe. Word soon spread, and in 1967, Quickborner crossed the Atlantic, securing their first US commission with Du Pont.

Many cornerstone features of today's modern workplace were incorporated in Quickborner's projects. The careful placement

> Innovation comes from people meeting up in the hallways.
> **Steve Jobs**
> **"The seed of Apple's innovation"**
> *BusinessWeek*, October 2004

This Quickborner-designed office for Stadtwerke Karlsruhe shows how strategically placed plants enhance the interior and work with room dividers to direct the flow of traffic across the floor.

of large potted plants, screens, and cabinets to separate apparently random clusters of desks and chairs was in fact a deliberate effort to encourage increased movement and interaction, while respecting the necessary role that each person plays within a team.

Designing flexibility

In 1960, designer Robert Propst became president of US office furniture manufacturer Herman Miller, and set about improving the world of work. Propst was impressed by the Schnelle brothers' progressive approach and shared their egalitarian outlook. Using mobile screens and shelving units, Propst's Action Office adaptable furniture system helped to popularize some of the ideas behind the Bürolandschaft, and the concept spread. Indeed, the legacy of the Bürolandschaft is most evident in the variety of modular office furniture systems that dominate workspaces today. ▪

Egalitarian office space

In the aftermath of World War II, European countries like Sweden, Denmark, and Germany embraced a more social-democratic approach towards leadership and management. This was rooted in a culture of consensus and co-operation between governments, employers, and labour organizations. The concept of an egalitarian office where employees at all levels worked together in a shared space mirrored this outlook.

Bürolandschaft prioritized freedom and autonomy, with the creation of activity-based environments that allowed employees to choose how and where to do their best work. These might include quiet areas for focused tasks or collaborative spaces for team projects. A workplace with a more democratic use of space to encourage communication and collaboration has positive impacts on productivity and creativity, and the concept has become a central plank of many modern office designs.

The chaotic-looking floor plan for the Osram Headquarters in Munich shows groups of desks divided into sections by defined paths rather than by office walls.

WHISKERS IMBEDDED LIKE STRAWS IN BRICK

CARBON FIBRE

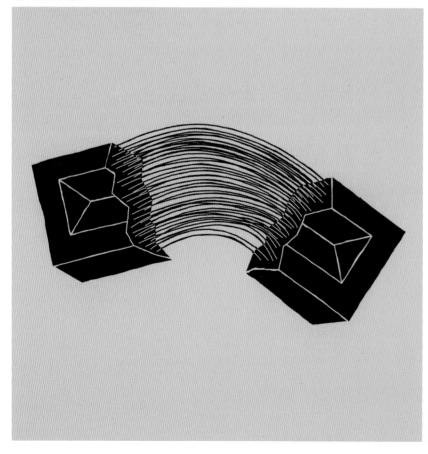

IN CONTEXT

FOCUS
A lightweight, strong design material

FIELD
Material design, product design, engineering, architecture

BEFORE
1855 British inventor Joseph Swan uses carbonized filaments while experimenting with incandescent light bulbs.

1879 US inventor Thomas Edison bakes cotton threads and bamboo slivers to create the first known carbon fibres.

AFTER
1963 Scientists at the British Ministry of Defence develop a process that greatly improves the strength of carbon fibre.

1984 US inventor and amputee Van Phillips designs the Flex-Foot running blade, a lightweight prosthetic leg made of carbon graphite.

Also known as graphite fibre, carbon fibre is composed of strong crystalline filaments of carbon that are twisted together like yarn. Although it is extremely thin – each strand is just 5–10 microns in diameter, or about the size of a single strand of spider web silk – carbon fibre is five times stronger than steel, twice as stiff, and about a third of the weight.

Carbon fibre can be woven into flexible cloth, or combined with resin or plastic and moulded to form solid components. Woven carbon fibre's strength lies in the

See also: Dawn of synthetic fabrics 194–95 ▪ Prosthetics and medical equipment 266–67 ▪ 3D digital printing 276–77 ▪ Smart materials 314–17

Scientists create carbon fibre and see great potential in its **weight, strength, and rigidity**.

Researchers continue to **develop techniques** for manufacturing carbon fibre-based materials.

Carbon fibre becomes highly sought after for everything from aerospace components to biomedical devices.

With an eye towards **sustainability**, 21st-century designers seek to create carbon fibre from **organic sources**.

Roger Bacon

Physicist and materials research scientist Roger Bacon was born in Cleveland, Ohio, US, in 1926. After studying for a PhD in solid-state physics, in 1956 he started working at the Union Carbide Corporation. Two years later, during laboratory experiments with graphite, Bacon accidentally discovered the first carbon fibres. These lab oddities were ten times smaller in diameter than a human hair, but when Bacon tested and measured them, he noted that their tensile strength was much higher than steel.

These early fibres, which contained about 20 per cent carbon, were fairly flexible but very expensive to produce. In 1964 Bacon developed stiffer rayon-based fibres that performed well at high temperatures, resisting expansion, and conducting very little heat. This material was soon in great demand by the aerospace, defence, and civil engineering industries.

Roger Bacon died in 2007. He was inducted into the National Inventors Hall of Fame in 2016.

complexity of its weave. As in a wire screen, carbon fibres are interwoven with each other at differing angles, then submerged in liquid plastic and pressed or heated until all the materials fuse together. The angle of the weave, as well as the type of resin combined with the fibre – usually epoxy, but sometimes polyester, vinyl ester, thermoplastic, or polyurethane – determines the strength of the finished composite.

Carbon fibre has numerous applications in the medical, aerospace, architectural, bicycle component, and sporting goods industries – or wherever a design material with minimal weight, high strength, and rigidity is needed.

Automotive applications
The physical properties of carbon fibre open up exciting possibilities in automotive design to reduce dependence on oil and gas. It is

estimated that replacing the steel components of the average vehicle with carbon-fibre elements would reduce a car's weight by 60 per cent, and its overall fuel consumption by 30 per cent, which would lower emissions by 10–20 per cent. Carbon-fibre car parts can also absorb large amounts of impact energy, increasing vehicle safety.

Due to the material's high cost, carbon-fibre body components are currently found mostly in Formula 1 race cars. A few consumer vehicles, however – including the BMW M6, the Lamborghini Aventador, and the Chevrolet Corvette ZR1 – use »

The carbon-fibre fabric shown in this macrophotograph has been woven in an over-and-under pattern. The tightness of the weave dictates the strength and stiffness of the material.

carbon-fibre components. In 2019, Aston Martin launched its first sport motorcycle, the limited-edition AMB 001, with a carbon-fibre structure.

Other forms of transport

Carbon fibre is a key ingredient in the design of other forms of modern transportation, from aircraft to bicycles and skateboards.

In the 1960s, engineers started to mix carbon fibres to protect the leading edges, noses, and wing tips of aircraft, missiles, and space vehicles. Almost every aircraft flying today contains carbon fibres in one or more of its components, most notably in the brakes on military and commercial jets.

Bicycle manufacturers use carbon fibre to make strong frames that are stiffer and a lighter weight than almost any other material.

Architectural uses

Carbon fibre has allowed architects to re-imagine traditional forms and building methods, and to move away from the rigid geometry of steel-frame construction and the massive weight of Brutalist concrete buildings. Because

> Carbon, in fact, is a singular element: it is the only element that can bind itself in long stable chains without a great expense of energy.
> **Primo Levi**
> *The Periodic Table*, 1975

carbon fibre does not need to be encased in as much concrete as steel rebar, it can carry a heavier load; in addition, unlike rebar, carbon fibre is rust-proof.

Cutting-edge uses of carbon fibre in construction include the Foster and Partners-designed Steve Jobs Theater, at Apple's headquarters in Cupertino, California. The airy lobby boasts the world's largest carbon-fibre roof, which requires only minimal structural support; the rest of the building is made mostly of glass.

In 2022, German architecture firm Henn completed the world's first building made of carbon concrete for the Technical University of Dresden. Called the Cube, its twisted arc facade is a reference to the flexible qualities of the carbon fibre that make the structure possible. The Cube's interiors are equipped with insulation pads, heating elements, and interactive touch surfaces, making good use of carbon fibre's electrical conductivity.

Medical applications

The medical industry relies upon carbon fibre for the production of prosthetics, lightweight surgical tools, and other equipment.

The lightness and flexibility of prosthetic limbs made from carbon fibre provide amputees with comfort and functionality. The material is also used to manufacture implants for spinal and orthopaedic surgery; one of the advantages is that these carbon-fibre implants are safe for use in MRI scanners and in medical procedures that require non-magnetic materials.

Crutches, walkers, and wheelchairs made of carbon fibre are easier for recovering patients to manoeuvre, and the material's durability ensures that the equipment can withstand hard daily use.

Design-led applications

The versatility of carbon fibre has also inspired playful approaches. In 2018, Zaha Hadid Architects reinterpreted Danish designer

The Steve Jobs Theater at Apple Park is a state-of-the-art glass pavilion. It is topped by a roof consisting of 44 radial panels made of carbon fibre that creates a lens-like effect.

Lusso's Vivere bath, the world's first tub made from forged carbon fibre, takes its inspiration from the sleek Bugatti Veyron sports car, which also uses this cutting-edge material.

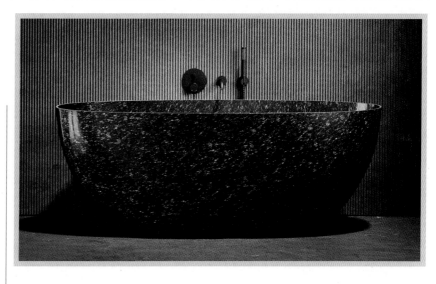

Hans J. Wegner's 1963 CH07 Shell Chair, which has a wing-like silhouette balanced on three tapered legs. While the original used wood and leather, Hadid's version combines the compressive properties of stone and the tensile properties of carbon fibre to achieve maximum thinness, lightness, and structural performance.

In 2023, British homeware company Lusso released the world's first bathtub made from a blend of carbon fibres and polymer resins. Scratch-resistant and durable, the tub weighs less than cast-iron or acrylic models, and it keeps bathwater warm for a long time due to its heat-retention properties.

Drawbacks of carbon fibre

Despite its many positive qualities, carbon fibre has several substantial downsides. One of the most significant is that it is difficult to mass-produce, which makes it a very costly material.

Carbon fibre is made from petroleum-based raw materials, and is about eight times more carbon-intensive to make than steel. The manufacturing process also produces hazardous gases such as ammonia, carbon monoxide, and nitrogen oxide.

Recycling carbon fibre is also difficult. The energy cost of processing carbon fibre via the main recycling methods –thermal, chemical, and mechanical – is disproportionate to the commercial value of the end product.

Recycling also presents a challenge because there are currently no mechanisms available to sort the origin of the fibres used in composite scraps. This means that recycled carbon fibre is not suitable for making products with structural applications. Hybrid yarns and non-woven products have a promising future for recycled carbon fibre, but current processes still yield a product with low mechanical performance.

To address some of these concerns, scientists are developing carbon fibres made from biomaterials such as cellulose and rayon instead of fossil fuels. Lignin, a byproduct of the paper industry, is a substance found in most plants that can be turned into carbon fibres. Its plant-based origin means that it removes carbon from the air during its lifecycle, rather than adding carbon from fossil sources such as oil or coal into the atmosphere. However, further research is needed to improve the quality of recycled carbon fibre and lower its environmental footprint and cost, as more and more design uses are found for this modern material. ∎

Resin transfer moulding

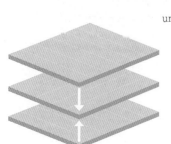

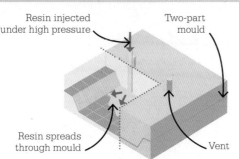

Resin injected under high pressure

Two-part mould

Resin spreads through mould

Vent

Carbon fibres are spun, wound onto bobbins, and woven into sheets. The sheets are stacked with the fibres running in different directions for maximum strength.

Sheets are added to a mould that is heated and placed under a vacuum. Resin is injected into the mould and cured to form rigid components.

BACK TO PURITY, BACK TO SIMPLICITY

BUILT TO LAST

After World War II, many Western countries enjoyed long periods of political stability and economic prosperity. As a result of people having a larger disposable income, affordability became a less immediate concern, and both manufacturers and consumers shifted their attention to quality and longevity instead.

The Mid-century Modern movement embraced clean, simple lines and functional aesthetics; at the same time, technological advances allowed the precision manufacturing of durable goods.

These factors – combined with a rising awareness of environmental issues – created a demand for products that minimized waste, ushering in the built-to-last era.

Prioritizing reliability
Emerging from the 1960s, an era in which there were broad societal and cultural changes, the built-to-last concept is characterized by a focus on durability through quality construction, craftsmanship, and timeless aesthetics.

In direct contrast to planned obsolescence – the controversial practice of designing a product with a limited lifespan that leads to repeat purchases over the years – the built-to-last philosophy resulted in items being designed with materials and techniques that withstood wear and tear, ensuring long-term usability.

Among those who best embodied the built-to-last ethos is the German electronics company Braun. With Dieter Rams as head

Stereo Steuergerät Atelier 3

Steuergerät ohne Lautsprecher mit Rundfunkempfangsteil für vier Wellenbereiche. Eingebauter Stereo-Plattenspieler. Hochwertiges, zweikanaliges Verstärkerteil. Für Stereo-Betrieb sind zwei Lautsprechereinheiten nötig. Braun L 20, L 40, L 45 oder L 50 sind besonders gut geeignet.

BRAUN

Designed by Dieter Rams, Braun's stylish Atelier 3 record player/radio arrived in shops in 1962 and is still highly prized among collectors.

See also: Bronzeware 42–45 ▪ Early mass production 64–65 ▪ Interchangeable parts 106–07 ▪ Plastic 148–53 ▪ Bauhaus 170–71 ▪ Design for social change 180–81 ▪ Mid-century Modern 216–21

Design must be functional, and functionality must be translated into visual aesthetics …
Ferdinand A. Porsche
Designer of the Porsche 911

of design from the early 1960s, the brand adhered to the Bauhaus approach, combining simplicity, functionality, and aesthetics. Braun's products featured clean lines, a minimalist style, and a dedicated focus on usability – values that both reassured and resonated with their customers.

To this day, Braun continues to promote its products – from electric shavers, to kitchen appliances – on a built-to-last basis, highlighting

aspects such as precision engineering, the careful use of top-of-the-range materials, and a rigorous testing regime.

Environmental policies

Repairability and recyclability are two elements that underpin the built-to-last philosophy. The ability to substitute a faulty part ensures that the lifetime of an appliance can be further extended. Repairing, rather than replacing, minimizes waste and lowers a product's carbon footprint.

A well-considered recycling strategy also contributes to a product's built-to-last credentials. Circular, or closed-loop, recycling, in particular, involves repurposing waste material instead of simply directing it to landfill – glass, for example, can be crushed, melted, and remoulded into bottles or jars. In 2009, designer Dirk van der Kooij opened a studio in Eindhoven, The Netherlands, where he creates durable furniture, such as his Meltingpot Table, from recycled plastic. ▪

Post-war **economic growth** leads to increased **disposable income**.

Affordability becomes a **less powerful driver** than quality when buying products.

At the same time, **environmental concerns** begin to emerge.

Companies respond to consumer demand for quality by manufacturing durable products.

Dieter Rams

Born in Wiesbaden, Germany, in 1932, Dieter Rams is an industrial designer renowned for his minimalist approach. After studying architecture and interior decoration at Wiesbaden School of Art, Rams joined Braun in 1955. Within six years, he had become head of design, and a key figure in shaping the company's design language.

Rams's design philosophy, summed up in his "Ten Principles for Good Design", advocates simplicity, functionality, and user-centredness. His creations for Braun, ranging from radios

to coffee makers, are celebrated for their clean lines and timeless aesthetics. His impact extends to his collaboration with furniture company Vitsoe, for which he designed the 606 Universal Shelving System, emphasizing adaptability and sustainability.

Throughout his career, Rams's focus has been on design as a means of improving a person's quality of life. He has inspired a generation of designers, and his legacy is assured as one of thoughtful, purposeful, and enduring design principles.

ONE THIN RUBBER MEMBRANE FROM DEATH

SAFETY FABRICS

IN CONTEXT

FOCUS
Fabrics engineered to provide protection and save lives

FIELD
Textile design, product design, engineering

BEFORE
400–300 BCE Etruscan artworks show soldiers wearing chainmail.

1850s Firefighters in Paris, France, wear asbestos helmets for protection against fire.

AFTER
1999 British materials scientists Richard Palmer and Philip Green develop protective clothing using a dilatant liquid, which becomes rigid upon impact.

2018 Researchers at Utah State University, US, use spider silk to create protective mesh.

For millennia, clothing has been designed to protect the human body from extreme temperatures, strong sunlight, water, and injury – yet be flexible and light enough to allow unencumbered movement. A number of different materials – both natural and synthetic – have been explored and developed in the quest to create effective safety gear.

Chainmail was an early example of protective clothing. Designed for battle in the 3rd or 4th century BCE, it was made of metal – which has obvious resistant properties – but structured like a textile. Modern equivalents of chainmail are still in

See also: Early textiles 24–29 ▪ Manufacturing textiles 84–91 ▪ Theory of colours 94–101 ▪ Dawn of synthetic fabrics 194–95 ▪ Smart materials 314–17

There are very few people in their careers that have the opportunity to do something to benefit mankind.
Stephanie Kwolek, 2007

use as components of stab-resistant body armour, shark-resistant wetsuits, and cut-resistant gloves for woodworkers.

Silk may seem a surprising material to use for protective clothing, but the delicate fabric is made with fibres that are extremely strong in proportion to their weight, and layers of silk have been shown to protect against great force. The material's resistant properties came to attention in the late 19th century. During a post-mortem in 1881, American doctor George E. Goodfellow found a silk handkerchief wrapped around the fatal bullet in one of his patients, which inspired him to explore the protective qualities of this material. However, the first successful attempt to create a bulletproof garment came from Polish-American priest and inventor Casimir Zeglen, who successfully tested such a vest in 1897. It was prohibitively expensive to make and was never produced on an industrial scale.

Fireproof fabric

By the 1930s, many firefighters and furnace workers were supplied with full-body, fireproof suits made of asbestos fabric. The fire-resistant qualities of asbestos have been known since at least the 3rd millennium BCE, and early 20th-century fire suits used asbestos fabric or incorporated fire-retardant chemical solutions such as baking soda or boric acid. These suits were effective but heavy and cumbersome. One »

Hard materials such as metal are used for **protective clothing**.

Lightweight, soft materials such as silk are shown to be **strong enough** to offer protection.

Chemists begin to develop **new protective fabrics**, largely in the field of **polymer research**.

New research explores the replication of natural materials such as spider silk.

Stephanie Kwolek

The daughter of Polish immigrant parents, Stephanie Kwolek was born in Pittsburgh, Pennsylvania, in 1923. She was a creative child, and grew up as interested in her mother's sewing as in her father's love of science. In 1946, she completed a degree in chemistry at her home city's Margaret Morrison Carnegie College.

Intending to go on to medical school, Kwolek took a temporary position at DuPont, a company already renowned for creating synthetics such as nylon. She enjoyed her work there so much, however, that she decided to stay – until her retirement in 1986. During that time, she registered at least 17 patents, including those for Kevlar.

Kwolek won many accolades and was inducted into the National Inventor's Hall of Fame in 1995. The following year, she was awarded the National Medal of Technology and Innovation. Kwolek also mentored many young scientists. She died in Delaware in 2014.

manufactured by Bells Asbestos and used by the British RAF, for example, weighed 12.7 kg (28 lb).

Polymer research

Also in the 1930s, textile developers turned to organic chemistry and research into long-chain polymers that produced strong, lightweight fibres. US corporation DuPont led much of the polymer research at this time. In 1935, one of its research scientists, Wallace Carothers, produced the first wholly synthetic fabric, nylon, which is both durable and relatively slow to ignite.

Later, polymer research would lead to the discovery of a whole new generation of safety fabrics. In 1961, Wilfred Sweeny, a Scottish chemist working for DuPont, discovered Nomex. This proved to be a major breakthrough because its aramid fibres form an impenetrable barrier to heat and flames and, crucially, do not melt at high temperatures. Instead, they form a carbon "char", which helps prevent the fire spreading to other parts of the garment. Firefighters and racing-car drivers wear Nomex clothing. Since 2020, Formula 1 racing suits have been

When you think of a space walker, you may visualize … advanced technology [but] I see a covey of little old ladies hunched over their glue pots.
Michael Collins
Apollo 11 astronaut, 1974

required to withstand 12 seconds of exposure to flames of up to 800°C (1,470°F) – and Nomex delivers this protection.

In 1965, while searching for a strong, lightweight fibre to replace steel in tyres, Polish-American research chemist Stephanie Kwolek, another DuPont employee, made an accidental yet dramatic discovery. One of her experiments, conducted at room temperature, produced a substance with unexpected qualities: it was cloudy, thin, and crystalline, rather than viscous

and clear, which is what she had expected. Normally, the substance would have been discarded, but Kwolek was intrigued and submitted it for testing. The colleague who was responsible for spinning materials into fibre at first refused, deeming the substance unsuitable and likely to damage the equipment. He eventually relented, and as Kwolek recalled, it created something "very strong and very stiff, unlike anything we had made before". The fibre – Kevlar – turned out to be at least five times stronger than steel but far lighter. It is the principle fabric for bulletproof clothing today.

Space programme

During the 1960s, a number of different companies competed for the high-stakes, high-budget project to design and make space suits for NASA's Apollo space programme. The eventual winner was American corporation ILC Industries, the parent company of Playtex, best known for its latex bras and girdles.

Although the experience of the pattern-cutters and machinists at ILC was in making lingerie, they were able to transfer their skills

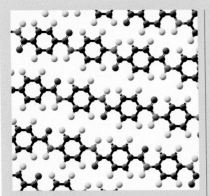

Kevlar is made up of long molecular chains of atoms: carbon (black), oxygen (red), nitrogen (blue), and hydrogen (white).

Kevlar's steel strength

The first fibre to reveal the benefits of its strength-to-weight ratio was natural silk, but it was the development of synthetic equivalents that led to the creation of Kevlar.

The extended and neatly aligned molecular chains within Kevlar fibre are what give it inherently strong protection against slashes, cuts, and punctures. It is one of a group of chemicals called synthetic aromatic polyamides, or aramids. They are very strong and fire-resistant: weight for weight, Kevlar is at least five times the strength of steel. It does not become brittle until -196°C (-321°F) and does not melt until 560°C (1,040°F). Kevlar also has great tensile strength and stretches at least 2 per cent before breaking, which allows it to absorb the kinetic energy from a fired bullet. Among its many other uses, Kevlar is incorporated into tyres to reduce puncture rates, in the body armour of military vehicles to protect against fire, and in the hulls of lightweight speedboats.

Designed to keep an astronaut safe in temperatures ranging from -157 to 110°C (-250 to 230°F), an Apollo spacesuit's many layers of protection included 12 synthetic materials.

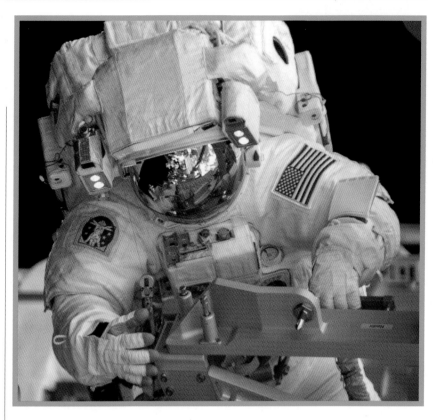

to tailoring space suits, working materials to fit body shapes perfectly. One innovation for the suit involved embedding a nylon mesh, previously used in Playtex bras, within the rubber of the suit to prevent it from ballooning dangerously in space.

Although made in the same factory as everyday items, the space suit was of an advanced design, with 4,000 pieces and 21 material layers, including cutting-edge fabrics such as Teflon-coated Beta cloth, light but tough polyesters Mylar and Dacron, Nomex, Kapton (a polyamide resistant to extreme temperatures), and Chromel-R, a woven stainless-steel fabric.

Safe when seen
The development of hi-vis, or high-visibility, material was a significant innovation in safety fabrics – for its preventative rather than protective qualities. Its invention came about in 1933, when American worker Bob Switzer was injured in a workplace accident that greatly affected his eyesight. While Bob was recovering in a darkened room, his chemist brother Joe entertained him with fluorescent paints. Realizing the commercial opportunities for the paints, the brothers experimented and later founded the Day-Glo Color Corp. Their products were the forerunners of hi-vis fabrics.

There are two main types of hi-vis fabric: fluorescent fabrics are effective during the day and at dawn and dusk, while retroreflective fabrics are more useful at night. Safety gear usually includes both elements: the fluorescent,

coloured fabric provides the base, and silver-coloured reflective strips are sewn on top.

Retroreflection works by reflecting a large percentage of directed light back to its source – for example, when car headlights shine on a cyclist's jacket, the light is reflected directly back to the motorist. Retroreflective materials were initially used in the 1930s for road signs and road paint but have since been incorporated into a variety of products. The leading manufacturer of retroreflective tape, 3M launched its Scotchlite material on clothing for the first time in 1951. These fabrics have silver backing combined with tiny glass beads in its surface that maximize its reflective qualities.

Hi-vis garments became widely used in the 1960s. For example, in 1964, Scottish Rail was the first

organization in the UK to require its workforce to use hi-vis. Today, hi-vis plays a vital road-safety role, helping cyclists, motorcyclists, and pedestrians increase their visibility in poor light conditions.

Future fabrics
Geotextiles that allow water to drain without washing away the soil have become a vaulable tool in construction, as well as in projects to mitigate coastal erosion; they include biodegradable options designed to last for a limited period. Meanwhile, the development of new and more effective protective fibres continues. Scientists in India have produced a fabric stronger than Kevlar by adding carbon nanotubes, while researchers in the US and China are hoping to produce an even tougher – and sustainable – material using spider silk. ∎

THE ART OF MAKING PLACES
URBAN DESIGN

Coined in 1956, the term "urban design" refers to how towns, cities, and streets are designed. It shapes the everyday environments where people live and work, and explores the way buildings, spaces, and the natural landscape fit together.

How urban spaces are formed depends on the values and priorities of planners, the resources and technologies available to them, and the climate of the space. The largest urban spaces are often the outcome of countless small acts by different people over time, but some have been intentionally shaped – either from the top-down by city planners, or from the bottom-up by communities and activists.

Top-down design

Inaugurated as the capital of Brazil in 1960, Brasília was designed from the top-down by urban planner Lucio Costa and architect Oscar Niemeyer during the 1950s. They were inspired by Le Corbusier's modernist urban planning ideals of geometry and uniformity. As a result, the city was designed in the shape of a bird in flight, with – according to Costa – a "monumental axis" and 96 superquadras, or super blocks,

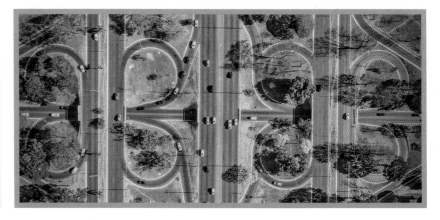

Roads that loop and flow together on the north wing of Brasília's bird-shaped plan allow traffic to merge onto the raised highways, or move off towards the superquadras.

See also: The Arts and Crafts movement 112–19 ■ Streetscape 172–73
■ Hospitality design 178–79 ■ Mid-century Modern 216–21

Necessary activity, such as people going to work or school, takes place in any **environment**.

→

Adding **facilities** such as pedestrian areas and parks **encourages optional activities**.

↓

The space between buildings becomes meaningful because of the variety of activities that occur there.

←

People spend **more time** in the space, which leads to spontaneous **social activities** such as children playing, or people greeting each other.

Legible cities

The concept of a legible city – a place that is easy to navigate and understand – is not just about way-finding. It is also about how people use the sights and sounds that they experience to create a mental map of the city. This approach to the cityscape was informed by the work of urban planner Kevin A. Lynch, who analysed how people navigated three US cities in the 1960s. Lynch realized that people used a variety of symbols and cues to "read" the city. Those cues included anything from scents and smells to paths and landmarks. Today, urban designers recognize the value of having uninterrupted views of landmarks as well as the significance of desire paths. These paths are routes that people naturally wish to take, such as a shortcut over a road that is close to a shop, rather than using a distant crossing. Accommodating these factors helps to make cities both legible and humane.

stretching out from the centre. Each superquadra was intended to be a self-sufficient neighbourhood.

Brasília was conceived as a utopian city of the future, a fresh start for Brazil, that presented a concept of city life that prioritizes the symbolism of the state. However, early residents of Brasília described its architectural repetition and uniformity as disorientating, and complained that its zoned spatial logic lacked the bustle of street life found in other Brazilian cities. Today, Brasília is a UNESCO world heritage site celebrated for its innovative town planning.

Prioritizing people
In the 1960s, urban planner Jan Gehl was tasked with redesigning the car-heavy central shopping street, Strøget, in Copenhagen, Denmark, into a pedestrian-friendly zone. Gehl's approach sought to infuse the city with humane values, by putting people at the heart of urban planning, providing places to congregate and making it easier to move around on foot or by

bicycle. This philosophy is reflected in Gehl's seminal book *Life between Buildings* (1971), which led to a period of urban development that prioritized making cities easier to live in. Gehl's ideas about place-making, the value of public space, and prioritizing people over cars can be seen in urban development projects across the world.

City branding
Today, an increasingly important element of urban design concerns city branding, particularly with the development of cities such as Dubai and Abu Dhabi in the United Arab Emirates. As they manage their expansion, both cities are focused on embracing their identities as urban spaces surrounded by desert and sea while remaining desirable places to live by providing green spaces and integrated services. Similarly, in Astana, Kazakhstan – which rises up from flat plains alongside rivers and lakes – global architects including Norman Foster and Zaha Hadid have sought to shape the city's identity through unique architecture. ■

It is that shape, colour, or arrangement which facilitates the making of vividly identified, powerfully structured, highly useful mental images of the environment.
Kevin A. Lynch
The Image of the City, 1960

GIVE ME PANTONE 123
PANTONE COLOURS

Colour plays a key role in design and visual communication – it helps establish mood, convey emotion, and influence perception. During the 20th century, advances in chemistry, printing, and manufacturing led to a surge in colour possibilities. This expanded the creative horizons for all types of designers, but it also created the challenge of ensuring consistency across different media and materials.

Until the 1960s, achieving accurate colour reproduction was a trial-and-error process, often reliant on personal judgment. The absence of a universal colour language meant that it was complex and time-consuming to communicate specifications across different regions and industries.

A new standard

In 1962, Lawrence Herbert bought M & J Levine Advertising, the small printing company in New Jersey where he worked. It was a watershed moment in the history of colour matching. Applying his skills as a chemistry graduate, Herbert began to streamline the company's pigment inventory and simplify its coloured ink production.

Under his stewardship, the firm evolved into an international authority on colour and colour systems. In 1963, Herbert rebranded the company as Pantone and introduced the Pantone Matching System (PMS). This simplified the science of colour-mixing and established a numeric code for each colour, creating the first standardized colour language. Printers were able to reduce their

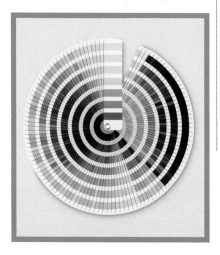

The Pantone Matching System (PMS) allows designers to easily identify a colour. It consists of a "fan deck", with each tab bearing a range of related shades.

See also: Pigments and colours 20–21 ▪ Theory of colours 94–101 ▪ Plastic 148–53 ▪ Dawn of synthetic fabrics 194–95 ▪ Branding 200–07

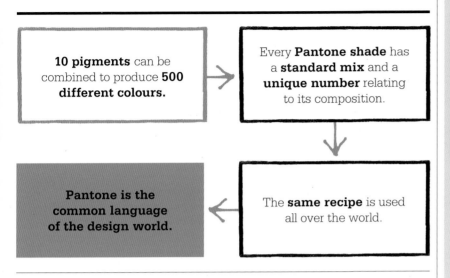

10 pigments can be combined to produce **500 different colours.**

Every **Pantone shade** has a **standard mix** and a **unique number** relating to its composition.

The **same recipe** is used all over the world.

Pantone is the common language of the design world.

Lawrence Herbert

Born in 1929 in the United States, Lawrence Herbert is a visionary figure in the world of design and colour. He is best known for his pivotal role in the development and popularization of the Pantone Matching System (PMS).

Herbert studied at Hofstra University, New York, majoring in biology and chemistry, before graduating in 1951. Five years later, Herbert began working as a printer at M&J Levine Advertising, where he skilfully matched the colours brought to him by clients and their designers.

By 1962, Herbert was running the ink and printing division at a profit, while the commercial advertising half of the business was in debt. That year, Herbert purchased the company and renamed it Pantone, a fusion of the Greek word "pan" (meaning "all" or "every") and "tone", as in the shade of a colour.

Herbert's company revolutionized the way colours were understood, specified, and reproduced across various design industries. He retired in 2007, after selling the company for $180 million to X-Rite.

basic pigment stock from around 60 to just 12. This was accomplished with the help of the Pantone Guides, compact sheets of cardboard or plastic, bound into a "fan deck". These precisely detailed the proportions in which the pigments should be mixed to achieve a full range of 500 coloured inks. This breakthrough enabled designers, manufacturers, and printers to achieve consistent results. As Herbert explained, if somebody wanted something printed in Tokyo, they could

say, "Give me Pantone 123!" and be confident that 123 – a daffodil yellow – would look exactly the same around the world.

Herbert then contacted prominent ink producers, proposing a licensing agreement for them to produce Pantone's core inks. Within two weeks, all but one had signed on, beginning a revolution in colour printing.

Beyond printing

Throughout the 1960s, Herbert expanded the basic matching system beyond printing to other industries. In 1964, he introduced a tool for designers, followed by an application for artists' materials the next year. Ten years later, Pantone ventured into the digital world with a data system for computerized colour. In 1988, it introduced its textile system, followed by a plastics system in 1993. Today, the system is used in fields as diverse as food science and medicine, to describe everything from the colour of wine to blood samples, and its colours are found everywhere – from the flags of countries to lines of makeup. ▪

God created the world in seven days… And on the eighth day, he called Pantone to put colour into it.
Lawrence Herbert
New York Times Magazine, 2013

INTEGRATED CIRCUITS WILL LEAD TO SUCH WONDERS
MAKING THINGS SMALLER

IN CONTEXT

FOCUS
Making devices more compact and powerful

FIELD
Product design, electrical engineering, computer engineering

BEFORE
1946 The first programmable computer – the ENIAC – uses 17,468 vacuum tubes.

1961 Robert Noyce patents the first silicon-based integrated circuit, or microchip.

AFTER
1977 The first mass-market personal computers – Apple II, Commodore PET 2001, and Tandy TRS-80 – are released.

1981 The first successful portable computer – the Osborne 1 – is launched.

1988 The first battery-powered laptop debuts.

Engineers and technologists are constantly searching for ways to make electrical components on a smaller scale. When space is saved, more parts can be packed into devices, and their design can become more efficient. This process is called miniaturization, and – especially since around 1965 – it has enabled electronic equipment to become more streamlined and portable. It has also led to computers becoming exponentially more powerful.

Between the late 1940s and the mid-1960s, several breakthroughs in the field of electronic engineering kickstarted the electronic age. The invention of the silicon-based

Gordon Moore

Born in the California town of Pescadero in 1929, Gordon Moore graduated from the University of California, Berkeley, with a degree in chemistry. In 1954, he received a PhD from the California Institute of Technology and then carried out post-doctoral research at Johns Hopkins University, Baltimore, before working at the Shockley Semiconductor Laboratory.

In 1957, Moore was one of the "traitorous eight" scientists who left Shockley to establish Fairchild Semiconductor in Silicon Valley.

In 1968, he and Robert Noyce – co-inventor of the integrated circuit – founded the Intel Corporation, which in the 1970s became a manufacturer of memory chips and semiconductor computer circuits.

Moore was awarded the US National Medal of Technology in 1990. He and his wife later established the Gordon and Betty Moore Foundation to raise funds for environmental conservation. Moore died in Hawaii in 2023.

transistor – a miniature version of a semiconductor that amplifies and switches electronic signals – in 1947 by American physicists Walter Brattain, John Bardeen, and William Shockley was particularly significant. In the following decades, it became an essential component of technology in every field from aviation to telecommunications.

Age of the microchip

The early 1960s saw the emergence of silicon-based integrated circuits, or microchips. These brought together all the components of an electronic circuit, including transistors, on a minute scale. From bathroom scales to jet planes, nearly every electronic device today contains a microchip. These tiny components – and other inventions in microelectronics – replaced vacuum tubes and wiring, creating new possibilities in electronics and computing. Every year, scientists and engineers were able to fit more transistors onto ever-smaller chips and circuit boards, using silicon as a base material. Many major

electronics companies making silicon-based products sprang up around Palo Alto, California, which became known as Silicon Valley.

Moore's law

In 1965, the journal *Electronics* asked Gordon Moore, director of research and development at Silicon Valley electronics company Fairchild Semiconductor, to predict developments over the next decade.

He forecast that the density of transistors on a microchip would continue to double every year, and the cost of making them would decrease. Moore speculated that this would lead to new technologies including "such wonders as home computers" and mobile phones.

The press quickly named this prediction Moore's law – an idea that symbolizes the power of miniaturization. Ten years later, »

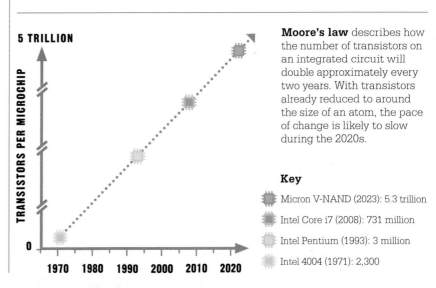

Moore's law describes how the number of transistors on an integrated circuit will double approximately every two years. With transistors already reduced to around the size of an atom, the pace of change is likely to slow during the 2020s.

Key

- Micron V-NAND (2023): 5.3 trillion
- Intel Core i7 (2008): 731 million
- Intel Pentium (1993): 3 million
- Intel 4004 (1971): 2,300

Moore revised his estimate, saying that transistor density would double every two years. The technology sector used this timeframe to set new targets in microelectronics, making Moore's law a self-fulfilling prophecy.

Nanotechnology

Since the 1960s, transistor density has increased exponentially – and with it, computing power. The first commercial integrated circuit, released in 1964, had 120 transistors. Today, a smartphone processor may have billions of silicon transistors packed into it, each of them as small as 5 nanometres (nm); as a comparison, a sheet of paper is 100,000nm thick.

Nanotechnology allows manufacturers to manipulate the materials for these minuscule transistors on a near-atomic scale. Researchers working to reduce their size even further are reaching the natural limits of physics – as Moore had expected – meaning that the pace of transistor miniaturization has recently begun to slow. However, corporations and research units are exploring the possibilities of using different

minerals or elements in place of silicon to improve energy efficiency and condense even greater computing power into chips.

Until only a few decades ago, many of the devices that now use nanotechnology – including smartphones and smart watches – were the domain of science fiction. These devices are effectively tiny supercomputers, with vast amounts of memory and processing power. Apple's iPhone 12, launched in late 2020, can perform 11 trillion

The first programmable computer, ENIAC was built by scientists at the University of Philadelphia and used in the creation of the first hydrogen bomb.

operations per second, giving it 22 billion times the processing power of the first programmable and general-purpose computer, the Electronic Numerical Integrator and Computer (ENIAC). When completed in 1946, ENIAC weighed 30 tonnes (27 tons) and took up 167 sq m (1,798 sq ft) of space.

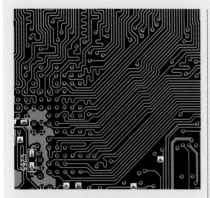

A close-up of a PCB shows many lines of thin, conductive copper bonded to a substrate of non-conductive fibreglass.

Printed circuit boards

Almost every electronic device now has a printed circuit board (PCB) inside. This comprises a thin conductive layer on an insulating surface, in a pattern that links components such as fuses, transistors, and sensors.

Engineers first began to develop flat circuit boards to replace conventional wiring to save space and weight in electronic devices. Initially, these were soldered by hand, but after World War II, more reliable circuit boards were printed by machines.

Combined with other new microelectronics technologies such as transistors, PCBs enabled designs for all kinds of devices to become smaller, more efficient, and more powerful.

PCB production may involve various graphic arts procedures, including screen printing, acid etching, electroplating, and photolithography. PCB templates were once designed manually, but manufacturers now use computer-aided design (CAD) to achieve the most efficient layouts and print them on an industrial scale.

The ENIAC was a world apart from our contemporary computers. A team of programmers would spend a day physically rewiring the machine for each complex problem it needed to solve. ENIAC – and others like it – was cumbersome, expensive, and mainly designed for military use and scientific research. The first commercially available laptops, released in the 1980s, were specialist items for mathematics-heavy roles and weighed up to 23 kg (51 lb). In the 2020s, laptops have become user-friendly, lightweight, and ubiquitous.

Creative possibilities

Accompanied by rapid evolution in programming and software, microelectronics helped to bring the power of computing into everyday life for billions of people. Other areas have been affected by miniaturization, too. Portable music players – from Sony's cassette-playing Walkman, to digital mp3 players – were only made possible by the miniaturization of electronic components. These microelectronic parts fundamentally shaped the product design of every modern electronic device, whether it's a shower radio, wireless headphones, a Furby robotic toy, or a drone.

As more and more functions can be included in a single device, miniaturization opens up new creative possibilities for electronics engineers and product designers to explore. While some of these – light-up trainers, for example – are simply fun and expressive, other products have altered the way that we understand and interact with

the world. Recently, small and smart chips have enabled the growth of the "Internet of Things" (IoT) – objects with processing power, software, and sensors that are connected to the Internet and able to exchange data. From farm monitoring systems to Fitbits, IoT technologies are now firmly embedded in many livelihoods and lifestyles.

Medical technology has seen some of the most impactful design progress enabled by miniaturization. Shrinking silicon-based components allowed medical designers to develop small, implantable devices that can improve and save lives. Pacemakers are a prime example; they were bulky, mains electricity-operated devices until the late 1950s, when American electrical engineer Earl E. Bakken developed the first wearable, battery-operated version using transistors. Multiple medical inventors then developed and improved even smaller implantable pacemakers that freed patients from external machines and reduced discomfort.

A changing world

Designers are now able to reduce the environmental impact of an item, since miniaturization means fewer materials are required, and a device functions on substantially

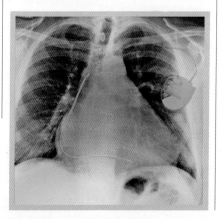

A colour-enhanced X-ray reveals a pacemaker (pale blue) in the patient's chest. These devices have decreased in size over the years and now weigh just 28 g (1 oz) or even less.

In this competitive era, if a product is to achieve market success, it is essential for it to be small, lightweight, and power-efficient.
Apurva Kulnarni
Electrical engineer, *Benchmark*, 2019

less energy. Nonetheless, the rapid development of nanoelectronics fuels the consumption of more devices in our booming digital age. This drives plastic production, the mining of minerals such as copper, lithium, gold, and silicon, and means that older generations of technology quickly become obsolete. When electronic devices are replaced and discarded, their complex composition of metals, plastics, and modified minerals produces e-waste, which is hard to recycle and often ends up being burned or languishing in toxic landfill waste.

Miniaturization has transformed the way that people interact with technology, opened up access to information via the Internet, and allowed us to connect with other people around the world, bringing innumerable human benefits. This tendency is a key part of the story of the electronic era – but like many aspects of design in the consumer age, it has also contributed to the large-scale generation of waste. The challenge for designers is to develop even more efficient technologies while avoiding negative impacts on our planet. ∎

IMMEDIATELY UNDERSTOOD
PICTOGRAMS

IN CONTEXT

FOCUS
Universal symbols that transcend language

FIELD
Visual communication, graphic design, information design

BEFORE
1909 The first international system of road signs is established in Europe.

1963 GINETEX, a European association based in France, develops a set of universal symbols to represent laundry care instructions.

AFTER
1979 Japanese graphic designer Yukio Ota designs an emergency exit sign, featuring a running figure.

2020 New pictograms with symbols related to mask-wearing and social distancing are introduced in response to the COVID-19 pandemic.

Pictograms are visual symbols that can represent an idea, object, or action. They are an essential part of modern life, communicating across languages and cultures, and are widespread in contexts ranging from clothing labels to medicine bottles. Pictograms are especially useful in global settings such as airports, where they bridge language barriers with ease.

A common language
Sign systems came of age in the 1960s, as globalization and the growth of international travel created a demand for clear communication in multilingual environments. One of the pioneers responding to this demand was Japanese graphic designer Yoshiro Yamashita, who crafted a set of easily interpreted pictograms for the 1964 Olympic Games in Tokyo, each representing a sport. Eight years later, a German graphic designer and typographer, Otl Aicher, created the visual identity for the 1972 Olympics in Munich. Aicher's streamlined pictograms,

Otl Aicher's pictograms depicting different sports are displayed on a wall at Munich Olympic Park. His designs for the 1972 games revolutionized ideas about the use of pictograms in signage.

See also: Written communication 34–41 ▪ Visualizing data 108–09 ▪ Information design 144–45 ▪ Bauhaus 170–71 ▪ Corporate identity 234–35

representing various sports and disciplines, were ground-breaking in their clarity and consistency.

That same year, Aicher's innovative directional signage was unveiled at the new central terminal at Frankfurt Airport. The pictograms drawn in his distinctive geometric style were combined with colour to represent different parts of the airport. His work on these high-profile projects received international attention, which helped him to build up an inventory of more than 700 symbols.

Setting the standard

It soon became clear that it was inefficient for every institution to create a separate set of symbols for similar purposes. In the US, the Department of Transportation was among the first bodies to develop a standardized system of signs. A committee of designers compiled an inventory of symbols used at transport hubs around the world, and several of Aicher's designs – including his geometric man to represent male toilets – were described as "a good starting

The intent of the project was to produce a consistent and interrelated group of symbols to bridge the language barrier and simplify basic messages.
American Institute of Graphic Arts
1974

point" for development. Finally, the shortlist was redrawn in a uniform graphic style by designers Rajie Cook and Don Shanosky.

The resulting set of 34 symbols for passengers and pedestrians was published in 1974 and expanded to 50 in 1979. The images were released into the public domain, and are now found around the world. As a result, they are often described as the "Helvetica" of pictograms. ▪

Otl Aicher

Born in Ulm, Germany, in 1922, Otl Aicher studied sculpture at the Academy of Fine Arts in Munich. In 1953, Aicher co-founded the Ulm School of Design with his wife, Inge Aicher-Scholl, and Max Bill, a Bauhaus alumnus. Aicher played a pivotal role in shaping the school's philosophy, placing a strong emphasis on the importance of interdisciplinary collaboration and functionality.

Aicher gained recognition for his role as the chief designer for the 1972 Summer Olympics in Munich. The visual identity that he created for the event – characterized by bold colours and geometric shapes – remains a milestone in sporting design history. The clear, uncluttered pictograms were praised as being democratic, universal, and inclusive.

Aicher also made significant contributions to corporate design, working with companies such as Lufthansa, Braun, and ERCO. Aicher died in 1991, but his legacy continues to influence design in both the corporate and public spheres.

Successful pictograms are immediately understood and easy to replicate because they meet three criteria:

Semantic
The symbol closely relates to its meaning. People from cultures around the world can understand it.

Syntactic
The parts of the symbol make sense together. The whole symbol makes sense alongside other symbols.

Pragmatic
The symbol is easy to reproduce and is clear to read at a distance. The sign is functional.

SUSTAINABILITY TAKES FOREVER

ECO DESIGN

IN CONTEXT

FOCUS
Minimizing the impact on the planet

FIELD
Industry, architecture, and engineering

BEFORE
1907 Leo Baekeland, a Belgian chemist, invents Bakelite, the first fully synthetic plastic.

1927–29 American architect Buckminster Fuller develops plans for an environmentally efficient house that can be mass produced, transported, and assembled on-site.

AFTER
1988 British authors John Elkington and Julia Hailes write *The Green Consumer Guide*, outlining how readers can make their purchasing habits environmentally friendly.

2021 Single-use plastic plates, cutlery, straws, and more are banned from sale in the EU.

Buckminster Fuller's Dymaxion Deployment Unit was designed in the 1940s as a low-cost solution for housing in wartime. The metal shelter could accommodate a family of four.

W hile often portrayed as a revolutionary concept born of the growing environmental concerns of the late 20th century, the fundamental principles of eco design were once the norm. Prior to the Industrial Revolution, before the buzzwords surrounding environmentalism were ever muttered, green design existed in the sense that furniture and utility items were produced locally in the workshops of highly skilled craftspeople.

Woodworkers, blacksmiths, wheelwrights, tailors, weavers, and seamstresses created the everyday objects and garments needed by their communities, often using materials procured nearby. In the absence of machine-making and affordable international transport, the labour and costs associated with this type of design were unchallenged by the cheaper, faster, disposable alternatives a future of mass-manufacture would bring.

New developments

Technological developments central to the Industrial Revolution ushered in the machinery, automation, and increased power that were needed to facilitate mass production. While these advances were welcomed by many, some groups of designers, architects, artists, and educators noted a degradation of quality in the products emerging out of these new processes, as well as the negative impact on the planet itself.

From the 1860s, the founders of the British Arts and Crafts movement were among the first to explore production techniques that combined increased output with a lower environmental impact. Their philosophy paved the way for Modernist design principles that were further refined and defined during the 20th century by the Deutscher Werkbund and the Bauhaus school in Germany, the Secession and the Wiener

There are professions more harmful than industrial design, but only a few.
Victor Papanek
Design for the Real World, 1971

See also: Streetscape 172–73 ▪ Material-led furniture design 186–87 ▪ Flat-pack furniture 228–29 ▪ Sustainable materials 302–07 ▪ Smart materials 314–17

Modern office complexes increasingly include green spaces with natural features to address concerns about sustainability.

Eco design and business

The 1990s was a pivotal decade in the story of eco design, with environmental issues becoming worryingly apparent, and the looming new millennium inspiring socioeconomic predictions for the future – in particular, how the economics of design would affect the planet.

In 1992, the United Nations Commission on Sustainable Development (UNCSD) declared business to be a central part of sustainability strategies. It explained that environmental criteria had to be integrated in procurement policies, a strategy known as green procurement.

In 1995, the 120 international companies that formed the World Business Council for Sustainable Development (WBCSD) published *Sustainable Production and Consumption: A Business Perspective*. This report called for unified thinking across business, governments, communities, and individuals. It recognized that businesses must drive the transformation to deliver more sustainable products and services.

Werkstätte in Austria, and De Stijl in the Netherlands. Particularly at the Bauhaus, a focus on the economy of materials dictated that to minimize waste and reduce the cost of resources, the form of a product must follow its function, and that designs should be simplified to allow mass-manufactured items to be produced to a high standard.

Emerging from the Bauhaus school of thought, the Mid-century Modern style addressed the users' ergonomic and emotional need for connections between the built environment and nature by bringing together natural materials and innovative craftsmanship. The biomorphic bent-plywood furniture produced by Charles Eames and Eero Saarinen in the 1940s is one example.

Nature and simplicity

Biomorphism is a design approach that takes nature as a primary source of inspiration. Designers blend aesthetics of the natural world with the built environment. This style typically features sinuous, irregular, flowing forms that evoke the non-mechanical movement and fluidity of living organisms and their environments. Biomorphism is popular in architecture: notable examples include Antoni Gaudí's Sagrada Família in Barcelona, Spain; Saarinen's TWA flight centre at the John F. Kennedy International Airport in New York; Fariborz Sahba's Lotus Temple in Delhi, India; and a number of works by Iraqi-British architect Zaha Hadid and British architect Thomas Heatherwick.

The period of austerity and shortages that followed World War II – from 1945 to the mid-1950s – inspired a renewed appreciation for simplicity and efficiency. While Americans enjoyed a short-lived celebration of the post-war economic boom with large, fuel-thirsty cars, European »

The Nativity Facade of the Sagrada Família in Barcelona is a celebration of biomorphism, with a multitude of statues inhabiting cave-like spaces that echo the natural world.

car manufacturers, such as Fiat in Italy and British Leyland, traded on the virtues of smaller vehicles, selling their audiences an enduring dream of relatively low-cost and fuel-efficient vehicles that almost anyone could own.

Alternative lifestyles

With the 1960s came the arrival of the consumerist-sceptic hippie movement. Seeking to free themselves from capitalism, members of this widespread subculture returned to nature in search of tools that would help them to become more self-sufficient. This involved exploring the rituals and habits of nomadic people and embracing a do-it-yourself approach to everyday life. Responding to the reality of applying idealistic values to a less-than-ideal modern world, a movement of so-called alternative technologists was born.

Alternative technologists advocated the use of forms of technology that minimized harm to the environment. By the early 1970s, the threat of an energy crisis and the peaking of oil prices saw alternative technologists working

> I want things designed so well, there is no need for regulations.
> **William McDonough**
> *Vanity Fair*, 2010

on pragmatic solutions to a heavy reliance on fossil fuels. They began to design products that would consume less energy, triggering the first coherent attempts to make cradle-to-grave assessments – considering the energy and environmental impacts at each stage of a product's life cycle. Life-cycle analysis (LCA) has become the cornerstone of cradle-to-grave design thinking.

Promoting change

In 1971, Austrian-American designer and educator Victor Papanek published *Design for the Real World*. The book focused on the impact that design could have on society and the environment. He urged the design industry to prioritize the needs of people and the planet, and to use their design skills in socially responsible ways to help alleviate modern ills such as pollution, overcrowding, starvation, and waste. The very next year, 1972, saw members of what is now known as the European Union acknowledge the need for unified policies to address the borderless impact of environmental issues.

By the 1980s, new legislation and increased public awareness of environmental issues saw greener shopping, greener thinking, and greener design swing to the fore of the consumer mindset. With pressure finally coming from the most powerful place of all – the household purse – designers and manufacturers began to prioritize eco design in an attempt to secure their place at the top of the modern consumer's shopping list.

Spurious claims

Unfortunately, the 1980s also saw the beginning of a greenwashing epidemic that is only now starting

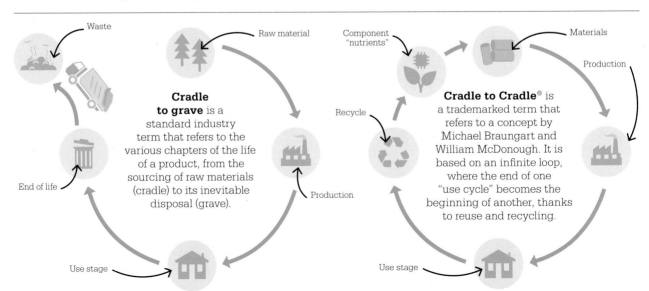

Cradle to grave is a standard industry term that refers to the various chapters of the life of a product, from the sourcing of raw materials (cradle) to its inevitable disposal (grave).

Waste

End of life

Use stage

Raw material

Production

Component "nutrients"

Recycle

Production

Use stage

Materials

Production

Cradle to Cradle® is a trademarked term that refers to a concept by Michael Braungart and William McDonough. It is based on an infinite loop, where the end of one "use cycle" becomes the beginning of another, thanks to reuse and recycling.

to be unravelled. Recognizing the significant marketing power of "environmentally friendly" products, but without the impetus or presence of a framework to regulate the credentials behind the labels, supermarket shelves and household appliances were draped with vague sentiment and dubious claims of eco supremacy that would damage the legitimacy of this messaging for decades to come. However, some brands did take the matter seriously, willing to show that they had a part to play in sustaining the planet.

In the early 1990s, leading Dutch electronics brand Philips partnered with the country's government and the University of Delft on a groundbreaking project to standardize eco design practices. Together, the three parties blended their agendas and expertise to develop a life-cycle analysis suitable for any designer – but particularly those in the field of industrial design. The Idemat LCA software allowed a set of defined eco-indicators to quantify a product's all-inclusive impact on the environment. Today's numerous packaged iterations of the software are available to manufacturers and

designers who wish to analyse and streamline their products' cradle-to-grave environmental credentials.

Product life cycles

Reducing the environmental impact of products and services is a significant design challenge. Examining product life cycles allows us to quantify the scientific and material impact of items and also inspires conversations about how, when, and why we use certain things in certain ways. Balancing the perceived value of an item against its impact on the planet allows the consumer or end user

The recycling of electronic waste (or e-waste) has become a hot topic because many electronics contain potentially hazardous materials such as lead and mercury.

to make informed choices based on sustainability. Vehicles, especially cars, are some of the most environmentally taxing products, but they are also one of the most "essential", providing freedom and safety in the form of everyday travel, resource and product transport, and vital mobile and emergency services. The ideal solution would be to eradicate the use of cars »

William McDonough

Born in Tokyo, Japan, in 1951, American architect and academic William McDonough spent much of his childhood in Hong Kong, where his father was a foreign service officer. When McDonough's father later became an executive at the Canadian multinational conglomerate Seagram, the family lived in Canada and Westport, Connecticut, US.

After graduating from Dartmouth College, New Hampshire, in 1973, McDonough put himself through architecture school at Yale and visited Jordan to work on the Jordan River Valley redevelopment project.

In 1981, he founded William McDonough + Partners architecture practice in New York City. He moved the practice to Charlottesville, Virginia, when he became dean of the School of Architecture at the University of Virginia in 1994. In 2002, in partnership with Michael Braungart, McDonough defined the concept of cradle-to-cradle design in a book titled *Cradle to Cradle: Remaking the Way We Make Things*.

completely so as to prevent further damage to the planet, but the reality of our societies' infrastructure means that we must explore alternative options.

For several decades, the "car of the future" has been pop culture's touchpoint for speculating on advanced innovation and aesthetics, but electric alternatives to the internal combustion engine car have only been available on the mass market since the mid-1990s. In 1997, Toyota marketed the Prius – the world's first gasoline/electric hybrid car for mass production. With rising fuel prices and increased environmental consciousness, the Prius model has been continually developed to cater for increased demand. In 2008, Tesla Motors answered cries for an electric supercar by unveiling a prototype Roadster, the first road-legal, all-electric car to use lithium-ion battery cells. Designers worked to reduce the environmental impact of the car, and they also created branding and messaging to appeal to an audience resistant to change.

The plastic problem

One of the hardest habits to break in the 21st century is the world's addiction to plastics. When polymers arrived in the 1900s,

We need to figure out how to have the things we love and not destroy the world.
Elon Musk, 2012

they were sold as a cheaper, more durable alternative to materials that are costly to source and manufacture, such as wood, metal, and glass – and consumers loved them. Plastics have since infiltrated every aspect of our lives – from furniture, tools, and machinery, to appliances, clothing, and toys. While they are certainly better from some perspectives, their low cost and convenience have created a culture of disposable, single-use items that is environmentally catastrophic.

Even plastics that are considered recyclable require significant resources to become usable a second time around. This means that it might be just

as damaging to the planet to repurpose a particular item as it is to discard it. While some examples of plastic design have become collectors' items – including Verner Panton's Panton Chair, Saarinen's Tulip chair, and the Eames DSW chair – billions of single-use plastic products, such as drinking straws, beverage bottles, and food packaging are polluting the oceans, shores, and soils. Metal straws, glass bottles, cardboard packaging, and textile shopping bags are all viable alternatives to their plastic counterparts, but it has often proved difficult to communicate their value. Designers are therefore looking to branding and aesthetics-led design for strategies that will transform the mindset and habits of users to incite a massive worldwide change.

Inevitably, some countries and corporations progress faster than others in specific areas of eco design shifts. Change-makers increasingly take note of their successes and failures to inform future policies around the design and use of products.

The first-generation Roadster (2009) by car manufacturer Tesla could travel almost 400 km (250 miles) on a single charge of its battery pack.

Single-use plastics have contributed to an ecological catastrophe. Not only do they litter beaches, but they also kill marine animals that mistake the items for food.

It would be untrue to claim that plastics and disposable designs are inherently bad. In the fields of medical design and science, the availability of single-use equipment has significantly improved hygiene and reduced contamination. In many countries, intravenous-drug users have been provided with free access to disposable syringes, significantly decreasing the likelihood of transmitting blood-borne diseases such as HIV and hepatitis C. This means that the complete eradication of single-use plastics is not a viable option, but designers are exploring more compostable plastics for their manufacture.

Looking forwards
Throughout all of history, and particularly in the 20th century, design movements have anchored themselves to a single manifesto or set of principles that is to be followed closely and without significant deviation. While this has carved a path for distinctive aesthetics and important reactionary movements, it ignores the value of difference, refusing to cater to cultural, environmental, and geographical factors, and so limiting their global reach and implementation.

Many designers, educators, and commentators now subscribe to an eco-pluralistic approach to design, which embraces all manifestations of eco design – from modifying products and designs to reduce their environmental impact, to radical concepts that wholly reimagine how we live, such as car-free cities. Championing a more accessible and unrestricted approach to eco design allows innovators around the world to make positive change on all levels. This might be as simple as replacing the material used to build a product with a more sustainable, recyclable alternative, or as complex as using design to interrupt traditional processes in a bid to foster more sustainable societal habits. ∎

The **invention of Bakelite** leads to product design based on a **strong and affordable** new material: **plastic**.

Plastic debris detected in oceans during the 1960s raises **ecological issues**.

Designers and industries begin to consider the **environmental and social impact** of the products they make.

Laws are created to **increase ecological design** in industries that are **slow to adopt it** themselves.

Many countries ban single-use items made from plastic.

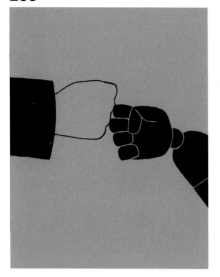

EMPOWERED AND ENHANCED
PROSTHETICS AND MEDICAL EQUIPMENT

IN CONTEXT

FOCUS
Designs for life

FIELD
Product design

BEFORE
1927 The iron lung is created by Philip Drinker and Louis Agassiz Shaw at Harvard University. The machine can maintain respiration, pulling air in and out of the lungs by changing the pressure in an airtight metal box.

1958 Wilson Greatbatch accidentally invents the implanted pacemaker, which regulates heartbeats, while trying to make a device to record heart sounds.

AFTER
1992 Jerome Schentag and David D'Andrea patent the smart pill – a computer-controlled medical device that can be ingested. The patient swallows the tool needed for diagnosis or treatment.

Medical design is one of the foremost frontiers of design innovation, encompassing single-use products and protective equipment, implantables and prosthetics, as well as surgical, laboratory, and diagnostic testing equipment. The primary focus of medical design is to support people in living longer, healthier, and happier lives – either by delivering the safe and effective treatment of disease and illness, or through the development of prostheses and mobility aids for those living with disabilities and long-term conditions.

Where once there was stigma, amputees are now empowered and enhanced.
Richard Springer
The Guardian (film),
2018

Prostheses through history
The evolution of prostheses has transformed the lives of people who have had amputations or who have a limb difference. The first known wearer of a prosthetic hand was the Roman general Marcus Sergius Silas in around 200 BCE, who wore a prosthesis made of iron. Wood, leather, and iron remained the main materials used for artificial limbs until the 16th century, when French doctor Ambroise Paré invented prosthetic limbs with hinges, including a leg with a locking knee joint. In 1861, US engineer James Hanger built on Paré's vision by creating the Hanger Leg – a more comfortable, flexible iteration that had hinges at the knee and ankle and could be mass produced for casualties of the US civil war.

In 1975, Mexican-American Ysidro M Martinez invented the concept of a below-knee prosthesis, which was light to wear and solved issues related to an unnatural gait when walking with a heavier prosthesis. Martinez's design laid the foundation for the below-knee leg prosthetics still used today.

Recent advancements in the design of prostheses have included the use of electro-mechanical

See also: Carbon fibre 238–41 ▪ Making things better 286–87 ▪ The online user experience 294–99 ▪ Smart materials 314–17

Prosthetic legs from history

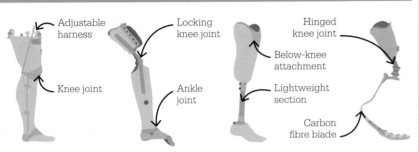

Adjustable harness

Knee joint

Locking knee joint

Ankle joint

Hinged knee joint

Below-knee attachment

Lightweight section

Carbon fibre blade

16th century
Ambroise Paré's prosthetic leg has a harness to fit the limb to the body and hinged joints.

19th century
The Hanger leg has knee and ankle joints that can flex and lock for stability.

1975
A below-knee prosthesis with a high centre of mass improves gait and agility.

1984
A flexible blade prosthesis allows the wearer to use their bodyweight to spring forward.

technology to create physically articulate bionic limbs, while developments in manufacturing, such as 3D printing, have allowed for bespoke design features to suit the wearer.

Implantable materials

Advances in material science have also been pivotal to the creation of new and improved medical devices. In 1891, when German surgeon Themistocles Gluck made the first recorded attempt at hip replacement surgery, he used implantable man-made hip joints that were made from ivory and fixed with nickel-plated screws. Today, more biologically compatible metals such as titanium and cobalt-chromium are considered the best options for implantables as they are tolerated well by the human body with minimal risk of adverse reactions – an essential material requirement that is unique to the field of medical design.

Designs for life

Medical devices are central to the everyday lives of millions of people, but many of them have only been developed since the mid-20th century. For example, Dr Arnold Kadish invented the insulin pump in 1963, and it was only in 1971 that Dr Godfrey Hounsfield developed the first commercial CT scanner. In 1987, robots became part of laparoscopic surgery (known as keyhole surgery) and lasers were brought into use to correct vision.

Medical design is design for life, and it is ethically, scientifically, and economically complex. From the impact of how expensive the manufacture of equipment is to the patient or health services, to how the movement and aesthetics of a prosthesis influences the wearer's relationship with their body – every design decision comes with human consequences. A well-designed medical device can change lives. ▪

Biomimicry

Designers have long found inspiration in the natural world. The replication of the processes found in animal and plant life – referred to as biomimicry – has been central to many inventions. One example is Velcro's hook-and-loop fastening, which Swiss engineer Georges de Mestral created after studying how cockleburs attached themselves to his dog's fur.

In medical design, where sensitivity to the limitations and delicacy of the human body is paramount, nature has been pivotal to product development. Gecko adhesive – developed in the 2000s by professors from MIT Institute and Harvard Medical School – creates a biodegradable bandage for organ and tissue repair inspired by the surface of a gecko's foot. More recently, an international team of researchers at the Universities of Michigan, Fribourg, and California-San Diego took inspiration from the electric eel to build a synthetic organ that can produce up to 100 volts – potentially enough to charge small devices such as pacemakers.

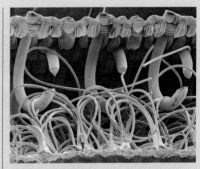

A sheet of hooks is secured to a sheet of loops in this micrograph of a fastening. The mechanism imitates the way in which cocklebur seedpods attach themselves to animal fur.

PERFECTLY EXECUTED JOY
MEMPHIS MILANO AND MAXIMALISM

IN CONTEXT

FOCUS
Rejecting modernist values in favour of humour and playfulness

FIELD
Product design, architecture, furniture

BEFORE
1960s Pop Art flourishes, drawing inspiration from popular and commercial culture. It shows that art can be brash and colourful.

1968 In Italy, students occupy the XIV Triennale di Milano, criticizing an exhibition seen to embody the design establishment.

AFTER
1985 Ettore Sottsass leaves Memphis Milano in order to focus on his design and architecture firm.

1980s–1990s Postmodern design around the world is greatly influenced by the Memphis Milano style.

By the late 1960s, many designers and architects were growing tired of the functionality and minimalism of modernism. They were drawn towards a concept of maximalism, embracing an aesthetic of excess that unashamedly celebrated flamboyance and playfulness.

In 1966, Italian design and architecture groups Archizoom Associati and Superstudio

Fashion designer Karl Lagerfeld transformed his Monaco penthouse into a shrine to Memphis Milano design, complete with a Masanori Umeda Tawaraya boxing ring.

came together to present a new theoretical framework called *Superarchitettura* at an exhibition in the city of Pistoia. It marked the beginning of Italian Radical Design, a provocative architectural and design movement characterized by bold, unconventional, and anti-establishment designs, such as the Pratone lounge chair (1971), a bright green seat that resembles blades of grass. This brash style began to influence other designers.

Memphis revolution
During the 1980s, designer and architect Ettore Sottsass emerged as one of the most influential

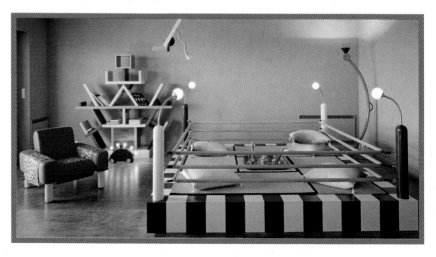

See also: Bauhaus 170–71 ▪ Modernism 188–93 ▪ Dawn of synthetic fabrics 194–95 ▪ Mid-century Modern 216–21

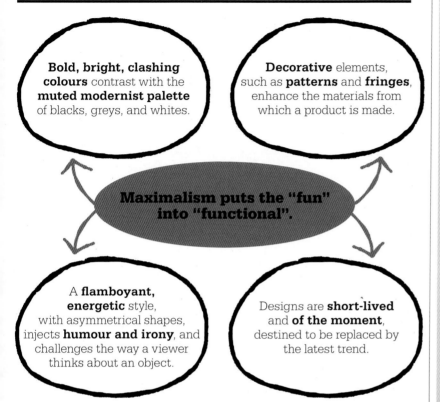

Bold, bright, clashing colours contrast with the **muted modernist palette** of blacks, greys, and whites.

Decorative elements, such as **patterns** and **fringes**, enhance the materials from which a product is made.

Maximalism puts the "fun" into "functional".

A **flamboyant, energetic** style, with asymmetrical shapes, injects **humour and irony**, and challenges the way a viewer thinks about an object.

Designs are **short-lived** and **of the moment**, destined to be replaced by the latest trend.

figures in Italian design. Sottsass had previously worked with modernist designer George Nelson in the 1950s before moving to Olivetti, where he designed the Valentine typewriter (1969), but by 1980 he was ready to take a new approach. Sottsass invited a group of emerging designers and architects to come together to discuss the future of their fields. United by their desire to refocus the primary objectives of design, they formed a collective and – inspired in part by the title of a Bob Dylan song – named it Memphis Milano.

Iconic irreverence

The collective burst onto the scene with an eye-popping debut collection in 1981, presented at the Salone del Mobile furniture fair in Milan. Bright colours, asymmetrical shapes, and plastic laminate came to the fore, and a number of pieces were immediately proclaimed design classics – among them Sottsass's multicoloured Carlton shelf / room-divider and Peter Shire's sharp-angled Brazil desk. The collection challenged established ideas of "good taste", and each piece was designed to be playful and fun. Sottsass's work was described as "perfectly executed joy".

Memphis Milano produced some of the most prominent examples of design from the postmodernist movement. Although the group disbanded in 1987, its aesthetics continue to influence contemporary design today. ▪

Radical Design

Originating in Italy in 1966, Radical Design stood for a fresh approach to design. Unlike many movements, it did not present a single, unified manifesto, but preferred to communicate its values through reviews, articles, films, and teaching.

As part of the growing critique of the modernist movement, Radical Design stood against minimalist functionalism in design and architecture, preferring vibrant colours and the use of diverse materials.

Central exponents of Radical Design included avant-garde design groups, Archizoom and Superstudio. These groups aimed to bring about social change through design and architecture, and their projects ranged from large-scale plans for future cities to household furniture, such as sofas and lamps. Its designers and architects were politically motivated and interested in ecological issues and sustainability.

An exhibition held at New York's Museum of Modern Art in 1972 helped to introduce many of the movement's values to a wider audience.

The interlocking waves of the Superonda sofa (1967) could be put together in different ways to make a sofa, bed, or chaise longue.

PEOPLE ARE ONLY PART OF THE PROCESS
SERVICE DESIGN

IN CONTEXT

FOCUS
Using design thinking and insights to improve a business

FIELD
Service design

BEFORE
1868 American door-to-door salesman Joseph "J.R." Watkins offers a money-back guarantee on his home-cooked liniments.

1960s The widespread adoption of the telephone leads to the first call centres to respond to customer queries.

AFTER
1986 The book *User-Centered System Design*, by American authors Donald A. Norman and Stephen W. Draper, introduces the concept of products or services based on users' needs.

2004 The Service Design Network (SDN) is established. It has since become a leading institution in the field.

In the consumer age, customer service is the link between a business and the client's experience with it – whether buying a drink at a coffee chain, shopping online, or taking a flight.

All these experiences involve multiple brand touchpoints – that is, customer interactions with the business's operations, products, and employees. They range from marketing and social media content, to point-of-sale elements such as packaging and service, as well as post-purchase feedback requests and customer support.

Service design choreographs processes, technologies, and interactions within complex systems in order to co-create value for relevant stakeholders.
Birgit Mager
President of the Service Design Network, 2012

How well these touchpoints function determines the smoothness of the customer experience – and ensuring a positive interaction between a business and its customers is the focus of service design.

A user-centric approach
The concept of service design emerged in the early 1980s. The term is usually attributed to American business theorist and consultant Lynn Shostack. In two landmark articles – "How to Design a Service" for the *European Journal of Marketing* (1982) and "Designing Services That Deliver" for the *Harvard Business Review* (1984) – Shostack emphasized the need for businesses to focus on designing and improving customer services.

A customer-centric approach is fundamental in delivering a successful service. In order to understand and anticipate customers' needs, designers review the user experience through a range of tools – from field research, to identifying user personas. They might also use a customer journey map, which is a detailed breakdown of when and how the user interacts with

See also: Design catalogues 82–83 ▪ Visualizing data 108–09 ▪ Visual merchandising and retail design 124–31 ▪ Hospitality design 178–79 ▪ Branding 200–07

The user-centred design process

Gauge how the user uses the product → **Understand the needs of the user** → **Create solutions** → **Check proposed solutions against user needs**

the service. These touchpoints may be virtual or face-to-face interactions. For a restaurant, they might include customers reading about the establishment on social media, making reservations, and their entire dining experience – from arriving and being seated, to perusing the menu, ordering food, and being given the bill.

At each stage of the customer journey map, designers might be able to identify potential pain points, or concerns that need to be addressed – for example, an overly complicated online booking system, or confusion in the dining room as clients search for tables.

After identifying the issues and implementing positive changes – streamlining the booking procedure, or placing signs at the entrance instructing customers to wait to be seated –

designers test and refine those solutions, making improvements iteratively, based on feedback and changing needs.

Business benefits

Enhancing the user experience of a product or service results in improved customer satisfaction, positive brand perception, and increased loyalty. Consequently, businesses – both large and small – have much to gain from this business strategy.

A collaborative environment in which businesses actively engage with their end users can deliver more effective problem solving and lead to the introduction of time- and money-saving ideas, as well as a more impactful market presence.

Service-design techniques are now deployed across many business sectors – including healthcare, hospitality, retail, finance, and technology – as a way to stay competitive, meet the evolving needs of customers, and improve environmental and social standards. ▪

Creating user personas

User personas are fictional profiles of a company's target user based on data collected in the exploration and discovery phase of a service-design project.

These composite characters usually come with detailed information, including a name, a picture, and demographic data, as well as descriptions of needs, goals, preferences, motivations, and behavioural patterns.

Having a comprehensive and tangible representation of a target user engenders empathy,

which helps service designers to ask the right questions and create design solutions that respond to those needs more holistically.

In addition, user personas can help the business client to relate to the design process, understand their customer needs in more detail, and respond to design solutions with more insight.

The creation of user personas can therefore play a pivotal role in service design. It ensures a human-centric approach to decision making that results in empathetic solutions and a seamless user experience.

Accessing user personas offers designers the opportunity to fine-tune and tailor the consumer experience according to the needs of the service provider.

REALITY IS BROKEN. GAME DESIGNERS CAN FIX IT

COMPUTER GAMING

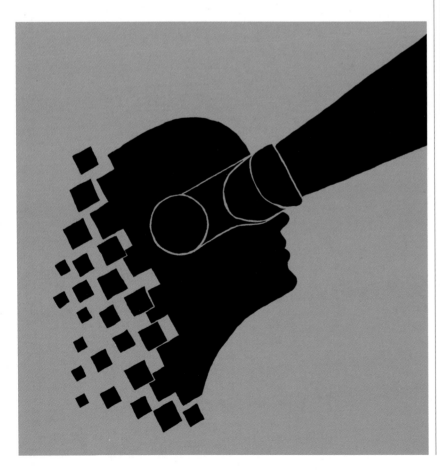

D esign in computer games is a diverse field that incorporates multiple disciplines under the umbrella of game content design. The early history of computer gaming started as far back as 1952, when British computer scientist A.S. Douglas created *OXO* – which simulated noughts and crosses, or tic-tac-toe – as part of his doctoral dissertation at the University of Cambridge.

Other basic computer games followed, including *Tennis for Two*, created by American physicist William Higinbotham in 1958, and *Spacewar!*, created by American computer scientist Steve Russell

See also: Planned obsolescence 176–77 ▪ Youth culture 230–33 ▪ Corporate identity 234–35 ▪ Ergonomics 278–85

Arcade games such as *Pong*, *Space Invaders*, and *Pac-Man* enjoy a **golden age** during the 1970s and 1980s.

Computer **game consoles** Nintendo and Sega, and later PlayStation and Xbox, make **home gaming** possible, alongside home computers.

Internet connectivity enables gaming to move online. **Games for multiple players** allow users to connect with friends and create **online communities**.

The development of the smartphone, augmented and virtual realities, and other innovative technologies leads to new types of game, played in new ways.

in 1962. These games could only be played on large computers at universities and other institutions.

Mainstream games

In the 1970s, the invention of coin-operated arcade games and home consoles used in conjunction with television screens brought computer games to mass audiences for the first time. American electrical engineer Nolan Bushnell, the founder of Atari, released the first arcade machine, Computer Space, in 1971, while the first home console was developed by German-American inventor Ralph Baer, whose Magnavox Odyssey was released in 1972. *Pong* – often

remembered as the first computer game – was released by Atari as an arcade game in 1972; the home version followed in 1975. The game could not have been simpler – a virtual game of ping-pong with two white lines bouncing a white ball back and forth – but it was extremely popular and the beginning of something big.

Other arcade games also became immensely popular – probably the most famous being *Space Invaders* (1978), a game that involves shooting lines of spaceships as they gradually descend, and *Pac-Man* (1980), in which the eponymous character moves through a maze avoiding »

Shigeru Miyamoto

Born in Kyoto, Japan, in 1952, Shigeru Miyamoto is a video game designer and creator, responsible for some of the most influential and best-selling game franchises. Having graduated with an industrial design degree, Miyamoto joined Nintendo in 1977. Following the success of *Donkey Kong* (1981) and *Mario Bros* (1983), which introduced the brothers Mario and Luigi, *Super Mario Bros* (1985) – probably Miyamoto's best-known game – popularized the side-scrolling video game genre, where the action moves along the screen left and right.

Miyamoto's *The Legend of Zelda* (1986) pioneered nonlinear, open-world gameplay. The storytelling in his games made them best-sellers, and Nintendo became a giant of the industry. Miyamoto was also involved in the launch of the Wii, a console that popularized motion control capture, and its first game *Wii Sports* (2006).

Key games

1981 *Donkey Kong*
1983 *Mario Bros*
1986 *The Legend of Zelda*
2006 *Wii Sports*

There are plenty of skills I've learned from playing video games. ... You're using your brain.
Shaun White
Olympic snowboarder

or eating ghosts. These and other popular titles created a golden age for arcade games in the 1980s, led by Atari and followed by a range of other companies, mainly from the US and Japan.

In 1977, home computers entered the market with the Radio Shack TRS-80, Commodore PET, and Apple II followed by dozens of competitors, including the BBC Micro, Sinclair ZX Spectrum, Atari 800XL, and Commodore 64. Each model had its own games, and many were authored by only one or two people; these were the original indie games.

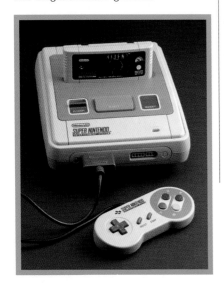

The Super Nintendo games console (SNES) sold almost 50 million units between its initial release in Japan in 1990 and being discontinued in 2003.

Donkey Kong **became** Nintendo's first international success after its release in 1981. The game features a gorilla throwing barrels at characters called Mario and Pauline.

In Japan, Nintendo was a games and toy business whose first foray into computer games was to create toy guns for a game called *Shooting Gallery* on the console Magnavox Odyssey in 1972. Five years later, the company launched its first two video game systems, Color TV-Game 6 and Color TV-Game 15, followed by the arcade game *Donkey Kong* (1981). *Super Mario Bros*, a platform game, arrived in 1985.

Nintendo also became a leading manufacturer of handheld video games between 1980 and 1991. In the late 1980s, the company made two more historic releases. The first of these (1987) was the adventuring game *The Legend of Zelda*, inspired by the childhood of designer Shigeru Miyamoto. Then followed *Tetris* (1989), which was created by Russian computer engineer Alexey Pajitnov and designed for the Game Boy console.

The console wars
Games consoles developed rapidly, with each generation of the product improving on hardware, software, and game design. The rivalry between Nintendo and Sega during the 1990s is often referred to as "the console wars". In the US, Sega's answer to the success of *Mario* was *Sonic the Hedgehog*, a super-fast, blue hedgehog who could curl into a ball to attack its enemies. Sonic first appeared in the arcade game *Rad Mobile* (1990) before making his full debut in *Sonic the Hedgehog* the following year. By 1994, both companies faced new competition with the arrival of the Sony PlayStation console, followed by the Microsoft Xbox in 2001.

Many home computer games were still played on PCs during the 1990s, with 1993 seeing the launch of *Doom*, a first-person shooter game developed by id Software, in which the player is a space marine fighting hoards of demons and the undead. *Doom* has its origins in the original first-person shooter game *Wolfenstein 3D* (1992), in which the enemies are Nazis. Other famous games for PCs include *Lemmings* (1991), *SimCity 2000* (1993), *Warcraft* (1994), and *Age of Empires* (1997). The mid-1990s marked the emergence of three-dimensional graphics across all platforms.

Online multiplayers
While early game types were simple, including puzzles, platform games (where a player moves through an environment),

Multiplayer online gaming has spawned a whole new industry of ergonomic gamer furniture, including multitilt chairs with adjustable armrest and backrest recline.

simulations, and fighting and racing games, the emergence of new technologies has produced more sophisticated kinds of game. Massively multiplayer online role-playing games (MMORPG) emerged in the 1990s and led to the creation of online communities of users playing the game together.

The best-known MMORPG, *World of Warcraft* (2004), created opportunities for players to explore an open game world and socialize online through play. More recently, *Fortnite* (2017) has a number of different player modes, including a cooperative game, battle mode, and sandbox mode – in which the players create the world themselves. Other sandbox games include *The Sims* (2000), *Minecraft* (2010), which is also a MMORPG, and *Animal Crossing: New Horizons* (2020), which allowed separated friends and family to interact during COVID-19 lockdowns in 2020.

The widespread use of mobile phones, then smartphones, also created a new gaming category. Simple games like *Snake* (1997) could be played on Nokia mobile phones, while *Angry Birds* (2009) and *Candy Crush Saga* (2012) were designed for smartphones. In 2016, smartphone game *Pokémon Go* incorporated augmented reality to create a new type of game using GPS technology to allow players to track, capture, train, and battle virtual Pokémon characters in the player's real-world location. Modern gaming incorporates virtual reality headsets, voice and facial recognition, gesture control, AI, and monetization.

A burgeoning industry

Computer gaming is now larger than the film industry and one of the most popular and complex forms of art and virtual reality in the 21st century. Consumers can choose to game on Xbox, Nintendo, or PlayStation consoles, on PC or Mac home computers, via smartphone or tablet, or in person through arcades or tournaments, called ESports. ∎

World of Warcraft, which was released by Blizzard Entertainment in 2004, is one of the best-selling MMORPG video games.

Community games

While gaming is often regarded as solitary, it can also be highly social. In particular, the invention of online gaming allows players to meet or battle each other and form teams, creating large online gaming communities. The term MMORPG emerged in the 1990s to describe immersive games populated by large numbers of online players. Early MMORPGs include *Ultima Online* (1997) and *EverQuest* (1999). In these virtual worlds, players interact with other users, with some games encouraging the creation of organized groups – called guilds or clans – that regularly play together. The most successful and famous of these is *World of Warcraft* (2004). In this game, players take on the roles of druids, priests, rogues, paladins, and other fantasy characters to complete various quests, battle, and missions, alone or in groups. Launched one year earlier, *SecondLife* (2003) was also very popular and became famous because it was more about socializing and world-building, with no fighting.

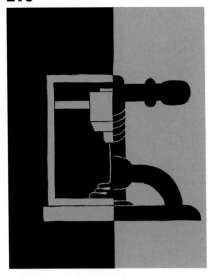

A GUTENBERG-LIKE RENAISSANCE
3D DIGITAL PRINTING

IN CONTEXT

FOCUS
Rapid prototyping

FIELD
Industrial design, product design, architecture

BEFORE
1960s Newly developed computer-aided design (CAD) systems allow designers to create digital models of objects.

1969 German company Bayer patents a process for rapid prototyping called reaction injection moulding (RIM).

AFTER
2003 Dr Thomas Boland, a professor at the University of El Paso, Texas, US, develops a method for printing living cells using an inkjet printer.

2011 Engineers at the University of Southampton, UK, create and fly the world's first 3D-printed unmanned aircraft, known as SULSA (Southampton University Laser Sintered Aircraft).

The process of designing a new product starts with conceptualization and sketching form and function. It then moves on to digital modelling and the creation of a prototype, ideally using the desired materials. Small-scale models are crucial for testing and refining designs before full-scale production. Three-dimensional (3D) printing has revolutionized the prototyping process, cutting costs and allowing additional testing stages to check the functionality, aesthetics, and user satisfaction in the product's final design.

Homebuilding has seen no significant changes since the Middle Ages. It's time for a paradigm shift.
Jason Ballard
Co-founder and CEO of Icon, 2022

In computer-enabled 3D printing, a three-dimensional object is created from a digital file. The 3D-printing process is often referred to as additive, or desktop, manufacturing, because the item is created layer by layer, through depositing, joining, fusing, or solidifying materials such as plastics, metals, liquids, or powders.

By using 3D printing to create prototypes, or small batches of customized finished products, manufacturing companies can bypass traditional – and often expensive – processes such as machining or moulding. Three-dimensional printing is an effective, low-cost way to produce objects on a small scale, and it empowers everyone – from individual designers, to small- and medium-sized enterprises and large-scale industry – to be more proactive and innovative.

From CAD to RepRap
Three-dimensional printing is closely linked to computer-aided design (CAD), in which digital technology assists in the design and production of objects. CAD software facilitates the precise physical realization of a detailed

See also: Industrial design 146–47 ▪ Plastic 148–53 ▪ Eco design 258–65 ▪ Prosthetics and medical equipment 266–67 ▪ Sustainable materials 302–07

digital model by using information such as proportional geometric shapes, precise dimensions, materials, and essential printing specifications.

The first 3D printer was invented in 1981 by Japanese lawyer Hideo Kodama. It was a rapid prototyping machine able to create objects layer by layer using a resin that could be polymerized – that is, made into a chain of molecules – by ultraviolet light. When his invention failed to gather any interest, Kodama abandoned the project, destroying both his prototype and his notes.

In 1986, US engineer Chuck Hull patented stereolithography (SLA), a 3D-printing technology now known as resin printing. The following year, Hull co-founded 3D Systems, the company that produced the first commercial 3D printer – the SLA-1 – and developed the STL file format, which is the most common file type now used for 3D printing.

During the 2000s, British engineer Adrian Bowyer's RepRap project made 3D printing more accessible with the introduction of

a low-cost self-replicating 3D printer that can print most of its own components. Bowyer's decision to make the RepRap printer freely available for the benefit of everyone laid the foundations for the open-sourced 3D-printer revolution.

Multiple applications

Many professional settings – from healthcare to construction – now use 3D printers. High-profile projects include the two-storey Office of the

The MX3D Bridge, installed over a canal in Amsterdam, The Netherlands, in 2021–23, was part of a project on the viability of 3D-printed infrastructure.

Future building in Dubai, UAE, and *3Dirigo*, a 7.6-m (25-ft) boat created at the University of Maine, US.

Three-dimensional printers have a role in the domestic environment, too: they can be used to create new utensils, or to print parts to repair items such as drawer handles. ▪

This two-storey house in Beijing, China, is the world's first 3D-printed building. It was constructed over a period of six and a half weeks during 2016.

Printing in construction

Additive construction is an innovative building method that is transforming the construction industry. This technology utilizes large-scale 3D printers to layer construction materials – in most instances, concrete – creating entire buildings step by step.

In 2021, the US construction tech company Icon unveiled the Vulcan printer, which is capable of producing a 186-sq-m (2,000-sq-ft) home in less than 24 hours. The advantages of this process include design flexibility,

reduced construction time and waste, and lower costs, leading to the potential for affordable housing solutions. Notable projects – such as a 3D-printed housing development in Austin, Texas, US – showcase the technology's viability.

Although challenges such as scaling and material optimization still persist, additive construction stands as a transformative innovation, redefining building methods and offering sustainable, cost-effective solutions for the future of housing.

TRUE COMFORT IS THE ABSENCE OF AWARENESS

ERGONOMICS

Ergonomics – from the Greek *ergon*, meaning "work", and *nomos*, meaning "natural law" or "control" – is the study of the human body and its interaction with machines, systems, or environments to the betterment of human productivity and health. Since computer-based work became dominant in the 1980s and 1990s, the focus of ergonomics has been on the design of the workplace, how its furniture and accessories fit the body, and how to prevent strain or injury. However, ergonomics is a vital consideration in all workplaces, and in the design of every aspect of our world.

Time and motion studies

In the late 1890s, US engineer Frederick Winslow Taylor carried out a time study, using a stopwatch while observing factory workers to establish the quickest way of completing a certain job. At the Pennsylvania-based Bethlehem Steel company, for example, Taylor was able to increase production by matching the shovel with the type of material being shovelled (ashes, coal, or ore), as well as issuing detailed instructions to the

> Ergonomics is the study of the interaction between people and machines and the factors that affect the interaction.
> **R.S. Bridger**
> *Introduction to Ergonomics*, 1995

workers regarding their pace and even their water breaks. This system of scientific management, which became known as Taylorism, had an important impact on synthesizing workflows and rethinking productivity.

Between 1908 and 1924, also in the US, engineers Lillian and Frank Gilbreth looked into efficiency in the workplace by counting and timing the movements required to carry out specific tasks, such as bricklaying. The goal of the Gilbreths' motion study was to create a physically

Time and motion studies in the workplace assess how to increase **productivity and efficiency**.

The advent of the **Information Age** leads to **innovative seating designs** for a largely sedentary workforce.

Designers start to create products with **the human factor** in mind.

Ergonomics **extends beyond seating** to encompass **all aspects** of computer-based office work.

Ergonomic principles are applied to an ever-growing number of fields and industries.

The J-3 Hudson locomotive was designed, inside and out, by Henry Dreyfuss. The streamlined exterior was matched by a stylish interior with ergonomic seats and few corners.

streamlined process for the workers, which would reduce time and effort while achieving results of the same quality.

Designing for the body

During the mid-20th century, research on how to design to suit the body in the workplace gained momentum. US industrial designer Henry Dreyfuss was the first to champion the "human factor", which put the user before the design. From 1931 until his death in 1972, Dreyfuss created a diverse range of items for the Machine Age designed around the user and utility – from alarm clocks, typewriters, and a lightweight vacuum cleaner, to tractors, an aircraft, and even an ocean liner.

In 1949, British psychologist Hywel Murrell founded the Ergonomics Research Society in Oxford, UK, to investigate the impact of seating and equipment on the human body, as well as considering the effects of environmental and organizational factors. A few years later, in 1957, the Human Factors and Ergonomics Society was established in Washington, DC, US. The society examined how effectively human operators performed their work, and whether improvements could be made in the design of machines and processes to help them to do it better and more comfortably.

The age of computers

From the 1980s, ergonomics became an increasingly important discipline as a direct result of the popularity of computers – first in the workplace and then in the home. During the 1990s, as access to the Internet and the use of email became more widespread, people »

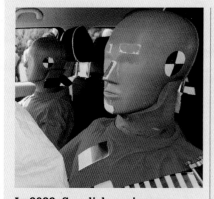

In 2022, Swedish engineers developed anatomically correct female crash-test dummies. Male dummies have been used since the 1950s.

Gender bias

Ergonomics, like many fields of study developed during the 20th century, has an implicit gender bias in much of its research. In 2019, design historian Jennifer Kaufmann-Buhler wrote about sexism in the design of US office furniture. She argued that a one-size-fits-all approach to chair and desk design does not work for people – especially women – whose bodies do not conform to an idealized norm. The misfit is acutely apparent and can cause discomfort and even pain.

British author Caroline Criado-Perez's 2020 book *Invisible Women: Exposing Data Bias in a World Designed for Men* details more examples of gender bias. These include "unisex" uniforms for the armed forces designed for male anatomy; personal protective equipment designed for man-sized faces, hands, and bodies, which means that it is comfortable for just 5 per cent of women; and cars tested with male crash-test dummies that do not consider women's height, weight, or differences in bone structure.

Bill Stumpf

A furniture designer who helped to bring ergonomic science to chair design, Bill Stumpf was born in St Louis, Missouri, US, in 1936. He studied industrial design at the University of Illinois at Urbana-Champaign, before earning a master's in environmental design from the University of Wisconsin–Madison. In the course of his studies, Stumpf conducted extensive research into the ergonomic aspects of sitting.

In 1970, Stumpf joined the research team at Herman Miller, where he studied the design of office seating. Six years later, he introduced the Ergon chair. In the 1980s, Stumpf and fellow designer Don Chadwick created the Equa chair; this was followed in 1994 by the revolutionary Aeron chair, for which they dispensed with upholstery in favour of a breathable, supportive fabric mesh. The Aeron became an immediate classic, chosen for the design collection of New York's Museum of Modern Art even before it went into production. Stumpf won the 2006 National Design Award in Product Design. He died the same year.

began spending more and more time sitting at a desk as their main mode of work. Indeed, for the first time, white-collar office work, conducted in front of a computer, was more common than farming or factory work.

However, as computers became more widespread in the workplace, the number of injuries related to their use also began to rise, especially repetitive strain injuries (RSI), caused by repeated physical movements over a prolonged period of time. Companies were forced to investigate and adjust the design of workstations and equipment to encourage correct posture. This marked the start of modern ergonomics, and it became an extraordinarily rich time in the design of equipment for human–computer interaction (HCI), especially with regard to office chairs, but also the height and shape of desks, mice, and keyboards.

Seating solutions

Adjustable chairs became a fundamental requirement of the office environment. The first swivel chair is attributed to US inventor Thomas E. Warren (1849), and the

Having held any posture for a while, the best posture is always the next one.
Peter Opsvik
Norwegian designer

first height-adjustable chair to US architect Frank Lloyd Wright (1904). However, these early examples of adjustable chairs were a far cry from the modern office, or task, chair, which is designed for support, comfort, adaptability, and to minimize the strain on the body.

The Aluminum Group chair, designed by Charles and Ray Eames for US office furniture company Herman Miller in 1958, had many of the hallmarks of later task chairs, including a cast aluminium frame and seat-back suspension with mesh. Throughout

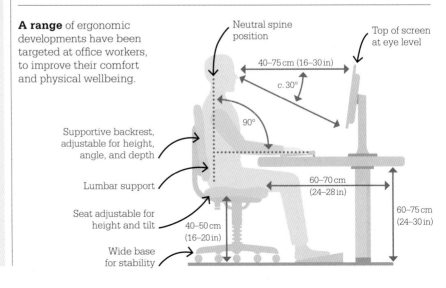

A range of ergonomic developments have been targeted at office workers, to improve their comfort and physical wellbeing.

Neutral spine position

Top of screen at eye level

40–75 cm (16–30 in)

c. 30°

90°

Supportive backrest, adjustable for height, angle, and depth

Lumbar support

Seat adjustable for height and tilt

40–50 cm (16–20 in)

60–70 cm (24–28 in)

60–75 cm (24–30 in)

Wide base for stability

the 1960s, similarly innovative chairs were released, including Charles Pollock's Executive Chair from Knoll (1963) and the Oxford Chair designed by Arne Jacobsen for Fritz Hansen (1965).

Task chair development

The true age of innovation in task chairs began in the 1970s. Herman Miller hired ergonomics expert Bill Stumpf, whose in-depth research included data collection, X-rays, and product testing, and his theory was that, far from there being a "correct" posture to sit in, a task chair should support the body in a variety of different positions. The result of this research – the Ergon – was released in 1976. This was the start of something new: the first chair whose design factored in ergonomic performance, as well as the very first gas-lift swivel chair.

Other task chairs released around the same time included the Vertebra armchair, designed by Emilio Ambasz and Giancarlo Piretti (1976), which was meant to mimic the shape of the spine; the Supporto chair (Frederick Scott, 1976), with its simple, clean lines, and adjustable back and arm rests; and the FS chair (Klaus Franck and Werner Sauer for Wilkhahn, 1980), which featured simultaneous yet distinct movement of the backrest and seat. In 1979, Norwegian designer Peter Opsvik invented a kneeling chair called the Variable; Galen Cranz, professor of architecture of the University of California, Berkeley, called it the most radical seating design of the 20th century. A firm believer in

breaking the norms of seating, Opsvik later designed the Capisco chair (1984), also known as the saddle chair, in collaboration with Norwegian furniture company Håg.

A new generation

In the early 1990s, Herman Miller commissioned Bill Stumpf and industrial designer Don Chadwick to develop the next generation of task chairs. The pair had previously worked together on another

Herman Miller commission – the unreleased Sarah, which was an improvement on the La-Z-Boy recliners. After consultation with ergonomics experts and orthopaedic specialists, Stumpf and Chadwick created the Aeron chair (1994). This actively dealt with postural health problems through a suspension system that distributed the user's weight evenly over the seat and back, reducing pressure on the spine and »

The Aeron chair established such a widespread reputation for ergonomic quality that it appeared on a 2005 episode of *The Simpsons* TV show, "Thank God, It's Doomsday".

muscles. The semi-reclining mechanism that moved the seat and chairback at the same time helped equalize pressure on the user's body and was informed by their work on the Sarah. The frame was made from die-cast aluminium and glass-reinforced polyester, the legs from recycled aluminium, and the pads from polyurethane foam; the fabric mesh webbing (Pellicle) on the seat and back allowed air to flow around the body.

The Humanscale project

Another game-changer in the development of ergonomics was the founding of Humanscale in 1983. Focused on improving the comfort and health of office workers, this New York-based brand began with the design and sale of articulated keyboard systems, before commissioning US industrial designer Niels Diffrient to create its first task chair. The Freedom chair (1999) mimics the body's natural contours, with a pivoting backrest that promotes movement throughout the day; it also has a separate headrest.

The chair embodied what Diffrient had learned while collaborating with Alvin R. Tilley,

> The best way to know what people want and need is not by asking them but by understanding them.
> **Niels Diffrient**
> **Humanscale designer**

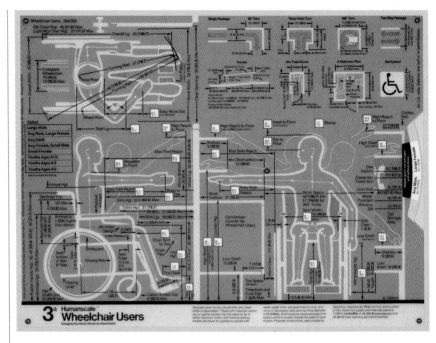

3a Humanscale™
Wheelchair Users
Designed by Henry Dreyfuss Associates

David Harman, and Joan C. Bardagjy in the Humanscale manuals, published 1974–81. Aimed at "everyone who designs for the human body", this toolkit of information includes a vast amount of human-engineering data compiled and organized by Henry Dreyfuss Associates. Different sections cover seating, wheelchairs, helmets, and more. They provide designers with measurements for the most ergonomic designs for men, women, children, disabled people, and the elderly.

Desks and keyboards

Most workplace ergonomics research has focused on creating the perfect task chair, but designs have also been engineered to make the office a more comfortable place to work. These include height-adjustable desks to cater for the long- or short-limbed, and for those who prefer to work standing up.

Standing at a desk is not a new concept – historical figures such as Marie Antoinette, Ernest

This plate from a Humanscale manual focuses on wheelchair design. By rotating the dial on the right, designers can see the measurements needed for comfort in various environments.

Hemingway, and Charles Dickens may have preferred to write at a standing desk. However, it was in 1998 that the first electric height-adjustable desk was introduced by German carpenter and furniture maker Herwig Damzer.

The 1990s and the years that followed also witnessed the development of other ergonomic office accessories. Building on Humanscale's articulated keyboard, a number of other ergonomic designs were released, including split and angled keyboards. The computer mouse was also made more ergonomic, with the introduction of vertical and trackball versions. The monitor mount, patented by American designer Rob Mossman in 2006, allowed the monitor to be angled for correct posture.

In the 21st century, as the workplace considers wellness above and beyond posture, the focus on ergonomics has not waned. Early brands such as Herman Miller, Wilkhahn, Håg, and Humanscale, along with others like Steelcase and Haworth, have released more ergonomic products, ranging from rocking footrests to adjustable desk lighting and storage compartments that reduce the need to bend. They have also commissioned research, such as Steelcase's Global Posture Study, published in 2013.

The 2020 COVID-19 pandemic saw a huge rise in working from home as a result of enforced lockdowns. In the years since, many people have adopted a hybrid working pattern, with one or more work-from-home-days per week. This has created an increased demand for ergonomic work arrangements in the home office and meant a boost in the sale and variety of ergonomic task chairs, desks, and accessories such as monitor arms.

Out-of-office applications

Although the focus on human–computer interaction appears to be the most common, the principles

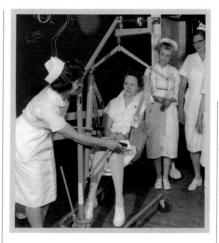

of ergonomics are relevant to many different work situations. In his 1996 publication *Good Ergonomics Is Good Economics*, Hal W. Hendrick identified applications in fields as far apart as the forestry industry, transport aircraft, and the handling and storing of industrial materials. According to the nature of the work required, each field has different needs – whether it is to relieve stress and fatigue, improve air quality, consider gender and cultural differences, or prevent accidents.

Ergonomics is also vital in the healthcare industry. Examples include devices designed to help

The Hoyer hoist is a patient lift that was developed by Ted Hoyer in the 1940s. As a 16-year-old, American Hoyer had been left paralysed from the waist down following a car accident.

healthcare professionals to lift a patient, reducing the likelihood of injuring the patient or themselves. Hospital hoists are a good example: not only do they increase patient safety, comfort, and dignity, but they also greatly reduce the risk of staff injury.

Design methodology

Within the broad umbrella of ergonomics are disciplines such as design for human factors, human-centred design, and user experience design, all of which draw on engineering, design, psychology, medicine, and social sciences to create products, environments, services, and systems. In order to create ergonomic products, designers must do extensive research on the item and the user to fully understand the interaction between the two and be able to bring that knowledge to bear on the item's form and function. ∎

Utensil design

Ergonomic design has improved a broad range of utensils, both in the workplace and at home. Adapted cutlery – that is, cutlery designed for those who have difficulty using standard cutlery – includes left-handed utensils, wide forks, and items with heavy-weighted or curved handles. Ergonomically designed cutlery for children can make learning easier.

One of the most readily recognized ergonomic designs is the orange-handled scissors

created in the 1960s by Finnish company Fiskars. In Sweden, Ergonomi Design Gruppen was particularly concerned with ergonomic design for disabled people. Its combination cutlery (1979) was created for people with single-handed function, while its support cane (1983) had an ergonomic handle that alleviated pressure on arthritis sufferers' wrists and shoulders. In the 1990s, Sam Farber launched the OXO Good Grips range in the US after seeing his wife struggle to peel apples as a result of her arthritis.

The Fiskars scissors, developed by Finnish designer Olof Bäckström, have curved handles that fit more comfortably with the user's grip.

SURPRISING INVENTIONS THAT DEFY CONVENTION
MAKING THINGS BETTER

IN CONTEXT

FOCUS
Using design to improve everyday objects

FIELD
Product design, industrial design, engineering

BEFORE
1907 The first portable electric vacuum cleaner is invented by James Murray Spangler from Ohio, US.

1911 The first motorized washing machine is invented by Frederick L. Maytag.

AFTER
2000s Advances in battery technology mean portable devices such as cordless vacuum cleaners become more efficient and reliable.

2012 The SOL, a rugged, waterproof solar-powered laptop computer, is designed by WeWi Telecommunications. It is aimed at providing computing in regions with limited access to electricity.

Design plays a crucial role in enhancing the functionality of everyday objects. Changes vary in scale, with some being small, incremental improvements, while others represent significant, transformative leaps in design and technology. The vacuum cleaner is an excellent example of this – over the years, it has undergone numerous redesigns, resulting in increased power, greater efficiency, and more ease of use.

The vacuum cleaner was invented by British engineer Hubert Cecil Booth in 1901. Nicknamed the "Puffing Billy", Booth's machine was the first device capable of sucking up dirt rather than merely blowing or brushing it away. It was a large, petrol-driven device with an internal combustion engine that powered a piston pump to draw air through a cloth filter. Due to its size, it had to be pulled by a horse.

Vacuum cleaners have evolved significantly from their initial, cumbersome form. The Hoover model 700 electric made them available to families in the 1920s. Later, in the 1980s and 1990s, manufacturers such as Dyson made them more efficient and stylish.

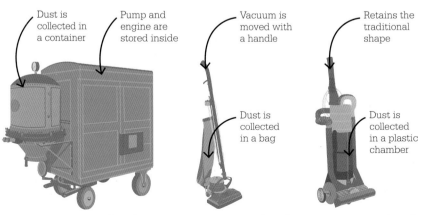

Dust is collected in a container

Pump and engine are stored inside

Vacuum is moved with a handle

Retains the traditional shape

Dust is collected in a bag

Dust is collected in a plastic chamber

"Puffing Billy" (1901)   **Hoover 700 electric (1926)**   **Dyson G-Force (1983)**

See also: Prosthetics and medical equipment 266–67 ▪ Ergonomics 278–85 ▪ The Internet of Things 300–01 ▪ Topology optimization 312

We don't have industrial designers. All our engineers are designers and all our designers are engineers.
James Dyson
The New Yorker, 2010

Over the years, inventors and engineers worked to improve the design and functionality of the vacuum cleaner. These resulted in making it smaller, lighter, more practical, and better suited for cleaning tasks – ranging from household floors and industrial spaces to the intricate nooks and crannies of car interiors.

Cyclonic revolution

In the late 1970s, inventor James Dyson was impressed when he witnessed the suction power of a local sawmill's industrial cyclones. He began thinking about a new type of vacuum cleaner, and over the following years, created thousands of prototypes. An early model was released onto the Japanese market in 1983. It was a success, and a decade later, Dyson launched his DC01 bagless vacuum

Dyson vacuum cleaners are compact and engineered for efficiency. The motor is in the centre of the machine. The filters are washable, which reduces waste and ensures easy maintenance.

in the UK. Dyson had added a motor and collection bin to his model, and removed the bag found in most vacuum cleaners. The motor created a high-speed air vortex – a powerful cyclone that forces dust and dirt particles into the collection bin, which removed the need for a disposable bag.

Not only was Dyson's invention more efficient at capturing fine particles, it also maintained consistent suction throughout the cleaning process. Removing the bag meant cost savings for the user, as well as reducing the amount of waste.

Constant progress

Dyson has since created many more designs and manufactured a range of household appliances, such as air purifiers, bladeless fans, hair dryers, and headphones. Designers across industries continue to innovate, making existing products ever more user-friendly, efficient, and aesthetically pleasing. The car industry, for example, benefits from constant progressive improvement. The driving experience has been improved with redesigned chassis; hybrid technology has reduced emissions; and interiors have been enhanced by new materials. ▪

Sir James Dyson

Sir James Dyson was born in Norfolk, England, in 1947. He is a British inventor and industrial designer, best known as the inventor of the bagless vacuum cleaner. After graduating from the Royal College of Art in London, Dyson began a career in design and engineering. His first major invention was the Ballbarrow, a modified version of a wheelbarrow replacing the wheel with a ball, which made the barrow easier to manipulate on soft ground. He established Dyson Limited in 1991. His multi-national technology company, based in the UK and Singapore, researches and designs new technologies. It has gained global recognition for its engineering and dedication to innovative design. Dyson was Provost of the Royal College of Art from August 2011 to July 2017 and opened the Dyson Institute of Engineering and Technology in 2017 in Wiltshire, England.

Key works

1974 Dyson Ballbarrow
2009 Dyson fan
2016 Dyson Supersonic hair dryer

THE FINAL EXHIBIT
EXIT THROUGH THE GIFT SHOP

Museums and art galleries are the locations where culture meets commerce. The earliest museums were set up in the ancient world, but the impetus for establishing museums got under way in the 17th century, when traders and colonialists in Europe and North America started to amass private collections of artwork and create "wonder rooms" of items with scientific or cultural interest. An increasingly leisured and educated public led to the founding of national museums and galleries such as the British Museum in London, the Louvre in Paris, and the Smithsonian Institution in Washington, DC.

Modern museum design
Today, the most famous museums attract millions of visitors a year from all over the world. Displays therefore need to engage a wide audience – as well as keeping valuable exhibits safe from potential damage.

Exhibition design involves more than simple siting and protection of artefacts. The initial task for curators and designers is to define the overarching idea and purpose of the exhibition. Is the aim to stimulate the intellect, or to excite the imagination? Is the display intended for in-depth education or for fun?

The next step is to identify key themes, and to define the target audience – for example, an interactive science display for children, or a journey through the work of an abstract artist, or the history of ancient China. The team will pick out capsule quotes or concepts to form a framework for the information. The sequence of displays will also be defined –

In **"Michelangelo: Divine Draftsman and Designer"** at New York's Metropolitan Museum of Art, the artist's drawings, paintings, and sculptures were arranged to give a sense of his thought processes.

See also: Visual merchandising and retail design 124–31 ▪ Hospitality design 178–79 ▪ The online user experience 294–99

An **initial plan** identifies the **main idea** of the exhibition, **key goals**, and **target audience**.

A **content brief** plans how to present the **exhibits** with **displays**, **audio** and **video**, and **interactive** elements.

An **outline** divides the content into **sections**, identifies **key items**, and defines how visitors **move through** the display.

The **overall look** of the exhibition is defined – **colours**, **lighting**, **typography**, and the nature and style of **souvenirs**.

for example, whether an artist's work will be laid out chronologically or grouped thematically.

The concept is then fleshed out with the choice of key objects and images, and decisions are made on how best to display the artefacts – whether in display cases, on walls, or using technology such as videos, projections, digital displays, or hands-on interactive elements. Text for signage, labels, and captions, scripts for audio recordings, videos, and aids for visitors with visual, hearing, or mobility impairments also need to be created.

In addition, lighting, wall colours, and display equipment are chosen to give the desired ambience, and a "pathway" is designed for visitors to follow, with pauses for key objects and quieter areas where people can sit and rest.

Lasting impressions

The final consideration is the memory that visitors will take away with them. For most, souvenirs are the most tangible mementos, and many visits to museums and galleries end with a trip to the gift shop. Institutions

typically locate their shops at the end of the pathway through the exhibition space, just before the exit. The range of goods displayed is selected to reflect the themes of the exhibition and will often include its key images and typographic style used in the exhibition. As well as catalogues, souvenirs may include models of important objects, clothing, stationery, food, and furnishings. Even the carrier bags for purchases may leave a lasting impression of the pleasure and interest generated by an exhibition. ∎

Immersive experiences in museums and galleries

From the 1930s, exhibition designers began to move away from traditional methods of displaying artefacts on walls or in display cases, to using bold, modern graphics, concealed lighting, and even projected film to create more immersive experiences.

Exhibitions today often feature audiovisual displays and hands-on activities to create immersive experiences that give multi-sensory stimulation. Many science exhibitions use

interactive devices and displays to engage visitors. The technique can even be used for showing art. One particularly striking example was Icelandic artist Olafur Eliasson's "Weather Project" in the Turbine Hall of Tate Modern, London in 2003. There was just one item: an artificial sun, created with mirrors and lights, with artificial mist. Viewers could lie on the gallery floor and "bask" in the sunlight, or could walk behind the exhibit to see how the effect was created.

In 2023, David Hockney used video, music, and his own words to share insights into his way of working in "Bigger & Closer (not smaller & further away)".

DIGITAL TO SUST
2000 ONWARDS

AINABLE

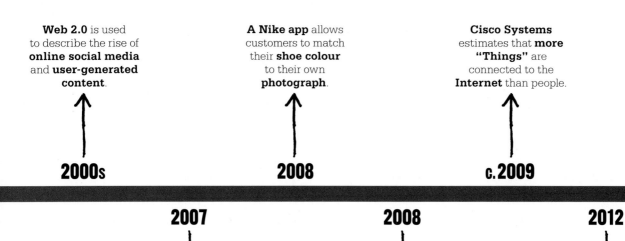

Web 2.0 is used to describe the rise of **online social media** and **user-generated content**.

A Nike app allows customers to match their **shoe colour** to their own **photograph**.

Cisco Systems estimates that **more "Things"** are connected to the **Internet** than people.

2000s

2008

c.2009

2007

2008

2012

US technology company **Evocative** creates **sustainable materials** from **mushrooms**.

Architect Patrik Schumacher describes **Parametricism** in a manifesto for Venice Architecture Biennale.

Converse launches an **interface** that enables customers to **personalize** the design of their **shoes**.

The arrival of a new century brought fresh developments in computing and digital technology. The Internet began to reach maturity at about this time: as access increased, commercial businesses, private individuals, and state-run organizations all found themselves online. This, in turn, gave rise to an emergent, globalized digital culture, profoundly changing human connectivity, perceptions, and behaviour, while providing designers with whole new dimensions in which to apply creative imagination. Cultural critics, meanwhile, observed that the effects of the online world on users appeared to be reprising concerns about autonomy, control, and decency that are as old as popular culture itself.

User-friendly design
Social media – and the ability to access it via smartphones from practically anywhere – created new opportunities for businesses to get to know and interact with their customers. As companies gained more insights into their client base, they also realized the value of clearly designed, well-structured information architecture that allowed their users to find their way around the website with ease, but also encouraged them to engage with any new products and services that might be on offer, perhaps by including facilities such as 1-click purchases.

Part ergonomics, part way-finding, graphic design, and service design, optimizing the User Experience (UX) has become an essential part of Web design.

However, UX design remains an important field in the real world, too, as the terrestial retail, hospitality, and events sectors continue to compete for attention and custom.

Digital ecosystems
One revelation of the 21st century is that the digital environment is no longer just for people. Your washing machine, fridge, kettle, watch, and home thermostat may also be online. The number of connected devices on the Internet of Things is thought to outnumber the human population by some distance. The data that is captured can be used by manufacturers and product designers to troubleshoot issues and perhaps improve the performance of the next generation of the product.

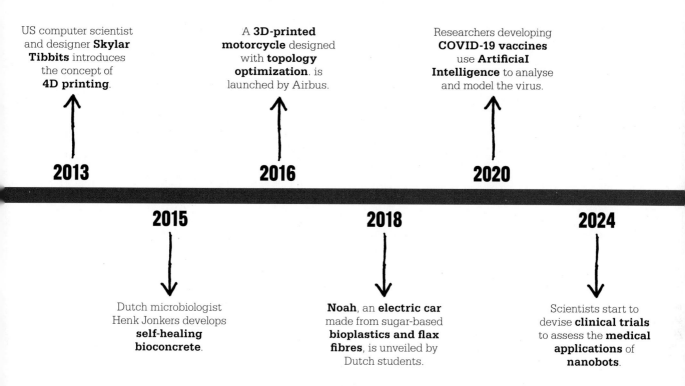

US computer scientist and designer **Skylar Tibbits** introduces the concept of **4D printing**.

A **3D-printed motorcycle** designed with **topology optimization**. is launched by Airbus.

Researchers developing **COVID-19 vaccines** use **Artificial Intelligence** to analyse and model the virus.

2013

2016

2020

2015

2018

2024

Dutch microbiologist Henk Jonkers develops **self-healing bioconcrete**.

Noah, an **electric car** made from sugar-based **bioplastics and flax fibres**, is unveiled by Dutch students.

Scientists start to devise **clinical trials** to assess the **medical applications** of **nanobots**.

Artificial Intelligence (AI) has an increasingly significant part to play in this arena. Many of us already interact with AI without really knowing it: for example, recommendations for new books, films, or products to try are often generated by an AI algorithm analysing your browsing history data and content consumption. AI can process vast amounts of data at speed; this speed of analysis and ability to model data helped scientists to track the COVID-19 virus during the 2020 pandemic.

Sustainable practices

In 2019, China was responsible for more than 25 per cent of the world's manufacturing output. China's ability to make goods at a lower cost than its western counterparts has long been an attractive economic proposition. However, making and transporting commodities long distances consumes huge amounts of energy. It also produces large quantities of carbon dioxide and other undesirable emissions. With economic models relying on never-ending growth, many people are increasingly apprehensive about the sustainability of this approach.

As early as the 1960s, designers such as Austrian-American Victor Papanek had voiced concerns about the conflict between design and the environment. Papanek argued that most consumer goods were unnecessary and that design should instead be focused on real environmental and human needs. It is thought that around 80 per cent of a product's ecological impact

is fixed at the design stage, so the onus is on designers – whether working in fashion, product design, graphic design, or construction – to adopt sustainable materials and manufacturing practices.

Processes such as topology optimization can not only produce some extraordinary and intriguing designs, but the technique may also help designers to conserve resources and reduce waste by identifying excess material that is not strictly necessary for the product's optimum performance. A computer algorithm runs through the various configurations of mass and volume when subjected to a range of different stresses to produce a structurally efficient design that places the material resources at the points where they are needed. ∎

SIMPLIFY, SIMPLIFY, SIMPLIFY

THE ONLINE USER EXPERIENCE

IN CONTEXT

FOCUS
User-oriented design and accessibility on the Web

FIELD
Information design, communication design

BEFORE
1946 The first programmable computer (ENIAC) is built in the US.

1969 ARPANET (Advanced Research Projects Agency Network), a precursor to the Internet, is first used in the US.

1984 Apple launches its first Macintosh computer, popularizing graphical user interfaces and facilitating desktop publishing.

AFTER
2007 Apple launches the iPhone smartphone.

2016 Around 230 companies globally are working on virtual reality-based projects.

I n August 1991, the first website went live. It was created by British computer scientist Tim Berners-Lee at CERN (the European Organization for Nuclear Research) and dedicated to outlining a new "universal linked information system" – the World Wide Web. In 1993, the project was released to the public, and by the end of the year, 623 websites were online; NASA was an early adopter.

In its infancy, the Web was simply a network of linked texts relying on HTML – codes that tell Web browsers how to display a Web page's words and images – to structure content. Design options were limited by low-resolution monitors and default system typefaces. Colour schemes were restricted by the capabilities of early browsers, and while JPEG and animated GIF files were soon supported, dial-up Internet speeds dictated that they were used sparingly and at small sizes. During the mid-1990s, new programming languages, such as JavaScript, gave Web designers more control, but aesthetics remained a secondary consideration, with priority given to content and functionality. By

Tim Berners-Lee stands with his NeXTcube workstation computer, on which he developed the first Web server – and the World Wide Web.

the 2020s, the Web had adopted a whole new design discipline – online user experience, or UX.

The scope of Web design changed dramatically in 1996, when American company Macromedia's Flash software allowed developers to create multimedia elements incorporating video, text, sound, animation, and graphics. Flash encouraged experimentation and creative expression – the Internet was a playground of possibility, and

Jakob Nielsen

Born in Copenhagen, Denmark, in 1957, Jakob Nielsen is a computer scientist and usability consultant. In the early 1990s, after completing a PhD in human–computer interaction at the Technical University of Denmark, Nielsen began work as a software engineer. He recognized the need for a more systematic, user-centric approach to Web design.

In 1993, Nielsen published the field's defining text, *Usability Engineering*, which has since been cited in many academic papers.

Nielsen's "heuristic evaluation method" – a technique that he developed in 1994 – is still widely used to identify and solve problems with user interfaces. In 1998, Nielsen co-founded the Nielsen Norman Group (NN/g) with American cognitive scientist Donald Norman. NN/g specializes in consulting, training, and research related to computer user experience and interface design. Among NN/g's achievements is eye-tracking analysis, which allows designers to structure content more effectively for consumers.

See also: Written communication 34–41 ▪ Visualizing data 108–09 ▪ Information design 144–45 ▪ Design for social change 180–81 ▪ Pictograms 256–57 ▪ Computer gaming 272–75 ▪ The Internet of Things 300–01

Web design was regarded as an emerging artform. "Interaction" was a new medium for storytelling, realized through dynamic content, immersive games, and visual richness. While this transformed static websites into engaging experiences, Flash-based platforms often suffered from usability issues: they were slow to load, frequently chaotic, and difficult to navigate.

User experience evolves

Web 2.0 is a term that materialized around the year 2000 to represent a second generation of Web development and design, with a greater focus on user-generated content, social networks, and e-commerce. As the number of people using the Internet increased, Web 2.0 also marked a shift towards standardization and usability. The early 2000s saw the rise of "information architecture" as a distinct discipline, and the first formal UX roles began to emerge. The term "user experience" was coined by the cognitive psychologist and engineer Donald Norman in 1993, but the basic principles drew on ergonomics – considering how the design and arrangement of systems could optimize the relationship between people and their tools.

By the 2010s, with the increasing popularity of smartphones and mobile browsing, the value of UX was more apparent, and the field expanded rapidly. Big companies – including Amazon and Apple – established dedicated UX teams to research, prototype, and test digital products, resulting in significant advancements in usability. Responsive design was introduced to accommodate the diverse range of devices used to access websites, and the concept of "mobile-first" design gained prominence, ensuring that sites performed effectively on small screens.

Touchscreen interaction

The importance of inclusive design also gained recognition, leading to the development and promotion of Web accessibility standards (WCAG 2.0). This included

Effective communication depends on the use of resources that are intrinsically connected with aesthetics.
Gui Bonsiepe
"Design as Tool for Cognitive Metabolism", 2000

guidance for designing interactive elements for people with differing dexterity levels, acknowledging that mobile devices often rely on touch interactions – tapping, swiping, and pinch gestures – that could exclude certain users. Addressing these concerns helped to ensure that the latest online platforms remained accessible to all, fostering inclusivity and diversity in the digital realm. »

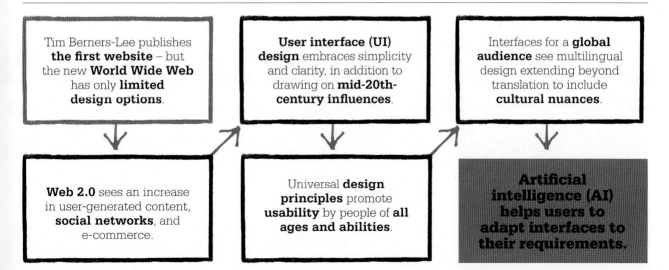

Tim Berners-Lee publishes **the first website** – but the new **World Wide Web** has only **limited design options**.

User interface (UI) **design** embraces simplicity and clarity, in addition to drawing on **mid-20th-century influences**.

Interfaces for a **global audience** see multilingual design extending beyond translation to include **cultural nuances**.

Web 2.0 sees an increase in user-generated content, **social networks**, and e-commerce.

Universal **design principles** promote **usability** by people of **all ages and abilities**.

Artificial intelligence (AI) helps users to adapt interfaces to their requirements.

Meanwhile, user-interface (UI) design – a subset of UX that is concerned with visual features and functions – embraced simplicity and clarity, with clean layouts, intuitive navigation, and a minimal aesthetic. Icons were widely adopted to convey information quickly. There was a backlash against the prevailing trend of skeuomorphism – for example, elaborate icons that looked more like realistic objects than navigational devices – in favour of "flat" design that rejects unnecessary embellishment.

Reductionism

In many ways, Web 2.0 can be seen as a successor to mid-20th-century design principles. Its information architecture draws heavily on Modernist information design and visual communication. The origins of its graphic icons can be traced to the pictograms and sign systems developed from the 1960s, while its user-friendly interfaces inherit a legacy influenced by International Typographic Style, with its emphasis on universal understanding.

The Bauhaus school's tenet of reductionism also has modern relevance. The philosophy of "form follows function" has gained traction since the mid-2010s as growing evidence shows that streamlining content, simplifying interfaces, and minimizing distractions contribute

> The total experience of a product covers much more than its usability: aesthetics, pleasure, and fun play critically important roles.
> **Donald Norman**
> *The Design of Everyday Things*, 2013

to a more enjoyable and efficient user journey. Embracing white space, using a limited colour palette, and focusing on essential features enhance visual appeal and facilitate quicker comprehension of information. Websites and apps that adopt this approach benefit from improved user engagement.

Seamless storytelling

In today's fast-paced digital era, the foundation of a successful online user experience lies in the harmonious integration of design, functionality, and usability. A methodology called design thinking is commonly used to achieve this. According to British designer Tim Brown, this is a

"human-centred approach to innovation that draws from the designer's toolkit to integrate the needs of people, the possibilities of technology, and the requirements for business success." Unlike ergonomics and cognitive science, a holistic approach to design thinking involves considering aesthetics in conjunction with the product or message.

Consistency is also significant. Successful brands use design to tell a story that embodies their identity and values across platforms to create a unified experience. This means taking a cohesive approach to interfaces for everything from websites, apps, and software, to home appliances, car dashboards, and wearable tech. Design systems can provide a centralized resource for teams to create coordinated work across these varied touchpoints. This is a structured set of principles, patterns, and components for visual and functional consistency; unlike design guidelines, design systems are inherently iterative and dynamic, and they include code.

Designing for all

Universal design can be defined as the design of products and environments to be usable "to the greatest extent possible by people of all ages and abilities", and this is an important consideration for designers of all disciplines. In Web design, ensuring accessibility involves making conscious choices. For example, high-contrast colour schemes – with sufficient definition between text and background – are more legible, benefiting users with

Instagram's original icon (left) was a skeuomorphic virtual representation of a physical camera. The simpler, "flat" replacement developed in 2016 is both memorable and ubiquitous.

visual-cognitive difficulties such as dyslexia and autism. Designers should avoid relying solely on colour to convey information – especially red–green distinctions – because this can be challenging for users who are colour blind.

It is also crucial that typefaces are easy to read and can be adjusted in size: online, fonts with a large x-height are considered best practice. A clear hierarchy of information with context-setting "alt text" for images, descriptive links, and navigational aids assists users of all abilities. To create a truly inclusive online environment, however, websites must be compatible with screen readers, for users with visual impairments. In multimedia contexts, they should include closed captions for those with hearing difficulties. The larger the potential audience, the more urgent it is to consider accessibility to reduce the number of people excluded from participation.

The world on screen

In the interconnected world of the 2020s, designers also face the challenge of creating interfaces that resonate globally. Truly multilingual

The five elements of UX design were described by Canadian-born UX designer Jesse James Garrett in his 2002 book *The Elements of User Experience*, which advised companies on how to incorporate UX into their communication strategies.

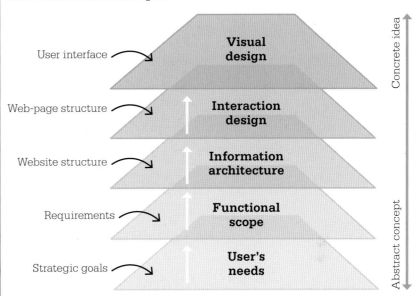

design goes beyond translation, encompassing cultural nuances and preferences. In computing, this is known as "internationalization and localization", or i18n. For companies seeking an expert perspective, accessibility and cross-cultural consultancy services are becoming more widely available.

Since at least 2010, artificial intelligence (AI) and machine learning have become pivotal forces in digital design. From personalized recommendations to intelligent chatbots, these technologies adapt interfaces dynamically, tailoring content according to the user's behaviour. This enhances engagement and creates new opportunities for designers to craft platforms that learn and evolve with users over time, so creating a more intuitive experience.

Augmented reality (AR) – where computer-generated information enhances real-life objects – and virtual reality (VR) are also reshaping the boundaries of Web design. From online showrooms to product previews, AR and VR allow designers to transcend the conventional two-dimensional confines of user interfaces with rich content that captivates all the senses in a virtual space. These concepts are set to become ever more commonplace. ∎

The digital landscape

Both UX and UI have crucial roles in shaping the digital landscape. Although they are interconnected and often conflated, they represent different aspects of the design process. UX can be thought of as the architecture, focusing on the overall flow and functionality of a product. It is concerned with understanding the needs, behaviours, and preferences of users to ensure that they can easily navigate the site and achieve their goals.

UI design brings this blueprint to life, concentrating on the look and feel – the colour schemes, typography, and components that consumers interact with. The end goal is to create an aesthetically pleasing interface that aligns with the brand and enhances the overall user experience. UI is detail-orientated, considering every button and icon to ensure a cohesive and engaging visual language. UI designers use tools such as Sketch, Figma, and Adobe XD to achieve their desired results.

AN ECOSYSTEM OF INFORMATION
THE INTERNET OF THINGS

IN CONTEXT

FOCUS
Everyday objects that can exchange data over the Internet

FIELD
Digital design, product design

BEFORE
1982 Students at Carnegie Mellon University in Pittsburgh, US, connect a vending machine to the Internet.

1988 US computer scientist Mark Weiser develops his concept of "ubiquitous computing", in which computing is entirely integrated into everyday life.

AFTER
2002 Amazon Web Service launches, offering services that allow other companies to develop IoT systems.

2009 Google tests a self-driving car. It relies on a network of sensors and devices that collect and exchange data.

Coined in 1999 by computer scientist Kevin Ashton, the term "Internet of Things" (IoT) describes a network of devices embedded with sensors and software that collect and exchange data. Over the past two decades, it has transformed the way we interact with the world around us.

The IoT has become an integral part of our daily lives. For example, an office worker heading home from work might use their smartphone to interact with their smart home system. They can turn on the heating and hot water, and set the oven to warm up shortly before they are due to arrive. Upon entering the house, they use a voice-controlled system to adjust the lighting and play music, to create a welcoming environment, and then proceed to the kitchen to warm up a meal.

Digital connectivity
It is the IoT that allows these objects to connect and communicate with each other and the Internet. At home, devices such as fitness trackers, smart meters, and smart doorbells simplify our lives by sharing information and performing intelligent actions autonomously, with minimal human intervention. Smart meters, for example, share information with the supplier and allow energy consumption to be monitored in real-time, leading to more accurate billing and the potential for energy savings.

An IoT system uses technology such as WiFi or Bluetooth to connect devices to the Internet so that they can communicate with each other. Each device is equipped with sensors and

A smartphone app allows a child to unlock a door. Devices such as smart door locks and smart doorbells have revolutionized home security, offering users convenience and control.

See also: Visualizing data 108–09 ▪ Information design 144–45 ▪ Service design 270–71
▪ The online user experience 294–99 ▪ Customization 310–11 ▪ Artificial Intelligence 313

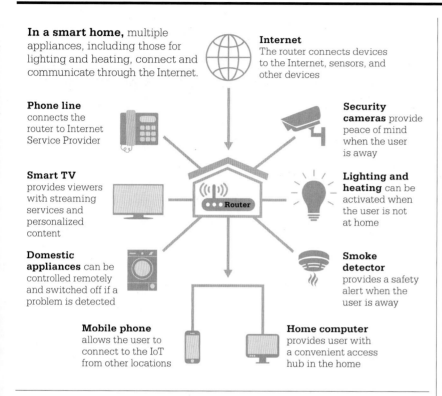

In a smart home, multiple appliances, including those for lighting and heating, connect and communicate through the Internet.

Internet
The router connects devices to the Internet, sensors, and other devices

Phone line
connects the router to Internet Service Provider

Security cameras provide peace of mind when the user is away

Smart TV
provides viewers with streaming services and personalized content

Lighting and heating can be activated when the user is not at home

Router

Domestic appliances can be controlled remotely and switched off if a problem is detected

Smoke detector
provides a safety alert when the user is away

Mobile phone
allows the user to connect to the IoT from other locations

Home computer
provides user with a convenient access hub in the home

actuators that collect information about how the device is used: sensors monitor changes, while actuators cause a physical change, such as switching a device on. Once the device is connected to the Internet, the IoT system may also use cloud computing to store and analyse data, or make use of advanced analytics tools to interpret the data that it collects.

Data-driven design

The data and information exchanged through IoT systems provides real-time insights into human behaviour and how people interact with spaces, products, or processes. This helps designers to gain a holistic understanding of a user's experience through their preferences and usage patterns. These insights

allow designers to respond to a user's needs and create better products or services that are more appropriate to them. For example, interface designers can use IoT data to understand which aspects of a system are underused. This in turn can help the developers to redesign the interface or improve a website.

Data exchange inevitably poses privacy and security risks. Given the sensitive nature of IoT data, protective measures – such as implementing regular software updates – are essential to guard against unauthorized access and data breaches. Industries and governments may use encryption, secure protocol guidelines, and regulatory frameworks to address broader concerns about privacy. ▪

Smart cities

A smart city uses technology and data to improve the quality of life for its residents. It does this by managing resources efficiently and streamlining urban services. This is achieved through the use of interconnected devices, data analysis, and automation. The ultimate goal is to create an urban environment that is sustainable, efficient, and liveable.

Smart cities employ sensors and data-driven insights to tackle urban issues, including transportation, waste management, and public safety. They prioritize sustainability, aiming to reduce environmental impact.

Singapore, a pioneering smart city, is known for its comprehensive Smart Nation initiative. This programme integrates cutting-edge technologies, including smart transportation systems, digital government services, and sustainable urban planning.

It's about embedding intelligence so things become smarter and do more than they were proposed to do.
Nicholas Negroponte
Speaking about IoT at a conference in 2005

SUSTAINABILITY HAS TO BE A DESIGN CHALLENGE

SUSTAINABLE MATERIALS

IN CONTEXT

FOCUS
Ensuring a healthy environment for future generations

FIELD
Graphic design, product design, architecture, interior design

BEFORE
1862 British chemist Alexander Parkes creates Parkesine, the first artificial bioplastic, from cellulose.

2002 Michael Braungart and William McDonough promote a circular model of recycling and upcycling products and their components in their book *Cradle to Cradle*.

AFTER
2018 Students at the Eindhoven University of Technology, The Netherlands, unveil Noah, an electric car made from sugar-based bioplastics and flax fibres.

The need for sustainable materials and methods started to gain attention in the mid- to late 20th century. Sustainability pioneers such as American architect Richard Buckminster Fuller and designer Victor Papanek began calling for ways to reduce the impact of produced goods and services through design in the 1960s.

Four decades later, American architect William McDonough and German professor Michael Braungart took that concept further, identifying the conflict between industry and environment as a critical design problem. As much as 80 per cent of the ecological impact of a product is locked in at the design stage, which makes it imperative for designers to adopt sustainable materials and manufacturing practices.

Sustainable printing

In the 1970s, political turbulence in the Middle East caused oil prices to rise. This led the Newspaper Association of America to look for alternatives to the petroleum-based inks on which the printing industry had historically relied. In 1987,

The global printing industry is increasingly relying on environment-friendly inks based on soy or on vegetable oils like linseed or sunflower.

The Gazette, a daily newspaper based in Iowa, introduced the first successful practical printing run using soy-based inks. Today, more than 90 per cent of US daily newspapers are printed with colour soy ink.

A longer drying time and higher degree of rub-off transfer make soy inks less suitable for use on glossy paper. However, there are other advantages besides lower cost, including more accurate colour reproduction. From a sustainability

Sustainability woes

The higher cost of sustainable alternatives is often offputting to consumers. For instance, refuse bags made of linear low-density polyethylene (LLDPE) are about a quarter of the price of biodegradable bags made from polylactic acid (PLA), a bio-resin typically made from corn starch or other plant-based starches.

Bamboo – currently used for everything from eco-friendly textiles to flooring – also has its drawbacks. Some issues are tactile: bamboo sheets and T-shirts have a slippery feel that some people find unpleasant; conversely, bamboo-based paper products are rougher to the touch than wood- or rag-pulp papers. Other difficulties are related to performance: bamboo flooring can wear out quickly in high-traffic areas and become stained with ground-in dirt that can only be removed by sanding it down and refinishing.

Sustainable products have definite advantages over their non-sustainable equivalents, but they are not always better.

There is no need for shampoo bottles ... and other packaging to last decades (or even centuries) longer than what came inside them.
Michael Braungart and William McDonough
Cradle to Cradle, 2002

See also: Industrial design 146–47 ▪ Plastic 148–53 ▪ Material-led furniture design 186–87 ▪ Dawn of synthetic fabrics 194–95 ▪ Eco design 258–65 ▪ 3D digital printing 276–77

point of view, soy inks are easier to remove than their petroleum-based counterparts, making soy-printed paper easier to recycle.

More recent developments in the printing industry include the 2013 launch of an algae-based ink by the Living Ink company. Algae Black is a viable alternative to carbon black, the petroleum-based black pigment that generates a large carbon footprint, as well as being unsafe for humans. Algae Black pigments can be used in a range of commercial applications including printing, plastics, cosmetics, and textiles.

Fashion and bioplastics

Algae have also found their way into the world of haute couture, thanks to a sequinned dress by American designer Phillip Lim. Sequins are usually made of either a polyester film called Mylar or polyvinyl chloride (PVC); additionally, they are often coated with synthetic materials to give them their shine. In 2021, Lim worked with researcher Charlotte McCurdy to create bioplastic sequins made from algae. They were sewn onto a biodegradable base fabric made of plant fibres, resulting in a dress entirely free of crude-oil derivatives.

In 2023, British designer and sustainability champion Stella McCartney created a dress covered in BioSequins, made from polymer cellulose extracted from trees. The cellulose naturally reflects light, making the sequins sparkle without any additional treatments.

Cellulose-derived sequins made by British company Radiant Matters are a plastic- and colourant-free option for sparkling party dresses.

Bioplastics are increasingly used in the packaging and music industries, too. In 2020, Australian biomaterials company Great Wrap created a compostable cling film made of starch extracted from potato peel, recycled cooking oil, and cassava root.

In 2023, UK-based music and sustainability collective Evolution Music designed a 12-inch vinyl record made of bioplastics. Evovinyl is compatible for use in existing record-pressing machinery, and it works on all record players.

Construction materials

A strong, flexible, and renewable material that produces very little waste, bamboo has been employed for construction scaffolding in tropical latitudes for centuries.

Untreated bamboo – which burns rapidly and rots within two to three years as insects and fungi attack the sap within the canes – was not deemed practical for modern architecture. That changed in the 1990s, when Irish designer Linda Garland teamed »

Extraction of materials requires the use of **natural resources** and has an impact on biodiversity.

↓

Production and **processing** use energy and create pollutants.

↓

Distribution necessitates packaging and also leads to **emissions** and **energy** use.

↓

Once in the hands of the consumer, the product's packaging **creates waste**.

↓

At the end of the product's life, the **disposal process** leads to further waste, emissions, and pollutants.

up with German scientist Walter Liese at the University of Hamburg to treat bamboo and turn it into a viable building material. The technique involves drilling through the centre of the canes, soaking them with insect repellent and fire-resistant chemicals, then curing and drying them.

Bamboo is now being adopted globally in large-scale architecture, flooring, furniture, and textiles. The entire stem of a bamboo tree can be used in construction, and leftover pieces are biodegradable and compostable. Bamboo plywood and particle board have similar properties to conventional plywood, with the additional advantages of affordability and eco-friendliness.

Most of the world's bamboo forests are found in Asia, with China having the richest resources. According to the World Wide Fund for Nature (WWF), the industrial variety of bamboo used for flooring

The Millennium Bridge at Green School Bali has a bamboo structure and a thatched cover. Stretching 23m (75ft) across the Ayung River, it is Asia's longest bamboo bridge.

and furniture is not the same as pandas feed on, so the ecological impact remains negligible.

Concrete developments
Another sustainable advancement in the construction industry is that of Engineered Cementitious Composite (ECC). Also known as bendable cement, this is a type of concrete reinforced with small, polymer-derived fibres. Although it contains many of the same ingredients as its traditional counterpart – Portland cement, made of sand, stone, and water – ECC is more sustainable. It can be infused with carbon dioxide to strengthen it, while reducing the amount of cement in the mix, which lowers carbon emissions.

Bioconcrete, a self-healing concrete product, contains biodegradable plastic capsules of calcium lactate and bacteria within a wet concrete mix. When activated by water, the capsules expand to fill any cracks.

Due to continued advances in 3D concrete printing, it is now possible to digitally design any component of a building and print

> We can't just continue living as if there was no tomorrow, because there is a tomorrow.
> **Greta Thunberg**
> *Time* magazine, 2019

it on-site, saving time, money, and energy. Additionally, since the formwork is reusable, 3D-printed concrete produces less waste.

Inspired by nature
In their search for sustainable solutions, designers often turn to the natural world for inspiration.

In 2017, California-based company Bolt Threads launched Microsilk, a fibre created by mimicking the DNA in spider silk. Spider proteins are inserted

Sir Norman Foster

Born in Stockport, UK, in 1935, Sir Norman Foster has maintained a focus on sustainable building methods and materials throughout his five-decade career as an architect. His firm's environmental research teams work hand in hand with architects to develop liveable, breathable buildings.

A key element of Foster's philosophy is the retrofit – that is, transforming old office buildings into flexible workspaces. In 2006, he expanded an existing structure in New York into the 44-floor Hearst Tower. Rather than demolish the 1928 six-storey sandstone building, Foster retrofitted it, saving tons of rubble from landfill and creating a new landmark for the city – New York's first gold-rated structure under the US Leadership in Energy and Environmental Design (LEED) programme. The steel used was 85 per cent recycled, and the structure's diagrid pattern uses 20 per cent less steel than a conventional frame.

into yeast cells, which then produce liquid silk protein during fermentation. After processing, the mixture can be wet-spun into fibres, in much the same way that acrylic and rayon are made.

One of the most popular natural materials used by eco-conscious designers is hemp, a healthier alternative material for use in insulation, wall systems, textiles, and more. The plants even nourish depleted soils as they grow. When blended with lime, hemp absorbs carbon dioxide from the atmosphere, and hemp-lime products are naturally resistant to pests, mould, and fire, which makes them an attractive option for architectural interiors.

Mycelium, first derived from mushrooms in 2007 by US-based company Ecovative, is another sustainable material with myriad uses. It can be moulded into bricks for use in construction, grown into vegan leather hides, shaped in the form of bicycle helmets, or used for biodegradable packaging, a solution already adopted by IKEA and Dell. This natural polymeric substance is highly durable and resistant to mould, water, and fire.

Mycelium can also be used to make plant-based "meats". Meati, a Colorado-based alt-meat brand, claims that its mycelium-based products require less than 1 per cent of the water and land needed for industrially produced animal meat, and also emit 99 per cent less carbon.

Design opportunities

The impact of adopting sustainable materials is most visible at a large, industrial scale – in manufacturing,

This 3D-printed vase by biodesign studio Biomatters is made of mycelium and clay. The company specializes in creating biodegradable decorative items out of organic and waste materials.

agriculture, shipping, and construction. However, designers are becoming more aware of the role they can play in guiding individual consumers towards sustainability.

Huge strides are being made in packaging. Toothpaste is now available as tablets sold in refillable glass jars or aluminium containers; deodorant comes in fully recyclable cardboard or in refillable cases instead of plastic containers; and household cleaning products are packaged in refillable glass bottles.

A major success story in planet-friendly packaging concerns the humble water bottle. To prevent an estimated 60 million disposable bottles entering US landfills every day, designers created reusable water bottles in a wide array of appealing colours, sizes, and sustainable materials such as glass and aluminium, encouraging consumers to make the simple switch from carrying water packaged in plastic to having their own refillable container. With 54 per cent of Americans drinking bottled water, this small individual effort towards sustainability is having a notable impact. ■

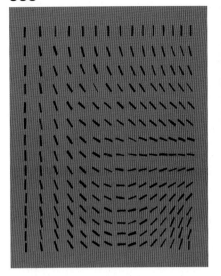

EVERY ELEMENT IS SUBJECT TO VARIATION
PARAMETRICISM

One of the most striking styles within contemporary avant-garde architecture, Parametricism is most associated with dynamic, fluid, and complex forms and spaces. It is derived from the parametric modelling approach, in which computer programs and algorithms dictate the form of the building. The concept rose in prominence during the early 21st century, with the development of advanced parametric design.

The use of computer-aided design (CAD) software and hardware technology in the design process, dates as far back as the 1950s. But since the 1980s, the use of parametric design, which relies on sophisticated software and algorithms to generate designs and create models, has steadily increased. Today, it is an essential tool in a range of fields including urban and furniture design. Its adoption marked the shift from hand-drawn design methods to computer-based practice.

Celebrating complexity

The term "Parametricism" was first coined by German-born architect Patrik Schumacher, of Zaha Hadid

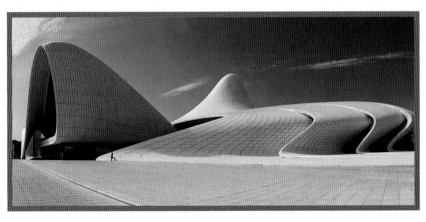

The Heydar Aliyev Centre in Baku, Azerbaijan, was designed by Zaha Hadid. The curved, flowing form of the building is almost seamlessly integrated with the piazza that surrounds it – a typical feature of Hadid's style.

See also: Futurism 175 ■ Modernism 188–93 ■ Streamlining 196–99 ■ Urban design 248–49 ■ Artificial intelligence 313

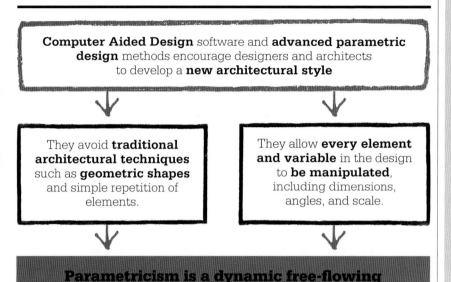

Computer Aided Design software and **advanced parametric design** methods encourage designers and architects to develop a **new architectural style**

They avoid **traditional architectural techniques** such as **geometric shapes** and simple repetition of elements.

They allow **every element and variable** in the design to **be manipulated**, including dimensions, angles, and scale.

Parametricism is a dynamic free-flowing architectural style with exciting possibilities.

Architects. In a manifesto written for the Venice Architecture Biennale in 2008, Schumacher claimed that Parametricism is unique in its ability to articulate increasingly complex social processes and institutions. In other words, its approach would allow for the design of buildings and urban spaces that could adapt to their context and reflect the complexity of modern life. The difference between a Modernist architect using parametric design and Parametricism, he suggested, is in the acknowledgement and expression of this complexity. Rather than absorbing it, as in Modernism, Parametricism calls on the architect to emphasize complexity and maximize differentiation.

Practical applications

Schumacher made extensive use of these principles in his works. His own designs for Zaha Hadid

Architects – including some co-authored by Zaha Hadid herself – are among the best-known examples of Parametricism. These include the Opus Tower (2019), a mixed-use block in Dubai with an irregular-shaped void in its centre, and the London Aquatics Centre (2011), built for the 2012 Olympics, which has a wave-like roof.

Examples of Parametricism by other architects include the Museo Soumaya (2011), a private museum held in a metallic shell in Mexico City designed by Fernando Romero, and the Louis Vuitton Foundation (2014), an art museum and cultural centre in Paris, designed by Frank Gehry.

In many cases, the buildings designed in the Parametricist style have a distinctive architectural aesthetic that includes sweeping forms and irregular shapes created by combining complex geometries, such as spheres, cubes, cones, or cylinders. ■

Blobitecture

Blobitecture is an architectural movement characterized by free-flowing, organic forms, created through advanced 3D modelling software. The term is both a blending of the words "blob" and "architecture", and a reference to "binary large object", a form of data storage used by design software.

Notable examples include the Selfridges Birmingham department store (2003) in the UK and the Kunsthaus Graz (2003), an art museum in Graz, Austria. Both buildings have an abstract undulating shape covered with unusual adornments: Selfridges is covered with 15,000 anodized aluminium discs, while the Kunsthaus has an iridescent blue skin.

Blobitecture has a counterpart in industrial design, known as Blobjects. Created with the help of computer-aided design, its products are tested for safety, durability, and performance before manufacture. Famous blobjects include the Embryo chair by Marc Newson (1988), and the Blob Wall by Greg Lynn (2008).

The Selfridges building in Birmingham, UK, epitomizes Blobitecture. There is an absence of sharp geometry, and like other examples of the movement, it has an undefined, undulating surface covered in detailed ornamentation.

EXPRESS YOURSELF
CUSTOMIZATION

IN CONTEXT

FOCUS
Digital tools that offer increased individuality

FIELD
Product design

BEFORE
17th–18th centuries Posie rings engraved with quotations from courtship stories are given as tokens of love.

1973 German sporting goods company Puma produces a pair of custom-made shoes for basketball star Walt "Clyde" Frazier of the New York Knicks.

AFTER
2008 Nike launches the Nike PHOTOiD app, which analyses photographs uploaded by users to create custom shoe colours.

2014 New York-based company Normal uses 3D digital printing technology to manufacture bespoke earbuds moulded to each customer's ear size and contours.

A significant trend in consumer culture since the late 20th century, customization has its roots in traditional bespoke craftsmanship.

The process – enabled by both changes in consumer tastes and technological advances – allows end users unprecedented control over the look and feel of their purchases. Customization gives individuals the ability to personalize certain items according to their own specific needs or whims, tailoring them to create something unique.

Two-way benefits
Product customization has clear advantages for both consumers and the businesses that provide it. For consumers, being able to personalize a product means having something that aligns perfectly with their style and preferences, fostering a strong emotional

Consumers can create a product that better **serves their needs**.

Businesses offering customization have a **unique selling point**.

The product is unique to each **customer**, making it **more personal**.

Increased revenue can be brought in through a **premium charged for unique items**.

Customization benefits both business and customers.

Shoe brand Converse offers customers a vast range of possibilities in its online customization tool. This means that every resulting product has the potential to be completely unique.

connection. Breaking down product designs into modular components that can be selected empowers consumers to create products that are truly one-of-a-kind.

Moreover, the ability to personalize products addresses the growing demand for individuality in a world saturated with mass-produced goods. Consumers seek items that help them to stand out from the crowd, and personalization caters to this desire, offering a path to self-expression.

From a business perspective, customization offers a competitive edge, provides a unique selling proposition, and engenders customer loyalty.

The shift from standardized to personalized products has made the consumer experience more engaging, emotionally resonant, and reflective of an individual identity that aligns with a customer's values.

Consumer creators

Among those that have adopted consumer customization are US footwear brands such as Converse, maker of the hugely popular Chuck Taylor All-Star sneakers. In 2012 Converse launched a user-friendly interface to facilitate the process of personalizing their shoes. Digital tools now allow online customers to choose from a variety of elements – including shoe style, materials, colours, print patterns, logos, and embroideries – as well as to add individual touches such as initials or a short inscription.

This level of customization goes beyond mere selection – it transforms consumers into co-creators and gives them a sense of ownership and uniqueness in the products they purchase.

Personalized marketing

Companies in other sectors have also come up with ways to customize their products to commemorate events or special occasions. For example, Coca-Cola allows its customers to personalize the classic glass Coke bottle with names, messages, and special design themes – from birthday candles, to graduate caps, and from Pride rainbows, to Lunar New Year imagery. In the US, the company also produces customized bottles that bear the logos of college football and soccer teams, or with labels that mark sporting occasions such as the Daytona 500 car race.

Similarly, Apple products such as iPhones, iPads, and Airpods can now be customized with engraved messages, while customers at LEGO can build a figurine in their own likeness by selecting from the company's vast catalogue of looks and accessories. ▪

Apple products were designed to foster innovation. This approach goes beyond product design, affecting your brand's design.
Steve Jobs
Co-founder of Apple

WHERE TO PUT THE HOLES
TOPOLOGY OPTIMIZATION

Topology optimization is an algorithm-based computer-aided design process that has transformed how products and structures are conceived and engineered. It uses complex mathematics to calculate the best way to distribute material within a given space, allowing for the simplified creation of more efficient and lightweight structures. First used in the biomedical field for modelling implants to match the human skeletal structure, it

has since become an invaluable tool in the fields of automotive, aeronautical, and civil engineering.

Efficiency in design
The algorithmic software created to complete topology optimization explores all possible configurations of mass and volume under a range of stresses. This helps to guarantee structural efficiency and reduce wasted resources when creating objects such as the wings of an aeroplane, where even a fraction of a gram can be the difference between success and failure. Today, topology optimization is also undertaken during the conceptual phases of product design. The results of the process are often organic, free-form shapes that are difficult to make. This means its use is sometimes confined to the early stages of the design process. ∎

The Bone chair (2006) was designed by Dutch designer Joris Laarman. He uses topology optimization to create furniture that simulates natural growth patterns, such as those found in bones.

See also: Industrial design 146–47 ▪ Streamlining 196–99 ▪ Built to last 242–43 ▪ 3D Digital printing 276–77 ▪ Ergonomics 278–85 ▪ Parametricism 308–09

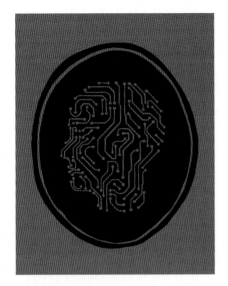

AI IS A MIRROR
ARTIFICIAL INTELLIGENCE

Artificial intelligence (AI) is playing a transformative role in the design world. It is revolutionizing how designers create, innovate, and interact with users, and has already reshaped key parts of design processes.

From fantasy to reality

The creative industries have flirted with the potential of AI for decades: it has been the subject of films such as Spike Jonze's *Her* (2013) and Alex Garland's *Ex Machina* (2014). The reality of its integration into everyday life has been much slower, but the emergence in the 2020s of generative programs that can create entirely new text, images, and audio – such as Midjourney, ChatGPT, and Adobe Firefly – has democratized AI, and made it available to anyone with a computer and an internet connection.

In design, AI is used at every stage of the creative process – brainstorming ideas, generating prototypes, and helping designers to visualize products in real-world situations. Personalization has been

A computer would deserve to be called intelligent if it could deceive a human into believing that it was human.
Alan Turing
Computing Machinery and Intelligence, **1950**

a notable application. By analysing datasets and identifying patterns, AI can make predictions and tailor designs. For example, a streaming service can use AI to suggest new films in genres the viewer likes to watch. And in manufacturing, AI can streamline machine-making and resource usage by calculating the most efficient production method in a matter of seconds. ∎

See also: Service design 270–71 ▪ The online user experience 294–99 ▪ The Internet of Things 300–01 ▪ Customization 310–11

REWRITE OUR RELATIONSHIP WITH THE PHYSICAL WORLD
SMART MATERIALS

IN CONTEXT

FOCUS
Materials that can autonomously respond to their environment

FIELD
Product design, textiles, engineering

BEFORE
1932 Swedish physicist Arne Ölander demonstrates the shape memory effect with gold-cadmium alloy.

2012 The innovative Self-Assembly Lab is established at MIT in the US.

2013 Skylar Tibbits outlines the concept of 4D printing.

AFTER
2024 Scientists researching the use of nanobots to deliver drugs automatically to targeted parts of the body via the bloodstream begin to develop clinical trials.

Smart materials change their physical or chemical properties in response to external stimuli, such as heat, light, acidity, or electricity. Examples include metals that lose their deformities and bounce back into shape when they are heated, and photochromic sunglasses, which grow darker in sunlight.

Traditionally, objects are made in the optimal form for their function; they may be susceptible to wear and tear – which can lead to their breakdown – but other than that, they are not expected to change. In contrast, an object made from a smart material is designed to adapt to different circumstances. It may

Six primary external influences cause smart materials to respond in a variety of ways.

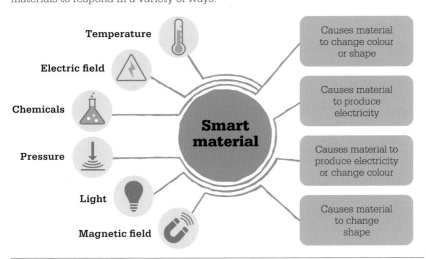

- Temperature — Causes material to change colour or shape
- Electric field
- Chemicals
- Pressure — Causes material to produce electricity
- Light
- Magnetic field

Smart material — Causes material to produce electricity or change colour

Causes material to change shape

> All the things that make something quote-unquote "smart", you can do it with materials themselves. … All materials are active in some way or another.
> **Skylar Tibbits**
> *New Civil Engineer*, 2016

even be capable of building itself in the first place, or healing itself when broken, without the need for new parts, material, or labour. That ability is preprogrammed into the material itself.

Transformative materials

The prefix "smart" often suggests that electronics or sensors are embedded in a product, and connected devices such as smart home thermostats have become increasingly common since British entrepreneur Kevin Ashton coined the term "Internet of Things" in 1999. However, "smart" solutions also include innovations that remove the need for human or electronic intervention, because the material itself is designed to perform the required function.

Familiar examples of materials that react to stimuli include non-Newtonian fluids, whose viscosity changes when stressed, and shape-memory materials. Quicksand (water-saturated sand), for example, reacts in an

unexpected way when pressure is applied: the more a person struggles, the more they sink, as the pressure caused by movement turns solid to liquid. In artificial non-Newtonian fluids such as tomato ketchup, this property helps to get the sauce out of the container – it becomes runnier when the bottle has been given a vigorous shake. Potential applications for materials made with non-Newtonian fluids include paint that does not clump and protective clothing that stiffens on impact.

Shape-memory alloys (SMAs) were among the first shape-memory materials recognized as being "smart". They "remember" their form and return to it when energy is applied or removed. One popular demonstration, the magic paperclip trick, illustrates their behaviour, when a seemingly normal paperclip – in fact made of the nickel and titanium alloy nitinol – is twisted and contorted, then springs back into shape when heat is applied.

The shape-memory effect was first recorded in the 1930s, using an alloy of gold and cadmium, but it did not become commercially viable until the properties of nitinol were discovered in 1959. Today, there are numerous applications for the use of SMAs and shape-memory polymers – from car »

As the Bayeux Tapestry (*c.* 1070s) shows, the treacherous nature of quicksand has long been known. Scientists are now looking to exploit its characteristics in smart materials.

bumpers and wing mirrors that can regain their shape after a minor collision, to splints and stents in biomedicine.

Manipulating molecules

Materials can be manipulated to become smart through the use of nanotechnology. This works at a molecular level, where particles behave differently and exhibit changed properties due to quantum effects. The molecular structure of a fabric, for example, can be altered to make it waterproof or stain resistant. American physicist Richard Feynman introduced the concept of controlling atoms and molecules in this way in his 1959 lecture "There's Plenty of Room at the Bottom", and Japanese scientist Norio Taniguchi coined the term "nanotechnology" in 1974.

Nanotechnology is now an active area of cutting-edge research, but some of its techniques have been in use for centuries, long before the science behind them began to be understood. Roman artists of the 4th century CE discovered that adding gold and silver to glass could stain it in different colours;

Self-healing bioconcrete incorporates microcapsules that contain dormant bacteria and a food source. When cracks allow water to enter, the bacteria are activated and produce calcium carbonate ($CaCO_3$).

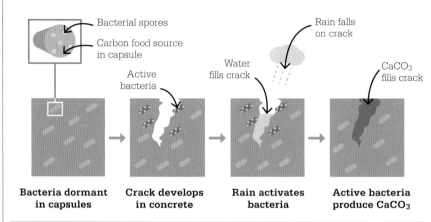

| Bacteria dormant in capsules | Crack develops in concrete | Rain activates bacteria | Active bacteria produce $CaCO_3$ |

a famous example is the Lycurgus Cup, which appears green but glows red when lit from within. Similarly, lustrous pottery glazes in 9th-century Mesopotamia were achieved using nanoparticles of silver and copper. Nanotechnology was also behind the mysterious Damascus steel – famed for its strength and durability – that was produced in parts of Asia from the 1st millennium BCE. In 2006, microscopy revealed the presence of tiny carbon nanotubes in the material.

Researchers are also looking at the molecular properties of the natural world – such as insect shells that are particularly hard, or unique colouring – to inspire the next generation of smart materials.

4D printing

In 1984, American engineer Charles Hull invented 3D printing to speed up prototyping in design. It is now widely used to print objects of all kinds, in materials from plastics to natural tissue, as long as it can be extruded layer by layer through a

Skylar Tibbits

Born in the US in 1985, Skylar Tibbits graduated from Philadelphia University with a degree in architecture before continuing his education at MIT, where he gained qualifications in computer science and design. Best known for the concept of 4D printing, which he first proposed in 2013, Tibbits is the founder of MIT's Self-Assembly Lab.

Through the Self-Assembly Lab, Tibbits has explored smart materials across applications ranging from fashion and furniture to civil engineering. He has designed large installations for the Museum of Modern Art in New York, the Centre Pompidou in Paris, and the Victoria and Albert Museum in London. His numerous awards include R&D Innovator of the Year (2015).

Key works

2017 *Active Matter*
2021 *Things Fall Together: A Guide to the New Materials Revolution*

nozzle. In 2013, American computer scientist and designer Skylar Tibbits introduced the concept of 4D printing. The additional dimension of time means that 4D-printed objects are preprogrammed with instructions that allow them to change in response to different circumstances or stimuli.

Designers choose materials to perform a specific function in response to a stimulus such as water or heat. The design process requires shaping the material so that this response happens in a controlled manner – aligning its particles and working with geometry to determine dimensions and visual effects.

Examples of preprogrammed materials in action include Nike's 2015 textile AeroReact, which used two types of material in its yarn to support the body's existing thermoregulatory capabilities. It functioned by reacting to moisture, opening up the structure of the knit to maximize breathability. Meanwhile, a 4D knit dress designed by the Self-Assembly Lab at the Massachusetts Institute of Technology (MIT) uses heat-activated yarns to tailor a garment – to change the fit for an individual body or to change the style – when targeted heat is applied. Smart materials can also be used in the built environment, where the colour of a building's facade may change to repel heat, or solar shades may close in response to bright sunlight. These responses regulate building temperature without recourse to energy-intensive heating and cooling systems.

The Self-Assembly Lab's 4D knit dress uses heat-activated yarns, computerized knitting, and robotic activation to tailor a dress and create a perfect personalized fit.

> Self-assembly is a process by which disordered parts build an ordered structure through only local interaction.
> **Self-Assembly Lab**

In biomedicine, the ability of smart materials to respond to environmental changes – such as temperature, light, acidity, pressure, and biochemical signals – means that they can mimic natural biological elements and processes. Areas of development include medical diagnostics and monitoring, where the material can react to specific biomarkers, drug delivery, and tissue engineering.

Self-assembly, self-healing

Tibbits describes working with programmed materials as a bottom-up process: "All of these things are designed and built from the bottom up, that they self-organize and self-assemble into this final structure that has

functionality." One of the areas that smart-material designers are investigating is self-assembly. The MIT Self-Assembly Lab has explored this with furniture that builds itself: a flat-pack table that unfolds into 3D form, or a chair that can autonomously unite its parts, removing the need to ship bulky items or decipher complex instructions. In aerospace, self-assembly would allow an antenna to shape itself in space's hazardous working conditions.

Beyond self-assembly, there is also self-healing, where – like skin after an injury – a material repairs itself. One application is self-healing bioconcrete, invented by Dutch microbiologist Henk Jonkers in 2015.

Smart materials have the potential to solve problems non-invasively. The Self-Assembly Lab has a project to tackle coastal erosion in the Maldives archipelago, which is under threat from rising sea levels. Current beach restoration techniques require the installation of permanent fixed barriers or ecosystem-disrupting dredging to reallocate sand. However, the Self-Assembly Lab is trialling submerged geometric structures, which are designed to work with natural wave patterns to build up sand – a strategy that works with and not against nature. ∎

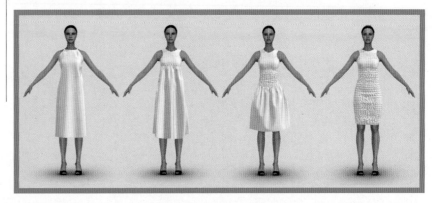

DIRECTO

RY

DIRECTORY

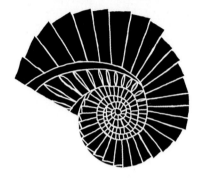

Design is a broad and constantly evolving area, and one that touches almost every aspect of the world: from the arrangement of towns and cities and the structure of buildings, to the shape of furniture and the way in which it is packaged for sale. Design even affects the appearance of different media – and the longevity of the devices on which media is consumed. Over the centuries, a large number of different design disciplines have emerged in response to the changing needs of our world, influenced by a vast and varied range of movements and ideas – far more than can be described in this book. The pages below explore some significant examples in chronological order from the 19th–21st century.

JAPONISME
1845–1920

Japonisme refers to the influence of Japanese culture on Western art and design following Japan's 1854 opening to trade. Artists and designers in Europe and the US were fascinated by the decorative patterns and asymmetrical compositions of Japanese art. Early works by the French artist Félix Bracquemond included the 1866 dinner services, which used Japanese artistic motifs, while British designers Christopher Dresser and Edward William Godwin produced works in the Anglo-Japanese style. In the US, the work of Frank Lloyd Wright and glassmaker Louis Comfort Tiffany was influenced by Japanese art.

CHICAGO SCHOOL
1890–1920

The Chicago school was formed of a group of architects and engineers from the US city, including Daniel Burnham, William Le Baron Jenney,

John Wellborn Root, and the firm of Dankmar Adler and Louis Sullivan. Also referred to as Commercial style, the tall buildings created by the Chicago school were made possible using the steel frame. Because the exterior walls were not load-bearing, they could be replaced by glass. The buildings were usually between six and 20 storeys, and typically rectangular with a flat, corniced roof. Chicago school skyscrapers still standing today include the Manhattan building, designed by Le Baron Jenney in 1890–91, and the Carson Pirie Scott & Co department store building, designed by Sullivan between 1898–1904.

GLASGOW SCHOOL
1892–1910

The Glasgow school refers to a group of artists and designers working in Glasgow, Scotland, whose style combined Celtic Revival, the Arts and Crafts movement, and Japonisme. With elongated sinuous forms, the Glasgow school made a major

contribution to the development of an international Art Nouveau style. Significant members included Charles Rennie Mackintosh, sisters Margaret and Frances Macdonald, and Herbert MacNair. The most famous of the group, Mackintosh, is known for being the architect of important Glasgow buildings such as the Glasgow School of Art, built between 1897–1909, and his furniture and stained glass window designs.

JUGENDSTIL
1895–1910

Jugendstil, meaning "youth style", emerged in mid-1890s Germany, encompassing graphic art, architecture, and applied art. Jugendstil had two phases, firstly featuring sinuous, organic forms, rooted in Art Nouveau, and later a more abstract, geometrical style, more suited to mass production. Initially Munich was the centre of Jugendstil, with advocates including Hermann Obrist, Richard Riemerschmid, Bruno Paul, and Peter Behrens. Around 1900 the

Munich group dispersed, heading for Berlin, Weimar, and Darmstadt. An artist's colony was established in Darmstadt by Jugendstil architects including Behrens and Joseph Olbrich. In 1907, Behrens rejoined Riemerschmid, Paul, and others to create the Deutscher Werkbund (see p.162).

FUNCTIONALISM
1896–1970s

Functionalism in architecture is a movement that prioritized the function of the building as the driver of its form and construction. A part of the Modernist movement, Functionalism rejected tradition and ornament in favour of a pared-back approach that saw buildings as tools for human activity. US architect Louis Sullivan, who coined the phrase "form follows function", is considered a founder of modern Functionalism alongside fellow architects Frank Lloyd Wright, Hugo Häring, Hans Scharoun, Alvar Aalto, and James Stirling. Although aesthetics were not prescribed, Functionalist buildings tended to be multi-storey, with simple geometric shapes and large amounts of glass.

VIENNA SECESSION
1897–1905

The Vienna Secession was formed in 1897 by a group of Austrian painters, graphic artists, sculptors, and architects. Led by Gustav Klimt, Josef Olbrich, Josef Hoffmann, and Koloman Moser, the group broke away from the traditional artistic styles that were fashionable in Vienna at the time. In 1898, the group started a journal,

Ver Sacrum, which published influential works of graphic art. Their main architectural work was the Secession exhibitions hall, a gallery designed by Olbrich as a venue for members of the group to show their works. In 1905, the group split, with Klimt, Hoffman, and Wagner resigning.

ORGANIC DESIGN
1908–

Organic design, or Organic architecture, is design inspired by nature. Distinct from biomimicry, which imitates nature, Organic design describes forms that incorporate nature's principles. Practiced since 1908, Organic design has resulted in low-lying, intuitive structures that are built into nature itself so that the environment and the building become one. The most famous example is the Fallingwater house, designed in 1935 by Frank Lloyd Wright, which was built above a natural waterfall. In 1941, the Museum of Modern Art put together an exhibition called *Organic Design in Home Furnishings*, which included works by Eero Saarinen and Charles Eames.

EXPRESSIONISM
1910–1933

Expressionism emerged in Germany in the early 20th century as one of the key early Modernist movements. In visual arts, film, theatre, literature, and architecture, Expressionism took the form of bold images, forms, and ideas that expressed strong emotions. Expressionism in architecture

rejected Functionalism – as was seen in the pagodalike Glass Pavilion, designed in 1914 by German architect Bruno Taut for the Deutscher Werkbund exhibition in Köln.

Films including the exaggerated horror *The Cabinet of Dr Caligari* (1920) and *Nosferatu* (1922), and early science fiction film *Metropolis* (1927) also embraced expressionism in their production and costume design.

RATIONALISM
1920–1949

Rationalism was an architectural movement that championed scientific advancement to bring about a new world order. Led by architects including Walter Gropius and Ludwig Mies van der Rohe, Rationalism subscribed to the machine aesthetic, with buildings made from steel, glass, and concrete. Part of the larger Modernist movement, Rationalism was also related to the New Objectivity style, a German movement that called for philosophical objectivity and its practical application. Rationalism was widespread in the Soviet Union in the 1920s and early 1930s, led by Nikolai Aleksandrovich Ladovskii, and in Italy under the Fascist regime between 1922–43.

SURREALISM
1924–1939

A 20th century art movement, Surrealism aimed to change perceptions of the world by exploring dreams, the unconscious and the irrational. Beginning with André Breton's 1924 manifesto,

Surrealism was embraced by artists including Max Ernst, Salvador Dalí, and René Magritte. In the 1930s, attention turned to the creation of objects, including Man Ray's iron with nails and Méret Oppenheim's bird feet table and fur teacup. Dalí's partnership with fashion designer Elsa Schiaparelli produced the Lobster Dress in 1937 and the Shoe Hat in 1938. With art patron Edward James, Dalí created the Mae West Lips Sofa in 1937 and the Lobster Telephone in 1938.

USONIAN ARCHITECTURE
1937–1959

Usonian architecture was a style conceived by Frank Lloyd Wright in the 1930s to address the need for affordable housing in the US. The Usonian-style house was simple and inexpensive: a single-storey house without a basement or attic, typically with a living space, bedrooms, and a kitchen-dining area. It was built on concrete slabs with piping for radiant heat, and the interiors had built-in furnishings. From 1937, Wright built more than a hundred Usonian houses, with the last one completed after his death in 1959. Usonian architecture played an important role in the evolution of Mid-century Modern homes, anticipating the Ranch-style home that became popular in the US in during the 1950s.

SWISS STYLE
1945–

The Swiss style, or International Typographic style, of graphic design originated in the 1940s,

taking elements from Bauhaus and De Stijl. The style was based on a mathematical grid, making type more legible, hierarchies more readable, and designs more harmonious. It also used sans serif typefaces like Univers, designed by Adrian Frutiger in 1957, and Helvetica, designed in 1960 by Eduard Hoffmann and Max Miedinger. Pioneers of the Swiss style include Ernst Keller, Max Bill, and Otl Aicher who opened their own school in Ulm, Germany, as well as Josef-Müller Brockmann, and Armin Hofmann, whose curriculum is still taught at the School of Design in Basel, Switzerland.

GOOGIE ARCHITECTURE
1945–1972

Googie architecture was a mid-century futurist style in the US, inspired by industrial progress, car culture, and the space age. It was most prominent in the 1940s and 1950s, especially in Southern California, where everyday buildings such as restaurants, coffee shops, bowling alleys, and petrol stations were built in the style. It featured curved roofs, cantilevered structures, geometric designs, triangles, and futuristic starbursts. The name derives from Googie's Coffee Shop in West Hollywood, California, which was designed by John Lautner in 1949.

Notable buildings include two that were completed in 1961: California's LAX Theme building, designed by Paul Williams and William Pereira, which had parabolic arches, and Seattle's Space needle – designed by Edward E. Carlson – with a

saucer-shaped observation deck held aloft by a slender tower to celebrate the space age.

PUSH PIN STYLE
1954–1980

Push Pin studios was founded in 1954 in New York, US by Seymour Chwast, Milton Glaser, and Edward Sorel. The distinctive Push Pin style created by the studio rejected the rigidity of modernism in favour of reinvigorated interpretations of historical styles such as comic books, Art Nouveau, Victorian typography, and German woodcuts. It was also characterized by bulging, exaggerated forms, bright colours, and playful juxtapositions.

Examples include Milton Glaser's 1966 *Dylan* poster, which showed the musician Bob Dylan in silhouette with psychedelic hair, and Seymour Chwast's *Visit Dante's Inferno* poster from 1967, which featured an orange Satan complete with waistcoat, cigarette, and monocle. The group published *The Push Pin Almanack,* then The *Push Pin Graphic,* to showcase their work.

SPACE AGE DESIGN
1957–1972

A mid-20th century US movement, Space Age design emerged amid optimism generated by the technological achievements in space exploration. Found especially in furniture, lighting, and household objects, it is typified by rounded, spherical, or angular shapes, often featuring plastic, fibreglass, and reflective metals. The style inspired a number of significant chairs, including Eero Aarnio's Ball chair, designed in 1963, which resembled a space capsule; Peter Ghyczy's 1968 UFO-shaped polyurethane Garden Egg chair; and Olivier Mourgue's 1963 Djinn chair, seen in the film *2001: A Space Odyssey*. Stilnovo's Sputnik chandelier, created in 1957, was shaped like the Sputnik satellite and Arthur Bracegirdle's Keracolor Sphere television from 1970 recalls a space helmet. In architecture, Matti Suurinen's 1968 Futuro House imitates a flying saucer, and Nova House, designed by Michel Hudrisier and M. Roma in 1972, is a metallic bubble.

CONCEPTUAL DESIGN
1960–

Conceptual design, like Conceptual art, is a work defined by its concept rather than by its eventual execution or appearance. It often takes the form of a prototype, proposal, or idea that is not in production or available to buy. Conceptual designs are often developed to meet a need or solve a problem. As a movement, Conceptual design began in the 1960s as a reaction to the commercialization of the design industry. Later, Conceptual design was important in the avant-garde Anti-design movement of Italy in the 1970s, and in the work of many Dutch designers in the 1990s, including the Conceptual design collective Droog design.

MINIMALISM
1960–

Minimalism is a movement that began as an art movement in the 1960s in the US. It consists of plain geometric shapes and negative space. In architecture, minimalist buildings prioritize clean lines and neutral colour palettes with no ornamentation, drawing inspiration from earlier Modernist architecture movements, such as Bauhaus and De Stijl. In graphic design, Minimalism has a similar aesthetic, with limited elements, negative space, and a small colour palette. Today, Minimalism is also used to refer to an entire lifestyle in which individuals reject clutter and embrace simplicity in their lives and homes.

METABOLISM
1960–1970s

Metabolism was a Japanese avant-garde architectural movement that combined visions of architectural megastructures with notions of organic growth. Group members – including Noboru Kawazoe, Kisho Kurokawa, Kiyonori Kikutake, and Fumihiko Maki – were all influenced by their professor, Kenzo Tange. The group's Metabolism manifesto, which was presented at the 1960 Tokyo World Design conference, envisaged modular buildings that could be replaced and renewed, and floating cities that could expand further onto the sea. The vision was to make Japanese cities more adaptable, however many of their designs were not realized due to technological limitations. Built examples include Kurokawa's 1972 Nakagin Capsule tower, which exemplified the group's modular approach with capsulelike apartment units attached to a central building core.

PSYCHEDELIC ART
1966–1972

Psychedelic art is a visual style that was inspired by the experience of taking psychedelic drugs like LSD. Culturally, it is the art movement associated with the late 1960s US counterculture. It first appeared in the work of San Francisco poster artists such as Victor Moscoso, Bonnie MacLean, Stanley Mouse and Alton Kelley, Rick Griffin, Bob Masse, and Wes Wilson. Influences include Art Nouveau, Victoriana, Surrealism, Pop art, and Op art. It featured intense, strongly contrasting colours, and busy compositions filled with spirals, flowers, curves, and winding lines. Graphics appeared on concert poster art, vinyl record album covers, and in light shows, murals, comic books, and newspapers.

HIGH TECH ARCHITECTURE
1970s

High Tech Architecture, or Structural Expressionism, was a futuristic architectural style that emerged in the 1970s as an extension of the Modernist's focus on new materials and technologies in a machine age. Architects exposed the structural elements of the building in their designs, creating high-rise buildings in steel, aluminium, and glass, with mechanical services – like air conditioning and electrical equipment – placed on the outside of the building. The aesthetic was industrial and emphasized transparency with reconfigurable interiors. The most famous examples include the Pompidou centre in Paris, France, designed by Richard Rogers and Renzo Piano, in 1977, and the Lloyds building in London, UK, designed by Richard Rogers in 1986. Other architects working in the style include Norman Foster and Santiago Calatrava.

AFROFUTURISM
1970s–

Originating in the US, Afrofuturism is a movement which reimagines alternative futures that celebrate African diaspora culture. Rooted in music, film, fashion, and literature, it combines science fiction and fantasy, empowering Black and African Americans to connect with their lost ancestry.

Examples of Afrofuturism include the UFO and fashion designs of punk musician George Clinton and his band Parliament, especially the album *Mothership Connection*, produced in 1975. More recently, Marvel's *Black Panther* franchise, launched in 2018, is set in the fictional African nation of Wakanda, which was never colonized and has developed advanced technology. The design for the film includes Afrofuturist architecture, fashion, and electronic devices that combine Space Age and African elements. Recent fashion and music videos of recording artists Janelle Monáe, Rihanna, and Beyoncé have also featured Afrofuturist designs.

POSTMODERNISM
1970–1990

Postmodernism emerged in the 1970s as a reaction to modern architecture's austerity, lack of ornament, and insensitivity to historic cultural contexts. In *Learning from Las Vegas*, published in 1972, US architects Denise Scott Brown and Robert Venturi proposed emphasizing the facade, incorporating historical elements, and considering the existing architecture of the area. Notable postmodern buildings include Piazza d'Italia, in New Orleans, US, which was designed by Charles Moore in 1978, the Portland building, in Portland, US, designed by Michael Graves in 1982, and the MI6 building, in London, UK, designed by Terry Farrell in 1994.

The postmodern style spread to product design, art, and fashion, emphasizing colour, bold patterns, artificial-looking surfaces, historical references, parody, and wit. Italy became a global design centre, with designers including Alessandro Mendini, who created the Proust chair in 1978, and Ettore Sottsass, the designer of the Carlton bookcase in 1981. Mendini and Sottsass formed the Memphis group in 1981 (see pp.268–69).

CIRCULAR DESIGN
1976–

Circular design is the concept of designing to keep materials in use, to limit the product's reliance on raw materials, and reduce waste and pollution. It advocates for the use of recycled or reconstituted materials, in addition to design for disassembly and recycling at the end of a product's usable life. The term comes from the concept of a circular economy – a system based on the reuse or recycling of products or their materials.

The concept of Circular design is also associated with the term Cradle to Cradle (see pp. 258–65), which was popularized by the German chemist Michael Braungart and US architect William McDonough in their book *Cradle to Cradle: Remaking the Way We Make Things* in 2002.

UNIVERSAL DESIGN
1977–

Universal design, or Accessible design, is a process for creating products, buildings, and services that are accessible to people regardless of their age, size, ability, or disability. The term was first coined by US architect Ronald L. Mace in 1985, after he developed his seven principles of Universal design in 1977.

US designer Patricia Moore also championed Universal design. Moore spent four years in her 20s travelling as an 80-year-old woman, wearing uncomfortable shoes to affect her walking, earplugs to muffle her hearing, and thick glasses to blur her vision as part of her Empathetic Elder Experience (1979–1982). She used the information gained from the experience to report on mobility.

DECONSTRUCTIVISM
1980–

Deconstructivism is a movement of architecture that developed in the 1980s as a combination of the terms Constructivism and Deconstruction. Constructivism was a Russian architecture movement from the 1920s that featured jagged irregular forms. Deconstruction was a form of philosophical analysis by Algerian-French philosopher Jacques Derrida that questioned meaning and truth.

In 1988, US architect Philip Johnson curated the exhibition *Deconstructivist Architecture* at the Museum of Modern Art with works by Peter Eisenman, Frank Gehry, Zaha Hadid, Coop Himmelblau, Rem Koolhaas, Daniel Libeskind, and Bernard Tschumi. Although the architects in question worked in this disruptive style, many did not accept their work as part of the movement.

RIGHT TO REPAIR MOVEMENT
1990–

The Right to Repair is a consumer rights and legislative movement arguing that consumers have the right to repair products when they break, rather than throwing them away and purchasing a replacement. The increasing complexity of goods, especially electronics, coupled with planned obsolescence, has made repair increasingly unaffordable and, in some cases, impossible. Right to Repair began as a movement in Europe in the 1990s and has gained momentum ever since, spreading around the world. A Right to Repair Europe coalition represents over 100 organisations from across Europe. In 2021, in the US, an executive order was signed pushing the Federal Trade Commission to make third-party product repair easier.

REGENERATIVE ARCHITECTURE
1996–

Regenerative architecture is an approach that considers the broader ecology of a project, seeking, not just to do no harm, but to actively restore and enhance the landscape or environment. This means undertaking a thorough analysis of the existing ecosystem including its flora and fauna, air, water, and soil, and then designing in order to regenerate the natural ecosystem. The concept comes from US landscape architect John Tillman Lyle who first set out his theory in the 1996 book *Regenerative Design for Sustainable Development*. A more recent example is the Bosco Verticale apartment block in Milan, Italy, designed by Boeri studio in 2014, which has hundreds of varieties of trees and shrubs planted on its facade.

FLAT DESIGN STYLE
2006–

Flat design is a minimalist user interface style for digital design that uses simple, two-dimensional shapes and bright colours. Because it consists of simpler shapes and colours with no three-dimensional elements, it is responsive to the size of the screen, is quick to load, and always looks sharp.

Flat design was first introduced by Microsoft in 2006 with the launch of the Zune MP3 player and was inspired by the Swiss style of graphic design. Flat design replaced skeuomorphism, a form of design where digital objects have a realistic, three-dimensional representation. Since 2012, Flat design has become the main style of digital design and is used widely by tech companies including Microsoft, Apple, and Google.

DESIGN ACTIVISM AND CRAFTIVISM
2008–

Design activism rejects design as a solely technical expertise and focuses on its use as a tool for social and environmental change. Increased engagement with politics in the 2000s led to a movement among graphic designers raising awareness on a range of different issues, fuelled by social media.

Activism is also strong in craft, and has led to the creation of a new term: Craftivism. One famous example of Craftivism in action was on show in the US in January 2017 when millions of women joined protest marches against the inauguration of Donald Trump wearing bright pink hand-knitted Pussyhats.

RADICAL INDIGENISM
2019–

The term Radical Indigenism was coined in 2003 by Eva Marie Garroutte, a Princeton professor and citizen of the Cherokee Nation. Garroutte calls for Indigenous knowledge to be reclaimed and strengthened, as well as for a greater understanding of how Indigenous knowledge has been misunderstood and made subordinate to the dominant culture in the US.

In the book *Lo–TEK: Design by Radical Indigenism* (2019), author and designer Julia Watson reframes Radical Indigenism in the context of contemporary architecture and design by re-evaluating the traditional construction techniques and materials used by diverse and remote populations.

GLOSSARY

Analogous colours Groups of colours that are close together on the colour wheel. For example: red, orange, and yellow.

Anthropometrics The measurement of bodily proportions that can be used to improve the functionality of products.

Arabesque Outlines of natural forms, such as plants and flowers, used to make rhythmic, flowing patterns. This form of decoration originated in Islamic art.

Biomorphic A design that references patterns or shapes that are found in nature, often in an abstract manner.

Cabinet-making The making of high-quality furniture.

Celluloid A tough type of thermoplastic, originally called Parkesine. Widely used from the mid-19th century, especially in photographic film, it became less popular as it is highly flammable.

Chrome Coated or plated with the metallic element chromium.

Classical Architecture based on principles established in ancient Greece and Rome.

Complementary colours Colours that have the greatest contrast, such as yellow and purple. They hold opposite positions on the colour wheel.

Crystal glass A type of glass that is composed of at least 20 per cent lead oxide. Also known as crystal or leaded crystal glass, it is softer and easier to shape or cut for decoration.

Cut glass A method of cutting decorative grooves and facets into glass. It is done with the aid of a rotating wheel hand-tool.

Demi-lune A French term for a half-moon or semi-circle shape.

De Stijl A Dutch movement from 1917 to 1931, founded by avant-garde artists, architects, and designers. Related to Bauhaus, the movement aimed to reduce design to its essentials using a limited colour palette, straight lines, and geometric shapes that did not intersect.

Earthenware Pottery made from a soft porous clay that can be shaped by hand. It can be made waterproof with a glaze.

Ebonized Wood that has been stained black to look like ebony. This technique is often applied to pianos and fine furniture.

Embossing A raised surface decoration made by punching out a relief, often with a hammer or stamp. The reverse technique, debossing, is an impressed pattern.

Enamel A type of coloured glass that is fused in a furnace to create a shiny, smooth decorative finish on a metal surface. It can be translucent and opaque.

Engraving A decorative technique where a design is cut into a surface. An engraving can also be a print made by cutting into wood or metal, covering the surface in ink, and pressing paper against it.

Ergonomics The practice of accounting for the relationship between a product and the user during designing. The aim is to make the design comfortable, functional, and user-friendly.

Facade The front or exterior of a building that has decorative elements or special architectural features .

Femme-fleur A French term for a motif that combines a woman with a flower. It was popular in Art Nouveau designs.

Fibreglass A type of plastic that is reinforced with glass fibres, making it strong yet lightweight.

Figuring The appearance of natural markings and graining on wood. It can be used to form a decorative pattern.

Finial A decorative element at the top or terminal of a building, piece of furniture, or ceramic. It often has the form of an acorn, pine cone, or urn.

Foliate A term for decoration that resembles leaves.

Gilding The use of gold leaf or powder applied to a surface as a decorative finish. Occasionally silver is used instead.

Golden ratio The mathematical ratio for proportions that are harmonious and aesthetically pleasing. The ratio of 1:1.618 occurs in nature such as nautilus shells and has been used in classical architecture, art, and design.

Hallmark A small mark that is stamped onto the surface of precious metals including silver, gold, and platinum. The mark shows the purity of the metal and signifies the manufacturer, as well as the date and place of manufacture.

Hue The true appearance of a colour. In painting, it can also refer to a pigment with a pure colour.

Inlay A type of decoration where an alternative material is embedded into the surface of a piece of furniture. Inlays are commonly a different colour of wood or sometimes made of stone or other materials.

Iridescence A surface that appears to change colour when viewed at different angles. Caused by differences in light refraction, iridescence is found in nature on fish scales and bird feathers.

Isometric A shape, such as a triangle, in which all the sides have equal dimensions.

Lacquer A resin made from tree sap, that is applied to furniture to form a hard, smooth water-resistant finish. It has been used on furniture since the 6th century, particularly in Japan and China, and later by Modernist designers.

Lancet A tall, pointed arch, most often used in windows and entrances.

Lithograph A printing technique in which an image is drawn on metal or stone with wax, and then treated with water and ink. The waxed areas repel the water but retain the ink, which can then be transferred onto paper. The technique is mostly used for making posters.

Marquetry A decorative furniture veneer made from thin pieces of wood that are pieced together to form a pattern or picture. Other materials such as ivory or mother-of-pearl are also used.

Modular construction A construction method in which parts of a building or large item are made in a factory and then assembled on site.

Moorish Architecture produced in western North Africa and parts of Europe during the Middle Ages. It follows Islamic design principles and often features horseshoe arches and geometric motifs.

Muqarnas A vaulted ceiling, found in Islamic architecture, that features rows of arches and niches, resembling honeycomb.

Obelisk A tall four-sided shaft of stone that tapers into a pyramid at the top.

Organic A design that has curves and free-form lines that are similar to those found in nature.

Pâte-de-verre A French term meaning "glass paste". Ground glass is mixed with liquid to form a paste that is pressed into a mould. The mould is then heated to fuse the glass into shape.

Patina A fine film or sheen on the surface of furniture that appears after years of handling, polishing, and wear. It can cause the furniture's colour to change.

Pattern A repeating, decorative design. The repeats can be made from lines or shapes that are regular or irregular.

Photolithography A process using light to etch lines into the surface of a light-sensitive material. It is often used to create electronic circuit boards and lenses.

Plywood A flexible material made of thin layers of wood fixed together. Each layer is laid at a right angle to the layer below, which provides extra strength.

Porcelain A type of ceramic first made in China in the late 6th century. It is translucent white, strong, dense, and

watertight. Porcelain is usually glazed and decorated; it is used for making vases and high-quality tableware.

Primary colour The hues red, yellow, and blue, which cannot be made by mixing other colours.

Quatrefoil A symmetrical motif of four overlapping circles that often resembles a four-leaf clover. It is used in both Gothic and Christian design.

Radial symmetry A symmetrical arrangement of lines or shapes around a central point. It is often used in designs for round objects such as plates and vases.

Rattan A material made from the vines of rattan palms. The fibrous strips are woven together to make furniture.

Relief A decorative element that is moulded, carved, or stamped to be raised out of its surrounding material.

Repoussé A French term for relief decoration on metal. It is made by hammering a design from the back or inside of the piece, creating a raised effect on the front or outside.

Revivalism In architecture, it is the practice of applying a historic style to a new building.

Rustication A masonry practice in which blocks with a rough surface texture are cut at the edges to give a smooth contrast.

Saturation The intensity and purity of a colour. When black or white is added, a colour's saturation is reduced.

Secondary colour A colour that is formed by mixing two primary colours together. Orange, green, and purple are all secondary colours.

Skeuomorph A decorative design that mimics the features of another object, such as plastic designed to look like marble or a digital button given 3D features.

Stoneware A type of durable ceramic that is fired at very high temperatures. Some stoneware has stone added to the clay mix, which makes it watertight and hard. Used to make decorative vases and tableware, it is often glazed with salt or lead.

Studio glass Fine art sculptures or objects made with the use of glass. It is often made by an independent glass-maker or artist, working in a small studio, using easily available materials. Studio glass frequently prioritizes artistic expression over commercial pressures.

Temperature In relation to colour, temperature is how warm or cool a hue is perceived to be. Red is the hottest colour, while blue is the coldest.

Terminal A decorative feature at the end of a structure or object.

Tertiary colour A colour mixed from a primary and a secondary colour, or from two secondary colours.

Texture The characteristic appearance, or tactile quality of a surface.

Thermoplastic A plastic polymer that becomes soft and mouldable when it is heated, and becomes hard when it cools.

Thermoset A plastic polymer that becomes irreversibly hard and set in shape when heat is used.

Tone In relation to colour, tone is how dark or light a hue is. Dark tones are shades, while light tones are tints.

Vault In architecture, a self-supporting arch that forms the ceiling of a building or structure.

Veneer A thin layer of decorative wood, ivory, or tortoiseshell that covers the surface of a piece of furniture constructed from an inferior wood.

Vernacular Architecture that has been designed and built to suit the local geography and cultural traditions.

Webbing Strips of woven fibres that form a strong fabric. Webbing is often used as the base of a chair seat.

Ziggurat A pyramid structure with stepped sides, such as the terraced temples of ancient Mesopotamia. Shapes based on this structure have the same name.

Zoomorphic A shape or decoration that is based on animal forms, such as a building with a roof structure resembling bird wings.

INDEX

QUOTE ATTRIBUTIONS

ACKNOWLEDGMENTS

Dorling Kindersley would like to thank: Shaarang Bhanot, Arshti Narang, and Aanchal Singal for design assistance; Tim Harris for editorial assistance; Ann Baggaley for proofreading; and Helen Peters for indexing.

PICTURE CREDITS

DK
BIG IDEAS SIMPLY EXPLAINED